If you are unable to obtain additional copies from your dealer,
write directly to:

TDF Publishing Ltd.
1299 Gilpin St., #4E, Denver, CO 80218

Your comments are always welcome. Send messages to Gabby:
gabbygourmet@gmail.com
www.gabbygourmet.com

Listen to and call Gabby on The Gabby Gourmet Restaurant Show,
Saturdays from 1-3 pm. on KHOW 630 AM
on iHeart Radio.

INTRODUCTION

Input from you, our readers, is always invaluable.

If you want to give us your opinions, please feel free to:

1. Call Gabby on KHOW's Gabby Gourmet Restaurant Show (630 AM) Saturday afternoons from 1 p.m. to 3 p.m. at 303-713-8255.

2. E-mail gabbygourmet@gmail.com

This book is gluten free, dairy free, fat free and sugar free. It's not, however, opinion free.

This is the region's longest-running, most definitive food chronicle featuring reviews of over 500 places to eat in Denver, Boulder, Aspen, Colorado Springs, and Glenwood Springs. We've been doing this book since 1984 and you're looking at the 29th edition right now!

Stay on top of the ever-changing restaurant scene with new and updated reviews. Learn more about great local food shops and resources. See our list of "To Die For" restaurants and discover the go-to places we love and head back to for special cravings and fun. It all adds up to the best insights on the latest and greatest dining trends in the area.

Get online and tune in for more. Go to **GabbyGourmet.com** to look for the weekly **Where's Gabby** blog and latest restaurant reviews. Follow Gabby on **Facebook** on the Gabby Gourmet page and check her out on Instagram. Listen in to Gabby on Saturday afternoons from 1:00 – 3:00 MT on KHOW (630 AM), on iHeartRadio, or by replaying the broadcast on our website. And please do share your experiences with us!

Remember, these are our reviews, rated by a select group of foodies. We want you to get out there and judge for yourself. Everyone's entitled to their own opinion! Use this book for guidance and as a terrific reference with addresses and phone numbers. Keep one at home, one at your office, one in your car, and share one with a friend.

Let's Eat!

Gabby Gourmet

2016

Restaurant Guide

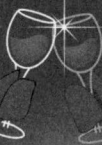

Where to dine in the Denver area by Pat Miller & Friends

2016 GABBY GOURMET RESTAURANT GUIDE

By
Pat Miller, The Gabby Gourmet and friends

Denver editors: Maria Lao, Kristen Kidd, Abby Reecer,
Jared Willey, Kristen Barden, Pat Blum

Thanks to all our friends and contributors! And special thanks
to this year's writers from Aspen, Glenwood Springs, Snowmass
and surrounding areas.

Special thanks to our regional writers and editors:

Aspen, Snowmass, Glenwood Springs and
surrounding mountain towns: Lucy Lea Tucker

Colorado Springs: Bob and Lisa Rennick and friends

This edition is dedicated to Mark Miller, loving husband
and constant supporter. We miss you and know you're being well fed.

COVER WRITER: Carol Miller/IdeaSource®

ORIGINAL COVER ILLUSTRATION: Bill Thomas

ORIGINAL COVER CONCEPT AND UPDATES: Steve Miller/
IdeaSource®

BOOK LAYOUT: Anita Jones/Another Jones Graphics

ADDITIONAL ILLUSTRATIONS by Bill Thomas and Steve Miller

Printed in the United States of America by Bang Printing
3323 Oak St. P.O. Box 587, Brainerd, Minnesota, 56401

ISBN # 978-0-918481-00-9

$18.95

ADDRESSES

Along with a street address, city and phone number for each restaurant, we have included approximate cross streets to help guide you to the area. Please note that these are not exact and generally were provided by the restaurants.

PRICES

$ .... INEXPENSIVE

$$ .... VERY MODERATE

$$$ .... MODERATE TO MORE EXPENSIVE (DEPENDING ON SELECTION)

$$$$ .... EXPENSIVE

The above scale is based on a three-course dinner, per person, excluding drinks and tip. It is impossible to be precise, as some restaurants are prix fixe, while others are à la carte or have daily specials. A fine bottle of wine might double the cost of your meal, or you may have no beverage at all. Nevertheless, we feel that the above is a good indicator of what you might expect to pay and provides a sound reference for the restaurant you might be considering.

OPEN

B: Breakfast, L: Lunch, D: Dinner, BR: Brunch

RESERVATIONS

"Yes" indicates that a restaurant will take reservations for small groups. Most places accommodate larger parties, so if you have six or more people, call ahead to see if you can have your table waiting.

MEET THE PIGS

We've returned to our roots with our original rating structure. Here's how to read the pig ratings.

TO DIE FOR

These restaurants are the few that are amazing in style, service and food, standing out above all others.

5 PIGS

One of the very best restaurants in the area.

4 PIGS

Highly recommended.

3 PIGS

Recommended.

NR

Fresh food markets and places too new to rate fall into this category.

There is also a list of our GO TO dining spots where my listeners, callers, AND I go and list our favorites. They may not be the highest pig but deserve the highest praise.

Pigs with a ".5" are somewhere in between.

Restaurants out of the Denver/Boulder and Colorado Springs areas have not been given pig ratings.

. . . .

Gabby picks special spots to visit.

The TO DIE FOR restaurants bring that final touch with food, service, and wine. The very few are in a special category.

BAROLO GRILL

FRASCA

MERCANTILE DINING AND PROVISIONS

ROOT DOWN

SHANAHAN'S

Read our reviews on these spectacular places.

We all have our GO TO restaurants that bring that special warm, friendly feel. Maybe not the priciest or in a top pig category but we find ourselves visiting often for fun and food.

ADELITA'S: The Mexican food here reflects dishes from Michoacan, Mexico, original home of chef. Breakfast, lunch and dinner are served all day every day! Prices are great and so are the drinks.

BAGEL DELI: You don't have to be Jewish to appreciate sandwiches like corned beef or Reuben. The latkes and everything you ever wanted are here, including turkey bacon.

BIJU LITTLE CURRY SHOP: Move down the counter as your bowl is filled by friendly staff with divine curry and all the trimmings at the best price and with the best flavors ever.

BOURBON GRILL: No inside here. Stand in line on E. Colfax to get the most fun and delicious bourbon chicken, piled high over rice with two sides. The mac and cheese a must. Take it home, to the park, or sit at one of two tables on site.

BRAZEN: Head to this funky place for late night dining. Enjoy great small plates and heavenly homemade ramen noodles. Dining is a treat anytime.

GAETANO'S: Back in the day, it was the headquarters for crime, but now it's a different mob scene. Delicious Italian food at affordable prices make this a must stop.

HIGHLAND TAP AND BURGER: Head here for sports, beer, a scene and awesome burgers. Try beef, bison, lamb and extraordinary veggie burger too.

KATSU RAMEN: Look at the plastic dishes of the choices outside because inside it's really busy. Not too much English here, but the ramen is so worth the visit. It's spicy, flavorful, delicious and inexpensive.

LEÑA: Latin American tapas are just fun in terrific surroundings, especially with signature cocktails and wine. The Octopus ceviche is outrageous.

LITTLE MAN ICE CREAM: See the milk carton building – and the line. Wait your turn for remarkable creamy ice cream. It's a happening any time of day and season.

THE MARKET: This is Larimer Square's signature spot for breakfast, lunch, dinner, carryout, coffee, ice cream, pastries... and for people watching.

OPHELIA'S: Time to be part of a brothel! The redesigned house of ill repute is awesome; and live entertainment and super food make this a place to hang out (pun intended).

PINCHE TACO: Nobody has tacos this good. Just order the one you want and prepare to be wowed. You'll wait in line but who cares. Have a margarita and enjoy.

SARTO'S: A bit more upscale than most on the list, but the Italian food is totally wonderful and the cicchetti bar is unique and special. Chef prepares surprises for you (with notations on your food restrictions). Enjoy the show and the one-on-one interaction with chef.

SHELLS AND SAUCE: This perfect neighborhood bistro has everything from delicious Italian food, excellent wines and drinks and super prices. Go for lasagna but just know everyone in town is part of this hood. One visit you'll be hooked.

WORK AND CLASS: Shipping containers come to life to make the setting for the most popular spot in town. Executive Chef Dana Rodriguez, her partners and staff turn out Latino/American fare that amazes. The atmosphere, the crowd and every detail in this wildly popular place is a must.

Ace Eat Serve

Cuisine: Asian/fusion
Open: L-D: Daily
aceeatserve.com

501 East 17th Ave.   303.800.7705
Denver, CO 80203
17th & Pennsylvania

Price: $$ **Patio:** Yes
Reservations: Yes   **Brunch:** No
Location: Uptown

The latest venture of Josh and Jen Wolkon is right next to the wildly popular Steuben's. The décor is awesome—and fun-and in this Asian/fusion inspired eatery. The use of old woods, fabulous items for lighting, high ceilings, huge windows, great tables, and fabulous bar areas, there is a special section for ping pong. These are some extraordinary ping pong tables and the setting for these rocks—as does every detail in the huge space. Outdoor dining, signage, it could take months to describe it all. And the food is fun where you can watch the chefs in the open kitchen. Start with soups such as coconut lemongrass, add Bao buns of chicken, pork, and short rib, and then enjoy dim sum. The veggie pot stickers are worth the trip. Still covering the world, the menu features cold plates of sweet and sour mango, papaya, greens or celery in the salad section. Hot plates offer many choices including tiger wings, naked chicken wings, Korean short rib, chile prawns and a whole crispy snapper. The chicken chow fun is just that with several flavors complementing each other. Share or not, the menu appeals to all. End with steamed chocolate cake for a real treat. The cocktails are a big part of the menu with a great list of mixology drinks—and of course, beer and wine. Service shines, and remember, you can ping pong the night away. Ace brings great fun to the neighborhood.

Acorn

Cuisine: Contemporary
Open: L: Mon-Sat, D: Daily
denveracorn.com/

3350 Brighton Blvd Suite 150   720-542-3721
Denver, 80216
The Source Building

Price: $$$-$$$$	**Patio:** Yes
Reservations: Yes	**Brunch:** No
Location: : RiNo	

Oak on Fourteenth in Boulder is one of the most outstanding places in Colorado and now Acorn brings the great food, drink, and ambience to Denver. The place is fabulous in design. Totally open as are all the spaces in the Source, high ceilings, exposed pipes, and huge open doors that go to the patio start the scene. The bar is great, the open kitchen amazing, and tables, booths, and seating are done in contemporary style set in the old brick where even the graffiti on the walls remains. Black colors accent the fun and it is great. The food is outstanding under the direction of the divine chef, Amos Watts. Start with tomato peach salad with mozzarella, olive oil braised octopus, pork belly, lamb Shawarma with shishito peppers, shrimp and grits, meatballs, short ribs and salmon, all designed to share with fabulous spices, accents and presentation. Carrots and a crispy egg in a salad are worth the trip. Big plates, served family style, are awesome: a huge steak, a fish of the day, and the best chicken ever with gruyere and shallot bread pudding, wild mushrooms and crushed potatoes to die for. Sweets bring s'mores, dark chocolate cake and coffee cremoso, and peaches and caramelized brioche. The wine, cocktail, and beer lists are great and service excellent. Acorn, in a word, rocks, and is a great addition to a neighborhood that has it all. What a treat for Denver to have Acorn.

Adelita's Cocina y Cantina

Cuisine: Mexican
Open: L-D: Daily, BR: Sat-Sun
adelitasdenver.com/

1294 S. Broadway   303-778-1294
Denver, 80210
Broadway & Louisiana

Price: $-$$	**Patio:** Yes
Reservations: Yes	**Brunch:** Yes
Location: South Broadway	

Great Mexican comes to Denver at Adelita's. The place is fun with lots of wood, a huge bar on one side of the room, a giant community table in the center and tables and booths throughout. Totally casual, the staff is great; friendly, informative, and making guests feel welcome. The food is not the typical cheesy Mex; but from the area that reminded us of great Santa Fe fare. The menu is huge and features the dishes of Michoacan, Mexican, and the original home of chef. Start with fabulous chips and sauces and enjoy guacamole, ceviche, quesadillas, sopes, and queso. The Comida section features enchiladas, pollo con crema, carne asada, and yummy fajitas. The mole, green chili, chili roja, and chipotle mushroom cream sauces rock. More dishes include shrimp with crema or diabla, tamales, pozole, pollo mole, and sope. Don't miss the great tortas and burritos, or a fabulous list of the best corn tacos with great fillings. There are so many sides as well and many vegetarian options to please all. The most fun part is a weekend brunch that one can really enjoy every day all day and night. That makes me a fan right there. Chilaquiles, huevos rancheros, diverclados, chorizo, Mexicana and breakfast tacos or burritos are divine. Portions are huge, prices are great, and don't forget some divine margaritas, mezcals, and more. Adelita's is just plain fun and delicious and a real treat for Mexican fare any time, and often.

Ale House at Amato's

Cuisine: American, Brewpub
Open: L-D: Daily, BR: Sat-Sun
alehousedenver.com

2501 16th St.   303-433-9734
Denver, 80211
16th & Central

Price: $$ **Patio:** Yes
Reservations: No   **Brunch:** Yes
Location: LoHi

Perhaps the best view from LoHi is at Ale House at Amato's with a perfect craft brew in hand. The upstairs outdoor lounge offers great sights by the fire pit as you sip your brew of choice and gaze at Denver's skyline. Downstairs, the modern interior stays warm and welcoming with large windows, wood accents and natural stone. The Ale House is a place that beckons comfort. The large horseshoe bar downstairs features forty craft brews on tap with many seats to watch a game or engage in chatter with the crowd. The dining room has great views as well and comfortable earth tones make dinner and conversation a pleasure. With a setting like this, the menu of American pub food is perfect for the scene. Start with appetizers, perfect for sharing - calamari, artichoke-spinach dip, chicken wings, and great meatballs served with bread start the list. The tomato mozzarella, Caesar and a terrific bacon, lettuce, avocado, and tomato salad make a great second course. Sandwiches tempt with chicken, apple brie, Portobello, veggie, and beef, all served with fries or salad. Top of the list are the mac and cheese, several pastas, and the burger selection. From buffalo and lamb, to beef with several toppings, these are a big hit. Add entrées like brined half chicken, pork, lamb kabobs, fish and chips, and sea bass and the decisions are difficult. It's impossible to pass up the decadent desserts of bread pudding, ricotta cheesecake and gelatos. The beer and wine lists rock—both in choices and price. Service is casual and informative. The Ale House at Amato's makes a big hit in LoHi.

Altitude Restaurant at the Hyatt Regency Denver Convention Center

Cuisine: Contemporary
Open: B-L-D: Daily, BR: Sat, Sun
denverregency.hyatt.com

650 15th St.   303-486-4434
Denver, 80202
Hyatt Regency Hotel

Price: $$$$ **Patio:** Yes
Reservations: Yes   **Brunch:** Yes
Location: Downtown

Altitude, the sleek restaurant located at street level within the Hyatt Regency at the Colorado Convention Center is a treat. The open-spaced venue features cool tones of stone and spectacular windows that overlook the plaza at the Convention Center. Diners can comfortably watch the Blue Bear (the iconic sculpture) peek into the Convention Center. Breakfast comes as a buffet or can be ordered from the menu. Lunch is also served with a themed lunch buffet that changes daily and includes non-alcoholic beverages. This is a restaurant that caters to the out-of-towner as well as to locals. Dinner can be quite a treat at Altitude. For starters, try the tortilla soup or the crab cakes. Bruschetta with housemade burrata is a must. The Caesar salad features luscious white anchovies and perfectly toasted croutons. Entrées include pecan crusted salmon, milk and honey Colorado lamb, elk medallions, and lobster mac and cheese. Great sides accompany all. There are lighter dishes available as well. Don't miss decadent desserts. On Friday and Saturday nights, there is a prime rib buffet. The setting is comfortable, service great. It is perfect before or after theater, for people and "bear watching", and some excellent food..

Ambli Gourmet Eatery & Wine

Cuisine: Contemporary, Mediterranean
Open: L: Mon-Fri, D: Mon-Sat
Amblidenver.com

600 S. Holly   303-355-9463
Denver, 80245
Holly & Leetsdale

Price: $$ **Patio:** Yes
Reservations: Yes   **Brunch:** No
Location: South East

Ambli is a terrific restaurant in an interesting area. The area is in need of dining choices and this is one. In a strip mall, the space as you enter is exciting, upscale, and welcoming. Contemporary in design with super seating, great chairs and tables, a focal open kitchen and fabulous bar area where you can enjoy drinks and dinner. The owners, Kelly and Parisa, came from different backgrounds and wanted to bring the food from Parisa's native roots with a twist, and showing the true flavors of the food. And then they added some tastes of Mexico too. Start with tapas of arancini, lobster shooters, tequila mussels, shrimp ceviche, samosa, steak flatbread and tacos. More selections include: saag chicken quesadilla, fig habanero flatbread and tuna tartar. A variety of soups and salads come next. Entrees range from steak two ways, kuku paka, chicken tikka masala and a vegetarian platter to Tandoori crab cake sandwich, enchiladas, pasta, tacos and trout. The list offers something for every taste. The wine list is very nice, service so friendly and prices affordable. Ambli brings the charm of divine owners and unique food making it a spot to stop in often.

Amerigo Delicatus Restaurant and Market

Cuisine: Italian, Deli
Open: L-Mon-Fri, D:Tues-Sat
americatus.com

2449 Larimer Street   (303)-862-9850
Denver, CO
24th and Larimer

Price: $$-$$$ **Patio:** Yes
Reservations: Yes   **Brunch:** No
Location: RiNo

Amerigo brings a vibrant atmosphere to lower Larimer. The space is super fun with a huge open kitchen, high top community table, and banquettes along the wall. The tables, chairs and all the accompaniments are made by Owner Ian

Chisolm who is also one super chef and does all the cooking. Brick walls are the background for huge colorful paintings that brighten the scene. The patio seats an additional 20 diners. During the day, indulge in sandwiches, cheeses, pastas, all made on premise for a casual lunch. Night brings the same casual feel with antipasto, primo, secondo, and dolce. The antipasto ranges from pistachios, bruschetta, and crispy risotto to a salumi plate and caprese with house-made mozzarella. The Caesar or house salads make a great second course. The main dishes are pasta: crespelle with cow's milk ricotta, shiitake and leeks that are worth the trip, gnocchi with braised pork that is equally delicious, linguini with house-made Italian sausage and red sauce, and beef shoulder tender with pappardelle. Each dish disappears quickly as the flavors and seasonings are so exciting. End with decadent desserts of peach pie a la mode, a dark chocolate brownie, cannoli, pannacotta, and cookies and cream. A short but nice wine list, beer, and liquor complement the food. Do not forget $5 Monday!!! Open only for lunch on Monday, everything-sandwiches and salads are only $5 and oh so good. So are the housemade chips. And enjoy the crowd enjoying the scene. With very affordable prices, fabulous service, and a totally family feel, Amerigo is on the list of neighborhood favorites.

Annie's Café and Bar

Cuisine: American, Breakfast
Open: B-L-D: Daily
annies-cafe.com/

3100 E. Colfax Ave.   303-355-8197
Denver, 80206
E. Colfax & St. Paul

Price: $-$$ **Patio:** No
Reservations: Yes   **Brunch:** No
Location: East Colfax

Annie's Café is a staple among the eateries in Denver. The old-school café brings back great memories of good times. The space is divided into several areas, with a very large bar serving as a focal point in a place decorated brightly with fun lunch boxes, paper dolls and memorabilia on the walls. The menu is extensive and breakfast, lunch, and dinner are offered to the happy diners. Begin with breakfast that is served all day and night: eggs any style, served with homemade scalloped potatoes and toast, omelets, Benedicts, burritos, oatmeal, French toast and fluffy pancakes. Burgers and sandwiches come next with many versions of each. The egg salad and bacon, tuna melt, French dip, and Reuben are some choices. Add fries, side salad, coleslaw or cottage cheese and you have a meal. The sweet potato fries are a small extra, but worth the charge. The next section is supper classics with beer-battered shrimp or fish and chips, salmon, meatloaf, and liver and onions. Entrée salads bring a tostada, Cobb, salmon spinach, oriental chicken and Caesar. Want Mexican? It's here with quesadillas, nachos, and burritos. This old-fashioned restaurant continues to please with a soda fountain list, espresso bar and lots of pies, chocolate cake, German chocolate cake, carrot cake, and gingerbread. Add wine and beer, very friendly service, and reasonable prices. Annie's Café pleases fans and remains a popular choice on East Colfax.

Angelo's Taverna

Cuisine: Pizza, Italian
Open: L-D: Daily, BR: Sun
http://angelosdenver.com/

620 E 6th Ave   303-744-3366
Denver, 80203
6th & Washington

Price: $$ **Patio:** Yes
Reservations: Yes   **Brunch:** Yes
Location: North Cherry Creek

Angelo's has been a long time Denver spot for Italian food but now it has been updated with new owners and new menu. Eric and Craig are great operators and together are focusing on oysters and pizza here. There's more too. The décor is great with big windows, the original old brick, a great wood focal bar with the kitchen located behind and comfortable seating throughout. There is a party room and a fabulous patio to add to the scene. The menu starts with calamari, arancini garlic bread, and antipasti platters along with traditional apps. Order oysters raw, charbroiled, bbq and special preparations. The pasta dishes bring bison or cheese ravioli in marinara or cream sauce, chicken or zucchini parmesan, meatballs, and lasagna. and calzone are super with your choice of fillings. The pizza offers many different versions or build your own. Leave room for delicious tiramisu, cheesecake, or zucchini ravioli sweetened and topped with ice cream. The wine, drink, and beer list is great to complement the food. Service is very friendly and casual to match the feel of this spot. Angelo's brings is perfect for a spot to drop in often and relax and enjoy.

Arabesque

Cuisine: Mediterranean
Open: B-L Mon-Sat
arabesqueboulder.com

1634 Walnut St.
Boulder, 80302
16th & Walnut

720-242-8623

Price: $$
Reservations: No
Location: Downtown

Patio: No
Brunch: Yes

You will be instantly charmed by the comfort, beauty and grace in the food and atmosphere at Arabesque. Manal Jarrar, a former ballet instructor, took her passion for art into the kitchen first as a personal chef and caterer and later as a chef and owner at this quaint restaurant in Boulder. The mood at Arabesque exudes the owner's love and appreciation for food. She cooks and serves with the purpose of bringing community together over tastes, smells, entertainment and warm conversation. Everything here is homemade, from the hummus to the chai and the flat breads. The sampler platter is a good overview of the delicious food with baba ghannush, tabbouleh, hummus, Arabic bread, chicken shawarma, 3 freshly stuffed dolmas. Or try the chicken shawarma plate with hummus, tomato slice, red onion, spring mix, chicken shawarma, yogurt sauce on the side, and Arabic bread. Look out for comforting soups like zucchini and lentils and never skip the heavenly syrupy baklava..

Arada Ethiopian Restaurant

Cuisine: Ethiopian
Open: L-D: Tues-Sat
aradarestaurant.com

750 Santa Fe Dr.
Denver, 80204
8th & Santa Fe

303-329-3344

Price: $
Reservations: Yes
Location: Downtown

Patio: No
Brunch: No

This little restaurant serves some of the best Ethiopian food in Denver. The staple of Ethiopian cooking is berbere, a combination of spices that include ginger, cardamom, coriander, fenugreek, nutmeg, cloves, cinnamon, allspice, red chili peppers, paprika, turmeric, and black pepper. Each Ethiopian restaurant offers its own combination and the one at Arada's is great, brought to Denver by owner and cook Haime Asfaw who learned this recipe from her mother in Africa. She combines flavors that excite the taste buds without burning them. Request it mild, hot or extra hot. Wot (sauce) comes with many different meat choices, chicken, beef and lamb, cooked to perfect tenderness. All meals are served atop injera, the spongy and tangy national bread of Ethiopia. Injera is used in place of forks and knives -- simply pull off a portion and scoop up your food. If you've never tried Ethiopian food, Arada is the place to go for your first experience. The restaurant is bright, cheerful, and fun.

Argyll Whiskey Beer, A Gastropub

Cuisine: Gastro pub, contemporary
Open: L-D: Daily BR-Sat-Sun
argylldenver.com

1038 E. 17th Avenue   303-847-0850
Denver 80218
17th and Downing

Price: $$-$$$ **Patio:** Yes
Reservations: Yes   **Brunch:** Yes
Location: Uptown

Argyll, originally in Cherry Creek, is now open in this great new Uptown area. The décor is super with a huge patio, closed in porch, a fantastic bar area with seating, great lighting and design, and super dining spaces throughout. There is wood, tile, and super wall décor, an "openish" kitchen, and a great looking private or club-like space with carpet and more upscale seating. The drink, beer, and whiskey list is huge, and a short wine list is offered as well. The Chef has created a menu to appeal to every taste. Start with pub snacks of Potted shrimp, pickled trout, spicy olives, and the signature Scotch egg. Crispy chips with a balsamic dip are served to all when seated. There are oysters on the half shell and a great array of Charcuterie as well to share. Salads include red endive and butter lettuce, beet and cucumber, orange, olive and mint. There are burgers of beef or lamb, a chicken sandwich, and ham sandwich all accompanied by fries. Entrees include bangers and mash, fish & chips, shepherd's pie, cauliflower chickpea curry, and orecchiette with sausage. Add fish of the day, a ramen bowl, salad Nicoise, and a Wagyu London broil for two and you just have to decide. Argyll brings a fun choice for dining in the hood.

Arugula Bar e Ristorante

Cuisine: Italian
Open: L: Wed- Fri, D: Daily
arugularistorante.com

2785 Iris Ave.   303-443-5100
Boulder, 80304
Iris & 28th

Price: $$ **Patio:** Yes
Reservations: Yes   **Brunch:** No
Location: Boulder

Arugula Bar e Ristorante brings upscale Italian dining with contemporary interpretations to Boulder. Chef/Owner Alec Schuler takes his inspiration in design using his antique collection for the art on the walls, sustainable wood floors, imported tiles and great lighting to create the background for dining. The dining room features comfortable seating, booths, and a great bar for dining as well. Start with calamari steak scampi, seared polenta and lamb, tomato-fennel bisque or gorgonzola mushrooms. The combinations of flavors in each dish are well-balanced and exciting. Fennel salad with orange, pine nuts and cheese, endive with walnuts, gorgonzola and herbs, and arugula with caramelized onions, roasted tomatoes and shaved Pecorino make the salad course a must. The squash and apple penne is awesome, as are other pasta choices that include pear and gorgonzola gnocchi, vodka shrimp gnocchi, chicken risotto, and orecchiette bison Bolognese. Entrées range from strawberry scallops with risotto, Dover sole "Francese," and chicken with garlic cloves and thyme to black pepper rubbed pork tenderloin with apple and grappa sauce, lamb sirloin, and hanger steak. Decadent desserts end the meal. The wine selections by the glass and bottle are excellent, and service is great. With comforting food, a warm feeling and affordable prices, Arugula Bar e Ristorante is a great Italian bistro.

Avenue Grill

Cuisine: American
Open: L & D: Daily, BR Sat-Sun
avenuegrill.com

630 E. 17th Ave.   303-861-2820
Denver, 80203
17th & Washington

Price: $$-$$$ **Patio:** Yes
Reservations: Yes   **Brunch:** Yes
Location: Uptown

Avenue Grill, a 17th Avenue restaurant, serves upscale food in classy yet casual surroundings. Take a seat at the large bar and enjoy signature martinis, beer and great wines. Gather with friends and indulge in dinner here as well. The scene is totally upscale and busy at this happening bar. Pictures of diners from opening days amuse patrons as they pick out folks they know. The menu appeals to those who want a casual lunch or dinner but also to those seeking something a bit more upscale. Start with chilled oysters on the half shell or seared chicken-and-spinach pot stickers spiced with soy, ginger and chile dip. Steamed mussels in red curry broth, wild mushroom strudel and clam chowder make other excellent choices. The Avenue Grill burger, accompanied with crispy fries, rates high. Mahi-mahi fillet and a roasted turkey BLTA make good entrées for lunch as do the grilled ham and cheese sandwich and the turkey club wrap. For pasta, try the grilled chicken ziti, with a light and spicy sun-dried tomato, basil and roasted pepper cream sauce. Asian barbecued half duck comes with orzo, vegetable spring rolls and hot mustard. Salmon, lamb, steak and more add to the entrée list. All are accompanied by complementary sides. Desserts are delicious with crème brûlée, decadent chocolate cake with caramel, chocolate mousse, berry cobblers and ice creams. Service is special, with friendly and informative staff. This oldie but goodie continues to bring in the crowd in the very popular Uptown.

Axios Estiatorio

Cuisine: Greek/Mediteranean
Open: L: Sat-Sun, D: Daily, BR: Sat-Sun
axiosdenver.com

3901 Tennyson St. 720-328-2225
Denver, 80212
39th & Tennyson

Price: $$ **Patio:** No
Reservations: Yes **Brunch:** Yes
Location: Berkeley

Denver is so ready for terrific Greek cuisine, and you will find exactly that at Axios, a fun addition to the Berkeley neighborhood. This Greek-style upscale trattoria lives in a space inspired by Greece with much blue and white throughout. The interior is warm and welcoming with comfortable seating and a nice bar. Owner Telly Topakas does everything right. His simple menu elevates Greek dishes to new heights. Start with great bread and olive oil and dig into the mezze course. This is the place to share many delights. The selection includes hummus, great lentil soup, amazing not-to-miss calamari, and a must have saganaki cheese. Spanakopita, tzatziki, dolmades, and lamb ribs are enough to keep diners happy and make them experience the Greek food ways. Several great salads come next and the not to miss selection of flatbreads. Try Greek, Skordo Kai Patates, meatball, or sliced tomato. Then come the entrées: lamb shank, kabobs of lamb or chicken, salmon, pork or stuffed pepper. Don't forget the pastitio, moussaka, Mediterranean pasta, and shrimp skewers on linguini. Leave room for dessert and pick from fig tart, baklava, and olive cake. The wine list features several surprising Greek wines, among others, to complement the food. The service is excellent, the prices affordable, and the vibe great. No matter what your neighborhood, this is well worth the trip.

Backcountry Provisions

Cuisine: Deli
Open: B-L: Daily
backcountryprovisions.com

444 17th St. Denver, 80202 17th & Glenarm	303-534-2100
1617 Wazee St. Denver, 80202 16th & Wazee	303-534-7900

Price: $-$$ **Patio:** Yes
Reservations: No   **Brunch:** No
Location: LoDo

LoDo welcomes a concept that offers diners a spot for breakfast and lunch. As you enter the restaurant, you feel that "back country" with wood walls, booths for seating, and that very casual feel. Read the menu on the board and place your order at the counter. Eat in or carry out, either way the food is great. The sandwiches are made on fresh breads matched with great fillings. The Pilgrim brings Thanksgiving every day with turkey, stuffing, and cranberries, or order plain turkey, club sandwiches, chicken, and more. There are tuna and chicken salads that fill the bread, tomato and mozzarella, beef, and so many choices that decisions are difficult. Several salads please the non-bread eaters. Order a cookie for dessert if you have a sweet tooth. Backcountry Provisions is a great alternative for really good food in LoDo for daytime dining

Bagel Deli and Restaurant

Cuisine: Breakfast, Deli
Open: B-L-D: Daily
thebageldeli.com

6439 E. Hampden Ave. Denver, 80222 Hampden & Monaco	303-756-6667

Price: $ **Patio:** No
Reservations: Yes   **Brunch:** No
Location: South East

Enjoy this classic deli that proudly wears the badge of the oldest continuously operated deli in Colorado, with a 32-year-old tradition under its belt. The comfortable atmosphere feels just like Mom's kitchen. Jewish or not, prepare yourself for some serious Jewish treats! Try everything from corned beef, to chicken soup with matzo balls, to chopped liver, or lox and bagels with cream cheese. The Reuben is piled high, as it should be, and couldn't be tastier. Breakfast lasts until 3 p.m. and includes such fare as latkes - potato pancakes, blintzes and a variety of egg dishes. Don't miss the egg salad! The sandwiches amaze both in taste and size. The Passover selection is the best in town. Dinners include roast beef, brisket and eggplant parmesan. Take home cheeses, meats, salads and desserts from the deli case. Catering is also available for any occasion and is excellent. The spot is so terrific that it was featured on the Food Network. Rhoda and Joe Kaplan have created the best deli, and the Bagel Deli remains a Denver favorite and staple.

Bangkok Café

Cuisine: Thai
Open: L & D: Mon-Sun
bangkokcafedenver.com

1225 E. Hampden Ave.   303-806-9354
Englewood, 80113
Old Hampden & Downing

Price: $-$$ **Patio:** No
Reservations: Yes   **Brunch:** No
Location: Englewood

Enter this small spot located in a strip mall and get ready to enjoy a real taste of Thai cuisine at its best. Family run, the food is what it's all about at Bangkok Café. Start with Thai egg rolls with plum sauce, steamed dumplings, chicken satay, or tasty crab cooked in garlic and black pepper. Thai hot-and-sour soup and chicken coconut milk soup make great entrées as well as starters. If you love Thai beef salad, the rendition here is very special. Traditional Pad Thai is a must, and the curries head the entrée choices. Yellow curry with shrimp, chicken, pork or vegetables is a flavorful and mild option, while red curry brings more spice to the dishes. Enjoy noodle and rice dishes as well as entrées of fish, chicken and beef, and you are set for a feast. End with bread pudding, sticky rice or Thai beignets. The prices are very reasonable, and the service is friendly and efficient. This neighborhood spot is definitely worth the trip.

Barolo Grill

Cuisine: Italian
Open: D: Tues-Sat
barologrilldenver.com

3030 E. 6th Ave.
Denver, 80206
6th & St. Paul

303-393-1040

Price: $$$$
Reservations: Yes
Location: Cherry Creek North

Patio: No
Brunch: No

As soon as you enter Barolo Grill, the energy of the happy crowd greets you, letting you know that you're in for a great evening. Wonderful Italian food, ethereal wines and excellent service make it a great spot for a special occasion or just a night out on the town. Casual but upscale, the bar is filled with guests who gather to enjoy a drink, eat dinner or wait for their table in the dining room. The personality of the restaurant begins with Owner Ryan Fletter, as he greets and charms all, adding a special touch to the experience. Chef Darrell Truett and staff are amazing and bring their great talents to the stove as they create exciting dishes with true Italian flair. The seasonal menu changes often. Start with the bread sticks and ever-changing dips. Then indulge in the divine, warm rolls served with your meal. A parmesan soufflé, prosciutto wrapped around savory doughnuts, prawns with vegetable relish, sweetbreads, duck liver pate, and the signature fritto misto are some of the incredible first courses presented by the chefs. Pastas are marvelous – ricotta cheese gnocchi with sprouts and leeks, risotto with seafood, tagliatelle with mushrooms and agnolotti with cheese. The signature braised duck with olives, pork tenderloin stuffed with dried fruit, Osso bucco, and bone-in sirloin bring raves. Grilled salmon with cauliflower puree and pan seared monkfish with lentil ragu are outrageous in taste and flavor. Decisions are impossible. Leave room for decadent desserts such as crème brûlée and the best chocolate cake with chocolate meringues. The wonderful nightly "tasting dinner" is served with or without wine. The new menu is totally amazing and divine. Under Ryan's expert hands, the incredible wine list boasts many exquisite Italian varietals. Enjoy the party rooms for special occasions, but grab a seat at the bar any night for a special dining experience. A night at Barolo Grill is perfect and will almost seem like the dream trip to Italy!

Bastien's

Cuisine: Steakhouse
Open: D: Daily
bastiensrestaurant.com

3503 E. Colfax Ave.   303-322-0363
Denver, 80206
Madison & Colfax

Price: $$-$$$ **Patio:** No
Reservations: Yes   **Brunch:** No
Location: East Colfax

Walking into Bastien's takes you back to a time when life was simple and oh so mellow. On any given night you can find a member of the Bastien family serving up a drink from the Cheers-like bar or a home-style meal from the kitchen. The ambience remains retro, with lots of updates including new chairs and carpet. The dining rooms include an upstairs area as well as seating on the main level. The food has gotten a facelift along with the décor, and traditional dishes now have a new touch. Baskets of the best cheese and sesame sticks, along with flavored butter for dipping, greet you at the table. Start with gnocchi with pine nuts or rich mascarpone and gorgonzola sauce, ravioli, shrimp cocktail, onion rings and deep-fried mushrooms. Dinners come with house salad with excellent dressing or homemade soup. The signature sugar steak, a 16-ounce New York strip with brown sugar and herbs pounded into the meat, is broiled on the open flame to caramelize the sugar with the natural juices of the beef. Other steak choices include a filet, T-bone, rib-eye or prime rib and come in two sizes, and are accompanied by vegetables and potatoes. Fish options include trout, catfish, tilapia or salmon. Desserts are mandatory, with decadent coconut banana cream pie, chocolate brownie à la mode, pecan pie, and apple, cherry or peach pie served à la mode in a sizzling dish topped with brandy sauce. With an "old school" feel Bastien's is a true classic.

Baur's

Cuisine: American/contemporary
Open: L-D: Mon-Fri, BR-D:-Sat-Sun
Baursrestaurant.com

1512 Curtis Street,   (303) 615-4000
Denver, 80202
15th & Curtis

Price: $$$ **Patio:** Yes
Reservations: Yes   **Brunch:** Yes
Location: Downtown

Baur's brings great fun to dining in downtown Denver.
Retaining the charm of the original, it shows the combination
of new with the old. The white tile floor is as old as Baur's, that
is about 100 years, with a fabulous bar designed to reflect the
tradition but is not really an antique. The dining room has
comfortable seating with booths and tables while lovely art
accents the white walls. There is bar seating and high top tables
as well in the lounge area. There's even a section of the space
with a stage for live entertainment that happens frequently.
The menu brings great options for all. Start with chips and a
veggie dip, fried calamari, beef marrow done with sweet and
sour shallots, a plate that includes berbere spiced duck, pork
ribs, chicken wings and chow chow. Do not miss the lobster
deviled eggs with bacon, avocado and potato chips. It's hard
to eat just one but save room for grilled asparagus salad with
brandade fritters, beet salad, and roasted cauliflower romesco.
Perfectly grilled octopus and fresh abalone are must haves.
Both are great in texture and taste and a real treat. Pasta dishes
of tagliatelle, gnocchi with mushroom gratin, and garganelli
Bolognese make a wonderful entrée or go for the list of main
dishes: halibut, pave of chicken, pork shoulder chop with green
chili, lamb chops, venison schnitzel, and steak frites. Decadent
desserts end the feast. Chef Robert Grant and front of the
house manager, Diane Kliendienst have done an amazing job
with food and staff to bring excitement to downtown dining.
And remember this spot when attending the DCPA. With the
warm welcome, excellent food and wine, Baur's is a special
place for dining.

Beast + Bottle

Cuisine: Contemporary
Open: D-Tues-Sun, BR: Sat-Sun
beastandbottle.com

719 E. 17th Ave
303-623-3223
17th avenue and Clarkson

Denver, 80203

Price: $$$-$$$$ **Patio:** Yes
Reservations: Yes   **Brunch:** Yes
Location: Uptown

Paul and Aileen Reilly finally have a place of their own, and what a delight it is. Enter through a welcoming patio and find bright white walls, a fabulous focal bar with white tile behind, beige touches and light colors and wood throughout. It is totally charming and a place you want to visit. The menu brings all sorts of great options, thanks to the creativity of Paul and his chefs. Small plates start with hamachi crudo, foie gras torchon, soft shell crab, octopus, a meat board and porcini mushroom gnocchi. The Greek style sausage with green garbanzo and cured pork with tuna aioli, and the sunchokes are the most outrageous dishes ever. The flatbreads are another must with a crispy crust with fabulous toppings. Eat your Vegetables brings lettuces, spinach potato soup, peas, and roasted beets. Next come the awesome plates. Lamb or pappardelle with lamb ragu, spinach garganelli, where the perfectly done spinach noodle is paired with mushrooms and rabbit meatballs, and an asparagus-porcini tart begin the list. Add a remarkable pork tenderloin with pork belly confit and green garlic spaetzle and yellowfin tuna with chorizo and peas and try to decide. Each presentation is a work of art to the eye, better to the taste. Leave room for chocolate dacquise, bruleed buttermilk tart, and pink peppercorn-chevre cheesecake. But you must have the "bite" of cardamom-caramel dumpling (cousin to a beignet). The wine list is as outstanding and carefully chosen as the cuisine and offered in different size portions at reasonable prices. Service is just as top notch as everything else. In a word-or two—Beast+Bottle is tops.

Beatrice & Woodsley

Cuisine: Small Plates
Open: D: Daily, BR: Sat-Sun
beatriceandwoodsley.com

38 S. Broadway Blvd.   303-777-3505
Denver, 80209
Ellsworth & S. Broadway

Price: $$$ **Patio:** No
Reservations: Yes   **Brunch:** Yes
Location: Baker

South Beach meets Coal Creek Canyon might begin to describe this fantastic, fanciful small plate restaurant. Begin with their story: Beatrice, a French woman, lover of wine, met Woodsley, a lumberjack who loved the outdoors. Together they began their journey in the woods and built a charming cabin. Beatrice & Woodsley was created in honor of their fairy tale love and the space feels romantic, charming and magical. With very high ceilings, Aspen trees throughout, kerosene lanterns hanging from the ceiling, curved boards (indicating pieces of the roof), twigs, and an awesome bar complete with chain saws along the back of the bar; the world of love and fantasy is created. Add gorgeous French bar stools in light pine, comfortable, very modern booths in beige and white, sheer curtains, and a marvelous wine cellar and this is the beginning of your adventure. Owners Kevin Delk and John Skogstad finished each detail in design, added small plates and stocked big wines to complete the picture. The wines are offered by the half or full glass, as well as by the bottle, and tastes are happily offered. Start with artisan cheese, braised pork belly with house pickles and mango mustard, sweet pea cakes of sautéed oyster mushrooms, yogurt and pea shoots, or vegetable mousses. Lamb loin, sweetbreads, duck rillette with shirred egg, diver scallops on Johnnycake, and cod with cockles are more options. End with sweets and a dessert wine. Weekend brunch and high tea are other exciting options. Beatrice & Woodsley is very unique and a place to see and a fabulous choice for a romantic date.

Biker Jim's Dogs

Cuisine: American
Open: L-D: Daily
bikerjimsdogs.com

2148 Larimer St.	720-746-9355
Denver, 80205	
21st & Larimer	
1601 Mayberry Dr. Suite 103	720-344-2100
Highlands Ranch, 80129	
Highlands Ranch Pkwy & Lucent	

Price: $-$$	**Patio:** No
Reservations: No	**Brunch:** No
Location: LoDo, Highlands Ranch	

Biker Jim took a step away from his famous carts and entered the restaurant scene with a big splash. Rev up that cycle and park in front of this great spot. The interior is high tech contemporary with high ceilings, exposed pipes, a brick wall, a nice counter, and comfortable seating with the open kitchen totally the focal point. Try to decide on what to order and they will call when your food is ready. We're talking choices that make decisions hard to make: the Alaskan reindeer, elk jalapeño cheddar, pheasant, wild boar, veal, Italian, Louisiana red hot and even an award-wining vegan dog! Combinations are outrageous with the duck dog, topped with wasabi aioli, caramelized apples and shaved cheddar; the bat dog, tomato cream cheese, avocado and caramelized onions; the rattlesnake and pheasant with roasted cactus, Malaysian curry jam, scallions, and onions. Those are just a few choices. The off-the-street burger is served with garlic aioli, seared poblanos, fried green tomatoes, fried onions and a basted egg. The buns are fabulous and sides rock. Try fried mac and cheese, charred tahini cauliflower, a great salad, fried green tomatoes, and homemade fries and chips. Beer, wine, soft drinks, and shakes complement the food. Service is fun, prices affordable, and wow, Biker Jim has a real winner in LoDo with this great spot.

Billy's Inn

Cuisine: American, Pub
Open: L-D: Daily, BR: Sat-Sun
billysinn.com

4403 Lowell Blvd.   303-455-9733
Denver, 80211
44th & Lowell

Price: $-$$ **Patio:** Yes
Reservations: No   **Brunch:** Yes
Location: Berkeley

A great neighborhood spot, Billy's Inn offers simple food, beer and good times. Inside there is a big bar with booths and tables and a great patio for dining. The garage doors open to let customers enjoy that indoor-outdoor feel that the Colorado weather allows for many months out of the year. Start with fried chicken nuggets or chicken wings, nachos deluxe, fabulous guacamole and salsa, or devilishly spicy deviled eggs. The taco list ranges from mahi mahi, shrimp, and lobster to chicken, veggie and rib-eye steak. There are also quesadillas and a good selection of salads like the chicken with spinach, apples, walnuts and bacon, the chop-chop salad, or the avocado Caesar. Burgers rock with Santa Fe, guacamole bacon, or Texas. Add fries, onion rings, or sweet potato fries and you are set. If you prefer sandwiches, don't miss the grilled chicken with avocado and pepper-jack cheese, roast turkey with provolone, grilled hot avocado melt and roast beef. Desserts entice with a hot fudge sundae, warm brownie and blondie, or warm apple pie à la mode. Service is friendly and the drink list fun.

Biju's Little Curry Shop

Cuisine: Indian
Open: L-D: Mon-Sat
littlecurryshop.com

1441 26th St   303-292-3500
Denver, 80205
26th & Walnut

Price: $ **Patio:** Yes
Reservations: No   **Brunch:** No
Location: RiNo

What a treat this little spot is! A bit hard to find on the block but so worth the look. There's a small patio with stools and high tops as you enter and then you are there dreaming of what's to come. The small space is industrial in feel with touches of India. Indian patterned fabrics on the backs of the banquettes, and the focal yellow counter has a pic of an elephant. You are given

a bowl and walk through the line with many choices. Start with plain or basmati rice, add chicken, beef, veggie or combo already in curry. This brings another choice-mild, medium, hot. The hot is divine but not so that you do not relish every flavor of the sauce. They call this one vindaloo-addictive-and there are medium and mild with different sauces. Add lentils, potatoes, beets, veggies, yogurt, cilantro, green onions, jalapenos, extra sauces, slaw, and poppadum chips. It goes on until you are finished with toppings and decisions. The homemade parata bread is just as perfect as all else and perfect to sop up sauces. Take a seat and enjoy every minute of your incredible dish. It is gourmet fast food-but extraordinary. There is wine, beer, and drinks to complement your meal as well. The staff is super helpful and come around to care for you. With fabulous food and affordable prices, the Little Curry Shop is so good that it could be an everyday happening for anyone.

Bistro Barbes

Cuisine: French
Open: D: Tues-Sat
bistrobarbes.com

5021 E. 28th Ave   720-398-8085
Denver, 80207
28th & Elm

Price: $$$-$$$$ **Patio:** No
Reservations: Yes   **Brunch:** No
Location: Park Hill

Bistro Barbes in Park Hill is one interesting and very popular spot. The well qualified chef/owners have created a short menu that changes often, the wine list is lovely and affordable, and the service is nice. The bread-if you ask-is great—and the appetizer list again rotates. The artichoke vichyssoise is special when available and on one occasion spring salad and octopus were other choices. There are four entrees each evening that range from duck confit, snapper, and escargot to flank steak and vongole. Desserts change constantly as well. On a night with your favorites, it is great fun. This is a tiny spot-casual in the neighborhood and a fun night out for dining in a super area.

Bistro Vendôme

Cuisine: French
Open: D: Daily, BR: Sat-Sun
bistrovendome.com

1420 Larimer St.   303-825-3232
Denver, 80202
14th & Larimer

Price: $$$ **Patio:** Yes
Reservations: Yes   **Brunch:** Yes
Location: Larimer Square - Downtown

Enter this French bistro with high ceilings, mustard faux-painted walls, mirrors, great lighting and comfortable seating for a true French dining experience. The sensational patio is awesome with great flowers, shrubs, seating, umbrellas and the perfect spot to be. Bistro Vendôme is situated in the back of the main street truly transporting the guests to Paris. Jennifer Jasinski and Beth Gruitch, owners of Bistro Vendôme (and the popular Rioja across the street,) charm diners with a marvelous menu. Start your meal with the French baguette served in a paper bag and choose from the selection of appetizers: soupe à l'oignon, mussels, foie gras with rhubarb and escargot are among the favorites. Crêpes filled with chicken and the excellent steak tartare bring more options for an appetizer. The beet salad or greens combined with a fried egg and bacon make for great flavors. Herb-roasted chicken comes with a rich cauliflower gratin, and duck confit with foie gras start the entrée list with other favorites of steak frites, halibut with fava bean ravioli, salmon with corn-bacon beignets, and stuffed quail as more choices to entice the diner. A very French wine list is nicely priced. Dessert alert: Bistro Vendôme features homemade ice creams and sorbets in sensational flavors. Apple cider date, pineapple orange, and caramel green apple ice creams or sorbets of pineapple, cherry tarragon, and blood orange add great choices to the dessert menu. Weekends bring a sensational brunch. With great service and a warm, friendly feel, Bistro Vendôme earns kudos as a great dining spot in Denver. Ooh-la-la, it's nice to be French.

Bittersweet

Cuisine: Contemporary
Open: D: Tues-Sat
bittersweetdenver.com

500 E. Alameda Ave.   303-942-0320
Denver, 80209
E. Alameda & Pennsylvania

Price: $$$$ **Patio:** No
Reservations: Yes   **Brunch:** No
Location: South Central

Bittersweet feels magical. As you drive up, you see magnificent flowers and gardens with guests enjoying their meals in this fairytale urban setting. Enter the restaurant and go to the other patio, to find herbs that Olav Peterson-Chef/Owner is growing for the restaurant. The interior is stunning and so beautiful. The front room is more casual with big windows, wood topped tables with white chairs and lovely place settings while the second room is a bit more formal with a fireplace and set with the beautiful silver and warmer colors. The staff, from the bar to the servers, is amazing and welcoming, charming, and efficient. Add great food and wine and you have one fabulous experience. The wines are great and reasonably priced, always including a divine rosé—a personal favorite in warmer weather. The menu changes but, when available, try beets with quinoa, pomegranate, and poached egg, root vegetable risotto, rabbit meatballs, octopus, mushroom consommé, sausage with veggies and a charcuterie plate. Each is so fabulous that you want one of each. Entrées start with sturgeon with clams, mussels, and octopus, divine cod with crab and hot chilies, Wague Hanger steak with bone marrow sauce and scallops. Add pork osso bucco, lamb cassolet, and a vegetable tasting and decisions are impossible. Each presentation is stunning and delights the eyes, just as the flavors delight the taste buds. Remember the entire menu changes often. Do not leave without dessert- and these also change constantly. The headings on one menu were Passion Fruit, Banana, Chocolate, Pineapple, and house made ice cream and sorbets. The pineapple brings caramelized pineapple, brown butter doughnuts, buttermilk foam, and dulce ganache. Again, the tastes are spectacular. It is charming, romantic, and wonderful at Bittersweet- don't miss out on one of the best dining experiences in Denver.

Blackbelly Restaurant and Market

Cuisine: Contemporary Grab & Go Breakfast
       & Lunch

Open: B - L: Daily D: Daily

blackbelly.com

1606 Conastoga St #3
Boulder, 80301
Conestoga & Arapahoe

303-247-1000

Price: $$-$$$
Reservations: Yes
Location: East Boulder

Patio: Yes
Brunch: No

Blackbelly brings very special dining to Boulder. Hosea Rosenberg, chef and owner, took a long time creating this amazing spot. During the day it is a grab and go spot for food and a terrific market that features special meats, goods, and produce. The space is great looking with black floors, a super huge open kitchen, two bars that are totally mobbed, and great seating. It is casual and comfortable and the place to be. The food is amazing. Start with Grateful Bread that wins every prize and then dig into marvelous oysters and a selection of charcuterie that rocks. Small plates range from house-made sausage, roast bone marrow, awesome wagyu beef tartare, and the best posole with hatch green chile and pork shoulder. Enjoy a Caesar, beet or greens with roasted pear salad for your next course. Large plates are so special: a burger with bacon and Swiss, steelhead trout with lentils, prawns with smoked cheddar grits, and seared duck breast. More great options add to the confusion of choosing with smoked lamb shank, ricotta cavatelli with mushroom, a half chicken with fries brings chicken to the level it should enjoy, and beef and pork dishes each day. There are great sides—and add an egg to any dish! OK I will. The desserts keep pace with the rest of the food with everything from chocolate to carrot cake. Presentation of every dish impresses and the tastes bring perfect balance. The wine and cocktail list are excellent and nicely priced, and service the best anywhere. Blackbelly has it all and is a must on any list for great dining and super fun as well.

Blackbird

Cuisine: Small Plates
Open: L: Mon-Fri, D: Daily, BR: Sat-Sun
blackbirddenver.com

305 S. Downing   303-733-3923
Denver, 80209
Downing & Alameda

Price: $$$ **Patio:** No
Reservations: Yes   **Brunch:** Yes
Location: Wash Park

Blackbird is located in a small strip mall in a great area for neighborhood casual dining. The space is great. Enter to a dining area and open kitchen and move into a huge bar with great lighting, TV, seating all around, and fun. Lots of wood and casual ambience and even a separate dining space for parties set the scene. The menu brings an interesting concept. One menu is for Tuesday through Saturday and another informal menu happens Sunday/Monday. Take your pick. The more formal list includes charcuterie board, brie hot pot, potted pig, steak tartare, blistered Brussels, and candies bacon. There's a soup of the day, frisee, roasted beets, smoked Caesar and simple salads next. Plates of vegetable hot pot, cauliflower steak, fried chicken and lamb ragu start the entrees. Arctic char, risotto paella, short ribs, lamb and hanger steak round out the choices. The pizzas are super and there are several options here. Add sides and some yummy desserts and you are set. The weekend menu is such fun with the charcuterie, smoked Caesar and soup. Pizzas are a must with a thin but chewy crust and great toppings; barbecue rib, charcuterie, Bianca, cheese, garden and a special one. Fried chicken skin, smoked wings, candied bacon, steak tartare, brie hot pot and blistered Brussels are for sharing while plates bring wheat berry fried rice, risotto, mussels, fried chicken, ribs and a burger. The wine and drink list is very nice and service amazing. The staff is some of the best in town and caring, pleasant, and wow. Blackbird brings a fun concept and a great addition to this neighborhood.

Black Pearl

Cuisine: Contemporary
Open: L: Mon-Fri, D: Daily, BR: Fri-Mon
blackpearldenver.com

1529 S. Pearl St.   303-777-0500
Denver, 80210
S. Pearl & Florida

Price: $$$ **Patio:** Yes
Reservations: Yes   **Brunch:** Yes
Location: Wash Park, Denver Old S. Pearl

Enter the great patio at Black Pearl, with its stone community table centered by a fire pit for warmth when needed. In the welcoming bar/lounge, you can enjoy drinks or a meal. The dining area is beautiful with large windows giving a view of the street, high ceilings, contemporary light fixtures, wood floors and putty-gray walls. Ultra-simple and striking wood tables and chairs, and printed fabric booths set the scene. Start with oysters, raw or fried, grilled romaine with anchovy, mussels with fries, or several cheese selections or try the sautéed calamari or mac and cheese with mascarpone. Entrées include gnocchi, sea bass, and lamb T-bone with eggplant and lentils. Desserts vary with the season but the brownie à la mode with caramel and chocolate is a winner. The wine list is nice with offerings by the glass or bottle. Black Pearl is part of the very popular South Pearl dining scene.

Blue Bonnet

Cuisine: Mexican
Open: L-D: Daily
bluebonnetrestaurant.com

457 South Broadway Blvd.   303-778-0147
Denver 80209
Broadway & W Alaska

Price: $-$$ **Patio:** Yes
Reservations: No   **Brunch:** No
Location: South Central

The Blue Bonnet has been around since the '30s and owned by the Mobel family for over 40 years. It remains a mainstay in Mexican dining in Denver, and now boasts an updated, contemporary menu to attract fans from all over the area. The place looks great, typical Mexican with a fun décor, a great bar, and a fabulous covered patio. Start with great guacamole and ceviche along with complimentary chips and salsa. The gazpacho is always a winner and available à la carte or served with tacos - a fun idea. The selection of tacos includes everything from veggie, chicken, and pork to shrimp and fish. Some of the tamales are vegetarian but there are also options for the meat-lovers. Do not miss the mango chicken salad in a crispy taco shell. Chili rellenos, enchiladas, fajitas, and all familiar dishes arrive in large portions and burst with flavor. There is a complete gluten-free menu. Do your best to try the poblano stuffed pepper—a delight—and end your meal with sopapillas, flan, fried ice cream or soft serve. Enjoy a mojito, margarita, beer or wine to accompany your meal. With great service, excellent prices, and lots of heart, the Blue Bonnet makes a great choice for Mexican dining.

Bonefish Grill

Cuisine: American, Seafood
Open: L-D: Daily BR: Sat-Sun
bonefishgrill.com

4948 S. Yosemite St.   303-741-3474
Greenwood Village, 80111
Also in Johnstown, Littleton & Westminster.

Price: $$-$$$ **Patio:** No
Reservations: Yes   **Brunch:** Yes
Location: Greenwood Village, Westminster, Littleton, Loveland

Bonefish Grill brings excellent seafood and a playful design. The space is large with casual but upscale décor including paintings, metal sculptures, and comfortable booths and tables. The bar area is furnished with community tables, perfect for conversation, along with additional booths for dining. The star here is the fish with choices that change daily depending on availability. Start with bang bang shrimp, where crispy shrimp are tossed in a creamy, spicy-sweet sauce. Crab cakes are filled with jumbo lump crab and served with a spicy sauce to accent the flavor. Other appetizers include ahi tuna sashimi, bacon-wrapped sea scallops and crispy calamari. Choose your entrée, as well as the accompanying sauce and side. Salmon, trout, tilapia, swordfish, tuna, sea bass, lobster tail and grouper are some of the options. Add your favorite sauce: lemon butter, lime tomato garlic, warm mango or pan Asian to complement the grilled fish. Sides include garlic-mashed potatoes, rich potatoes au gratin, angel hair pasta, island rice, or steamed vegetables. Pork, chicken and steak are available for those who are not seafood fans. End with the decadent chocolate macadamia nut brownie à la mode, key lime pie or crème brûlée. The wine, beer and martini lists are nice, and happy hour is a real bargain. Friendly service and reasonable prices add to the fun.

K: Good, not great food. Pricey. Good atmosphere.

Bones

Cuisine: Noodles Bar
Open: L: Mon-Fri, D: Daily
bonesdenver.com

701 Grant St.   303-860-2929
Denver, 80203
7th & Grant

Price: $$ **Patio:** No
Reservations: Yes   **Brunch:** No
Location: Capitol Hill

No "bones" about it, the Bones Noodle Bar is terrific—and a
perfect spot for this neighborhood. This small, 27-seat room
is upbeat and fun. There is black and white tile behind the
open kitchen/bar where the crowd watches the chefs prepare
great Asian-fusion food. Big windows, simple décor, tables and
booths, along with the bar seating, set the scene. Chopsticks
reign but silverware is in the background if one chooses.
Start with stunning steamed pork belly buns, duck confit
egg rolls, roasted bone marrow over toasted bread soaked in
the sauce, hamachi tartare, tuna sashimi, oysters Rockefeller
or escargot pot stickers. Noodles are the star here. Ramen are
complemented with poached lobster, edamame and miso,
very buttery and rich. Udon brings roasted pork with the wide
flavorful noodles and a poached egg, making a perfect dish.
There is a vegetarian offering and, with any dish, add a poached
egg to make the noodle bowl even better. Don't miss Frank's
soft-serve ice cream for dessert. The wine and cocktail list is fun
and the service is great. Frank and Jacqueline Bonnano have
done it again with Bones and several other big hits in Denver,
Bones is a winner for great dining.

Bourbon Grill

Cuisine: BBQ, Cajun, American
Open: L-D: Mon-Sat

1618 E. Colfax   303-355-3821
Denver, 80218
Colfax & Franklin

Price: $ **Patio:** Yes
Reservations: No   **Brunch:** No
Location: East Colfax

OK-not the usual spot that gets a review-but cannot resist.
There's a red awning with the name, a walk up window, and 2
tables outside-that's it!! Look into the kitchen and the décor
is the cooking arrangement where Tom takes the orders and
his wife Lynn and helpers heap up boxes of super chicken-and

more. It is a hoot. You can get sandwiches, entrees, or however you want but you will be a fan after one visit. The bourbon chicken is cut into small pieces, no bones, and marinated in great sauce—not too spicy but totally addictive. On the entrees, the chicken is piled on rice with lots of sauce and pick your sides. The mac and cheese is gooey, runny, and delicious. The roasted potatoes with Cajun spices and the spaghetti with the Cajun sauce are impossible to pass up. There is another seasoning offered for chicken but never got that far. You'll see pickles, veggies and more as well. Pack up your box-and the price is so cheap-and the box so heavy! I was not sure I could lift it-but did and return trips happen often. This is family fun and one popular spot in this hood.

Brazen

Cuisine: American
Open: D: Daily, BR-Sat-Sun
brazendenver.com

4450 W. 38th Ave. #130   720-638-1242
Denver, 80212
38th & Utica

Price: $$-$$$ **Patio:** Yes
Reservations: No   **Brunch:** Yes
Location: Tennyson-Berkeley

Brazen is a delightful spot that appeals to all in the area between West Highland and Berkley. Behind a dental office, walk by or enjoy a great patio complete with fire pit. Enter to a space that features both a great bar and open kitchen, seats 44 lucky diners, and is done with lots of wood, concrete floors, high industrial ceilings, and pillow accents on the banquettes for color. Owner Christopher Sargent teamed up with talented chefs to create a fabulous new American menu that is perfect for any taste. Start with oysters or Wahoo crudo, and then indulge in delicious Fancy Toast. The mushrooms with bean puree, bacon, and poached egg, and the lemon honey ricotta with sweet pea puree are worth the trip. Vegetables bring brown butter parsnip soup, baby carrots, zucchini squash latkes, turnip ceviche, beets, and a veggie and greens salad. Under Small Plates spicy deviled eggs, tomato meatballs, and duck confit are surpassed with the best butternut squash tortellini with brown butter sage, chanterelle, and cranberries, the veggies tartin, and cauliflower to die for. Large plates are designed for two: the best roasted chicken, whole fish, and pork chop and are terrific and enough for even more to share. End with donut holes or one super version of s'mores. The ramen served is another reason to get there. It is served late night and for brunch and unbelievably delicious. The cocktail and wine list rock and service is some of the best ever. A weekend brunch is great. Brazen is affordable and fun with exceptional food and the place to be at any time.

Brasserie Ten Ten

Cuisine: Contemporary, French, Brunch
Open: L & D: Daily BR: Sat-Sun
brasserietenten.com

1011 Walnut St.   303-998-1010
Boulder, 80302
10th & Walnut

Price: $$$ **Patio:** Yes
Reservations: Yes   **Brunch:** Yes
Location: Boulder

Brasserie Ten Ten earned its good reputation in the Boulder dining scene over years of service. The space is full of charm, reminiscent of a Parisian restaurant. Enter the bar area, then settle in the dining room to watch the kitchen at work. The wait staff guides you through the one-page menu, which features a variety of soups, seafood appetizers, salads and a cheese assortment. Entrées range from rack of lamb to the Brasserie burger—grilled tenderloin studded with Portobello mushrooms, caramelized shallots and rosemary served on a poppy seed buttermilk roll. Other great choices include coquilles Saint Jacques or pavé of salmon with cucumber salad and Thai curry rice. Desserts are a must with the dense chocolate terrine being a definite winner. The weekend brunch is exciting and features French classics like onion soup, escargot, and Lyonnais salad. Lunchtime sandwiches and breakfast items bring fabulous dishes of Belgian waffles, beignets, omelets so light and fluffy that one could not leave a bite behind, eggs Benedict at their finest, and scrambled eggs done with exciting fillings. Coffee and tea service is excellent. An extensive wine list, along with beers and other spirits, make Brasserie Ten Ten a great choice for dining.

Breakfast on Broadway

Cuisine: American, Breakfast
Open: B-L: Daily
breakfastonbroadway.com

2901 S. Broadway Blvd.   303-788-9998
Englewood, 80113
S. Broadway & Bates

Price: $ **Patio:** Yes
Reservations: No   **Brunch:** Yes
Location: Englewood

Breakfast on Broadway is the perfect spot for a casual and hearty breakfast or lunch. The building is bright and pretty with big windows, soft colors, comfortable seating, and a nice bar and simple food. There are great pancakes that include amaretto and peaches, s'mores, strawberries Romanoff, and peanut butter and jelly. Stuffed French toast, Benedicts, omelets or eggs your way offer more choices. Burritos, huevos rancheros, oatmeal and yogurt please all. There are burgers, grilled cheese sandwiches and tomato soup, club sandwiches, ahi tuna salad or Caesar salad if you want lunch. Leave room for a shake, mud pie, apple pie or praline crêpes. Along with coffee drinks, espresso and juices, wine and beer are available. Service is friendly and prices are affordable.

Briarwood Inn

Cuisine: Contemporary
Open: D: Tues- Sun BR: Sat- Sun
thebriarwoodinn.com

1630 8th St.   303-279-3121
Golden, 80401
6th & Hwy. 58

Price: $$$$ **Patio:** Yes
Reservations: Yes   **Brunch:** Yes
Location: Golden

The Briarwood Inn brings new excitement to the restaurant with executive chef Jeff Jones joining the team to create a more contemporary feel. Nestled on the outskirts of Golden, diners come here to celebrate special occasions or arrive just for a night out. Walk through elegant landscaping, over a little bridge and into the small mansion. Lovely accessories and china fill each dining room, and now a new menu. Ala carte offerings are so exciting. Start with shrimp ravioli, foie gras, pork belly, and sockeye salmon in beet puree. White gazpacho, tuna carpaccio, and a summer tart brighten the salad selections. Risotto and gnocchi are always a hit and all before entrees. They include filet, scallops, duck confit, rack of lamb, halibut, a ribeye, pork chop and vegetarian option. All are great in presentation and taste. Still available is the fixed price dinner that was the style here for years for those who want to indulge. Desserts are decadent as well. There is a wonderful wine list to complement the food. Briarwood in remains a great choice for special occasion or just because.

Brio Tuscan Grill

Cuisine: Italian
Open: L-D: Daily, BR: Sat-Sun
brioitalian.com

8441 Park Meadows Center Dr.   303-662-9727
Lone Tree, 80124

2500 E. 1st Ave.   303-329-0222
Denver, 80206
1st & University

Price: $$-$$$ **Patio:** Yes
Reservations: Yes   **Brunch:** Yes
Location: Cherry Creek, Park Meadows

Brio comes to Cherry Creek serving Italian food. The beautiful exterior and great patio are what you see first. Enter and find a welcoming bar and large dining room that seats 400. High ceilings, great lighting, Tuscan pillars to separate the large room into sections for comfortable seating with tables and booths, and drapes that soften the noise, set the scene. Fresh bread and crispy crackers arrive as you peruse the menu and enjoy wine from the lovely list with several choices by the glass. Start with bruschetta, flat bread pizza, rich lobster bisque, calamari, or beef carpaccio. Enjoy the Caesar, wedge or excellent chop salad. Pastas range from pasta with vodka and carbonara to Mediterranean penne, ravioli, and risotto. Beef entrées include tournedos, gorgonzola-crusted bistecca, Toscano, and Florentino. From the grill, favorites include brick chicken, pork chops, salmon, lamb, and steak. End with great desserts. Service is friendly, efficient and informative. Lunch and brunch are offered and there is valet parking. Brio brings a new option for dining in the popular Cherry Creek area.

The Broker Restaurant

Cuisine: American, Steakhouse
Open: L: Mon-Fri, D: Daily
thebrokerrestaurant.com

821 17th St.   303-292-5065
Denver, 80202
17th & Champa

Price: $$$$ **Patio:** No
Reservations: Yes   **Brunch:** No
Location: Downtown

Located in a historic bank building, The Broker is over 36 years old, an impressive streak in this business. Enter a living room-like setting before descending the staircase to the restaurant. A stock-exchange board hangs across the hoarse bar, plus you can dine in several areas, including the vault! Owner Jerry Fitzler has taken the "old" Broker and updated the menu with a "new" feel. The menu features à la carte dining with options to please all. Start with appetizers of tuna tartare, mussels, calamari and onion soup. Enjoy an entrée salmon salad or tuna niçoise for lighter fare. Grilled trout, eggplant Napoleon, and Dijon chicken are examples of the new entrées. Chicken piccata, grilled salmon, prime rib and several excellent steaks are more options. If you want the traditional of the "old" menu you can still enjoy the all-inclusive concept which includes the shrimp bowl, soup or salad, entrée and dessert. The wine list is extensive with great options. The staff will open almost any bottle of wine if you only want a glass. The varietals and several years of excellent vintages make for exciting choices and prices are very reasonable. Reserve the wine cellar downstairs for a special dinner. Open for weekday lunch, The Broker is a lovely setting for business or pleasure.

Brook's Steak House and Cellar

Cuisine: Steakhouse
Open: D: Daily
brookssteakhouse.com

6538 S. Yosemite Circle   303-770-1177
Greenwood Village, 80111
I-25 & Arapahoe Rd.

Price: $$$$ **Patio:** No
Reservations: Yes   **Brunch:** No
Location: Denver Tech Center

Tucked just off I-25 in the Denver Tech Center, this independent steakhouse serves some of Denver's best prime cuts of beef. One of the first steakhouses to open, Brook's does everything well. The sunken dining room sets the scene for those who come to enjoy steaks and more. A bar sits above the main area for people who want a glass of wine or cocktails and diners are welcome to enjoy their meals here as well. Elegant, but casual, the atmosphere complements the terrific meals. Start with excellent bread as you decide on wine or other beverages. The crab cakes with chile aioli and Dijon remoulade sauce are excellent. Or try escargot, shrimp, or a seafood combination appetizer. The Brook's salad brings greens, blue cheese, apple slices and nuts with walnut vinaigrette and makes a perfect second course. Other salads include tomatoes with mozzarella, blue cheese or a Caesar. Prime steaks are the feature and arrive cooked to order with a terrific pepper crust, plain or topped with gorgonzola. All entrées are served with potato and vegetable sides. Lamb chops come three to an order and are a staple for Colorado. For seafood lovers, indulge in halibut, salmon, sole or lobster tail. Sides include mushrooms, caramelized onions, creamed corn and asparagus. Do not leave without one of their scrumptious desserts such as crème brûlée, strawberry shortcake, pound cake topped with ice cream and warm chocolate sauce, carrot cake or great chocolate pudding. The wine list offers great choices by the glass or bottle. Great service reflects the caring of the owner.

Brothers BBQ

Cuisine: Barbecue
Open: L-D: Daily
brothers-bbq.com

105 Wadsworth Blvd Unit E   303-232-3422
Lakewood, 80226
Belmar & multiple locations in Denver, Broomfield & Greenwood Village.

Price: $-$$	**Patio:** No
Reservations: No	**Brunch:** No

Location: Belmar, Denver-South East, Denver-Central, DTC, Broomfield

Who would have thought two boys from England could pull off nationally recognized barbecue? Chris and Nick O'Sullivan prove they can, pleasing barbecue fans in every area of the city. From the original spot, a small room on Leetsdale and Monaco, to all the other locations, customers clamor for great ribs, chicken and more. The Broomfield location features a separate bar area with a great vibe, still keeping the casual design as a basis. The 6th and Washington location has a patio. All of the Brothers BBQ locations are welcoming and casual. Place your order and the cooks will call when your order is ready. Start with the terrific St. Louis-style pork ribs, beef brisket, hot links, pulled pork, chicken slices or half chickens. Beef ribs are the latest addition to the menu. All are lightly smoked, tender, juicy and full of flavor. You can get sandwiches, platters and half slabs in any combination. The sides—beans, potato salad and coleslaw—match the quality of the meat. Don't miss the fries: hot and crispy on the outside, soft and steamy on the inside. Experiment with Brothers' house sauces, sweet, zippy with vinegar, or hot. Whether you eat in or carry out, this is one terrific barbecue. Mother should be proud of these brothers.

Bruno's Italian Bistro

Cuisine: Italian
Open: L: upon reservation D: Daily
mybrunos.net

2223 S. Monaco Pkwy.   303-759-7025
Denver, 80222
Evans & Monaco

Price: $$ **Patio:** No
Reservations: Yes   **Brunch:** No
Location: South East

Bruno's Italian Bistro, the small trattoria on Evans and Monaco, has a terrific ambience with soft colors, banquettes along the wall, comfortable seating, a small bar and a tile waterfall. The menu is similar to the "old" Bruno's as the logo remains the same and Italian fare is the theme, but pizzas and sandwiches have been added as options for evening—a nice choice when one wants something light. Appetizers include fried mozzarella, bruschetta, fried artichokes, calamari, polenta or risotto. Pizzas come in several varieties, and minestrone soup and Caesar salad are popular items as well. In the pasta selection, pick spaghetti and meatballs, carbonara, fra diavolo, or a rich baked ziti with sausage, peppers and sage topped with crispy mozzarella. Entrées range from eggplant parmesan and salmon to chicken, veal saltimbocca and pork osso buco. End with tiramisù, cheesecake or ice cream. There is a nice wine list to complement your meal. Bruno's affords a nice choice for dining in the neighborhood.

The B Side Café

Cuisine: American
Open: L: Mon-Fri, D: Daily, BR-Sat-Sun
thebsided~~iver~~.com

1336 E. 17th Ave.   303-474-4960
Denver, 80218
17th & Humboldt

Price: $$ **Patio:** Yes
Reservations: Yes   **Brunch:** Yes
Location: Uptown

CLOSED

17th Avenue is the rage and new additions are really fun. The old Pasquini and Serioz is now The B Side and great looking. The front and back patios rock, while inside the casual décor is just fun. The bar area is terrific with lots of seating with some bright colors on the wall but more the theme of an upscale bar. It is a great place to hangout. The signature here is TV Dinners-retro comes to life again with hot crispy fried chicken, meatloaf Wellington, pork n'apples, salmon Florentine, and Salisbury steak. Sides of sautéed greens, fries, mashed taters, cheese corn, salad, and green chili add to the fun. Another menu features bar snacks with chicharonnes, meatballs, pickle n' veg plate, and salads. Sandwiches range from a burger, green chili slopper, and fried chicken baguette to roast chicken, salmon club, and fried bologna. Got the idea? Neighborhood fun is what they have in mind, and open till really late, this is the spot to go back in time right now.

Buckhorn Exchange

Cuisine: Steakhouse
Open: L: Mon-Fri, D: Daily
buckhorn.com

1000 Osage St.   303-534-9505
Denver, 80204
10th & Osage

Price: $$$$ **Patio:** No
Reservations: Yes   **Brunch:** No
Location: Denver - South of Downtown

This is Denver's oldest restaurant, where the train stopped and hungry cowboys, tycoons, rogues and even President Teddy Roosevelt stepped in for a steak and a beer. The certificate stating Colorado Liquor License No. 1 sits proudly on the wall, right alongside autographs of actors, presidents and Buffalo Bill Cody. The hunting trophies of original owner "Shorty Scout" Zietz stare glassily from the walls next to antique guns and other paraphernalia. Don't miss the annual Buffalo Bill

birthday celebration, where old timers and youngsters get rowdy and shout praises to this Wild West legend. Weekends feature cowboy songs, harmonica jams and knee-slapping good tunes. Steak dinners have always been Buckhorn's specialty, but you might prefer to indulge in a wide variety of game, including elk, pheasant, quail, duck or buffalo. Appetizers include a few exotic possibilities as well, from rattlesnake marinated in red chili and lime, and spicy buffalo sausage, to Rocky Mountain oysters. At lunch, grab barbecued baby back pork ribs, a buffalo Reuben sandwich or the buffalo philly. In winter months, start with a cup of Buckhorn's hearty bean soup. Finish with hot Dutch apple pie steeped in cinnamon-rum sauce.

Burt's Smokehouse BBQ

Cuisine: Barbeque
Open: L-D: Tues-Sun
bbqdenver.net

7470 S. University A-1   303-770-1875
Centennial, 80122
University & Dry Creek

Price: $$ **Patio:** Yes
Reservations: No   **Brunch:** No
Location: Denver - South, Centennial

And everyone loves BBQ, specially good stuff in terrific surroundings and that casual friendly spot to bring all. Enter Burt's and there you have it with lots of seating, big windows, great lighting of upside down olive buckets as shades, and the focal open kitchen with the huge pit where the goodies are cooked. Walk up and order and your food is delivered. As you place your order pick up beer or wine from the huge tub filled with ice or go for soft drinks. Grab some peanuts and pickles and onions to snack on while you wait. Take your seat and get ready for finger licking fun. Ribs star-either a whole or half rack, or if you prefer those yummy huge beef ribs make for a great meal. There's brisket, pulled pork, sausage, and chicken as well. Make any into sandwiches and enjoy or add to it and make a combo. Sides are a must with bbq, and the cornbread, potato salad, baked beans, pasta salad, brown sugared yams, and coleslaw complement the entrees. The sauce is super: the regular, sweet, or spicy are a delight. Leave room for berry cobbler and sweet potato pie for dessert. Burt's is a family of three generations working together and the family charms all and brings some terrific barbecue to the area. It's fun, so good, affordable, and worth the drive from wherever to be your spot for the food everyone loves. And they sell the bbq sauce too.

Butcher's Bistro

Cuisine: America, Steak
Open: L-D: Mon-Sat
thebutchersbistro.com

2233 Larimer St.   303-296-2750
Denver, CO 80205
Larimer & Park Ave

Price: $$$-$$$$ **Patio:** Yes
Reservations: Yes   **Brunch:** No
Location: Ballpark - LoDo

Butcher's Bistro brings great food, fun, ambience, and affordable prices to LoDo in the Ballpark area. It's just a treat. Enter and see a case of great sausage, meats, chicken, and more for sale for home cooks, or keep going and see the gorgeous focal bar with beautiful wood and comfortable seating, or take a seat at one of the banquettes covered with great fabric. There are some tables and more seats for dining at the bar. Wall décor is fun as it accents the theme of all sorts of meats and poultry butchered on premise and served in great style. Start with smoked deviled egg with homemade bacon crumbled; flash baked oyster, oyster shooter, or short rib crostini. Share olives, a sausage sampler, spinach croquettes, or chicken liver pate, pork terrine, and house ham. The greens include bacon and egg, butter lettuces with blue cheese, and grapes or a house salad. The Butcher Block shows off the real talent of the chef: dry-aged teres major, flat iron, crisp smoked chicken, braised beef shank, duck confit, pork chop, a burger, and a cut du jour. All are fabulous in presentation, size, and taste. Sides of wilted greens, cassoulet, pomme frites, and roasted vegetables give so many options. Lunch is super with some amazing sandwiches of Banh Mi, grilled chicken, grilled cheese, ham and egg, cheese steak, and smoked pork. Lunch gets a new meaning when it tastes this good. There's coffee, tea, beer, cocktails and wine to complete your dish. And some egg dishes appear on weekend menus as well. The staff is extraordinary, the prices affordable, and staff makes you feel like family in seconds. Butcher's Bistro is a great choice for dining any time on any day.

Café Aion

Cuisine: Mediterranean, Small Plates, Tapas
Open: L-D: Tues-Fri D: Tues-Sat BR: Sat-Sun
cafeaion.com

1235 Pennsylvania Ave.   303-993-8131
Boulder, 80302
12th & Pennsylvania

Price: $$-$$$ **Patio:** Yes
Reservations: Yes   **Brunch:** Yes
Location: Boulder - The Hill

Enter this funky, quirky spot and you know you are in for a good time. Named after the old bookstore that once occupied the space, Café Aion is simple and charming in every way. Walk up a few stairs to the bar and dining area – one large room - and nab a seat near the open kitchen to watch the chefs at work. No matter what time of day you come, the selection of house-made food is wide and all promise to please. For breakfast there are fresh pastries, buttery croissants, house-cured bacon or coppa, and eggs served the Turkish cold way or the Spanish way with warm polenta. For lunch bright and flavorful soups like pumpkin or lentil are always welcome but other items like roast beets with feta, quinoa salad with Turkish apricots, grilled artichokes with romesco, and chicken wings with cumin and spiced yogurt will definitely make you happy. In the late afternoon and evening it's all about tapas with a few large platters perfect for sharing. Start with house made sourdough bread, oysters, mussels, Moroccan spiced pork, lamb with grilled flat bread, sweet potato fries, and fried cauliflower with saffron yogurt. A vegetarian tagine, half chicken with harrisa, potatoes, and salad, whole bass, short ribs, and perfect paella complete the menu. Don't stop until you enjoy the chocolate torte with Noosa honey yogurt, pear tart, ice cream, and a plate of treats. The wine and beer list is excellent, service so friendly, efficient and caring, and prices are affordable. Whether in school or not take the trip to the "hill" and have a great meal at Café Aion.

Café Brazil

Cuisine: South American
Open: D: Tues-Sat
cafebrazildenver.com

4408 Lowell Blvd.   303-480-1877
Denver, 80211
44th & Lowell

Price: $$$ **Patio:** No
Reservations: Yes   **Brunch:** No
Location: Highlands

Café Brazil is a delight. Bright and colorful with walls of red, gold and purple, the tables are covered with blue cloths, and the art of one of the owners displayed on the walls. The staff is friendly, knowledgeable and always ready to make suggestions from the menu. Complimentary breads are brought to the table to start your meal. Fried calamari with hot sauce, ceviche, and grilled manchego cheese with salsa verde make great appetizers to share and the black bean soup is a must. Feijoada, the national dish of Brazil, is presented with or without meat. Shrimp and scallops are prepared many different ways: with coconut sauce, curried with a hint of Thai flavors or skewered and grilled with an array of Brazilian spices. Chicken arrives moist and perfectly cooked atop one of the exciting sauces. If lamb is offered as a special, it is a must! Entrées come on large plates with steamed rice and fresh veggies. Order mild or spicy and enjoy every bite. Save room for a piece of kiwi or blackberry cheesecake or fabulous mango torte. The decadent chocolate semifreddo mousse with mascarpone and the macadamia nut caramel ice cream are a great end to this meal. The wine list features varietals from Chile and Latin America at great prices. Specialty juices and mojitos are a perfect accompaniment to the flavors of the food. Café Brazil is a dining gem thanks to owners Tony, Marla, and Mauricio.

Café Jordano

Cuisine: Italian
Open: L: Mon-Fri, D: Mon-Sat
cafejordano.com

11068 W. Jewell Ave.   303-988-6863
Lakewood, 80232
Kipling & Jewell

Price: $$ **Patio:** No
Reservations: Yes   **Brunch:** No
Location: Lakewood

Despite its secluded shopping center location and long wait regulars have been coming back for years. Start with garlic bread, soups, tomatoes and mozzarella, and great shrimp appetizers. For your main course, order the pollo elegante or choose from several well-balanced pastas. Café Jordano uses buffalo instead of veal without losing an ounce of flavor. Be sure to try an Italian dessert.

Café Mercato

Cuisine: Italian
Open: L: Mon-Sat, D:Daily, BR-Sun
cafemercato.com

7561 East Academy Blvd   303-366-1315
Denver, 80230
Lowry

Price: $$-$$$ **Patio:** Yes
Reservations: Yes   **Brunch:** Yes
Location: Denver - Lowry

Café Mercato brings special Italian dining in the Lowry complex. Chef/Owner Giancarlo decided it was time for a sister restaurant to his Locanda del Borgo in a neighborhood that is perfect for his cuisine. The space is beautiful. Enter and enjoy a huge open kitchen complete with a tiled wood burning oven and a counter for dining. Peer at the chefs at work in the kitchen. Another huge bar is located in the rear where a wall of wine separates it from the main dining room. Warm woods, a great wood ceiling design, super lighting, banquettes and tables that are attractively set make for a warm and friendly scene. Start with house made burrata, beets and heirloom tomatoes, roasted pears and goat cheese or baby romaine salads. Next are the pastas where Giancarlo shines with his homemade noodles and sauces: spaghetti with eggplant and mozzarella, fettuccine with mushrooms, tagliatelle with clams, pappardelle with meat sauce, ravioli, and lasagna. The fish list includes risotto with seafood and zuppa di pesce while meat options include sausages, chicken breast, and meatballs and steak. Pizza rounds out the menu and the pie of a thin crust with many different toppings. Leave room for the special gelato served. The wine and cocktail list complement the food. Café Mercato is a nice choice for dining in the Lowry neighborhood.

Café Terracotta

Cuisine: American
Open: B-L: Daily, D: Mon-Sat
cafe-terracotta.com

5649 S. Curtice St.   303-794-6054
Littleton, 80120
Curtice & Main

Price: $$ **Patio:** Yes
Reservations: Yes   **Brunch:** No
Location: Littleton

You will not be disappointed with the warmth and charm of this old Victorian house in Littleton. The room is pleasing with comfortable seating and an open kitchen. The glass cases filled with baked goods are a treat to see and will make you want to eat dessert first. Exposed brick, soft lighting and a casual feel are the ingredients for a wonderful experience. Owners Levi Pike and Michael Tae Ludlam charm the guests and make each person feel like part of the family. Start with an artisan cheese plate, mussels in saffron broth, marinated shrimp cocktail or sweet chile buffalo calamari, crispy, delightful and complemented by a lemon remoulade. Caesar, cranberry feta with greens, Thai chicken and a simple house salad are offered as choices for your next course. Feta-crusted wild salmon with couscous, pan-seared tuna, and chicken Wellington top the entrée list. Don't miss the ancho-rubbed rib-eye with mac and cheese, grilled lamb T-bone, almond-crusted trout or barbecued pork chop. Spanakopita pie illustrates the variety of options for exciting main courses. Dessert includes white chocolate cheesecake, chocolate truffle cake, carrot or spice cakes, lemon bars and a cookie platter. The wine list is excellent, and service is friendly. With reasonable prices and the warmest welcome, Café Terracotta brings a great dining choice to the area.

Cake Crumbs

Cuisine: Café, Desserts
Open: B-L: daily
Cakecrumbs.com

2216 Kearnery   303-861-4912
Denver, 80207
Kearnery and 22nd

Price: $-$$ **Patio:** Yes
Reservations: Yes   **Brunch:** No
Location: Park Hill

Cake Crumbs is the bakery restaurant that produces the food, cupcakes, cakes and pies for The Denver Cupcake Truck and Denver Pie Truck. But stop by and eat here for a quick bite of some really good food. Displayed in cases, you can choose from all the sweets of course, but don't forget great croissants and savories. And the birthday or wedding cakes are specially designed for your occasion. The chicken salad is one of the best in town served with spinach salad and fruit. Tuna with quinoa, divine quiche, breakfast sandwiches, and more make a perfect lunch or carryout to enjoy at home. You can pick up until closing. Free WiFi, excellent NoVo coffee, and all sorts of appealing kiddie delights add to the charm of this place. And the carrot cake is the best anywhere. It's just a neighborhood treat.

The Capital Grille

Cuisine: Steakhouse
Open: L: Mon-Fri, D: Daily
thecapitalgrille.com

1450 Larimer St.   303-539-2500
Denver, 80202
Larimer Square

Price: $$$$ **Patio:** No
Reservations: Yes   **Brunch:** No
Location: Larimer Square - Downtown

The Capital Grille brings to Denver all the pomp and circumstance that one might imagine with its name. Arrive in Larimer Square and an army of valets greet you with complimentary parking for all guests. As you enter hosts are waiting to welcome and seat you. The décor is warm featuring lots of wood with wonderful paintings adorning the walls. The partitioned dining areas are excellent for conversation. The staff is professional and strives to make your experience memorable. Start with lobster and crab cakes, steak tartare, oysters or a terrific pan-fried calamari. French onion soup

is a must with excellent gooey cheese. Equally exciting is the creamy, rich lobster bisque. Steak is the star at Capital Grille: dry-aged sirloin, porterhouse, sliced steak, filet or delmonico. If you prefer try the veal chop, lamb, or one of several delicious seafood options including whole lobster. Sides for sharing round out the menu and complement your meal. Wonderful homemade desserts abound, including coconut-cream pie, flourless chocolate cake, mousse, crème brûlée and ice cream. The extensive wine list covers all price ranges with several nice wines by the glass. Dining at Capital Grille is a pleasant experience where no detail has been overlooked.

Carmine's on Penn

Cuisine: Italian
Open: D: Tues-Sun
carminescolorado.com

92 S. Pennsylvania St.   303-777-6443
Denver, 80209
Pennsylvania & Bayaud

Price: $$-$$$ **Patio:** Yes
Reservations: Yes   **Brunch:** No
Location: Wash Park

Carmine's has captured the hearts of Denverites for years. The atmosphere bustles with laughter and animated conversation drifting in from the bar while friendly servers hustle past with platters of food. The warm colors and a fabulous mural as a focal point in the dining room beckon you as menus are positioned strategically around the restaurant on chalkboards. If you don't feel like reading your server will guide you through the options. Portions are priced family-style and can easily feed a party of four. Start with a platter of roasted portobello mushrooms steeped in balsamic vinegar, plump mussels in marinara or a plate of spicy sausages and peppers. Sop up the sauce with a garlic knot—or two or three. Try the Caesar salad or the spinach salad with cheese and toasted nuts. Pastas include creamy chicken Montana, puttanesca with olives and seafood, or primavera packed with vegetables. Add seafood pasta, vongole, shrimp and carbonara, and decisions are difficult. Entrées include chicken parmesan, chicken with eggplant and a great chicken fontina with melted cheese. All the entrée preparations are available with chicken or veal. Be sure to order a glass of wine from the all Italian list to wash down your meal. Desserts include crispy cannoli with chocolate, tasty tiramisù or a light sorbet. Large parties are accommodated in the Blue Room a perfect place for special occasions.

Cart Driver

Cuisine: American, Pizza
Open: L-D: Daily
cart-driver.com

2500 Larimer Suite 100   303-292-3553
Denver, 80205
Larimer & 25th

Price: $$-$$$ **Patio:** Yes
Reservations: No   **Brunch:** No
Location: RiNo - Denver

When Kelly Whitaker and his partners decided to come to Denver (Basta is the original in Boulder), they first thought of fine dining. Instead, this 650 square foot storage crate is the home of some amazing oysters and pizza. Fun, fast food high style gourmet with organic, no GMO, super style and great taste is the word. The décor is terrific as you walk up in an open space to the counter. The interior has seats for 30 lucky people with wood booths that are all topped with stainless rails where your oysters and pizza go for sharing. Start with beer, wine, and cocktails-the last if you get some for the table arrive in a jar and glasses of ice-pour away on your own and have some fun. The oysters are fabulous, delivered daily and change. Mandatory: get the horseradish biscuit with lemon butter to go with. This is a dream combo of what a garlic knot and oyster crackers wish they were. Served freshly baked from the oven, no one can eat just one. There is a salad, a special crudo of the day, some other fun specials of the staff and then come the pizza. Basta has always been known for a great pie and the reputation remains untarnished here. There are five on the menu, and again specials each day. That's it except for rich dreamy soft serve for dessert. And that is enough to keep crowds coming back for more. It's open late night, eat in or take away, and just make Cart Driver part of your dining scene.

Casey's Bistro and Pub

Cuisine: Irish Pub
Open: L-D: Daily, BR: Sat-Sun
caseysbistroandpub.com

7301 E. 29th Ave., Unit 100   720-974-7350
Denver, 80238
29th & Quebec

Price: $-$$ **Patio:** Yes
Reservations: Yes   **Brunch:** Yes
Location: Denver-Stapleton

Casey's fills the need for an Irish Pub in Stapleton. With a well-stocked bar and a lunch and dinner menu that combines traditional Irish pub food with some bistro-type entrées it is a big hit. While the appetizer menu ranges from buffalo wings to pot-steamed mussels the real treat and value comes in the burger and Irish specialty sections. Casey's half-pound burger comes perfectly grilled on a toasted kaiser roll with lettuce, tomato and onion, accompanied with wonderful seasoned chips. The traditional salmon boxty, an Irish pancake stuffed with Atlantic salmon and roasted peppers in a sour cream dill sauce makes a terrific entrée. The bar menu has many traditional beers and a full complement of wines and hard spirits to add to the fun. Entrées include favorites such as fish and chips, chicken curry, grilled beef tenderloin, sandwiches and more. Casey's staff is friendly, and the minimal décor is pleasing. This pub is a popular choice in Stapleton.

Castle Café

Cuisine: Fried Chicken, American
Open: L: Mon-Fri, D: Daily
castlecafe.com

403 Wilcox St.   303-814-2233
Castle Rock, 80104
Wilcox & 4th

Price: $$ **Patio:** No
Reservations: No   **Brunch:** No
Location: Castle Rock

Here at Castle Café pan-fried chicken is what it's all about—pan-cooked in a black, cast-iron skillet to crispy, moist perfection and served with mashed potatoes, gravy, rolls and veggies. It brings back those childhood memories. Located in a historic landmark building the restaurant is full of homey, old-fashioned dining fun with a very casual décor, checkered tablecloths, memorabilia on the walls and a warm welcome for the entire family. Friendly efficient service, affordable prices, and full bar service adds to the scene. The blackened campfire trout has a bit of spice and a crispy skin, while the buffalo meatloaf arrives covered with gravy and is served with mashers and green beans. Don't forget to try the four layer chocolate cake, apple brown betty or bread pudding for a perfect ending to this family dinner.

Caveau Wine Bar

Cuisine: Wine Bar
Open: D: Daily
caveauwinebar.com

450 East 17th Ave.   303-861-3747
Denver, 80203
17th & Pennsylvania

Price: $$ **Patio:** Yes
Reservations: Yes   **Brunch:** No
Location: Uptown

Caveau Wine Bar is a sophisticated and at the same time relaxed place to find your new favorite wine. Located on the edge of Capitol Hill and Uptown this is the perfect place to stop before or after dinner. Happy hour is one of the best in town where any glass priced under $12 is $6 and anything over $12 is half price. This is a great way to sample some really amazing wines you may have thought were too expensive. If you have a beer lover in the group no worries. There are several bottle and draft beers from which to choose. Looking for a bite to eat? Start with the Wine Basket, a meat and cheese plate served with French bread — there's plenty to share with a group. Also on the menu are paninis, meatballs from an old family recipe, pizzas and salads. There is always something new at Caveau Wine Bar!

Celtic Tavern

Cuisine: Irish Pub
Open: B-L-D: Daily
theceltictavern.com

1801 Blake St.   303-308-1795
Denver, 80202
18th & Blake

Price: $$ **Patio:** Yes
Reservations: Yes   **Brunch:** No
Location: LoDo

This place could well be in Belfast. The décor is pure old Irish for lads and lassies to enjoy. The wait staff is very knowledgeable and friendly. Knowing the difference between single and double-malted Scotches is a real plus here. Tavern snacks include welsh potato skins filled with rarebit cheese sauce and smoked bacon, beer-battered oysters with red curry dipping sauce, and the ploughman's platter, a selection of cheeses, hard salami, crusty French bread, branston pickled relish and fresh fruit. For lunch don't miss the Black Mountain shepherd's pie: ground lamb and beef with carrots, onions and peas in a wonderfully rich brown sauce topped with a pile of mashed potatoes. Dinner entrées feature corned beef and cabbage, Jeremiah's steak, Murphy's pie, New England cod fish cakes, and chicken piccata. Top off your meal with coconut crème brûlée, strawberry-rhubarb crisp or bread pudding with a hot cup of coffee.

Central Bistro & Bar

Cuisine: Contemporary
Open: L: Wed-Fri, D: Tue-Sun, BR: Sat-Sun
centralbistrobar.com

1691 Central St   303-477-4582
Denver, 80211
17th & Central

Price: $$$-$$$$ **Patio:** Yes
Reservations: Yes   **Brunch:** Yes
Location: LoHi

Enter this great looking space in the wildly popular LoHi Neighborhood. The ambience starts with the warm colors and a nod to the woodsy atmosphere. The owners have used wood taken from box cars to furnish the dining area which includes the tables and walls. Black concrete floors, huge picture windows, a pressed tile ceiling with super lighting and a sensational focal kitchen area top off the dining area. But not before HOT is lit up in neon on the sign over the kitchen area. Terra cotta and a wonderful color palette is used with slits of wood paneling to warm the scene. White and beige upholstered chairs combined with bourbon barrels holding light fixtures give this place a unique vibe. Pictures of old time Denver on the walls pay homage to the people who brought the city to its great status. Chef Matt Selby brings a terrific menu that appeals to a cross section of patrons. Start with small plates of confit chicken wings, caramelized Brussels sprouts, pear and chevre ravioli, mac and cheese, and chicken fried sweetbreads. Enjoy soups and salads before you begin with entrees such as lamb bolognese, chipotle maple glazed scallops, monkfish, duck breast and pork shoulder. Add ribeye, acorn squash risotto, squab, and even a burger to make your decisions more difficult. Every dish is accompanied by exciting sides and presentation is beautiful. Don't leave without dessert especially when options include a Nutella waffle with banana butterscotch and pretzel ice cream, a mud pie of Oreo brownie, chocolate pudding, and meringue with spiced nuts. These are a dessert lover's heaven. Don't miss weekend brunch and lunch on select days. The wine list is good and service is great. Central brings a great option for dining in this fabulous area of Denver where everyone calls it "their" hood.

Central One

Cuisine: Greek
Open: L-D: Daily
petesrestaurants.com

300 S. Pearl St.   303-778-6675
Denver, 80209
Alameda & Pearl St.

Price: $-$$ **Patio:** Yes
Reservations: Yes   **Brunch:** No
Location: Wash Park

Immerse yourself in the rich flavors of Greece at this tiny spot on South Pearl Street. Try something unusual like pan-fried kasseri cheese dipped in parmesan butter sauce, flamed with liquor and doused with lemon juice. Order the caviar blended with olive oil and lemon juice for an intriguing spread or try boiled octopus flavored with vinegar and spices. For your main course choose from broiled lamb chops, grape leaves stuffed with rice and ground beef or shrimp baked with tomato and feta. Several combination plates allow you to sample many different items. Great prices are offered at lunch on sandwiches and platters. For dessert try the baked custard flavored with Cognac.

Centro Latin Kitchen & Refreshment Palace

Cuisine: South American
Open: L: Fri, D: Daily, BR: Sat-Sun
centrolatinkitchen.com

950 Pearl St.   303-442-7771
Boulder, 80302
10th & Pearl

Price: $$-$$$ **Patio:** Yes
Reservations: Yes   **Brunch:** Yes
Location: Boulder

This Latin-American eatery and bar offers great dining to the Boulder area. One of the Big Red F Restaurant Group created by the brilliant David Query, this is a loud, fun and great gathering place. Start with shrimp en adobo, an Anaheim chile

relleno, lamb taquitos, white sea bass ceviche verde or spiny lobster arepas. Baked red snapper, coffee and brown sugar crusted lamb with quinoa, chicken and clams, and pan-roasted scallops with curried rice salad start the list of entrées. There are tacos galore including habanero rotisserie pork, zucchini mushroom, griddled shrimp, and duck carnitas. Add desserts of fried bananas, pineapple upside down cake, warm chocolate stuffed crepes, and dulce de leche flan and enjoy. There are lots of specialty drinks to complement the food. Grab a seat inside or on the patio and enjoy this lively place.

Charcoal

Cuisine: Contemporary, Scandinavian
Open: L: Mon-Fri, D: Daily BR: Sat-Sun
charcoaldining.com

43 W. 9th Ave.   303-454-0000
Denver, 80204
9th & Broadway

Price: $$$-$$$$ **Patio:** Yes
Reservations: Yes   **Brunch:** Yes
Location: Denver - Central

Enter Charcoal and find a terrific looking free standing restaurant in a neighborhood in need of upscale dining. The ambience is warm with brick, fabric with lighting and chandeliers from Argentina creating a contemporary background for Chef Patrick's eclectic cuisine. Fabric covered booths, comfortable tables and a great bar set the scene. The large open kitchen has an additional bar with seating for guests to watch the chefs at work. A high tech Napa technology wine dispensary system and special Bincho (white charcoal) grills are more features—which lend to bringing the name "Charcoal" into focus. Start with wonderful homemade breads, osso buco style oxtail with gnocchi, mussels, prawns, and a charcuterie platter. Chicken liver pate and feta spread are perfect for sharing. Gravlox is a must showing off Patrick's Swedish heritage. The beet salad and arugula with cheese and nuts make a great second course. Lamb, chicken breast, a salmon tournedo, and halibut start the entrée list. The steak, crab cake, gnocchi, and pork make decisions difficult. End with bread pudding, chocolate chile mousse, and a wonderful apple tart. The wine list is well-crafted and service shines. Brunch has specialty dishes from Sweden to showcase more of Patrick's background. The private dining room brings a country French setting. Featuring upscale food and wine in casual surroundings, Charcoal Restaurant is a great addition to the Golden Triangle dining scene.

Chautauqua Dining Hall

Cuisine: American
Open: B-L-D: Daily, BR: Sat-Sun
chautauqua.com/dining-hall/overview

900 Baseline Rd.   303-440-3776
Boulder, 80302
In Chautauqua Park

Price: $$-$$$ **Patio:** Yes
Reservations: Yes   **Brunch:** Yes
Location: Boulder

When American history buffs hear the name Chautauqua they
think of William Jennings Bryant and his Cross of Gold speech.
When food buffs hear the name Chautauqua they think of
wonderful food and a setting that has few equals. Spend an
entire day at the historic grounds of Chautauqua Dining Hall
and the surrounding park and hiking area. Established over
100 years ago as a place to get away from the world and learn
something new Chautauqua remains one of Boulder's most
popular spots. Now the renovated restaurant draws more fans
for dining. Ask for a seat on the veranda where you can look
out across the gardens of Chautauqua Park. Start with white
bean hummus, guacamole, buffalo style chicken wings, a crab
cake or smoked salmon. Several sandwich choices include
burgers, pulled pork and a veggie wrap. For your main course,
enjoy mac and cheese, trout, pappardelle, fish tacos, shrimp
and grits and game hen. There is a pork chop or flatiron steak
for meat lovers. Desserts reflect the home-style theme. A walk
around the grounds after dinner provides a star-driven light
show that really drives home the beauty of the place. Breakfast
and lunch are a special way to start the day.

Cheese Importers   K:

Cuisine: Specialty, Deli
Open: Mon-Sat 9-6 and Sun 11-5
Cheeseimporters.com

103 Main Street   (303) 772-9599
Longmont, CO 80501
1st & Main

Price: $-$$$ **Patio:** Yes
Reservations: Yes   **Brunch:** No
Location: Longmont

Cheese Importers is the most amazing place - built in the old
power plant building in Longmont. This is a second generation
Longmont gem, founded in 1976, rivals anything in the state.
Run by siblings Samm and Clara White, Cheese Importers has

a full, walk-in-and-get-lost refrigerator (jackets are available for use there) with a global selection of cheeses, dried meats and sausages as well as other rooms full of other goodies - including a deep selection of locally produced products - and gourmet accouterment. Their BISTRO features fare that ranges from French onion soup to quiche, salads, and cheese plates (of course) and small-plate tapas to savor. Yum! Enjoy coffees, teas, a world-wide selection of beverages, cakes, pies and pastries as well as savory selections of meats and pâtés. Explore the more than 475 cheeses from dozens of countries - with special sections full of locally sourced cheeses and other products as well. From soft, fragrant to hard, grater-friendly favorites to cheeses made to be grilled without liquefying. You will also find olives, sausages, breads and crackers, spreads, preserves, tapenades and much more. They have a collection of housewares from around the world as well. You'll find Cheese Importers products in many of the best restaurants in Denver and Boulder as well. They do both wholesale and walk-in retail business. They host demonstrations and tastings throughout the year - follow them on Facebook for upcoming events. Get there soon to experience this very special place for yourself.

Cherry Creek Grill

Cuisine: American
Open: L-D: Daily
hillstone.com

184 Steele St.   303-322-3524
Denver, 80206
2nd & Steele

Price: $$-$$$ **Patio:** Yes
Reservations: Yes   **Brunch:** No
Location: Cherry Creek

This restaurant brings the taste of down-home American cooking to Cherry Creek. The large room buzzes with business people and young couples gathered around a U-shaped bar. Large, comfy booths accentuated by dark wood and exposed brick replace the usual dining room tables. The ambience is upbeat and fun. The young and energetic staff gets food out quickly, and the quality is great. Start off with the essential cast-iron skillet cornbread, served fresh from the oven and still in the skillet. For your meal, enjoy tender, wood-fired, spit-roasted chicken served with a mound of mashers. Other great choices include slow-roasted prime rib, beef ribs, Scottish salmon, beef filet, pork or fish of the day. For something lighter, grab a chicken sandwich, a cheeseburger or a blackened fresh fish sandwich, all served with homemade slaw and fresh potato chips. The salads are terrific as well. Desserts include crème brûlée, banana cream pie or an Oreo ice cream sandwich.

The patio brings additional seating—a precious commodity in Cherry Creek. This dog-friendly place features outside water bowls, and free bones to take home to Rover. Cherry Creek Grill is definitely a favorite in the area.

Cherry Cricket

Cuisine: American
Open: L-D: Daily
cherrycricket.com

2641 E. 2nd Ave.   303-322-7666
Denver, 80206
2nd & Columbine

Price: $-$$ **Patio:** Yes
Reservations: No   **Brunch:** No
Location: Cherry Creek

The Cherry Cricket has been attracting everyone from high-power executives to rowdy sports fans for decades. This place rocks; it is always busy and for good reason. Pool tables and dartboards keep the place jumping, but crowds come to enjoy terrific food and fun. Start with guacamole and salsa, a bowl of tasty green chili or white chili if you prefer chicken to pork. How about mac and cheese wedges with ranch, quesadillas or nachos to start the fun? Burgers are made to order with a list of toppings, from blue cheese and avocado to green chiles and bacon, and will keep you experimenting for many visits to come. Other favorite sandwiches at the Cricket include the hot avocado melt with fresh avocado slices and cheese on grilled sourdough bread, a fabulous turkey club, and grilled chicken with avocado, bacon and cheese. Big flavorful salads and an extensive array of Mexican dishes add excitement to the menu. With 23 beers on tap and 50 different bottled varieties, they are sure to have your favorite. Don't miss the decadent chocolate cake for dessert. Service shines in this casual setting, and no one minds the wait for a table. The Cherry Cricket is the perfect destination for out-of-towners and suburbanites who come to Cherry Creek North.

Chili Verde

Cuisine: Mexican
Open: L-D: Tues-Fri BR-D: Sat-Sun
Chiliverde.com

2311 Federal Blvd   720- 287-2296
Denver 80211
23rd & Federal

Price: $$ **Patio:** Yes
Reservations: Yes   **Brunch:** Yes
Location: Jefferson Park

Chili Verde is part of the Latino dining scene on Federal. You can see it on the main street but the back entrance offers some places to park as well. The big dining room is warm and welcoming with wood, brick, an open kitchen area and a huge bar that covers a side of the room. There is also a patio in the rear weather permitting. The brothers bring their style from the area they called home in Mexico. Start with chips and three different salsas for dipping. Tableside guacamole is fun as you pick the ingredients. There are queso, tamales, and more for appetizers and then several salads from which to choose. Two different versions of chicken mole start the entrée list, one with chocolate. The chili rellenos brings sweets to the filling, while beef and pork dishes offer more options. The special chicken crepe with a rich, thick béchamel sauce while fish tacos are a lighter option. Be sure to enjoy flan or tres leches for dessert. There is a fun cocktail, wine and beer list to complement the food. For a different twist on traditional Mexican fare, Chili Verde is a great choice.

Chianti Ristorante

Cuisine: Italian
Open: L: Mon-Fri, D: Mon-Sat

5121 S. Yosemite St.   303-796-0611
Greenwood Village, 80111
Yosemite & Belleview

Price: $$-$$$ **Patio:** No
Reservations: Yes   **Brunch:** No
Location: Greenwood Village

Chianti Ristorante has all the charm of Italy. Originally Venice, Chianti is owned and run by Allessandro and Sara Carollo. Chianti boasts a lovely décor with soft colors, wonderful murals and nicely spaced tables. The feel is casual but upscale and you certainly hear the noise - it's all part of the charm. Start with lightly fried calamari, mozzarella and tomatoes, or carpaccio. The panzanella salad is a must—the combination of

red and yellow tomatoes, cucumber, onion, basil and toasted ciabatta bread with red wine vinaigrette is perfect. Other great salads include mozzarella and tomatoes, and baby spinach with bacon, mushrooms and gorgonzola. Ravioli with squash, spinach tortellini, gnocchi and a simple tomato basil linguine are a few pasta choices. Entrées range from veal and steak to fish or chicken. Cacciucco, a combination of clams, mussels and calamari with spicy tomato sauce, brings great taste and flavors. Fish arrives with artichoke hearts, olives, tomatoes and capers surrounded by spinach or asparagus. All are delicious and beautifully presented. End with tiramisù, profiterole or spumoni. Service is very friendly and efficient. The wine list is excellent and prices reasonable. Chianti is a good choice for Italian dining.

Chinook Tavern

Cuisine: Contemporary, Fondue, German
Open: B: Coffee Bar Mon-Fri, L: Mon-Fri,
      D: Mon-Sat
chinookdenver.com

6380 S. Fiddler's Green Circle   720-266-6000
Greenwood Village, 80111
I-25 & Arapahoe

Price: $$$$ **Patio:** Yes
Reservations: Yes   **Brunch:** No
Location: Greenwood Village

The Chinook Tavern brings excitement to Greenwood Village with its beautiful look and excellent food. The large space is welcoming and warm with pine wood finishes, large windows, and fabulous lighting throughout the restaurant. The colorful art, two fireplaces, comfortable leather chairs and oversized tabletops built from reclaimed heart-of-pine complement the dining rooms. The bar area is a great gathering place. The menu is reminiscent of the original Chinook in Cherry Creek with new options. Start with baked brie, shrimp cakes, mussels, tuna tartar, mushroom strudel, and escargot. Several soups and salads delight diners for the next course. Coquilles St. Jacques, trout, salmon, and pizza tempt all. Entrées include wiener schnitzel, jaeger schnitzel, duck, beef, and rack of lamb, pork, and chicken. The choices are difficult as you notice the wonderful presentation on all plates. End on a sweet note with delicious desserts. You should also make room for raclette. The wine and beer lists are excellent and service exemplary. It's a family affair with the Georg family as Mansfield the architect, Lisa the artist, Clemons the front of the house and bar, and Markus bringing the food to the table. Chinook Tavern is a treat and a welcome restaurant in its luxurious home.

ChoLon Modern Asian Bistro

Cuisine: Asian, Contemporary
Open: L: Mon-Fri, D: Daily
cholon.com

1555 Blake St. #101   303-353-5223
Denver, 80202
Blake & 16th St.

Price: $$$$ **Patio:** Yes
Reservations: Yes   **Brunch:** No
Location: LoDo

ChoLon, in the Sugar Cube building in LoDo makes a great statement in design and cuisine. Enter the bright contemporary restaurant and enjoy drinks or a meal in the bar, a perfect place to gather. The dining room is modern with high ceilings, an open look, and big windows. Black walls with interesting art, a great community table with large chandeliers, and an open kitchen make your dining experience a joy. Seating is comfortable with tables, banquettes and lounge sofas. The menu is divided in small bites, small and large plates and wok. Start with a complimentary rice cracker with a spicy dip as you peruse the menu. Sweet kaya toast with coconut jam and soft egg is a signature from the bites along with the outrageous onion soup dumplings, pork belly stickers and chile crab rolls. BBQ chicken Bao buns, duck spring rolls and pork satay are other options. On the small plate list the green papaya salad with tamarind sorbet and butternut squash soup are favorites. Wok dishes bring curried fried rice, tofu, egg noodles, and oh-so-good Brussels sprouts with ground pork. Desserts shine with a decadent molten chocolate cake with salted peanut ice cream and mini toasted marshmallows, and spiced doughnuts with Vietnamese coffee ice cream. The wine and drink list is adequate and service good. ChoLon brings excitement to LoDo.

Chop Shop Casual Urban Eatery

Cuisine: Contemporary
Open: L-D: Daily
coloradochopshop.com

4990 E. Colfax Ave   720-550-7665
Denver, 80220
Colfax & Elm

Price: $$ **Patio:** Yes
Reservations: No   **Brunch:** No
Location: Denver - East Colfax

Chop Shop Casual Eatery is a great way to enjoy casual fast gourmet food. Chef/Owner Clint Wangnes has a great

reputation for upscale dining and super talent while partner/ front of the house Christian Anderson delights the guests and shows off his knowledge of wine, beer, and cocktails— all available to complement the super food. The décor is welcoming with a great sign out front followed by orange and green accents with natural colors, high ceilings and a wonderful open kitchen. Start with the divine 48 hour short rib over potatoes and carrots or the peach wood smoked pork chop, chicken breast, and top sirloin. Between the bread you can choose a great burger, chicken pastrami and more while salads inspire with so many choices and any protein available if desired. The onion bliss soup is extra tasty. There is a great kids' menu to please all. Do not leave without chocolate truffles and toffee candy. Prices are great, the staff terrific, and Chop House is perfect for lunch, dinner, and carryout anytime. What a great new addition to the hood.

Cho 77

Cuisine: Vietnamese, Asian Fusion
Open: D: Daily
cho77.com

42 S. Broadway   720-638-8179
Denver, 80209
S Broadway & Archer

Price: $$ **Patio:** No
Reservations: No   **Brunch:** No
Location: Denver - South Broadway, Baker

Cho 77 opened on South Broadway in this so popular block. Lon Symonsia of Cholon fame has opened his second spot and brings some excitement to the area. The decor is great. Long and narrow, most of the room is the bar with seating along the walls. Brick walls are accented with great art, the bar is awesome, and watching the chefs and bartenders great fun. Start with roti pizza, vegetable samosas, buffalo chicken buns, scallop ceviche, green papaya salad, and the best pork dumplings. Noodle soups come next with shrimp and octopus and rice noodles, Thai coconut curry with chicken and crisp egg noodles, Vietnamese beef noodle soup with meatballs, and bacon, egg and cheese ramen offer more choices. The wok section offers noodles with pork belly, stir fried scallop, lobster and shrimp, and Singapore noodles with mushrooms. End with a fruit plate, chocolate sticky rice pudding Vietnamese coffee affogato, and kaya ice cream sandwich. The cocktail wine and beer list are excellent, service very friendly, and prices affordable. It's very casual and a fun spot for dining in the hood.

Chowder Room

Cuisine: Seafood
Open: L-D: Tues-Sat
chowderroom.com

560 S. Broadway
Denver, CO 80209

303-777-3474 (FISH)

Price: $$
Reservations: Yes
Location: Denver - South Broadway

Patio: Yes
Brunch: No

Chowder Room on S. Broadway with Chef Matt and his wife Carrie doing the honors brings a new team to the area. The place is simple but warm and welcoming. It's one room with a nice bar and booths and tables around the space. Pictures of the sea and seafood, etc. are on the walls. The menu starts with oysters, peel and eat shrimp, and poke with yellowfin tuna. Chowder is the specialty of the house: New England style, spicy red seafood, or chowder of the day. There is a green curry-coconut vegan choice as well. All are excellent and you can order a cup, bowl, in bread, or a combo tasting. The salads are a choice of winter nicoise or hearts of romaine with blue cheese, bacon, egg and pecans. For sandwiches the baker burger has the works and secret sauce, pan-fried chicken, filet of crisp North Atlantic cod, or fried shrimp po'boy. Finally there are choices of calamari, crab cakes, deep fried shrimp, and the catches of the day. End with desserts of bread pudding with ice cream, chocolate parfait or a bourbon pear trifle. There is wine and cocktails, coffee, and friendly service. It's an all-day/all night menu with nothing too heavy. The folks are lovely and the place a spot for that yummy soup and more.

Citron Bistro

Cuisine: American
Open: L: Mon-Fri, D: Daily, BR: Sun
citronbistro.com

3535 S. Yosemite St.
Denver, 80237
Hampden & Yosemite

303-771-5800

Price: $$
Reservations: Yes
Location: Denver - South East

Patio: Yes
Brunch: Yes

Citron Bistro brings fun dining to the neighborhood in the south Denver area. As you enter the free-standing building, casual décor and comfort immediately make you feel welcome. The space is large but divided into small rooms, with a fireplace and big chairs in the lounge, an open kitchen, and a bar area in front. Start with delicious homemade bread served with pesto olive oil as you select from several specialty drinks and wine. Appetizers include shrimp nachos, meatball sliders, mussels, fried calamari and hummus. Asian lollipops and chicken drumettes with Hunan chile cilantro sauce are unique choices. Entrées bring several options. For lighter fare, choose adobe grilled chicken salad, tenderloin gorgonzola salad, a focaccia chicken sandwich or burgers. There are several pastas or lamb chops, lamb shank, pork chop, New York strip steak, trout and salmon. End with a pleasing selection of desserts. The wine list is nice and service is friendly in this neighborhood bistro.

City Bakery Café

Cuisine: Bakery, Sandwiches
Open: B-L: Mon-Sat
citybakerydenver.com

726 Lincoln   303-292-3989
Denver, 80203
7th & Lincoln

Price: $-$$ **Patio:** Yes
Reservations: No   **Brunch:** No
Location: Central Denver

Finally, Michael Bortz, the genius of City Bakery—master of bread and sweets, has opened a place to enjoy great breakfast and lunch. It's City Bakery Cafe on 7th and Lincoln and even has parking. Enter the one room space and place your order at the counter and your order appears at the table. They are open for breakfast and lunch. There are egg sandwiches for breakfast-and then the fun of lunch starts. There are fabulous soups, really good salads such as the cobb, mixed blue, Tuscan, and Caesar. The sandwiches are over the top served on the great bread here. There are many versions of fresh turkey, chicken, ham and cheese, and specialty of the day. You can build your own too. Pick your chips and a freshly baked cookie comes with the entrée too. The panini of grilled tomato and cheese, roast turkey and artichokes, ham and cheddar and cubano round out the menu. Every ingredient is top quality, fresh, and so good. Michael actually was a chef years ago and now gets to have some fun again. There's a fabulous coffee list and cold drinks abound. It is a real treat and thrill to have City Bakery Café here. At the bakery you can find all the great breads and sweets served in the restaurant.

CityGrille

Cuisine: American
Open: L-D: Daily BR: Sat-Sun
citygrille.com

321 E. Colfax Ave.   303-861-0726
Denver, 80203
Between Grant & Logan on Colfax

Price: $-$$ **Patio:** Yes
Reservations: Yes   **Brunch:** Yes
Location: Capitol Hill

Looking for some really good food along with a Cheers-like atmosphere? Head over to City Grille. The bar/lounge area and dining room are bright with terrific lighting, nice colors and comfortable seating. The fresh food brings new meaning to bar fare. Start with gorgonzola cheese toast, hunks of toasted bread laden with wonderful cheese and garlic, or the hot artichoke dip and chips. Homemade soups are excellent, and the green chili rates tops in all the town's magazines. So do the burgers which are so big you can barely take a bite. Monday night brings "burger madness," where a burger with fries and a beer is a bargain. Chicken enchiladas, chiles rellenos, sandwiches and salads add to the options. Grill favorites include rib-eye steak sandwiches and London broil. Nightly specials, like barbecue rib Wednesday and prime rib Saturday really bring in the crowds. Don't leave without the warm brownie à la mode topped with either hot chocolate fudge or caramel pecan sauce. Good food, affordable prices, late-night service and friendly staff keep City Grille high on the list for very casual dining.

Colore Italian Restaurant

Cuisine: Italian
Open: L-D: Daily, BR: Sat-Sun
coloreitalian.com

2700 S. Broadway   303-761-4332
Englewood, 80113
Broadway & Yale

Price: $$ **Patio:** Yes
Reservations: Yes   **Brunch:** Yes
Location: Englewood

A visit to Colore Italian Restaurant is a real treat. The place is a neighborhood treat on South Broadway for Italian fare, pizza and wine. The space is warm and friendly with big windows, a fantastic bar as you enter and warm colors with lots of table seating with wood tables and red chairs for accent and booths for comfort as well. Owner Chris Millette, a veteran in the business brings this place to new heights and great fun. Start with crisp calamari, fritto misto, caprese, bruschetta, jalapeno artichoke dip, mussels, and burrata. Several salads include grilled shrimp, cobb, veggie, spinach and grilled chicken, salmon, and a very special Caesar. Sop all the dressings and sauces with the delicious rolls. Classics range from vongole or mussels, fabulous eggplant rollatina to spaghetti and meatballs and eggplant or chicken parm. The pastas include penne arrabiata, bolognese and baked pasta of lasagna, veggie lasagna, baked chicken, penne, and Bolognese. There's more with chicken, salmon and veal favorites and of course, pizza and calzone with divine toppings or create your own. The super dessert menu ends the meal. The famous peach bread pudding is a perfect choice. Add excellent wines, super service, and affordable prices and Colore Italian Restaurant becomes the place for all the family any time.

Colt & Gray

Cuisine: American
Open: D: Tues-Sun
coltandgray.com

1553 Platte St., #120   303-477-1447
Denver, 80202

Price: $$$$ **Patio:** Yes
Reservations: Yes   **Brunch:** No
Location: Platte Valley

Colt & Gray brings enjoyable dining to the Platte area with both cocktails and food. The place is beautiful with a fabulous patio and a perfect view of the walking bridge as well as downtown. Enter and enjoy the bar area with classic seating and lighting that adds to the sophisticated yet rustic feel. A second room is a bit more formal with white linens but both feature the chairs, table trim and framed mirrors done with wood finished with resin that has the look and feel of tortoise shell. Fireplaces add to the scene. The bar features an excellent cocktail program with Kevin Burke at the helm since opening. The contemporary food matches the décor and brings interesting options. Bar snacks include fried oysters, crispy pig trotter, blue cheese dusted gougère, and bacon cashew caramel corn. Charcuterie and cheeses delight with a changing selection. Small plates include oysters on the half shell, a grilled scallop, grilled octopus and mussels. Entrées like cioppino, chicken, rack of lamb, New York steak and trout are prepared with the chef's touch. Add items from the grill with burgers of beef or turkey. Pick a side of veggies or a plate of offal. Decadent desserts end the meal. Colt & Gray is a good choice for a special evening or just a late night snack and drink.

Colterra

Cuisine: French, Italian
Open: L: Mon-Fri, D: Daily, BR: Sat-Sun
colterra.com

210 Franklin St.   303-652-0777
Niwot, 80302
Franklin & 2nd Ave.

Price: $$$$ **Patio:** Yes
Reservations: Yes   **Brunch:** Yes
Location: Niwot

Colterra, the former Le Chantecler, is the place to enjoy a delightful evening. The victorian house glitters with tiny white lights which creates a wonderful ambience. Enter the wonderful bar area and then dine in one of the several rooms with comfortable seating, elegant art and beautiful table settings. The open kitchen area is a perfect spot to observe Chef/Owner Bradford Heap and his staff create remarkable meals. Start with roasted golden beet salad with chèvre, toasted walnuts, grilled bread and raspberry vinaigrette, a marvelous Caesar, or an arugula salad with spiced pecans, pears, chèvre and balsamic vinaigrette. Smoked wild salmon with crisp pasta, escargot l'orangerie, mussels, buffalo carpaccio, and lobster ravioli are other perfect appetizers. The tuna tartare is a must with shallots, lemon, chiles and olive oil, as is the crab cake with slaw. Braised lamb shank with garlic mashed potatoes, sea scallops, crispy duck breast with polenta, and flat iron steak with gorgonzola gnocchi start the list of incredible entrées. Pork tenderloin, barramundi and mussels with tomatoes, lobster gnocchi, ahi tuna, and mahi mahi with caramelized sweet potatoes are more temptations. Each presentation is picture perfect to see and more amazing to taste. End with a chocolate tasting of pot de crème, biscotti, mousse and gelato, pumpkin spice cake with maple ice cream, fruit tart or crème brûlée. The wine list keeps pace with outstanding choices by the glass at reasonable prices. Excellent and family friendly service completes the picture. For an experience that meets every expectation for a perfect meal, Colterra is the place to be.

Comida Denver

Cuisine: Mexican
Open: L-D: Mon-Sat, BR: Sun
eatcomida.com

3350 Brighton Blvd. #105   303-296-2747
Denver, 80216
The Source

Price: $$ **Patio:** Yes
Reservations: Yes   **Brunch:** Yes
Location: RiNo District - Denver

Comida is a popular choice in the Source Building in the RiNo District. The building is great looking and the restaurant awesome in design and food. Start with contemporary, unfinished high ceilings, open pipe, stainless, black and red and totally wide open. There is a huge bar that opens outside to the patio and is the focal inside with the open kitchen behind. It is just stunning and a knockout. Rayme Rosello already has the wildly popular Comida in Longmont and a food truck and this food follows suit with fabulous tastes at great prices. Start with queso fundido, the best guacamole ever, jicama and cucumber, nachos with smoked gouda and asadero and add ons of protein. Tacos on soft corn tortillas include pork, marinated fish, skirt steak, shrimp, sirloin and chorizo, each done with great sauces and seasonings. The tortas (sandwiches) do not disappoint and come on a crusty warm Mexican roll with pickled veggies. Tostadas and gorditas are more options bringing great selections on crispy flat corn shell or warm masa pocket. The chicken with poblano, roasted poblano and onion with cream, the shroom, and chorizo are addictive. Add super quesadillas and decisions are impossible. The sides are mandatory with sweet potato mash, orange jalapeño slaw, grits, rice, beans and guacamole perfect to complement the tacos. Do not leave without indulging in the flan. The cocktail, wine, and beer list are terrific. With super service, great ambience, and delicious food, Comida brings a treat to dining at The Source.

Coohills

Cuisine: French, Contemporary
Open: D: Mon-Sat
coohills.com

1400 Wewatta St.   303-623-5700
Denver, 80202
14th & Wewatta

Price: $$$$ **Patio:** Yes
Reservations: Yes   **Brunch:** Yes
Location: Downtown - Denver

Enter through a patio with an open fireplace, great design and welcoming feel and walk into the restaurant. As you enter see the open kitchen where the chefs are busy working, a wine table to the right, a chef's table in front (a perfect place to watch the action, and a community table as well). Above it, an actual grape vine tree makes a gorgeous chandelier complete with twinkling lights. Move on to the lounge with a large bar, sofas, tables and booths and large windows. Stop in for a drink or spend the evening. The dining room is beautiful with comfortable seating and a great view. Chef/Owner Tom Coohill is creative and experienced and the menu shows his talent. Start with warm homemade epi bread as you peruse the wine list and menu. Starters include blue crab cakes, duck confit, pate, cheese, foie gras and snails. All are wonderful to see, better to eat. If the salmon terrine is on, get it. Salads range from crunch parmesan egg and bacon, Caesar, and living lettuce to the soup du jour. The entrée list starts with chicken, New York strip, and lamb. Then add salmon, monkfish, halibut and vegetarian dishes and just decide. Rich decadent desserts are a must. The wine list is designed to pair perfectly with your meal. Service, under the direction of the charming Diane Coohill, complements the talent of her husband along with a fabulous staff. Coohills does many events in their stunning setting and is close to Pepsi Center too, adding to the reasons for dining here.

Cool River Café

Cuisine: Steakhouse
Open: L: Mon-Fri, D: Daily
coolrivercafe.com

8000 E. Belleview Ave.   303-771-4117
Greenwood Village, 80111
Belleview & Ulster

Price: $$$-$$$$ **Patio:** Yes
Reservations: Yes   **Brunch:** No
Location: Denver Tech Center

This place is massive. A white stone fireplace rises to almost
two stories in the dining room and the domed ceiling glows
like gold leaf in the evening light. Tables fill a balcony
surrounding the main room and the entire space could easily
accommodate 250 people. At night a separate bar area the
size of many restaurants fills with people looking for a good
time. Live bands hit the stage at least once a week. Cool River
combines a classic steakhouse with southwestern flavor. Start
with shrimp cocktail, a pound of steamed mussels, or crab-
stuffed portobello mushroom caps. Entrées feature several
cuts of steak, lamb chops, barbecued ribs and a pork chop.
Other possibilities include salmon, lobster tail and swordfish.
For dessert try a slice of pecan sweet potato pie or mile-high
chocolate cake.

Cooper Lounge

Cuisine: Cocktail Bar, Cafe
Open: B-L-D:Daily
cooperlounge.com

1701 Wynkoop St   720-460-3738
Denver, 80202
Wynkoop & 17th

Price: $$$ **Patio:** No
Reservations: Yes   **Brunch:** No
Location: Union Station - Downtown

In the Union Station, upstairs from the lobby, is Cooper
Lounge. Make a reservation to be sure it is not full, and then
go and enjoy. It is spectacular—white, comfortable seating,
fabulous lighting and overlooks the hubbub below. The bar is
gorgeous and service great. Head bartender Marcel pleases all
with a great selection of drinks---and lots of charm. The food
is from Lon Symensma of Cholon and he is doing breakfast,
lunch and nighttime tapas. Breakfast is bagels, smears, and fun
while lunch adds salads and sandwiches. Cheese, charcuterie

and more bring nighttime excitement with all the beverages in beautiful surroundings.

CoraFaye's Café

Cuisine: Southern
Open: L-D: Tues-Sat
corafayes.com

2861 Colorado Blvd.   303-333-5551
Denver, 80207
29th & Colorado Blvd.

Price: $-$$ **Patio:** No
Reservations: Yes   **Brunch:** No
Location: Park Hill

If you're looking for what might be the best southern/soul food in Denver get yourself into CoraFaye's Café near the Denver Museum of Nature and Science and the Denver Zoo. The outside of the restaurant doesn't hint at the treat in store for you but once inside you feel as if you have been transported to an adorable southern country kitchen. Owner/Chef Priscilla named the restaurant after her mother, CoraFaye. Priscilla does the cooking, greeting customers as if they were guests in her home. The southern comfort food is outstanding. This is some of the best fried chicken anywhere—crispy, not greasy, and perfectly seasoned. The smothered pork chops and fried catfish are big hits as well. Ribs ends, brisket, and other delights tempt the diners. Sides of candied yams and collard greens receive rave reviews. Don't miss fried okra, the yummy coleslaw and potato salad, and mac and cheese please all. If you're looking for true soul food, you'll find frog legs on the menu as well as pig ear sandwiches, pig's feet, neck bones, beef ox tails and smothered rabbit are daily specials. Try one of the homemade desserts such as sweet potato pie, banana pudding, peach cobbler, and cakes that include coconut cream cheese or caramel. Like any good southern restaurant there is plenty of sweet tea to drink. Some of the servers are family members which gives the restaurant even more of a homey feel. Priscilla is doing her mother proud! And fried chicken lovers are very happy.

The Corner Office & Martini Bar

Cuisine: Contemporary
Open: B-L-D: Daily, BR: Sat-Sun
thecornerofficedenver.com

1401 Curtis St.   303-825-6500
Denver, 80202
14th & Curtis

Price: $$ **Patio:** Yes
Reservations: Yes   **Brunch:** Yes
Location: Denver - Downtown

Exciting things are happening in the downtown area of the DCPA and the Corner Office and Martini Bar in the Curtis Hotel is one of the popular spots for dining around the theaters as well as for the bar crowd. The separate entrance makes a perfect start to this terrific-looking spot where the feel is upbeat and the food offers so many options. The bright modern décor sets the scene with terrific graphics on the walls, large windows, fun seating and a bar highlighted with backlit blue Lucite. The large space is divided with several areas for dining. The martini list is impressive and a great way to begin your meal. The cuisine billed as "global comfort," starts with fried shishito peppers, hummus with pita, and crispy calamari with rock shrimp or chorizo quesadillas. The Vietnamese barbecued-pork sandwich, turkey club and a burger served on fresh bread are excellent choices for sandwich lovers. For total decadence, don't miss fried chicken on a waffle with syrup, or try the short ribs with mashed potatoes for real comfort food. Desserts include cheesecake, chocolate-almond tart and chocolate cake. Service is casual and friendly. Breakfast, lunch, dinner and brunch, all served at reasonable prices in this fun atmosphere make The Corner Office a fun choice for downtown dining.

Corridor 44

Cuisine: Wine Bar, French
Open: D: Daily
corridor44.com

1433 Larimer St.   303-893-0044
Denver, 80202
Larimer Square

Price: $$-$$$ **Patio:** Yes
Reservations: Yes   **Brunch:** No
Location: Larimer Square, Downtown

Part of the Larimer Square scene Corridor 44 is unique in concept and design. As you would expect with its name Corridor 44 features a terrific bar area as you enter, with a long corridor of additional seating that leads into a lounge where guests enjoy a fabulous selection of champagne as well as wine and cocktails. Along with that list of bubblies, enjoy some of the small plates to go. Start with Marcona almonds, olives, and oyster shooters. Share the cheese or charcuterie plates, smoked salmon and caviar potato chips, mussels in curry coconut broth, lamb chop lollipops and shrimp cocktail. Buffalo sliders, grilled tuna, and prosciutto are more options. Large plates of chicken breast, scallops, salmon, filet and surf-and-turf complement the wines. What fun to enjoy the great champagnes at Corridor 44 and a spot for a night of fun in the Square?

Crema Coffee House

Cuisine: Coffee House, Contemporary
Open: B-L: Daily
cremacoffeehouse.net

2862 Larimer St.   720-284-9648
Denver, 80205
28th & Larimer

Price: $-$$ **Patio:** Yes
Reservations: No   **Brunch:** No
Location: LoHi

The coffee culture in Denver got a serious boost when Crema Coffee House opened its doors. It's a funky and comfortable environment on the trendy north Larimer Street. Crema brews the best cup of coffee in the city. For the beans the coffee fanatics behind Crema go far and wide across the country to handpick only the best. You will find beans from Four Barrel in San Francisco, Herkimer from Seattle, the fabulous Novo and also local favorite Boulder-based Boxcar being ground to order and turned into flawless lattes and cappuccinos. The menu at Crema is simple and perfected. In the morning find pastries and breakfast items like homemade 5 spice granola with rich Noosa yogurt and fresh fruit as well as surprisingly amazing sweet potatoes waffles. Come lunch you can get the daily quiche that changes with the seasons or the awesome banh mi, a simple Vietnamese sandwich that comes on a soft bun slathered in aioli, filled with pork belly, and topped with crunch carrot, daikon radish, and cucumber and just a few sprigs of cilantro. Fresh juice is available all day in one healthy and pleasing combination: carrot, beet, apple with just a hint of ginger. Crema is a real treat.

Crêpes 'n Crêpes

Cuisine: Breakfast, Crêpes, French
Open: B-L: Daily, D: Tues-Sun
crepesncrepes.com

2816 E. 3rd Ave.	303-320-4184
Denver, 80206	
3rd & Fillmore	
1512 Larimer St.	303-534-1620
Denver, 80202	
Larimer Square	

Price: $$ **Patio:** Yes
Reservations: No **Brunch:** No
Location: Cherry Creek, Larimer Square

This delightful restaurant is the place where good things come in small packages. The eatery is very French and charming in décor. The room is made up of one long counter with pretty fabric-covered bar stools and soft faux-textured walls. Patios in front and rear provide additional seating for dining on premises. Take out is available as well. The real story here is the crêpes' batter, spread thin on the imported iron crêpe griddles, cooked perfectly and rolled with your choice of fillings. Savory crêpes feature buckwheat or wheat flour, add chicken, turkey, ham, eggs, cheese, spinach and mushrooms, with sauce or plain. The sweet crêpes, made with wheat flour, are truly heavenly, especially with Nutella, the distinctly Italian chocolate hazelnut filling that delights every time. Other choices include fruit, chocolate, whipped cream and crêpes suzette. The menu features other fare, including several soups and salads, as well as hot and cold drinks. After one visit, you'll be hooked. Crêpes 'n Crêpes—it's bonjour, but never au revoir.

CRU, a Wine Bar

Cuisine: Contemporary
Open: D: Daily, BR: Sun
cruawinebar.com

1442 Larimer St.	303-825-0881
Denver, 80202	
Larimer Square	

Price: $$-$$$ **Patio:** Yes
Reservations: Yes **Brunch:** Yes
Location: Downtown - Larimer Square

CRU, a Wine Bar, features an excellent wine list (wine is the only alcoholic drink on the menu) for fans stopping by Larimer Square to enjoy their personal favorites while sharing specialty and cheese plates. The space is attractive, with high ceilings, a central bar, walls decorated with various wine bottles and wonderful canvas "wallpaper" featuring hand-painted wine labels. Shades of dark purple, gray, black and mahogany create the ambience in the upstairs dining area, while comfortable sofas and more seating are offered on the lower level. Flights of wine bring combinations for those wanting to experience the differences in one varietal or several. Then enjoy your favorite by the glass or bottle. Start with shrimp and chicken pot stickers, fried calamari, steamed mussels or blue crab cakes. Sesame-crusted ahi tuna, roasted artichoke, crab dip with fontina cheese and a five-cheese pizza are other options. The chef's specialties include seared citrus salmon, paella, roast chicken and beef tenderloin. Roasted pomegranate-glazed pork chop with risotto, and lamb sirloin with ratatouille are excellent entrée choices. For that sweet tooth, and for port pairings, try the flourless chocolate cake or lemon tart. With a friendly staff, CRU brings a new dimension of wine and food to this very popular area.

The Crumb Café

Cuisine: Cafe, Breakfast
Open: B-L-D: Daily
cafecrumb.com

217 S. Holly   720-459-7158
Denver, 80246
Cedar & Holly

Price: $ **Patio:** Yes
Reservations: No   **Brunch:** No
Location: Hilltop - Denver

The Crumb Café in Hilltop brings great fun to the area where Moms with kids in tow, families, and singles can stop in for some good food and yummy sweets in the hood. The one room features a counter where one orders and displays of cupcakes and goods that are hard to pass up. Food is delivered to the tables. Huge windows, old wood on walls, and a wall of quilted cushions as seatbacks set the scene. Breakfast is served all day with egg and cheese sandwich, a breakfast buffalo, bagel and cream cheese, lox and bagel, a frittata and a sausage strata. Lunch and early dinner add many more choices. Chicken pot pie, mac and cheese, tuna or chicken salad or sandwiches, a French dip, and Reuben start the list. Add the Italian, bagel, tomato and cheese melt, cobb salad and wedge so there is something for every taste. There are kiddie choices that keep the young ones happy. Sides include potato salad, chips, fruit or a mini cupcake. Bet you know which is the most popular. The desserts and cakes are fabulous to eat or order for any occasion. Novo coffee drinks, tea and sodas complement the food. Owned by the folks of Cake Crumbs and the Denver

Cupcake Truck, this is a happy place with affordable prices, and welcoming to every age.

Cuba Cuba Café & Bar

Cuisine: Cuban
Open: D: Mon-Sat
cubacubacafe.com

1173 Delaware St.   303-605-2822
Denver, 80204
12th & Delaware

Price: $$-$$$ **Patio:** Yes
Reservations: No   **Brunch:** No
Location: Golden Triangle

Take an old Denver duplex, paint it bright tropical colors, "plant" an iron palm tree in the front yard and you have one of the hottest Cuban restaurants in town. Step into the cozy lounge area, slide up to one of the bongo-drum tables and order a pitcher of mojitos. Sample the ceviche with shrimp and roasted tomato served with corn chips. You'll think you have just been transported to Havana. Other delights include empanadas with beef, chicken croquettes and plantain chips with mojo. The Cubana salad with fresh avocado, hearts of palm, red onions and tomatoes is a must. The Cuban home-style ground beef with potatoes and raisins captures the essence of Cuban cooking. Paella Cuba Cuba, chicken topped with onion and served with rice, grilled skirt steak with an amazing chimichurri sauce and yucca fries, shrimp, pork and ahi tuna are more choices. Save room for the special tres leches cake, chocolate or plain, flan and crème brûlée. Cuba Cuba has a great patio to enjoy the outdoors. Whether stopping in for a drink or staying to enjoy a tasty meal, Cuba Cuba is a sure thing for a fun night out. Cuba Cuba Sandwicheria is open in Boulder and City Set in Glendale. Fun sandwiches, plates and salads are the fare as you place your order and then are served. Prices are great here.

Cucina Colore

Cuisine: Italian
Open: L-D: Daily
cucinacolore.com

3041 E. 3rd Ave.
Denver, 80206
3rd Avenue & St. Paul

303-393-6917

Price: $$ **Patio:** Yes
Reservations: Yes   **Brunch:** No
Location: Cherry Creek

Cucina Colore, with its upbeat dining room and bar, offers guests contemporary Italian cuisine in the heart of Cherry Creek. The space has been redone and enlarged and it looks terrific. The design is modern, warm and friendly. A huge horse shape bar takes over a large portion of the room with tables for dining on all sides. Beautiful glass separates the dining areas as people enjoy their meals or savor a drink at the bar. Behind a wall of glass windows and doors a small sidewalk patio offers a front row seat for people watching. A plate of bread with herb dipping sauce arrives as you are seated. Follow with a light caprese salad or try the beef carpaccio with arugula. Wood-oven fired pizzas are served with traditional Italian toppings in contemporary combinations. Pastas make great entrées, especially the ravioli steeped in rich brown sugar and balsamic sauce. The most exciting "pastaless" lasagna combines eggplant, roasted tomato, spinach and smoked mozzarella, satisfying any taste with its combination of veggies topped with a perfect marinara. Meat eaters will enjoy the New York strip or juicy pork chops, while the fish preparations please all. For dessert, indulge in vanilla bean mascarpone custard or the decadent chocolate oblivion, but don't miss the peach bread pudding in rich caramel sauce. With friendly service and an excellent wine list, Cucina Colore well deserves its status as a favorite for dining in the Cherry Creek North area.

Cured

Cuisine: Specialty Foods, Sandwich Shop
Open: L-D: Daily
curedboulder.com

1825 Pearl St.   720-389-8096
Boulder, 80302
18th & Pearl

Price: $$ **Patio:** Yes
Reservations: No   **Brunch:** No
Location: East Pearl - Boulder

If you are looking for high quality ingredients, exceptional service and a vibrant and inspiring atmosphere, go to Cured. This meat, cheese, and artisan products store located centrally on the Pearl Street Mall is charming and reminiscent of the days when big box grocery stores were not part of the daily lives. The selection of food here is great. There is always fresh bread and produce from Isabel Farm, a wide selection of oils, vinegars, jams, and preserves, but most importantly there is cheese and cured meat like nowhere else. With a balanced selection of domestic and imported cheese and cured meats, this shop can provide the best little afternoon snack, a cheese platter for a party, or a basic daily cheddar. Ask to sample whatever catches your eye and look as the meats are sliced on the spectacular Italian meat slicer that cannot be missed. Pick up fresh farm eggs, prepared small dishes, and give the daily lunch sandwiches a try—they are always spot on. Etalia gluten free bread, the best anywhere, is also available here. While you are there visit and patronize the small but carefully stocked wine and spirit store in the back and ask the friendly owners, Will and Coral Frischhorn about their picnic baskets and party platter choices. This place is charming and outstanding in its service – don't miss it.

The Curtis Club

Cuisine: Contemporary, Gastro Pub
Open: L: Tues-Fri, D: Tues-Sat, BR: Sat-Sun
thecurtisclub.com

2100 Curtis St.   720-420-9898
Denver, 80205
21st and Curtis

Price: $$-$$$ **Patio:** Yes
Reservations: Yes   **Brunch:** Yes
Location: LoDo

The Curtis Club, is one fun spot. Enter to the space that starts with a touch of country western at the focal bar, wagon wheels, adds reclaimed woods brings on the contemporary feel, and finished with touches of the Victorian era with a bit of red wallpaper and settee. The community table has funky barstools but there are booths and tables for more comfort. It adds up to a mishmash décor that works as a background for some excellent food. Start with the house salad, soup of the moment, oysters, a divine winter vegetable salad, and deviled quail eggs. Whatever you order from the share list, there is enough for many. Do not miss the Brussels sprouts petals with toasted almonds, currants, and queso de mano. The entrée list is fun: bison bolognese, foraged mushrooms, rack of lamb, beef tenderloin, and lobster and grits start the list. The hickory smoked trout with quinoa, rabbit wrapped in bacon, and duck with faro cakes. Accompaniments add to the flavors, and all priced reasonably. Desserts include toffee pudding, chocolate cake, fruit desserts and more. The service is lovely, the wine and cocktail list good. It's casual and funky. The Curtis Club is a great choice in this area.

D Bar Denver

Cuisine: American, Desserts
Open: L-D: Tues-Fri Brunch: Sat-Sun
Dbardenver.com

494 E. 19th Ave   303-861-4710
Denver, 80203
19th & Pennsylvania

Price: $$ **Patio:** Yes
Reservations: Yes   **Brunch:** Yes
Location: Uptown - Denver

Yeah, D Bar is back and Keegan and Lisa are home again. The new Uptown location is spacious, bright, and delightful. Enter and find the same ocean blue and brown color scheme, large windows, and lots of dining space. This location is a real restaurant with a great bar, an open kitchen to watch the chefs, with a rear kitchen to round out the space. The look is contemporary and stunning. The new take out area is wonderful with coffee and homemade breakfast rolls along with the other delectable pastries available from 6.30 AM. The menu, wine list, coffees, teas, and cocktails are numerous and now D Bar has food for every meal and taste. Start with crispy Brussels, crue fries, D Bar dates, crispy pork wings, and duck nachos. The tomato soup is terrific and salads are seasonal autumn with beets, squash, pepitas and cheese. Entrees include grilled tahini salmon, pizzas, salad, sandwiches, mac and cheese, veggies, shrimp and grits, scallops and steak and fries. The chicken dishes are the best with buttermilk fried chicken between bacon and maple sugar waffles and sweet potato fries, plus the crispy half chicken with Frank's red hot and maple glaze is a delicious southern item. The dessert list it awesome and really shines. D-Bar always means dessert and chef/partner Lisa Baily has won top 10 pastry chefs in America. With the chocolate cake and shake, crème brulee, lava cake, tarts, pies, cookies, and anything sweet and heavenly just pick your craving and be delighted. The drinks complement the food and are great options on their own. And don't forget breakfast treats, brunch and lunch. Keegan and Lisa have brought a new dimension and caring to their food preparation and bring in the crowds. Denver is happy to have D Bar back.

DJ's Berkeley Café

Cuisine: American
Open: B-L: Mon-Fri, BR: Sat-Sun
djscafe.biz

3838 Tennyson St.	303-482-1841
Denver, 80212	
38th & Tennyson	
865 Lincoln	303-386-3375
Denver, 80203	
9th and Lincoln	

Price: $-$$ **Patio:** Yes
Reservations: No   **Brunch:** Yes
Location: Berkeley, Central Denver

DJ Berkeley Café is a comfortable spot for breakfast and lunch in this ever popular neighborhood. It's casual and airy with the bar, tables and booths nicely spaced and a beautiful patio open when the weather cooperates. Breakfast begins with fluffy pancakes and waffles, omelets, scrambles, eggs Benedict and bagels. The breakfast potatoes are perfectly fried and the green chili is a must. All breakfast dishes are very tasty with homemade sauces. Lunch offers many choices starting with an enticing array of salads including Caesar, cobb, beets, and spinach. Sandwiches vary with cold, hot and panini. There's a club, roasted eggplant, grilled cheese, a crab cake and the quintessential burger. Enjoy bagels, specials, and the signature chicken pot pie, chicken parmesan and fish and chips. Service is excellent, prices affordable, and a brunch menu adds to the variety. DJ Berkeley Café is a fun neighborhood spot.

DaGabi Cucina

Cuisine: Mediterranean, Spanish, Tapas
Open: D: Daily
dagabicucina.com

3970 N. Broadway Blvd.   303-786-9004
Boulder, 80304
Broadway & Quince

Price: $$ **Patio:** Yes
Reservations: Yes   **Brunch:** No
Location: North Boulder

Hidden in a little-known Boulder strip mall this tiny eatery offers a comfortable place to relax and enjoy a fresh meal. Start with steamed mussels flavored with garlic and citrus or fried calamari with spicy tomato sauce. Enjoy a cup of spicy carrot-ginger soup and munch on a salad of mixed greens with goat cheese. Wood-oven pizzas offer something more familiar for kids and also make an excellent appetizer. Nicely-flavored pastas range from spinach-stuffed ravioli with butter sage sauce to spaghetti with marinara and veal meatballs. Follow your pasta course with double-cut pork chops sweetened with brown sugar, salmon sautéed with rock shrimp, or the popular veal saltimbocca. The wine list offers some great Italian varietals at reasonable prices. Finish with the refreshing taste of homemade gelato.

Da-Lat

Cuisine: Vietnamese
Open: L-D: Daily
dalatdenver.com

940 S. Federal Blvd.   303-935-4141
Denver, 80219
Federal Blvd. & Kentucky Ave.

Price: $-$$ **Patio:** No
Reservations: Yes   **Brunch:** No
Location: Denver - South West

Da-Lat stands out as one of the best amid the countless ethnic eateries on South Federal. The casual dining room is open with wood wainscoting, and mirrors that visually expand the space. The top-notch staff will happily guide you through the extensive Vietnamese menu. Start with the mouth-watering appetizer combination consisting of grilled beef, chicken, pork and shrimp served with an overflowing platter of fresh lettuce, bean sprouts, rice noodles, cucumbers and rice papers. Mix and match to create your own wraps for dipping into tangy homemade fish sauce. Both the chicken with lemongrass and the beef stir-fried with garlic, black pepper and soy sauce really satisfy. Other great choices include shrimp with cashews, shrimp noodle bowls, curry pork and catfish. Upon request, the chef will prepare something special just for you. Wash it all down with one of the thirst-quenching exotic fruit smoothies.

Darcy's Bistro & Pub

Cuisine: Irish Pub
Open: L-D: Daily, BR: Sat-Sun
Darcysbistroandpub.com

4955 S. Ulster St.   303-770-0477
Denver, 80237
Ulster St. & Belleview Ave.

Price: $-$$ **Patio:** Yes
Reservations: No   **Brunch-Yes**
Location: Denver Tech Center

Welcome to Darcy's, an Irish pub with upscale décor and a menu that offers more than just the usual pub fare. The front of the restaurant focuses on a massive, great-looking bar usually lined with happy customers. Bar tables as well as regular seating create a delightful place for dining. For a more subdued ambience ask to be seated in the library, with its beautiful red walls, bookshelves and comfortable seating. Service is friendly and efficient. Start with steamed mussels, flash-fried calamari, a crab claw cocktail or crab cakes. Sandwiches make a meal with corned beef on rye, a Reuben, grilled Irish cheddar cheese with sautéed onions, the grilled chicken "Pub Club," and a very special tuna melt. Don't forget the long list of burgers and chicken sandwiches. All come with choices of coleslaw, soup, salad or chips. Entrées include Bass Ale-battered cod fish and chips, corned beef and cabbage, lamb stew, shepherd's pie and Irish whiskey chicken. Desserts include carrot cake, chocolate caramel cake, cheesecake and a luscious chocolate brownie sundae. The wine list is varied with offerings at three price levels. The beer and whiskey choices are fantastic. A tapas menu, happy hour and late night menu add to the dining experience.

Dazzle

Cuisine: American
Open: L: Fri, D: Daily, BR: Sun
dazzlejazz.com

930 Lincoln Ave.   303-839-5100
Denver, 80203
9th & Lincoln

Price: $$ **Patio:** No
Reservations: Yes   **Brunch:** Yes
Location: Denver - Central

Dazzle has found its niche in the Denver scene, drawing crowds from a diverse population to enjoy the happenings. The late night art deco lounge entices patrons to enjoy a meal, listen to nightly live music or just sip a cocktail in the sensationally designed surroundings. Martinis are shaken ice-cold and the wine list is varied and nicely priced. Live entertainers, both local and national, add to the ambience. Some are very well known and the shows are a must. The food is more than an added thought with a menu worth the trip. Start with the fried green tomatoes with goat cheese, mussels or addictive French fries. The list of pizzas is terrific; the mac-n-cheese is addicting and the pies are delicious. The dinner salad with candied walnuts and goat cheese, the spicy Asian chicken and the Caesar are great ways to kick off the meal. Entrées include chicken, fish, beef and sandwiches. The grilled cheese sandwich with tomatoes and bacon is the perfect comfort food. Great burgers and the mahi mahi topped with coleslaw, lime and spices are special treats. Save room for delicious desserts. The weekend brunch is very popular and not to be missed.

D'Corazon

Cuisine: Mexican
Open: L-D: Monday-Saturday
dcorazonrestaurant.com

1530 Blake St. Unit C   720-904-8226
Denver, CO 80202
15th & Blake

Price: $ **Patio:** Yes
Reservations: No   **Brunch:** No
Location: LoDo

In the heart of LoDo is D'Corazon. The family owned restaurant is always busy but the owners and staff make you feel like family as soon as you enter. Get here early to beat the lunch crowd. Bright yellow wall, vibrant and authentic artwork greet you in this neighborhood favorite. The complimentary chips and salsa ease your hunger pangs as you peruse the menu. The staff is attentive and friendly. Entrées range from juicy carnitas, to flavorful steak tacos especiales, to crispy or crunchy chili rellenos or sizzling fajitas. These choices make coming to a decision difficult! Luckily--you can't go wrong. D'Corazon offers both lunch and dinner combo options if you are unable to pick just one item. There is a short beer list and house margaritas are always an option to pair with your meal. Save room for sopapillas, tres leches cake or fried ice cream. Next time you find yourself in LoDo after a game, before a play or out for lunch with a friend, escape to D'Corazon where you will have delicious food at an affordable price, served quickly and always with a smile.

Del Frisco's Double Eagle Steakhouse

Cuisine: Steakhouse
Open: L: Mon-Fri, D: Daily
delfriscos.com/location/Denver

8100 E. Orchard Rd.   303-796-0100
Greenwood Village, 80111
Orchard & S. Willow

Price: $$$$ **Patio:** No
Reservations: Yes   **Brunch:** No
Location: Denver Tech Center

Del Frisco's is the "prime" dining experience in the DTC. This popular steakhouse serves marvelous steaks and does an equally wonderful job with the rest of the menu. The warm, rich woods create a comfortable setting in which to sit back in one of the several dining areas and be pampered with exceptional service. Sip one of the hundreds of outstanding wines on the extensive wine list as you peruse the menu. Start with delicious crab cakes, shrimp and fresh oysters. Specials include crab claws, soft-shell crab and other seasonal seafood. The lettuce wedge with blue cheese is a classic, but the house salad with heavenly honey-smoked bacon is not to be missed. Pick your favorite cut of prime steak, or choose perfectly cooked lamb chops or the decadent veal chop. Fish lovers will be pleased with Del Frisco's selection of lobster tail, salmon or fish of the day. All made for sharing, sides delight. Don't miss Del Frisco's famous lemon cake for dessert. Lunch is also a treat at Del's. This is a perfect spot for that high-powered business meeting, special occasion, or group function. Private party rooms, a fabulous bar and a cigar room are also available.

Denver ChopHouse and Brewery

Cuisine: Steakhouse
Open: L-D: Daily, BR: Sat-Sun (Denver only)
chophouse.com

1735 19th St.   303-296-0800
Denver, 80202
19th & Wynkoop

921 Walnut St.   303-443-1188
Boulder, 80302
9th & Walnut

Price: $$-$$$ **Patio:** No
Reservations: Yes   **Brunch:** Yes (Denver)
Location: LoDo, Boulder

Housed in the old Union Pacific building in LoDo, Denver Chop House's atmosphere gives the original railroad décor a modern, sophisticated feel. Large booths and tables offer views of the kitchen and the brew tanks behind the gigantic bar. The ambience and feel are upbeat as you settle in for a night of great food and frivolity. Start your feast with one of the best mussel renditions in town: a bowl of plump, juicy mussels in a delicious marinara sauce that's perfect for sopping up with bread. Other great choices include a tower of homemade onion rings, grilled portobello mushrooms and the best crab cakes around. Each entrée comes with cornbread in a black iron skillet, a great house salad in a bottomless bowl, and potatoes or rice. Try the famous 22-ounce porterhouse, cedar-plank grilled salmon, or an incredible rack of lamb. The tuna chop is awesome and the fontina cheese-stuffed pork chop a must. Filet, Delmonico, beef tips and lobster tail add to the entrée choices. Don't forget the deliciously cheesy mashed potatoes. Save room for the dessert especially the warm chocolate lava cake à la mode. The wine list is generous with many choices by the glass or bottle. Lunch and weekend brunch are a wonderful option. Nobody leaves this perennial Denver favorite hungry and everyone looks forward to their next visit to the ChopHouse.

Devil's Food

Cuisine: American, Bakery
Open: B-L: Mon-Fri, D: Tue-Sat, BR: Sat-Sun
devilsfoodbakery.com

1024 S. Gaylord St.   303-733-7448
Denver, 80209
Tennessee & S. Gaylord

Price: $-$$ **Patio:** Yes
Reservations: No   **Brunch:** Yes
Location: Wash Park

Devil's Food brings great life to the South Gaylord Street area where fans come to shop and dine. This funky spot features a bakery where luscious pastries fill the shelves and homemade breads are available for purchase. The dining area, with 15 tables, boasts red walls, interesting paintings, hanging doors and windows, and vintage lamps with old-fashioned shades that will make you smile. Simple tables and chairs, paper napkins and no-frills china set the scene. Breakfast and lunch offers delightful egg dishes, waffles, pancakes and sandwiches. There is an assortment of homemade breads and dishes for every taste. Desserts excel with decadent mocha cake, chocolate-glazed donuts, fruit tarts and cookies. Wines are available by the glass or bottle. Service is friendly, efficient and in complete harmony with the ambience. Dinner is a delightful experience as well. Devil's Food has a unique identity that brings people back for more.

The District

Cuisine: American
Open: L-D: Daily, BR: Sat-Sun
districtdenver.com

1320 E. 17th Ave   303-813-6688
Denver, 80218
17th & Humboldt

Price: $$ **Patio:** Yes
Reservations: Yes   **Brunch:** Yes
Location: Uptown

Another new addition to E. 17th Ave. is The District. It is an interesting place with an inviting patio, windows that open wide to the inside, an expansive bar area, and ample tables for dining. It is simple, wood, exposed brick, and contemporary in feel, and Jason Sorrell and Kerry Condon make you feel welcome. Start with mussels, grilled scallops, and a Mediterranean platter. The "salad" district has house made pastrami salad with Russian dressing, grilled Caesar, pickled beet, avocado chop, orange

berry, and dates and goat cheese. Shareables range from the charcuterie plate, the bacon 3 ways, ratatouille fritter and wings to Reuben fries, bacon, and mexi fries. The "sandwich district" tempts with a burger, sausage, pulled pork and BBBLT, smoked turkey and avocado, pastrami, tempeh, and grilled cheese. Entrees of fish and chips, fried chicken, cuban smoked squash and mahi fish tacos please. And of course, mac n cheese, and chicken fried steak sliders are comfort dishes. At dinner ribeye, pork loin, salmon, gnocchi and grilled vegetable pappardelle are offered. There is a brunch menu on weekends, cocktails, beer and wine anytime. The servers are super and the place is open very late. Have some fun at The District anytime with comfort food and super surroundings.

Domo Restaurant

Cuisine: Japanese, Sushi
Open: L-D: Daily
domorestaurant.com

1365 Osage St.
Denver, 80204
13th Ave. & Osage St.

303-595-3666

Price: $$$-$$$$
Reservations: Yes
Location: Denver - Downtown

Patio: Yes
Brunch: No

K: Awesome experience, cool atmosphere! Very traditional, great Japanese food.

J: Superb Japanese food and beautiful Zen garden to dine in. Amazing sushi and courses.

4½

The informal Japanese word for thanks is "domo," and most patrons owe a big "domo" after feasting on this restaurant's outstanding Japanese cuisine. Located in the Japan House Culture Center, Domo will make you feel as if you've been transported to the countryside of Japan. The beautiful garden provides the perfect locale for dining under the stars, while walls covered in Japanese fabrics, rock-slab tables, and seats made of padded logs all work to create a striking atmosphere inside. Wander through the museum and fascinating spaces within the building to learn a bit about Japanese culture then settle down for the exciting dining experience. The food is Japanese country-style and starts with seven different small bowls that are served with all meals—spicy chicken with onions, salmon with broccoli, green beans, spinach, eggplant and cauliflower, crab with slaw, and pork with veggies. Entrées include light and smoky chicken, salmon teriyaki, nabemono, stewed meats with seaweed and vegetables, and sake kasunabe, salmon and vegetables in miso broth. The grilled fish with rice, udon noodle bowls and amazing presentation of sushi make for difficult choices. The sushi preparation of fresh fish served atop sticky rice in small bowls is quite unique for the area. As in Japan, soy sauce is not a main ingredient here; each dish has the perfect blending of spices, so soy sauce is not offered. Twenty different kinds of sake are offered. Dining at Domo affords an extraordinary opportunity to experience the amazing food and charm of Japanese culture right here in downtown Denver!

Duo

Cuisine: American, Contemporary
Open: D: Daily, BR: Sat-Sun
duodenver.com

2413 W. 32nd Ave.   303-477-4141
Denver, 80211
32nd & Zuni

Price: $$$ **Patio:** Yes
Reservations: Yes   **Brunch:** Yes
Location: Denver - Highlands

Duo brings excitement to the Highlands area. Actually one of the first to bring popularity to the area, it remains a top choice as it continues to bring great food, wine, and ambience to all. The space is an eclectic combination of old and new. Wood tables, black chairs and a semi-open kitchen are complemented by exposed brick walls, plank wood floors and a wonderful bar. The cuisine is creative and delicious. The new chefs have created menus that are innovative, exciting, and perfect for a night of great flavors and taste. Start with the complimentary plate of assorted marinated olives and crackers as you peruse the excellent wine list and menu that changes often. Appetizers include prosciutto wrapped apple slivers, sweet potato wedges, clams in vermouth, cornmeal crusted rabbit with smoked mustard, gnocchi in a taleggio fonduta, and house smoked sturgeon. The sweet potato soup and butter lettuce salad with sliced pickled eggs, garlic croutons and aged cow's milk cheese and bacon vinaigrette are awesome. The duck confit with golden beets and mustard greens and arugula are two more terrific salad choices. Entrees include divine rock fish with wild rice and quinoa with raisins and curry carrots, mussels and linguini, and cassoulet. Add a divine pork chop, chicken with walnut bread pudding, lamb shank, hanger steak, and faro and decisions are impossible. Each dish is beautiful to see, better to taste. Don't leave without desserts: chocolate ganache cake, sticky toffee pudding, ice cream pie and gelato. While the restaurant can be packed with happy diners the service keeps pace with the food and wine. With its upbeat feel and great food and wine Duo remains on top in this popular. It is a place that boasts repeat customers and you will be one of them. It's a great treat in the Highlands.

Dushanbe Teahouse

Cuisine: Contemporary
Open: B-L: Mon-Fri, D Daily, BR-Sat-Sun
boulderteahouse.com

1770 13th St.
Boulder, 80302
13th & Arapahoe

303-442-4993

K: Great tea, great atmosphere, good food (not fantastic and a little pricey)

Price: $$
Reservations: Yes
Location: Boulder - Downtown

Patio: Yes
Brunch: Yes

At last, the perfect place for a tea party in the park. The spectacular Dushanbe Teahouse was brought to Boulder from Tajikistan in crates and then erected over three years by native craftspeople. Magnificent flowers surround a patio overlooking Boulder Creek, and the walk to the front doors feels as if you are wandering through a garden paradise. Enjoy lunch or dinner every day but Sunday, when a delicious brunch is served. Tastes range across the globe from Indian samosas and African plantain fritters to Thai curries and Italian pastas. Don't miss the Mediterranean salad, a bed of greens with hummus, cucumbers, dolmas, tomatoes, feta and olives with red-wine vinaigrette. Other possibilities include korean pan-fried noodles, cuban salmon, and blue-corn enchiladas stuffed with spinach, tomatoes, cheese and onions. Your server can help you decide on a tea from the long list of possibilities. Drink a cup or two with your apple crisp or chocolate cake. When you decide to try the popular afternoon tea, complete with white linens and pastries, make a reservation.

J: Beautiful building and awesome tea times!

Earl's

Cuisine: American
Open: L-D: Daily
earls.ca

1600 Glenarm Pl. #140
Denver, 80202
16th & Glenarm

303-595-3275

Price: $$
Reservations: Yes
Location: 16th St. Mall, Denver - Downtown

Patio: Yes
Brunch: No

Earl's is a charming and vibrant dining establishment. On any given evening you will see busy bar areas filled with guests enjoying wine, drinks and food. Large dining rooms with big windows, wood, and black and brown colors throughout set a very comfortable mood. The spacious booths with black cut velvet backs make diners feel at home. Start with spinach and artichoke dip, grilled shrimp or chicken tacos, pork pot stickers, shrimp rolls, tuna, and wings. Soups include clam chowder and green chile soup and several breads are on the menu. Hot chicken Caesar, Santa Fe chicken and Mediterranean spinach salads make great entrées or perfect for sharing. Sandwiches range from a selection of burgers and ahi tuna to chicken and pulled pork. Pastas and big bowls bring more choices. Grilled salmon, Cajun blackened chicken, ribs, and a variety of steaks top the entrée list and several sides please all. End with brownies, chocolate sticky toffee pudding, cheesecake or sundaes. The wine list is great and the service terrific.

Early Bird Restaurant

Cuisine: Café, Brunch, American
Open: B-L: Daily
earlybirdrstaurant.com
11940 Bradburn Blvd.   303-469-9641
Westminster, 80031
120th & Bradburn

Price: $-$$ **Patio:** Yes
Reservations: No   **Brunch:** No
Location: Westminster

When Daniel and Kristen Cofrades decided it was time to leave the big restaurant scene and open a place of their own, Early Bird was their dream. It is delightful with a super ambience of yellows, greens, wood, large community tables, and a great focal open kitchen. On the wall, enjoy great pics of their daughter and related kids' stuff, hung up with clothes pins. The menu is breakfast, lunch, lots of great sweets, and excellent coffee and tea. Start with several versions of early bird risers, an open faced puffed omelet with potatoes, arugula salad and toast. Huevos, burritos, a breakfast club, granola, oatmeal, muesli, and breakfast breads are great beginnings. Add pancakes, French toast and waffles and pick your toppings. The lunch options include fried oyster cobb, prosciutto and arugula salad, corn and chicken chowda, and greens. Sandwiches of chicken salad, oyster po'boy, pulled pork, and toasted cheese and tomatoes make decisions difficult. All the ingredients are fresh from local farmers, and the resulting tastes show the attention to detail. Sweets of dark chocolate brownies and ice cream and sorbets complete the menu. Service is great and the captivating owners are there to charm all. You'll be delighted to start your day when Early Bird Restaurant is the destination.

Eat + Drink

Cuisine: Specialty foods, Café, Wine bar
Open: L-D: Daily
eatdrinkincdenver.com

1541 Platte St.   303-477-3288
Denver, 80202

Price: $$ **Patio:** Yes
Reservations: Yes   **Brunch:** No
Location: Platte Valley, LoHi

Eat+Drink comes to Denver and is a total delight. Located in the ever popular Platte Street this is a great restaurant with excellent food. The space is one large room, bright and cheery with big windows, high ceilings, funky lighting along with fabulous cases of exciting cheeses, sausages, and all sorts of goodies that are irresistible both in the case and lining the walls. You will want one of everything. Food and wine served from 11am till 8pm adds to the scene with a fabulous selection of wines by the glass and bottle. The menu is limited but the quality and presentation is top notch. Start with an olive boat, fabulous burrata, buttery with olive oil and fleur de sel. The soup changes daily. Choose the simple salad or a divine chicken salad. Or go for one of the many bruschetta, cheese plates, or charcuteries. Flatbreads are another choice. The paninis and sandwiches are outstanding. Grilled cheese, turkey with taleggio, pear and fig preserves, prosciutto and mozzarella, artichoke hearts with lemon ricotta, and smoked ham with raclette make panini choices impossible. The simple sandwich served on a baguette is great with your choice of protein. Panini and sandwiches come with salad, chips, or even fruit. The arugula salad that accompanies the dishes has a great taste and is almost a stand-alone meal. Pollyanna and Chris Irving have places in Vail and now bring this special place to Denver. Go to this hood and enjoy a fabulous treat.

East Moon Asian Bistro & Sushi

Cuisine: Asian, Sushi
Open: L-D: Daily
eastmoon8.com

10431 Town Center, #C101   303-635-1888
Westminster, 80021
Westminster Town Center

Price: $$ **Patio:** Yes
Reservations: Yes   **Brunch:** No
Location: Westminster

Enter the space and be wowed by the warm interior. Soft and inviting with lovely table settings, a focal sushi bar, fabulous chandeliers of multicolored glass, and fun artwork on the walls this is a must see restaurant. The star is the food with a terrific variety of Asian dishes and sushi. Sushi rolls include the Sunny Roll, the Hot River Roll with spicy crabmeat, and the Ninja with shrimp tempura and spicy tuna. These are a few of the exciting combinations. Appetizers from the Asian side include pork or chicken dumplings, chicken in lettuce wraps, coconut shrimp, mussels and tempura. Enjoy noodle and rice bowls and curries. The panang with chicken and vegetables is a perfect combination of spices. Don't miss sizzling beef, soft-shell crab in karee curry, crispy duck, sea bass, and rack of lamb with asparagus. There is a very nice wine, sake and beer list to complement the food. Located close to the movie theatres this is a great stop before a night at the cinema.

Eddie Merlot's

Cuisine: Steakhouse
Open: D: Daily
Eddemerlots.com

10110 E. Dry Creek Rd.   720-744-2622
Englewoood, 80112
I-25 and Dry Creek

Price: $$$$ **Patio:** No
Reservations: Yes   **Brunch:** No
Location: Englewood

Eddie Merlot's is a chain that debuts in Denver in a free standing building that is huge. So big that it seems like Vegas. The bar area is to the left but there are dining areas all over. The main dining room is very Vegas with a 90s feel. Huge chandeliers, colors in the panes and wall panels in bright colors, huge paintings on the walls, nicely upholstered chairs and booths in gold and orange, and white linens on the tables. The wine list is again, very big, with several selections by the glass.

Start with bread and butter (they offer if desired which is fine) and decide on your first course. Shrimp cocktail, bbq shrimp, escargot, mussels, and crab cakes are a few options. There are several interesting salads that include beet, Caesar, wedge, and chop. The main feature is steak of every kind and several sauces are offered to accompany your choice. Pork, lamb, chicken, and veal are more choices. A long list of seafood includes salmon, sea bass, tuna, crab, and lobster. The variety of sides to accompany your entrée is full of potato choices, vegetables as asparagus and creamed spinach, and rice. Decadent desserts end the meal. Service is very nice, knowledgeable, and efficient. Edie Merlot's expects you to enjoy your experience so relax and spend the evening. Prices are on the high side as in all steakhouses. Eddie Merlot brings another fun option to those very many beef lovers in the area.

Edge Restaurant & Bar

Cuisine: Contemporary, Seafood, Steakhouse
Open: B-L-D: Daily, BR: Sat-Sun
Edgerestaurantdenver.com

1111 14th St.   303-389-3343
Denver, 80202
Four Seasons Hotel, 14th & Arapahoe

Price: $$$$ **Patio:** Yes
Reservations: Yes   **Brunch:** Yes
Location: Denver - Downtown

Edge is the anchor restaurant in the Four Seasons Hotel. The space is huge with expansive windows, beautiful woods and tables, and comfortable seating that features three private dining areas perfect for a meeting or party. The see-and-be-seen bar located in the lobby is sensational. The glass-enclosed wine wall at the entrance of the restaurant makes a major statement and features some exceptional finds. Special wines by the glass and by the carafe programs enable guests to taste various wines from different countries and regions. Regional, seasonal and artisanal describes the menu. Start with the "epi" bread, very French and crusty, as you peruse the menu. Appetizers include crab cakes, shrimp, crispy pork belly with baby root vegetables and an ahi tuna tartare. Spring onion soup is topped with a goat cheese bruschetta with duck confit, while Caesar, a wedge, mozzarella and tomato, and prosciutto with melon, mâche, and manchego cheese are some of the salads. Entrées include steaks, lamb chops, veal and chicken with several fish selections. The pan-seared halibut with citrus-braised fennel and Colorado lamb with morel mushrooms and minted spring potatoes are favorites. Sides include mac and cheese, potatoes, and seasonal veggies. A knowledgeable and friendly staff adds to the dining experience. The Edge Bar is an all-day and late-night bar at the

Four Seasons Hotel. The bar serves tapas-style menu items for sharing with a global influence to pair cocktails, beer and wine with food. From complimentary valet to every detail of dining, the Four Seasons and Edge Restaurant are a terrific addition to Denver.

Efrain's Mexican Restaurant

Cuisine: Mexican
Open: L-D: Sun-Mon, Wed-Sat
efrainsrestaurant.com

101 E. Cleveland St.   303-666-7544
Lafayette, 80026
Cleveland & S. Public Rd.

Price: $ **Patio:** No
Reservations: No   **Brunch:** No
Location: Lafayette

For years, this tiny Mexican joint has retained a loyal group of fans. The décor is simple and the service can be slow, but people here just want good Mexican food. The large menu includes all the popular favorites from tacos and gorditas to burritos and fajitas. What the food lacks in presentation, it makes up for in flavor. Green chili comes hot. Smother everything with it. Popular favorites include chicken enchiladas, huevos rancheros and Mexican ribs. Even with rice and beans à la carte, the prices are amazing.

The Egg & I

Cuisine: American, Breakfast
Open: B-L: Daily
meetateggandi.com

560 S. Holly St.   303-577-9050
Denver, 80246
Leetsdale & Holly

8025 Sheridan Boulevard   303-577-0070
Arvada, 80003
80th & Sheridan

Price: $ **Patio:** Yes
Reservations: Yes   **Brunch:** No
Location: Denver, Arvada

The Egg and I is a franchise that brings breakfast fare at affordable prices. The Leetsdale and Holly location is a favorite. It's bright and cheery with comfortable seating. Families, kids and seniors are welcome. The menu is the same at all The Egg and I locations. Omelets, Italian-style frittata, eggs Benedict, pancakes and French toast make up some of the menu. Skillets are a specialty as are breakfast chiles rellenos, huevos rancheros and burritos. Several choices for non-egg eaters, as well as sandwich and salad offerings, round out the menu. In fact, the numerous options make choosing difficult. Enjoy pots of hot coffee and tea, friendly service and conversation to make rising early a good choice. There are party rooms available at both locations.

Eggshell of Cherry Creek

Cuisine: American, Breakfast
Open: B-L: Daily
theeggshell.com

235 Fillmore St.   303-322-1601
Denver, 80206
2nd & 3rd & Fillmore

Price: $-$$ **Patio:** Yes
Reservations: Yes   **Brunch:** No
Location: Cherry Creek

The Eggshell is a spot for breakfast or lunch in Cherry Creek North. The space is open, light, and bright with soft colors, a focal bar, and white linens on the tables. There is a patio to enjoy your meal and watch the busy street scene. The brightness of this Cherry Creek restaurant will help immediately, as will the cup of freshly brewed coffee that arrives when you take your seat. Choose from many breakfast entrées, including meats and eggs, omelets, hot and cold cereals, waffles, pancakes, and even breakfast pasta. The expanded lunch menu includes panini, soups, sandwiches and salads, and Mexican dishes. Or just grab a cup of Joe and a pastry for a takeout breakfast. There is wine and your favorite morning cocktails to complement your meal.

El Camino Community Tavern

Cuisine: Mexican
Open: L-D: Daily, BR: Sat-Sun
elcaminotavern.com

3628 W. 32nd Ave.   720-889-7946
Denver, 80211
32nd & Meade

Price: $-$$ **Patio:** No
Reservations: Yes   **Brunch:** Yes
Location: Highlands

El Camino calls itself a Mexican community tavern, welcoming everyone to come and eat. It's bright, busy, with comfy tables, lots of banquette seating and a great focal bar to enjoy your drinks and food. Pictures adorn the walls and beer cans are used to create some really interesting fixtures. It is so friendly with great staff and a menu that pleases all including vegetarians. Chips and salsa, guacamole, Aztec soup, and quesos start the menu. Add grande nachos, ceviche, a salad, and really great green chili and you are off to a great beginning. Mains range from enchiladas, shrimp tacos, and Mexican pizza to breakfast all day—and a quirky weekend brunch. Come early, stay late, and enjoy the good Mexican fare at every affordable prices.

El Jardin, Mexican Restaurant

Cuisine: Mexican
Open: B-L-D: Daily
iloveeljardin.com

6460 E. 73rd Ave.   303-288-3500
Commerce City, 80022
72nd & Hwy 2

Price: $-$$ **Patio:** Yes
Reservations: Yes   **Brunch:** No
Location: Commerce City

El Jardin a delightful Mexican eatery gives Commerce City something to brag about. Enter the freestanding building and the feeling is warm, casual and welcoming with booths, tables, and art on the walls. There is a large banquet room to one side where guests can be seated on very busy nights. The menu is lengthy with many great choices. Start with chips and salsa, and don't miss the terrific guacamole. Other choices include nachos, shrimp cocktail, quesadillas and mini rellenos. Fajitas are a specialty. Choose from lamb, chicken, beef or pork with all the fixings. Tacos please in both soft and hard shell versions and come as sides or as dinners. El Jardin's version of Indian tacos is original, comprised of two toasted flour tortillas filled with chicken or beef, melted cheese, lettuce and tomato, and served with beans, rice and pico de gallo. Enchiladas with green chile, seafood quesadillas, tilapia, burritos and steak ranchero make decisions difficult. Add burgers, salads and even breakfast specialties for more options. Desserts make a perfect ending with flan or cinnamon sprinkled sopapillas. With good service, a kids menu and affordable prices, El Jardin is a favorite in the area.

El Noa Noa

Cuisine: Mexican
Open: L-D: Daily
elnoanoadenver.com

722 Santa Fe Dr.   303-623-9968
Denver, 80204
7th & Santa Fe

Price: $ **Patio:** Yes
Reservations: Yes   **Brunch:** No
Location: Denver - Downtown

For years El Noa Noa has been treasured by Denverites for
its tasty Mexican fare. Daily specials keep customers coming
back for their favorites. Don't miss Tuesday's pork chops
smothered in green chili. The regular menu includes all the
Mexican classics of smothered burritos, enchiladas, beef tacos,
tamales and tostadas. Accompany your food with a margarita,
an imported beer or a tall glass of horchata. If you like outdoor
dining, grab a seat on the secluded back patio.

El Taco de Mexico

Cuisine: Mexican
Open: B-L-D: Daily
eltacodemexicodenver.com

714 Santa Fe Dr.   303-623-3926
Denver, 80204
7th & Santa Fe

Price: $ **Patio:** Yes
Reservations: No   **Brunch:** No
Location: Denver - Downtown

Looking for one of Denver's most authentic Mexican
restaurants? Go no further than the corner of 7th Avenue
and Santa Fe Drive. El Taco de Mexico is housed in a small,
bright yellow building with a few bar stools and a smattering
of booths. The menu is large and varied. Burritos, enchiladas,
tacos and some of the best green chili in town await you. Chile
rellenos are soft and very flavorful. Mini tacos are made of a
double corn tortilla stuffed with anything from beef or fried
pork to slow-cooked chicken. Mexican breakfasts are served all
day long. Parking is no problem, as El Taco de Mexico has its
own lot. Complement your meal with the sweet cinnamon rice
drink, horchata, or one of several liquado de fruitas.

Elway's Cherry Creek

Cuisine: Salad, Seafood, Steakhouse
Open: L-D: Daily, BR: Sat-Sun
elways.com

2500 E. 1st Ave.   303-399-5353
Denver, 80206
1st & University

Price: $$$$ **Patio:** Yes
Reservations: Yes   **Brunch:** Yes
Location: Cherry Creek

Elway's definitely takes a very special place in Cherry Creek. Enter the space to be greeted by a large granite water wall. To the right is a beautiful bar for gathering or dining, with warm woods and burgundy upholstered bar stools to set the scene. The dining area is warm and inviting, with brown and burgundy tones throughout, stunning chairs and booths, and soft lighting. Executive Chef Tyler Wiard is an amazing talent in the kitchen, creating the fabulous food that sets Elway's apart from other restaurants. Start with fried calamari, tuna tartare with avocado and lamb fondue, all fabulous in presentation and taste. The Caesar, wedge, and tomato and mozzarella make great salad choices. The steak entrées are all of the highest quality, prime grade beef. Most steaks are offered in two sizes for different appetites. Sirloin, porterhouse, filet, rib-eye and prime rib arrive cooked as ordered, full of flavor and tender to the bite. The best steak may be the bone-in filet. Several fish and shellfish options such as lobster, salmon, and more please. For sides, choose from a marvelous list and share. Desserts are decadent. S'mores, warm chocolate chip or oatmeal cookies, gelato and tiramisù cones are all great, but the ding dong and chocolate soufflé are even better. The extensive wine list with many by the glass list makes for delicious pairings. Service is top notch, with a well-trained, attentive staff to care for guests. The bar is the place to be and both the bar and patio are busy every day of the week. Live music makes it even more special. Lunch and weekend brunches continue in the same style as dinner. This dining experience adds up to a trophy for Elway's. Elway's also has a location in Vail at the Lodge.

Elway's Downtown

Cuisine: Steak, Seafood, Steakhouse
Open: B-L: Mon-Fri, D: Daily, BR: Sat-Sun
elways.com

1881 Curtis St.   303-312-3107
Denver, 80202
18th & Curtis

Price: $$$$ **Patio:** Yes
Reservations: Yes   **Brunch:** Yes
Location: Denver - Downtown

The Ritz Carlton Hotel puts on the glitz with Elway's Downtown. Enter the beautiful lobby of the hotel which opens into the space and can be seen while dining. The room is upscale, but also casual and welcoming, with wood walls and leather accents, fabulous tables, booths and table settings. The circular bar catches the eye, as does the wall of wine. The bar menu is outrageous and a great place to spend the evening or happy hour. At the bar indulge in the ribs which are worth the trip. The menu is similar to Elway's Cherry Creek. There is an appetizer tower of lamb riblets, empanadas and calamari. The familiar grilled artichoke is a big hit as are the lobster, crab and shrimp cocktails. Beef tartare or fresh oysters appeal to all. Traditional steakhouse salads include Caesar, the wedge, or John's favorite greens. The prime steaks star with filet, New York strip, rib-eye and prime rib. The fish menu features lobster tail, crab legs, salmon and sea bass. Each is done with a complementary sauce. Other options include chicken, short ribs, and the famous Elway's smash burger. For sides, cauliflower, potatoes au gratin, creamed spinach, sautéed sugar snap peas and creamed corn are musts. Decadent desserts end the meal. The wine list is terrific and the service impeccable. Dining at Elway's Downtown is fabulous—and although you are at the Ritz casual and elegant are welcome here.

Enzo's End Pizzeria

Cuisine: Pizza
Open: D: Wed-Mon
enzosend.com

3424 E. Colfax Ave.
Denver, 80206
Colfax & Madison

303-355-4700

Price: $-$$
Reservations: Yes
Location: East Colfax

Patio: No
Brunch: No

Just east of the Bluebird Theater on East Colfax sits a funky neighborhood pizzeria called Enzo's End. Customers come from every neighborhood to take home these tasty pies. The Neapolitan thin crust is the perfect base for Enzo's many fresh toppings. The pizza sauce is made fresh daily, with a hint of sweetness to bring out the richness. Toppings range from the usual to the adventurous. Try a red sauce pie with fresh basil, crushed garlic and sliced meatballs, or breaded eggplant with green chile and artichokes. The white pizza is topped with sautéed spinach, fresh garlic, sliced tomato and parmesan cheese. One bite and you'll become a white pizza lover for sure.

Euclid Hall, Bar & Kitchen

Cuisine: American, Pub
Open: L: Mon-Fri, D: Daily
euclidhall.com

1317 14th St.
Denver, 80202
14th & Larimer

303-595-4255

Price: $$-$$$
Reservations: Yes
Location: LoDo

Patio: Yes
Brunch: No

Euclid Hall brings a new twist for dining in Larimer Square. Located in Euclid Hall, an 1883 building that once housed the venerable Soapy Smith's bar, this American tavern focuses on high-quality and innovative pub food from around the world. The décor mixes an industrial feel with the original brick and ceiling tiles. Enter and the large bar and open kitchen can be seen along with comfortable seating and an open look to the upstairs dining room. From the second level, look down and get a full view of the dining scene as well. Start with house-made sausages, po' boys, poutine and schnitzels. Then indulge in oysters, cured salmon, hiramasa tartare, marlin crudo, fish and chips, and mussels from the "Dock" list. Sandwiches include the best camembert griddled cheese with peach preserves, a brat burger on a pretzel bun, and oyster po'boy. The Euclidian cheesesteak is a deconstructed version of an old favorite. Sides of pickles, mustard and more add to the fun. Desserts rock with pretzel fried pies, red velvet cupcake and sourdough waffle ice cream sandwich with salted butterscotch ice cream. An extensive beer selection and creative cocktails and wine complement the food. Terrific owners, Chef Jennifer Jasinski and General Manager Beth Gruitch are an incredibly talented duo with their very successful restaurants, Rioja and Bistro Vendôme. Euclid Hall, offers a unique spot for a different twist on their food plus lots of fun.

Fadó Irish Pub

Cuisine: Irish Pub
Open: D: Daily, BR: Sat-Sun
fadoirishpub.com/denver

1735 19th St. #150   303-297-0066
Denver, 80202
19th & Wynkoop

Price: $$ **Patio:** Yes
Reservations: Yes   **Brunch:** Yes
Location: LoDo

Tucked into the same building as both the Denver ChopHouse and Howl at the Moon this comfortable Irish pub just across from Coors Field is easy to miss. Workers constructed it out of bits and pieces from Ireland and then combined that with stonework, a fireplace and a large bar to create something delightfully authentic. Devoted fans arrive early to catch the latest live soccer game and have a breakfast of a traditional potato pancake wrap stuffed with seafood, sausage or just vegetables. Most nights feature live Irish music which gets fans to sing along or dance a jig between the tables. The entire space seems deceptively small, a feature that encourages guests to talk with strangers. That's what an Irish pub is all about - old and new friends, conversation, a pint of Guinness and a hearty meal. Appetizers include imported Irish oak-smoked salmon, baked brie in a phyllo crust, and chicken tenders with honey mustard. Enjoy a hearty bowl of fisherman's stew, or fish and chips. For dessert, try a slice of rhubarb custard pie—or just have another pint of Guinness.

Famous Dave's, Legendary Pit Bar-B-Que

Cuisine: Barbecue
Open: L-D: Daily
famousdaves.com

7557 E. 36th Ave.   303-399-3100
Denver, 80238
Quebec Square at Stapleton & multiple locations.

Price: $-$$	**Patio:** No
Reservations: No	**Brunch:** No

Location: Stapleton, Broomfield, Fort Collins

You can't miss Famous Dave's Legendary Pit Bar-B-Que. The space is massive, with lots of wood, paintings, posters and paraphernalia that give a country feel. Walk past the kitchen as you go from one big room to the next to settle in for a "messy" treat. The friendly staff wears T-shirts with great barbecue sayings. The fare is terrific. Start with rib tips, onion strings, catfish fingers, chicken tenders, and smoked salmon spread on fire-grilled flatbread. There are chicken wings, chili, soups and salads, as well as chicken or barbecued meat entrée salads. Or, choose from sandwiches and burgers. The cornbread muffins are delicious. Combo platters offer two or more options so one can taste all. The brisket is tender, juicy and a hit when served with excellent pulled pork. Chicken comes cooked perfectly, while the meaty ribs delight all. Sides of loaded baked potato, coleslaw, potato salad, beans, sautéed apples and corn-on-the-cob give diners many choices. Getting to the important part, the sauce is where the real flavor begins. Order your meat dry-cooked and sample from the six-pack of sauces on the table. Go for mustard, sweet Texas, killer spice, or sweet and spice combined. Do not leave until you have an outrageous chocolate brownie à la mode with vanilla ice cream and chocolate sauce, a piece of pecan pie or praline bread pudding. Dave's has pigs everywhere and that defines a great "pig out."

Farro, Italian Restaurant

Cuisine: Italian
Open: D: Tues-Sun
farrorestaurant.com

8230 S. Holly St.   303-694-5432
Centennial, 80122
S. Holly & County Line

Price: $$ **Patio:** No
Reservations: Yes   **Brunch:** No
Location: Centennial

Chef Matthew Franklin is the owner and host of Farro, a Cal/
Italian bistro. Small, casual and comfortable, the idea here is to
allow guests to enjoy food and wine at reasonable prices. The
space features a large bar, perfect for gathering or enjoying a
meal, an open kitchen and comfortable seating in the two small
rooms. Start with warm bread and a great dipping sauce as you
peruse the menu. Appetizers and small plates include flash-fried
calamari, beef carpaccio, an antipasti platter and Tuscan white
bean soup. Beefsteak tomatoes with mozzarella, tuna "crudo,"
and a baby spinach, pear, gorgonzola and walnut salad all shine.
Add mussels, farro salad, black pepper chicken wings and a trio
of Italian cheeses and you easily can make a meal from the list.
Pastas range from mushroom ravioli, lasagna, and linguine with
clams to capellini with shrimp, bucatini with pancetta, and
strozzapretti with chicken. If in the mood for pizza, indulge in
marinated tomato with mozzarella, prosciutto with gorgonzola,
artichoke, chicken Caesar, spicy shrimp or smoked salmon on
the thin, perfectly cooked crust. Entrées bring more options:
pork milanese, seafood "farro" stew, half chicken with rosemary,
flat iron steak, and meatloaf. End with decadent desserts.
With very affordable prices and an excellent wine list Farro is a
pleasant perfect neighborhood treat.

Fork & Spoon

Cuisine: Breakfast/American
Open: B-L: Daily
forkandspoondenver.com

341 E. Colfax   303-847-0345
Denver, 80203
Colfax & Logan

Price: $ **Patio:** Yes
Reservations: Yes   **Brunch:** No
Location: Capitol Hill

This is a tiny gem for breakfast and lunch on East Colfax.
The place is nothing fancy, big windows, simple tables and

chairs, no linens but paper napkins. The homemade delicious food makes up for the lack of elegance here. Even the coffee is special with a local guy providing it and his story very special. The menu is huge so start with breakfast. Chicken and waffles with a sweet potato waffle smothered in cayenne-pecan maple syrup, corned beef with potatoes, peppers and salsa, biscuits and gravy, and then the Benedicts: salmon, ham, veggie, and next comes stuffed French toast, a blueberry waffle sandwich filled with scrambled eggs, cheese and sausage, and a giant burrito with chorizo. Add a veggie or steak burrito, huevos rancheros, and a selection of scrambled egg dishes to keep one coming back forever. The caprese with mozzarella, tomato, and basil in the scramble and the spicy potatoes that come with are awesome. Don't forget homemade jams to go on your toast or biscuits too. If you prefer go for sandwiches of chicken, pastrami, turkey, grilled cheese or a French dip. Add gyro, club, smoked salmon BLT, chicken Caesar wrap, and veggie options and it's hard to decide. Salads include spinach, Caesar, Cajun shrimp, cobb, and more, all with homemade dressing. Service is impeccable, pricing is reasonable and the food a taste of Mom. Remember it is not much to see, but after one visit, you'll be a fan.

1515 Restaurant

Cuisine: Contemporary
Open: L: Wed-Fri, D: Mon-Sat
1515restaurant.com

1515 Market St.   303-571-0011
Denver, 80202
15th & Market

Price: $$$$ **Patio:** No
Reservations: Yes   **Brunch:** No
Location: LoDo

With a first-floor bar perfect for a meal or late night get-together and an upscale upstairs dining room, 1515 is a good choice for dinner. As you enter, the bar area features a large counter with scenic photos on the walls. The upstairs is elegant, soft and inviting, with exposed brick walls, terrific black-and-white photography, and beautifully set tables, booths and banquettes. A special section shows off the wines plus there is a large area for private parties as well. The chefs bring great food combined with delicious flavors and beautiful presentation. Homemade bread whets your appetite for the first course. Start with a foie gras-covered waffle, pork belly, or brioche flatbread topped with duck confit, tapenade and arugula. Salads with interesting ingredients are special. The entrée list starts with scallops, salmon, and sea bass. Chicken breast, buffalo short rib or tenderloin of beef offer more choices. Presentation is key here and you will not be disappointed. Finish a great meal with decadent chocolate crème brûlée, passion fruit panna cotta, coffee and donuts, or chocolate fondue. Enjoy the tasting menu for a special treat—with or without wine pairings. At the bar or at lunch, don't miss the Kobe beef burger. Owner Gene Tang takes great pride in an extraordinary wine list, matching the glassware to each selection. With excellent service, 1515 makes for a delightful time in LoDo. Ask for directions to the parking garage, as the restaurant will cover the expense.

Firenze a Tavola

Cuisine: Italian
Open: D: Wed-Sat
parisidenver.com/firenzeatavola

4401 Tennyson St.   303-561-0234
Denver, 80212
44th & Tennyson

Price: $$$$ **Patio:** No
Reservations: Yes   **Brunch:** No
Location: Berkeley

For a true taste of Florence, delight in the full-service dining experience at Firenze, downstairs from Parisi. The surroundings are lovely, and the ambience is reminiscent of below-street-level restaurants in Italy that resemble caves. With exposed brick, large wood tables and chairs, and a casual but upscale feel, relax for a night of wonderful food and fun. Pizza bread arrives as you peruse the extensive Italian wine list. Start with fritto misto with melted cheese, grilled artichoke, mussels, antipasti or calamari. Soups and salads are a lovely option to start your meal. Pastas shine with wild boar pappardelle, ravioli with seafood and cheese, pasta with pears and goat cheese, and tagliatelle with wild mushrooms and cheese. Entrées range from lamb shank, pork wrapped in pastry, and cioppino to chicken, porcini-crusted snapper and Tuscan steak. Each sauce and the accompanying sides complement the dish. Desserts are special with tiramisù, crème brûlée, and to-die-for calzone stuffed with Nutella and bananas. Service is extremely friendly and efficient. Food and wine in this setting make for a special night.

Flagstaff House

Cuisine: Contemporary
Open: D: Daily
flagstaffhouse.com

1138 Flagstaff Rd.   303-442-4640
Boulder, 80302
Baseline turns into Flagstaff

Price: $$$$	**Patio:** Yes
Reservations: Yes	**Brunch:** No
Location: Boulder	

Resting high above the chaos of Boulder and Denver the Flagstaff House is an excellent respite for special-occasion dining. The restaurant sits on a bluff and affords a spectacular view of Boulder and the plains beyond through picture windows that surround the dining area. Enjoy the crisp mountain air and the smell of pine on the heated outdoor terrace. Service is perfectly orchestrated, with a team of wait staff assigned to each table working in synchronized patterns to attend to your every need. A sommelier will guide you through the extensive wine list, which is awarded the Wine Spectator's Grand Award year after year. Private parties can dine in the vintner's rooms and get a peek at more than 20,000 wines from around the world. The view, service, wine and lush interior combine to create an extraordinary experience. A portion of the menu changes nightly, blending ingredients to match the season and emphasizing the best of what is available locally. Whet your palate with foie gras, tuna tartare prepared tableside with a quail egg, or braised lamb ravioli. For your main course, choose tender buffalo filet mignon, seasonal salmon, scallops or signature Colorado rack of lamb. For dessert, try the pineapple caramel crunch, soufflé with ice cream, or chocolate cake filled with hot liquid chocolate. Year after year, the Flagstaff House remains a top favorite.

Fleming's Prime Steakhouse and Wine Bar

Cuisine: Seafood, Steakhouse
Open: D: Daily
flemingssteakhouse.com

191 Inverness Dr. West
Englewood, 80112
County Line & Inverness

303-768-0827

Price: $$$$
Reservations: Yes
Location: Inverness

Patio: Yes
Brunch: No

Fleming's brings a steakhouse to Inverness. The freestanding building is warm and enticing, and the atmosphere is hearty and comfortable with an edge of sleek. Shades of brown and mahogany with wood accents, wonderful lighting, and an open kitchen trimmed in copper set the scene. The menu features prime steaks, as well as seafood, pork, lamb, chicken and veal. Start with the crispy toast and celery sticks served with cabernet goat cheese and brie cheese spreads. Appetizers include French onion soup, carpaccio, sweet-chile calamari, and shrimp and lobster cocktail. Prime steaks are juicy and cooked to order. The double-thick pork rib chop flavored with apple cider, creole mustard, julienne of apples and celery root is an excellent choice. Opt for beef "Flemington," triple-thick lamb chops, or double breast of chicken with mushrooms. The seafood selection includes salmon, tuna mignon, shrimp, scallops, lobster tails, and king crab legs. Sides complement the main and are sized for sharing. The Sunday night special of prime rib with salad, a side dish and dessert is a real bargain. Don't leave without trying the chocolate molten cake, key lime pie, fruit cobbler or crème brûlée. The wine list boasts 100 wines by the glass with selections in all price ranges. Excellent service enhances the Fleming's experience.

Fogo de Chao

Cuisine: Steakhouse
Open: L: Mon-Fri, Sun, D: Daily
fogodechao.com

1513 Wynkoop
Denver, 80202

303-623-9600

Price: $$$$
Reservations: Yes
Location: LoDo

Patio: No
Brunch: No

This place seats 300 and features a fabulous bar area upon entering. Enjoy gathering for drinks and conversation and then move into the dining room. Walls of wine, comfortable seating and an unbelievable salad bar are the focal points. The salad bar offers hearts of palm, artichoke bottoms, tomatoes, broccoli, asparagus, peppers and more. Smoked salmon, salami, and cheeses of every kind are other choices. Chicken or potato salad, beets, breads, and prepared salads fill the tables. The servers, dressed in gaucho pants, bring the main course. All entrées are served on skewers and 15 chefs each arrive with their specialty: filet mignon, sirloin, garlic sirloin, prime rib, pork ribs, leg of lamb, chicken, pork filets encrusted with parmesan, pork sausages and more. Cheese rolls, polenta, garlic mashed potatoes and caramelized bananas are served with your meal. The servers shave off your choice of meats until you turn your personal tab from green to red. End with decadent desserts, if you have room. The wine list is excellent, and service terrific from your waiter to the valet. Fogo de Chao is not an ordinary Brazilian steakhouse, but a step above in food and service.

The Fort

Cuisine: American
Open: D: Daily
thefort.com

19192 Hwy. 8   303-697-4771
Morrison, 80465
Hwy. 285 & Hwy. 8

Price: $$$$ **Patio:** Yes
Reservations: Yes   **Brunch:** No
Location: Morrison

In a replica of Bent's Old Fort, this restaurant summons the taste and feel of the Old West. Enter through the broad archway into a courtyard, where a fire burns in a nearby pit and a trading post features Native American crafts. The host guides you through the maze of rooms to your table. Owner Holly Arnold Kinney graces the floor with her irresistible charm. The chef brings great excitement to the menu with modern renditions of old favorites, along with totally new additions. The menu is based on years of painstaking research into the food of the Old West from black powder oyster shooters to the roasted marrow of bison bones. Start with rock shrimp ceviche, rattlesnake cakes or the infamous Rocky Mountain oysters. The lamb riblets are deliciously addictive. The duck quesadilla with coffee barbecue sauce brings new meaning to the familiar dish. House salad and muffins and rolls arrive complimentary with your dinner. Meat reigns on the entrée list, from elk medallions and a wild boar chop to broiled teriyaki quail and slow-roasted barbecue buffalo ribs. Buffalo selections remain the most popular items, offering a variety of cuts. Salmon and trout are wonderful choices for fish lovers, and the half chicken another treat. The spices and flavors of each dish reflect those of interior Mexico. A variety of desserts end the meal, ranging from chocolate negrito and cheesecake to chocolate-chile cake. The extensive wine list has won the Wine Spectator Award and enhances the feast. If it's your birthday, let them know; you'll get a different type of birthday wish. In the words of the late Sam Arnold, "Waugh."

Frasca Food & Wine

Cuisine: Italian
Open: D: Mon-Sat
frascafoodandwine.com

1738 Pearl St.   303-442-6966
Boulder, 80302
18th & Pearl

Price: $$$$ **Patio:** Yes
Reservations: Yes   **Brunch:** No
Location: Boulder

Frasca is widely recognized as the most prestigious restaurant in Colorado and it is does its magic while remaining humble and free of pretension. Hailing from the famed French Laundry, master sommelier Bobby Stuckey, James Beard-awarded chef Lachlan MacKinnon-Patterson, and divine Danette Stuckey created a stunning restaurant experience rivaling the nation's best restaurants. The name Frasca refers to a small, outside eatery specific to Friuli, a region in northeast Italy on which Frasca's cuisine is based. Décor is warm and inviting, high ceilings, exposed pipes, beautiful table settings, and comfortable seating start the ambience. Dining areas include spaces adjacent to the open kitchen where one can watch the chefs at work. The lively bar is the gathering spot or nab a seat and enjoy your amazing meal here. Start dinner with prosciutto, breadsticks, and olives. Next you might indulge in "laughing bird shrimp," polenta with brown butter, a salad of several lettuces, meyer lemon and bagna cauda, amazing calamari with cannellini bean, and kale, or pork belly with mushrooms and tardivo. Frasca's Primi, pasta course, features gnocchi with cheese and wild mushrooms, tortelloni with goat's milk cheese and mint, ravioli with ricotta, egg yolk, truffle and spinach, tagliatelle or pappardelle with beef ragu. The entrées bring petrale sole, grilled sturgeon, Colorado beef shank and ribeye, and pork. Each comes with special preparation and complimentary accompaniments that are awesome. End with inspired desserts of crostata with almond, chocolate torta, panna cotta, gelato, and more. The most amazing dessert is the chocolate macaroon with ganache. The menu changes often so expect new and exciting dishes when you visit. The wine list is outstanding, winning Frasca the highest accolades year after year. Frasca won the James Beard Award for Wine 2013 as well. Enjoy a wine pairing with each course or the incredible staff will help you decide. Your visit to Frasca will not disappoint, and it will be the special place to go for any occasion, or just because you want to feel very special. It truly is the best.

The French Press Café and Bakery

Cuisine: Café, Breakfast, Brunch
Open: B-L: Daily
myfrenchpress.com

7323 W Alaska Dr	303-984-5447
Lakewood, 80228	
W Alaska & S Vance	

15290 E. Iliff Ave	303-369-3111
Aurora, 80014	
Iliff & S Chambers	

Price: $ **Patio:** No
Reservations: No   **Brunch:** No
Location: Lakewood, Aurora

When you walk into the French Press Café and Bakery, you are surrounded by friendly neighbors who will soon become friends. Bobbi or Cisco Lopez, or one of their friendly staff members, will greet you with a smile upon arrival. Place your order at the counter after reviewing the daily specials and chalk boards around the restaurant with breakfast, lunch and beverage options. Start with an Americano or one of the many tea selections and pair it with one of the numerous delicious breakfast/lunch options. Try the M.A.M.A salad-- mandarin oranges, almonds, manchego cheese, and apples piled high on mixed greens with a delightful white balsamic and pomegranate dressing, or pick one of the mouthwatering sandwiches. For breakfast splurge on the zucchini pistachio pancakes or the sterling's sweet biscuits. The space is one room with an energetic atmosphere and lots of sunlight streaming in. Lounge in a sofa chair with a good book and sip an iced vanilla latté, or gather the family around a table and play Barrel of Monkeys while you wait for your lunch to be delivered. The French Press has the comfort of being in your own living room without the hassle of having to cook or do dishes. Regardless if you go to The French Press for your daily cup of coffee, breakfast with friends or lunch with coworkers, you will leave satisfied and excited to return.

The Fresh Fish Co.

Cuisine: Seafood
Open: L: Mon-Sat, D: Daily, BR: Sun
thefreshfishco.com

7800 E. Hampden Ave.   303-740-9556
Denver, 80231
Hampden & Tamarac

Price: $$-$$$ **Patio:** No
Reservations: Yes   **Brunch:** Yes
Location: South East

Fish tanks filled with colorful water denizens swimming in their beautiful environment capture the attention of young and old alike. Crowds flock to the place to eat, drink and have a good time. Light-hearted servers know their fish and will guide you through 30 varieties. Dine on halibut, ahi, lobster or an exotic Asian fish. Start with deep-fried calamari, a bowl of steamed mussels or shrimp on a skewer. For entrées, try crab-almond-pesto trout, halibut with lemon-caper sauce, coconut-battered shrimp, pistachio-pesto sea bass and various seafood skewers. Steaks please meat lovers, and the massive surf and turf makes big eaters happy. At the fabulous Sunday seafood brunch, enjoy an amazing assortment of shrimp, crab and other seafood favorites in addition to the usual breakfast fare. Don't miss the desserts, especially the giant strawberries. The feel and energy of the restaurant brings diners back often. Look for specials throughout the year from whole lobster and Copper River salmon, to king crab legs and more, and then enjoy the fare. And remember on your birthday the discount is your age!

Frijoles Colorado, Cuban Cuisine

Cuisine: Cuban
Open: L: Daily, D: Mon-Sat.
frijolescolorado.com

12095 W Alameda Pkwy.   303-716-4587
Lakewood, 80228
Alameda & S. Union

Price: $-$$ **Patio:** Yes
Reservations: No   **Brunch:** No
Location: Lakewood

Frijoles Colorado brings great cuban food to the area and it is a real treat. Enter this small spot with a counter displaying some of the great goodies and see the folks cooking right behind. The space may be simple and small but the food is outrageously great and authentic cuban fare that we all have been longing to have. The family, Ana, Roxanne and Sergio do the cooking and bring their recipes from their homeland. Start with the best empanadas anywhere: chicken, pork. Ham and cheese, and guava and cream cheese fill the wonderful crust. They make the cuban bread daily for sandwiches or just to dip in butter and savor. When available the potato tart is not to be missed. The red bean or black bean soups (the latter is vegetarian) are another treat bringing excellent flavor with the spices in each. The dishes of Cuba are savory but not spicy as is typical of this cuisine. Do not miss the cubano sandwich filled with ham, cheese, pork, mustard, and pickles on pressed cuban bread or choose turkey, pork, steak, chicken, and a burger. Entrées shine with arroz con pollo, seafood paella, a chicken creole, pulled pork with beans, chicken with beans and rice, and an amazing steak dish. The fried plantains, rice, and beans are delicious and complement the protein. Do not leave without flan, tres leche cake, and cheesecake. The pastries and the coconut macaroons are worth the trip. Portions are large and prices are reasonable. Frijoles Colorado will become your neighborhood favorite no matter where you live.

Fruition

Cuisine: American
Open: D: Daily
fruitionrestaurant.com

1313 E. 6th Ave.   303-831-1962
Denver, 80218
6th & Marion

Price: $$$$ **Patio:** No
Reservations: Yes   **Brunch:** No
Location: East 6th Avenue - Cherry Creek North

Fruition will fulfill every diner's wishes for a great evening in this charming neighborhood restaurant. Chef/Owner Alex Seidel creates sophisticated comfort food that is totally awesome. Now the whole world knows about the great talent of Seidel, as he was awarded one of Top Ten Chefs 2010 by Food & Wine, and deservedly so. The décor is all new as a revamp brings the space to a more modern and warm feeling. The colors are lighter and look terrific and the new wine rack console is stunning. Contemporary fabrics and tables of alder wood with lovely white china settings feel delightful. The well-trained and friendly staff adds to the experience. Start with wonderful breads from Grateful Bread as you peruse the menu. Spring-green garlic bisque with gruyere fondue brings new meaning to a bowl of soup. Potato-crusted oysters Rockefeller, a signature dish here, is a perfect way to begin the feast. Other delightful appetizers include seared alaskan halibut cheeks with English pea agnolotti, marinated beef carpaccio with crispy baby artichokes, pasta carbonara with pork belly, and the house salad of watercress, grilled asparagus, and red onion, grilled avocado and crispy shallots. Brussels sprouts will make you want to "eat your vegetables". The crab cakes far from traditional are a must. Entrées of grilled pork chop with fennel sausage, duck breast with risotto, and prime beef culotte are presented with combinations of flavors and texture that tantalize. Be enticed by barramundi with foraged mushroom, duck breast, a great pork dish, and always a vegetarian two course menu offering. Decadent chocolate pudding with bing cherry jubilee, carrot cake, and pound cake bring dessert to a new level. But the not to miss ending is the lemon meringue tart. An excellent wine list complements the food. In all, every moment dining at Fruition is a dream come true. Small, charming and delightful, Fruition is a perfect eatery that pleases every true "foodie."

Fuel Café

Cuisine: Contemporary
Open: L: Mon-Fri, D: Wed-Sat BR: -Sun
fuelcafedenver.com
3455 Ringsby Court # 105   303-296-4642
Denver, 80216
Taxi Campus (approx. I-70 & Washington)

Price: $$$	**Patio:** Yes
Reservations: Yes	**Brunch:** Yes
Location: RiNo	

What a total treat this place is! Fuel brings great fun, a funky vibe, and fabulous food to the Taxi development in the trendy River North (RiNo) neighborhood. As you enter you find a modern, casual spot with a large bar and comfortable seating in simple surroundings that say, "Welcome." The great-looking bar is the center of the dining room and for a little privacy there is additional space in a small room to enjoy your meal. High ceilings, wood and a bit of drapery set complete the ambience. The patio is perfect when weather permits. Owner/Chef Bob Blair brings creative, unique food that impresses all. Start with small plates of awesome pork belly with english peas, lamb kefta with grilled cucumber and flatbread, a fish fry, and burrata. The mushroom bruschetta with fried egg and salad of shaved asparagus, prosciutto and bibb lettuce are totally outrageous. Entrees are incredible: gnocchi, pappardelle with lamb ragu, and striped bass with white beans start the list. Flank steak with ramps, duck hash, and pork tenderloin make decisions impossible. End with rum cake, honey tart with gingerbread crust, and chocolate cake that is killer good—or a cookie that is the best ever. The menu changes often, but no matter what the choices every taste and presentation bring sighs of delight. The wine list is equally wonderful with great choices by glass or bottle at super prices. Service keeps pace with the friendly, informative, and delightful staff rounding out a perfect experience. Lunch is exciting with an amazing array of specialty dishes and salads. The chicken salad has wonderful taste and the grilled calamari salad divine. There are pork tacos, and a monthly changing menu. Brunch is the latest addition. They do it all right-really right. Fuel up that car with enough gas to get you there—and if you run out, just stay for the next super-leaded dining experience.

Gaetano's

Cuisine: Italian
Open: L: Mon-Fri, D: Daily, BR: Sat-Sun
gaetanositalian.com

3760 Tejon St.   303-455-9852
Denver, 80211

Price: $$ **Patio:** Yes
Reservations: Yes   **Brunch:** Yes
Location: Highlands

Gaetano's, an oldie in Denver for over six decades, has a new owner, Ron Robinson who carries on the tradition of fabulous Italian food made with finesse and quality. The décor is fantastic with historic photos on the wall of Denver's infamous Smaldone family- and the good guys. The bar is a fun place to enjoy the evening or pick a comfortable booth or tables. Gaetano's pays its respects to the past but is totally modern in style. Italian fare is what the menu is all about and there are myriad options. Start with risotto croquettes, white bean and garlic crostini, meatballs, or fonduta. Bruschetta explodes in the mouth and mini calzones with sausage delight. Antipasti platters, both meat and cheese and vegetarian are a must. The minestrone soup is the best- exactly what you want from an Italian restaurant. Caprese, shrimp and spinach and steak salads are wonderful. The Caesar salad is too but the grilled Caesar is even better. Bread is served with every meal, delighting the taste buds. More beginnings that tempt include scampi picatta, fritto misto, mussels, risotto and antipasto misto. Pastas such as excellent vongole, alfredo, piscatore and bolognese please the palate. Ravioli and gnocchi are done perfectly. A patron favorite is the carbonara classic style- or served with cream and peas. Entrées of lasagna, parmigiana, branzino, scaloppini marsala, pork chop, steak and salmon make for tough decisions. The roasted half chicken and chicken caprese are two divine choices. Pizza is back, exceptionally terrific, and always a treat. Yummy desserts finalize your meal. Many vote the tiramisu the best this side of Italy. The cocktail and wine lists are excellent and service shines. In addition to daily dinners, Gaetano's serves weekend lunch and brunch as well. "Frank Sinatra" sings live several times a month, and it's a blast. Gaetano's is just plain fun with exceptionally delicious Italian food at affordable prices, and with a unique ambience a must on your dining list.

Gaia Bistro

Cuisine: American, Breakfast, Contemporary
Open: B-L: Tues-Sun, D: Wed-Sat
gaiabistro.com

1551 S. Pearl St.   303-777-5699
Denver, 80210
S. Pearl & Florida

Price: $-$$ **Patio:** Yes
Reservations: Yes   **Brunch:** No
Location: Old South Pearl

Gaia theory requires an understanding that each organism on the earth is part of the whole. So, when Patrick Mangold-White and Jon Edwards put together a restaurant they wanted to respect the earth and provide a great dining experience. From the moment you walk into this charming Victorian home, the aromas entice you. The venue offers local produce, fresh juices and the best iced tea. Delicate crêpes, sandwiches, salads and soups are available. Be sure to start your morning with the scrambles served with a side of naturally raised bacon. Or, try the house-cured salmon with scallion cream cheese on brioche. Espresso coffees are available as is French press. Blueberry muffins and sticky buns are musts. The crêpes are the story at Gaia—you can make up your own or trust the menu. Lunch offers traditional sandwiches such as baked brie and tomato with basil pesto on brioche, or the peppered lamb loin salad with goat cheese on homemade bread. Dinner has been added for more dining choices. This delightful and busy restaurant will have you happy to be where you are, dining on wonderfully prepared food in a charming space!

Gallop Café

Cuisine: Breakfast, Café, Contemporary
Open: B-L-Br :Daily
gallopcafe.com

2401 W. 32nd Avenue   303-455-5650
Denver, 80211
32nd & Zuni

Price: $-$$ **Patio:** Yes
Reservations: No   **Brunch:** Yes
Location: Highlands

High ceilings, oversized windows and old world décor give Gallop Café the feel of a european café and create a welcoming space for diners. A partly shaded outdoor patio is ideal for enjoying a cool beverage and people-watching on a warm day. Originally just a coffee shop, you still can stop in for a cup of Joe but there is much more. A great spot for breakfast and lunch daily, the charming and delightful owners, David Grafke and Glen Baker, offer a terrific array of cocktails and excellent wines at very affordable prices. Start with nachos, quesadillas, perfect for sharing, or a bowl of onion soup. Breakfast is hearty with the sherpa bowl of granola and goodies topped with a poached egg, eggs Benedict over homemade biscuits, omelets, granola, breakfast wraps, biscuits and gravy, and several breakfast sandwiches. Lunch offers paninis that include a cubano, gobbler, roast beef, tuna melt and veggie. Moroccan chicken or tuna salad, a Caesar, and several soups make choices impossible. Leave room for bread pudding and carrot cake. With friendly service, good food, and affordable prices, Gallop Café is a treat and perfect neighborhood spot.

GB Fish & Chips

Cuisine: Pub, Seafood
Open: L-D: Daily
gbfishandchips.com

2175 Sheridan Blvd. Edgewater, 80214 Sheridan & 22nd	303-232-2128
1311 S. Broadway Denver, 80210 S. Broadway at Louisiana	720-974-0219
5325 E Colfax Denver, 80220 Colfax & Grape, Park Hill, Edgewater, S Central	303-333-4551

Price: $-$$ **Patio:** Yes
Reservations: No   **Brunch:** No
Location: Edgewater, Denver - South Central, Park Hill

This fun and terrific spot allows you to get your fill of fish and chips and english favorites. Decide on your dish and order at the counter. Limited seating is available on wooden benches at long tables. Carryout is another way to go. GB Fish & Chips features a tasty menu of perfectly battered and deep-fried cod, tilapia, prawns, oysters, squid and scallops offered as a single selection or in combinations. These may be ordered as a full or half order depending on your appetite. In addition they present english specialties such as bangers, perfectly spiced english pork sausage, shepherd's pie of beef and vegetables lightly spiced and topped with fluffy mashed potatoes, and pork pie with seasoned ground pork in a hot water pastry. Don't miss cornish pasties made with a variety of fillings wrapped in flaky pastry. Everything is made from scratch. The décor may be simple, but the food is simply delicious! It is a true favorite. You will love it.

Glaze

Cuisine: Bakery, Contemporary
Open: L:Tues-Sat, D:Thu-Sat, BR: Sun
glazebaumcakes.com

1160 Madison
Denver, 80206
Madison & 12th

720-387-7890

Price: $$-$$$
Reservations: Yes
Location: Congress Park

Patio: Yes
Brunch: Yes

Glaze now brings a contemporary menu to keep company with the famous Baum cakes produced here. The space is lovely with soft gray walls, huge windows, and a coffee bar area in the rear and tableside service in the simple surroundings. The dining area in front is small but there is bar service and some tables in the rear. Start with lobster bisque or French onion soup, the beet or wedge salad and small plates of scallops, salmon tartare, mussels, tuna, and spring rolls. One can even enjoy a baumkuchen pretzel with japanese mustard. The mains are lobster roll, short ribs, pan seared chicken, and catch of the day. Add pork udon bowl, a chicken and matcha waffle, and ravioli or steam buns and you are set. The desserts are decadent and wines lovely. Lunch is served as well with a similar menu and lots of coffee, tea and wine. Glaze is a fun choice for neighborhood dining.

Golden Europe

Cuisine: Czech, German, Polish
Open: L: Sat, D: Tues-Sat
goldeneurope.com

6620 Wadsworth Blvd.
Arvada, 80003
66th & Wadsworth

303-425-1246

Price: $-$$
Reservations: Yes
Location: Arvada

Patio: No
Brunch: No

This small, family-owned and operated restaurant is as shiny and clean as a grandmother's kitchen. The cuisine is a combination from America, the Czech Republic, Germany and Poland. For starters, try potato pancakes with sour cream and applesauce, or liver dumpling soup, chicken broth with large dumplings made of ground liver and bread crumbs with hints of garlic and herbs. Dinner choices range from roasted duck to wonderful weiner schnitzel and sauerbraten. If you can't make up your mind, Golden Europe also offers combination plates.

Seasonal specials include enchanting summer fruit dumplings of fresh peaches or plums wrapped in light dumpling dough and topped with a mixture of melted butter, cookie crumbs and sugar. Chicken paprika and roasted pork tenderloin are house favorites. Golden Europe offers a full bar that has many Czech Republic and German beers on tap. During the summer months, enjoy your meal on the cozy patio. Apple strudel, cream-filled horns, and cheesecake are all homemade. Be sure to bring a big appetite to this golden gem of a restaurant.

Gozo

Cuisine: Italian, Spanish
Open: L-D: Daily, BR: Sat-Sun
gozodenver.com

30 S. Broadway   720-638-1462
Denver, 80209
S Broadway & Ellsworth

Price: $$$ **Patio:** No
Reservations: Yes   **Brunch:** Yes
Location: South Broadway, Baker

Gozo on South Broadway brings great fun and super ambience to this fast growing hood. The space is great. The front windows open for summer, the interior is terrific. First you see the focal open kitchen with dining bar and it is super. The woods, brick, and great design are contemporary with high ceilings, great lighting and comfortable seating. The second focal point is the bar – it is great looking and super for cocktails or dining with high top tables for folks to enjoy the night. The kitchen has a great pizza oven to cook the pies, and all the chefs are busy turning out the creative dishes. Start with warm olives, a fabulous salad of shaved Brussels, egg, pecorino and Marcona almonds. The boquerones (white anchovies) with remoulade, egg and parsley on crostini and the beet salad with gorgonzola puree and hazelnuts are favorites. Other greats are acorn squash, cauliflower, octopus, calamari, manila clams, tender belly toast, meatballs and a pork terrine. Pizzas are thin crust cooked crisp in the hot oven and feature many different toppings. Pasta brings strozzapretti with spinach, orecchiette with butternut squash, torchiette with pork bolognese, and rigatoni with boar ragu. Entrees of prawns a la plancha, pork shoulder, and sea bass round out the menu. End with a delicious chocolate mousse. The wine, beer and cocktail list rock, and service is nice. The owners come from Napa and have brought their California twists to Colorado.

Grateful Bread Company

Cuisine: Bakery
Open: All day: Saturday
Gratefulbread.com

425 Violet Street   303-681-5406
Golden, 80401
Cross Streets: Colfax (Hwy. 40) and Violet Street in the 6 & 40
Business Park in Golden.

Price: $	**Patio:** No
Reservations: No	**Brunch:** No
Location: Golden	

Celebrating 10 years in business as a wholesale artisan bakery, this family owned gem in Golden is launching a regular Saturday retail store on-site while continuing to supply more than five dozen of Denver and Boulder's finest restaurants and hotels with fresh handmade breads and pastries crafted with all-natural and mostly local ingredients daily. Founder Jeff Cleary is now starting to mill his own specialty flours as well with Colorado grains for custom breads as part of the company's commitment to authentic old world bread baking techniques. Grateful Bread's Italian stone hearth steam-injected deck oven puts out an astonishing variety of breads including loaves of melt in your mouth ciabattas, French boules, pumpernickels, rosemary focaccias, rye, sourdough and red quinoa along with an array of rolls, pretzels, pastries and seasonal favorites like cranberry walnut batards, braided challah loaves and more. So good and so fresh with the impeccable flavor master european bakers established centuries ago. You'll be grateful every time you swing by on a Saturday to pick up a loaf or three of this amazing bread.

Greenbriar Inn

Cuisine: American
Open: D: Tues-Sun, BR: Sun
greenbriarinn.com

8735 N. Foothills Hwy.   303-440-7979
Boulder, 80302
Lefthand Canyon Drive & Hwy. 36

Price: $$$$	**Patio:** Yes
Reservations: Yes	**Brunch:** Yes
Location: Boulder	

Resting on a sprawling estate just outside Boulder, this restaurant is the perfect spot for special occasions. Dining rooms furnished in white linens, dark woods and candlelight recall a european elegance, while a spot on the patio offers a chance to soak up breathtaking views of the mountains. Appetizers range from pan-fried frog legs with lemon-sage garlic butter, to oysters on the half shell. Order a traditional Caesar salad for two, prepared table-side. Entrées include roasted duck glazed with eucalyptus honey, rabbit tenderloin wrapped in applewood-smoked bacon, and filet mignon with truffle butter. For dessert try white chocolate mousse, crème brûlée or apple-blackberry crisp. Don't miss the popular Sunday champagne brunch.

Guard and Grace

Cuisine: Steak, Seafood
Open: L - D: Mon-Fri, D: Mon-Sat
Guardandgrace.com

1801 California   303-293-8500
Denver 80202
18th and California

Price: $$$$ **Patio:** Yes
Reservations: Yes   **Brunch:** No
Location: Downtown

Guard and Grace brings a big splash to downtown and a huge hit. The space is big and gorgeous. As you enter walls of wine are displayed, 3500 or more to entice diners. Huge windows make for a great people watching scene – or those looking in! The bar is spectacular with comfortable seating of chairs, sofas, lounges done in great fabric and color, and stunning bar stools for gathering for drinks or dining at the long bar. Move on to an enormous open kitchen where chefs cook with oak wood fired grills, pizza ovens, and every imaginable kitchen appliance to turn out the exceptional food. Owner and chef Troy Guard has created a steakhouse to appeal to all. The menu starts with sashimi, tartars, and flatbreads to die for. The housemade potato rolls are worth the trip and this is only the beginning. Lamb sausage, sliders, pork belly, gnocchi with lamb, and crab cakes are a few of the first course options. Salads range from Caesar, wan chai, wood roasted beets, and house. Rack of lamb, pork chop, oak grilled chicken, and an ok grilled enchilada start the entrée list. Add divine cod, salmon, red snapper, and tuna for seafood lovers and you will be thrilled. Of course the star is the steak. All are rubbed in a special rub designed for them and then oak grilled, and the result is amazing. Desserts keep pace with chocolate peanut butter cake, butterscotch tart, mud pie, ice creams and more. The wine list is excellent and service shines. Guard and Grace is a steakhouse, but one with a unique personality and divine dining in a super setting.

Hapa Sushi & Sake Bar

Cuisine: Japanese

Open: L-D: Daily

hapasushi.com

1514 Blake St.
Denver, 80202
15th & Blake

720-354-5058

Price: $$
Reservations: Yes
Patio: Yes
Brunch: No
Location: LoDo, Boulder, Cherry Creek, Greenwood Plaza

High-tech modern décor meets terrific sushi, and the combination makes for a great night out. Food, drinks and a busy bar scene are sure to please. Enter the modern space, snag a seat at the sushi bar and watch the chefs create works of art that taste as amazing as they look. Start with any of the sushi rolls prepared before your eyes. For appetizers, try the spicy panko-crusted calamari with mango-chile dipping sauce, or salmon-wrapped avocado topped with japanese aioli and puffed under the broiler. Spicy tuna poke (chunks of very fresh tuna) served over seared taro cake combines great texture and taste. Enjoy traditional sushi rolls or some interesting varieties such as the "climax" and "orgasm" rolls. The grilled chicken on bok choy and hijiki rice makes a wonderfully flavorful cooked entrée. End with hot banana-bread pudding and caramel sauce for a touch of comfort to top off your evening.

Harman's Eat & Drink

Cuisine: American

Open: Brunch: Sat- Sun, L: Tues-Fri, D: Tues- Sun

harmanscherrycreek.com

2900 E. 2nd Ave.
Denver, 80206
2nd & Fillmore

303-388-7428

Price: $$
Reservations: Yes
Patio: Yes
Brunch: Yes
Location: Cherry Creek

Harman's in Cherry Creek is the latest creation by owners Mark and Larri Fischer. The place is one huge room wrapped in steel and wood with high ceilings, super lighting, comfortable tables and chairs with a sleek contemporary look. The bar is the focal point as you enter and there is a patio and upstairs dining as well. The menu offers a variety of choices at affordable prices. Start with snacks of truffled pork rinds, oysters, duck tacos, chicken liver pâté and english pea falafel. Small plates include brûléed figs with chevre and toasted bread, crispy pork belly and goat tostadas. For a small salad, choose the kale Caesar, wedge or sunchokes (artichokes and sunflowers). Entrée size salads include a delicious steak salad with grilled onions, blue cheese and bacon, grilled shrimp quinoa and a cobb. For large plates go for Thai fried chicken, hanger steak frites, moules frites, striped bass, lamb shoulder or porchetta. As with any great Denver restaurant there is a beef burger as well. End with salted chocolate pie, butterscotch budino, olive oil pound cake or the strawberry rhubarb crumble. Whatever you do, do not miss cake batter ice cream with crispy pork belly, rum caramel, blueberries and pork churros. The wine and drink list is excellent, and service fantastic. Lunch adds sandwiches and a brunch. Harman's Eat & Drink is a fun and satisfying choice for dining in Cherry Creek.

Hi*Rise handcrafted bread

Cuisine: Breakfast, Bakery
Open: B-L: Daily
hirisedenver.com

2162 Larimer St.   303-296-3656
Denver, 80205
22nd & Larimer

Price: $ **Patio:** Yes
Reservations: No   **Brunch:** No
Location: Lodo

Enter this bright, sunny place and you know you are going to have a cheery day. Big windows, bright colors and high ceilings welcome you to a large counter where you spy a myriad of wonderful baked goods. You'll find muffins, breakfast strattas, breads, rolls, cookies and freshly made bagels boiled Big Apple style, and all are divine. Read the menu behind the counter, place your order and your meal will be delivered to you. Breakfast fare includes several stratas (custard filled combinations of bread, eggs and goodies), and sandwiches of egg and cheese served on bagels, biscuits or brioche. Add bacon, ham or chorizo if you like. The bagels are perfect. Add cream cheese or smoked salmon and enjoy. At lunch, it's an array of sandwiches and salads. Pork shoulder, muffaletta, ham and brie, prosciutto and mozzarella, veggie, turkey club or tuna salad niçoise are all served on homemade bread. You can't miss with salads like mushroom and baby spinach, arugula with apples, walnuts and cheese, the wedge, and sesame pork with romaine and cilantro lime vinaigrette. Nine grain, focaccia, brioche, baguette and semolina breads are oven fresh and available for purchase. Do not leave without an outrageous cookie! Hot beverages and soft drinks are served to complement the food. Owners Doug and Kirstin Anderson welcome their customers to experience a new level of Hi*Rise cooking in Denver's LoDo district.

Hickory House Ribs

Cuisine: American
Open: L-D: Daily
Hickoryhouseribs.com

10335 S. Parker Rd.   303-805-9742
Parker, 80134
Lincoln & Parker

Price: $$ **Patio:** Yes
Reservations: No   **Brunch:** No
Location: Parker

Hickory House in Parker serves up some of the tastiest ribs around. A pleasant log cabin rustic atmosphere puts you at ease. Start with the homemade onion rings or the hot barbecue wings if you're really hungry, but you might want to save your appetite for their specialty, baby back ribs imported from Denmark, smoked over hickory and finished on the grill. Other barbecued options include chicken, smoked pork shoulder, smoked beef brisket, sausage, steaks, catfish, salads and sandwiches. On Tuesday and Thursday evenings enjoy smoked prime rib. A nice selection of sides is available to complement your meal. You can indulge in a milkshake, beer or wine. To end things right, try the skillet cookie sundae or one of the other yummy desserts. Be sure to check out their daily lunch, happy hour and early bird specials. Take-out and catering are available. This is barbecue worth the pilgrimage to Parker!

Hideaway Steakhouse

Cuisine: American, Steakhouse
Open: L: Mon-Fri, D: Mon-Sun
Hideawaysteakhouse.com

2345 W. 112th Ave.   303-404-9939
Westminster, 80234
W. 112th & Alcott

Price: $$$-$$$$ **Patio:** Yes
Reservations: Yes   **Brunch:** No
Location: Westminster

An ornate yet approachable interior creates a cool ambience at Hideaway Steakhouse in Westminster. This stand-alone building opened in an area in need of great restaurants. Enter into a beautiful lounge with a great focal bar, baby grand piano and casual seating. The main dining area features high-back fabric-covered booths, wood-topped tables, stunning tiered fabric drum shades throughout and soft earthy colors of brown and sienna. The room is spaced for conversation and carpet and fabrics add to this touch. The menu appeals to all and has more than just steak to offer. Delicious bread arrives as you peruse the wine list. Start with lobster tacos, crab cakes, oysters, mussels, escargot or chicken liver pâté. Soups include French onion and cauliflower purée while salad choices bring Caesar, iceberg wedge and spinach with herbs options. Steaks are the star and served with a house salad, choice of side and a sauce. Dry-aged, bone-in rib-eye, filet, New York strip, porterhouse, veal chop, pork chop, lamb chops and prime rib are favorites. If steak is not your thing, enjoy duck, ahi tuna, salmon, scallops and chicken. More options include a burger, penne, ravioli, short ribs and baby-back ribs. Sides of potatoes, sauces, and veggies complement the entrées. End with decadent desserts. Hideaway Steakhouse brings fine dining to Westminster!

Highland Tap and Burger

Cuisine: American
Open: Brunch: Sat-Sun, L-D: Daily
Highlandtapdenver.com

2219 West 32nd Ave   720-287-4493
Denver, 80211
32nd & Vallejo

Price: $$ **Patio:** Yes
Reservations: Yes   **Brunch:** Yes
Location: Highlands

"Fun and really good" best describes this fabulous eatery in the Highlands. You'll see the open pit with flames as you walk past, or stop to eat on the patio. Inside, the first room has a bar with lots of seating, warm wood accents and big screen TVs for sports enthusiasts. The second room follows in the same vein with garage windows that open in warmer weather. Settle down for fun in either room and enjoy a large selection of beers, wine and drinks at reasonable prices. Start with the best Stranahan's whiskey barrel smoked chicken wings, a cheese board, whole artichoke or mac and cheese. Soup or several great salads include arugula and spinach with sun-dried cranberries, sweet potato, goat cheese and lentil vinaigrette and an H.T.B. chop salad. The signature sandwiches of pulled pork, fish & chips in a sandwich, seared ahi and a great chicken club are king here. Burger choices include beef, veggie or lamb with your choice of bun and toppings, or pick one of their daily specials. These range from Shroom Luva's, with mushrooms cheese and truffled aioli, the Tap with root beer pulled pork, onion ring, cheeses, and special sauce, to the "Chimi" with white cheddar and chimichurri sauce, Mother Earth, or the Rocky

Mountain with ground lamb, goat cheese and tomato mint relish. All come with fries. The salmon entrée is a must with the best quinoa ever. Sides include duck fat fried zucchini fries, onion rings, apple slaw and salad. There is a kiddies menu to please the young ones. Service is great and prices affordable. Highland Tap and Burger is just what the neighborhood needs. It's totally cool, a real favorite of all, and worth the trip from anywhere at any time.

Hillstone

Cuisine: American
Open: L-D: Daily
Hillstone.com

303 Josephine St.   303-333-4688
Denver, 80206
3rd & Josephine

Price: $$$ **Patio:** Yes
Reservations: Yes   **Brunch:** No
Location: Cherry Creek

Hillstone is a welcome addition to the Cherry Creek neighborhood. With warm woods, a grand bar, sushi bar, comfortable seating throughout, great lighting and an open kitchen, this awe inspiring restaurant can be loud, but the ceiling is designed to allow conversation at the table. The menu features a soup calendar (du jour), cheese toast, spinach and artichoke dip, and salads for starters. Sides are listed in the same section with fries, veggies, couscous, dirty rice and a baked potato. You will find burgers, a fish sandwich, corned beef and French dip in the sandwich category with salads of spicy tuna roll with mixed greens, grilled chicken, Thai steak and noodle and Caesar for those looking for lighter fare. There is a sushi list and entrées that range from fish, crab cakes, and chicken to barbecue ribs, lamb sirloin, rib-eye and filet. Pick your veggie as a side to accompany your choice. End with brownies, apple cobbler or key lime pie. The wine list is excellent and service very friendly. The place is lively and has many devotees. Hillstone's is a casual, fun restaurant with straightforward food priced on the higher side. It's a big hit in the area.

The Hive Garden Bistro

Cuisine: American
Open: L: D Daily (seasonal)

1005 York St.
Denver, 80206
Denver Botanic Gardens

720-865-3501

Price: $-$$
Reservations: No
Location: Congress Park

Patio: Yes
Brunch: No

What a treat to have this charming, delightful cafe in the middle of the gorgeous Denver Botanic Gardens. This peaceful spot is a lovely place to relax and enjoy some really good food in the midst of a world class attraction. Order at the counter – there may be a line but it moves, and your food is delivered to your table. Plans are in the works for a wood-fired pizza menu, but for now the menu is ripe with salads and sandwiches made from herbs grown in the gardens. The Hive salad boasts greens, blueberries, feta, avocado mash, nuts and tomatoes in delicious vinaigrette. The poached pear salad is just as wonderful. All are available with chicken or bacon if desired. You would not expect a venue such as this to make more than an average sandwich but oh what a surprise. Fresh salmon, mahi mahi, turkey, chicken, a burger, vegetarian, beef- the list goes on and each done with great toppings and sauces. There are many choices of bread included. Don't forget to order a side of sweet potato fries. No alcohol, but the tea and coffee along with lemonade both regular and strawberry are refreshing. After 5 p.m. with a membership card you can bring your own wine. The soft serve for dessert is a big hit. Catering by Design is doing a terrific job feeding the patrons of this surprise hideaway at the DBG. Take time to experience this wonderful restaurant with its terrific staff the next time you're up for a nice nature hike within city limits.

Hoong's Palace

Cuisine: Chinese
Open: L-D: Daily
Hoongspalace.com

10333 E Costilla Ave.   303-792-5528
Englewood, 80112
Costilla & Havana

Price: $$ **Patio:** No
Reservations: Yes   **Brunch:** No
Location: Englewood

Enter this large Englewood restaurant and breathe in the aromas of the open kitchen while taking your seat at one of the nicely spaced tables. Tastefully done, fans are here to dig into huge portions of excellent Chinese food. Order drinks and sake to start and try to decide on your meal. Pages of offerings make decisions a challenge. Start with divine ribs, chicken wings, pancakes, dumplings or egg rolls. There are so many soups and dishes of beef, pork, seafood, poultry and of course vegetarian. Entrees include specially spiced and sauced crispy duck with a fantastic mango beef sauce. Sesame chicken, lo mein and fried rice are all tasty. Servings are very generous. Fresh fruit and fortune cookies end your feast. The lesson learned is you have to keep returning to try all the dishes on the menu. Hoong's Palace is a great choice for Chinese cuisine in the south Metro Area.

Hops and Pie

Cuisine: Pizza
Open: L-D: Tues- Sun
Hopsandpie.com

3920 Tennyson St.   303-477-7000
Denver, 80212
39th & Tennyson

Price: $$ **Patio:** No
Reservations: No   **Brunch:** No
Location: Berkley

Tennyson Street is the place to be these days and the anchor on the block is Hops and Pie. From game days to Friday nights, it is guaranteed you will have to wait for a table. While they are known for their beer (they have 2 dozen rotating on draft and many more in cans) and their pizza (where your creative juices can let lose as you design your own with their artisan toppings) you will want to make sure to try the cubano sandwich. If you are in the mood for pizza and not in the mood to make decisions, the pizza of the day is always guaranteed to please. On Saturdays you can get two slices of the pizza of

HotCakes

Cuisine: American, Diner
Open: B-L: Daily
Eathotcakes.com

1400 E 18th Ave   303-832-4351
Denver, 80218
18th & Humboldt

Price: $ **Patio:** No
Reservations: No   **Brunch:** No
Location: Uptown

The all-american charm of this Uptown breakfast house attracts customers from all over the metro area. It has earned its reputation by offering loads of value for the price. The breakfast menu is the main draw, featuring everything from flapjacks to delicious French toast, crêpes, waffles and the standard egg and meat dishes. At lunchtime, you'll find hospital staffers and visitors, neighborhood regulars and office workers enjoying home-style meatloaf, club sandwiches and burgers. Desserts make a perfect ending, especially with a good cup of hot Colombian coffee.

The House of Commons, an English Tea Room

Cuisine: British, Tea Room
Open: L: Daily
Houseofcommonstea.com

2401 15th St.   303-455-4832
Denver, 80202
15th & Platte

Price: $$ **Patio:** Yes
Reservations: Yes   **Brunch:** No
Location: Platte Valley

In the middle of the popular Platte area you will find this delightful english tearoom. It is petite and cozy with the wall displays of tea selections. Ask questions about the teas and the staff is happy to help. A counter filled with teapots, pastries and goodies (all made on the premises) set the scene for this charming space. There are so many varieties, from rare and aromatic to the more familiar. Tea arrives steeping in warm pots. Guests pour their selection through tea sieves into their cups. Add honey, milk or nothing at all and you are set. Several iced teas are offered as well. The menu is excellent, starting with roast beef, turkey with imported brie, roasted chicken, scottish smoked salmon, ham and vegetarian sandwiches. The salad list includes roasted chicken, turkey, curried chicken and

stilton and walnut. Don't miss the quiche of the day. Indulge in scones, complete with clotted cream and jelly, wonderful tea cakes, or chocolate dipped berries. A formal afternoon tea is served daily for those who want to enjoy the total traditional experience. The staff is charming and helpful. Prices are reasonable. This trip to "England" at the House of Commons would please even the Royal Family.

The Huckleberry

Cuisine: American
Open: B-L: Mon-Sun, D: Mon-Sat
Thehuckleberry.com

700 Main St   303-666-8020
Louisville, 80027
Main & Pine

Price: $$	**Patio:** Yes
Reservations: No	**Brunch:** No
Location: Louisville	

The Huckleberry, located in the middle of old-town Louisville, offers up a fine assortment for daily dining. The interior is quaint, with several rooms of seating in a historic building-actually two buildings connected by a sunny causeway. The staff is friendly and classic "Boulder," and the food is delicious. Tea is the main event at The Huckleberry, a sister restaurant to the Dushanbe Teahouse in Boulder, this location is more down-home. Enjoy a special afternoon tea with all the baked goodies. The assortment of tea is phenomenal. Be sure to try the iced tea of the day. Locals flock here for weekend brunch to enjoy "Scramlettes", Benedicts, French toast and homemade baked goods. Later in the day, meal options include flavorful salads and sandwiches. The avocado focaccia is a mouthful of great taste, as are the burgers and wraps. The hummus platter is a favorite, served with pitas, a mound of lemon-garlic spread, olives, roasted peppers and cucumbers. The Huckleberry stands out, not just because of its distinct lavender colored exterior, but also for its food and atmosphere. Stop by when you're in the neighborhood.

J:

K: Love the atmosphere, and it has good food and tea (not fantastic). Expensive, but a nice lunch/snack place.

Humboldt Farm*Fish*Wine

Cuisine: American
Open: BR: Sat-Sun, L-D: Daily
Humboldtrestaurant.com

1700 Humboldt St   303-813-1700
Denver, 80218
Humboldt & 17th

Price: $$$ **Patio:** Yes
Reservations: Yes   **Brunch:** Yes
Location: Uptown - Denver

Enter Humboldt in Denver's Uptown neighborhood and prepare for a delightful experience. We all remember Strings, but the new space brings a new look and new life here. The ceilings are high, wood floors warm, a great bar as you enter is well lit, large community tables and a huge open kitchen all set the scene. Gray walls are accented with turquoise and cognac colors with banquettes, comfortable seating and an area for parties or additional seating in the atrium. Start with oysters, fresh crispy fried, charbroiled or baked. Small plates of edamame, shrimp cocktail, calamari, mussels, crispy broccoli, steak skewers and tuna crudo are perfect for sharing. There are signature steaks including steak diane for a traditional presentation and several large plates that start with a terrific hamburger or fish sandwich. Add pork tenderloin, spiced tuna, whole crispy fish, chicken and scallops and your decisions become difficult. Don't forget the pastas and salads. The special page shows the fish selections daily which come with a side of your choice. Dessert items include chocolate caramel cake, bread pudding and key lime pie. The wine and cocktail list are adequate and service shines. The owners have done a superb job of bringing a new look and feel to a favorite neighborhood spot.

Il Posto

Cuisine: Italian
Open: L: Mon-Fri D: Daily
Ilpostodenver.com

2011 E 17th Ave.   303-394-0100
Denver, 80206
17th & Race

Price: $$$-$$$$ **Patio:** Yes
Reservations: Yes   **Brunch:** No
Location: Uptown - Denver

Andrea Frizzi, the talented Chef/Owner of Il Posto, brings a delightful Italian trattoria to the East 17th Avenue dining area. Along with his cooking, Frizzi charms the crowd as he greets diners while wandering through the restaurant. The open space is bright with exposed ceilings, white walls and hickory wood floors with a paprika finish, accented by Russian maple-topped tables with dark red and black trim. Weather permitting, garage doors open to a terrific patio. The kitchen where chefs interact with guests is trimmed in stainless steel. Small wine lockers and wine bottles arranged along the shelves pull your eyes upward. The Italian fare at Il Posto features an ever-changing menu with a few signatures. Fresh Grateful Bread with olive oil starts the meal. Appetizers include grilled calamari, a salad with greens and blackberry-ginger vinaigrette, lamb loin, buffalo mozzarella with prosciutto and ravioli. Pasta choices change nightly with variations. Risotto with grilled fennel or with mushrooms and fava beans are popular choices. If available, the carbonara is the best anywhere! Entrées such as salmon with arugula, scallops with radish and salsify, beef rib-eye and osso buco are delicious items. The signature stuffed chicken with mushrooms is always a winner. End with bombolini with sambuca, bread pudding or chocolate and white chocolate mousse. The all-Italian wine list complements the food perfectly. Service is super friendly. Il Posto makes an outstanding upscale neighborhood restaurant.

Imperial Chinese

Cuisine: Chinese
Open: L: Mon-Sat D: Daily
Imperialchinesedenver.com

431 S Broadway   303-698-2800
Denver, 80209
Broadway & Dakota

Price: $$ **Patio:** No
Reservations: Yes   **Brunch:** No
Location: S. Broadway

Imperial is one of Denver's favorite Chinese restaurants. The space is beautiful with a fish tank in the entry along with lovely pieces of oriental artwork. Partitions in the large dining room allow diners to enjoy an intimate dinner or feast with a big group of friends. Start with delicious scallion pancakes, coconut shrimp and chicken dumplings. Dim sum starters are terrific and include vegetable dumplings, shrimp dumplings and a chicken-shrimp combo. The menu offers many classics, but exciting new items make dining special. Order a whole sea bass smothered in szechwan, black bean or ginger sauce, salmon with Thai basil, mango chicken or grilled lamb chops. Imperial's spicy sesame chicken attracts many fans, as does the crispy game hen, steak wrapped in asparagus and spicy garlic shrimp. The peking duck is outstanding and always a treat. Refreshing mango sorbet, tiramisù, ginger and lychee nut ice cream make for perfect endings. The service is excellent, and the wine list nice. You'll hope your fortune cookie reads, "You will be back soon."

India's Restaurant

Cuisine: Indian
Open: L: Mon-Sat D: Daily
Indiasrestaurant.com

8921 E Hampden Ave   303-755-4284
Denver, 80231
Yosemite & Hampden

Price: $$ **Patio:** No
Reservations: Yes   **Brunch:** No
Location: Southeast

India's is a special place, starting with its fabulous surroundings. The new space is beautiful, upscale and inviting. It will remind you of the warm, cozy and welcoming original restaurant from so many years ago. It is pretty with lovely linens, super wine and beer, chai tea, and great food. India's is bright with beautiful art on the walls, Indian umbrellas and a nice patio. There is a party room as well. Start with a Taj Mahal or Flying Horse beer, plus black-peppered poppadums- crispy wafers made for dunking into sweet tamarind chutney or the hotter mint chutney. A nice selection of wines and beer perfectly complements the piquancy of the food. Delicious samosas and the onion fritters are to die for. Entrées run the gamut from shrimp vindaloo, tandoori-roasted shrimp in fiery hot tomato based gravy, saag paneer, chicken tikka masala to an excellent curry made with boneless tandoori chicken. Vegetarians will be especially delighted with the possibilities. Combo plates offer tastes of practically everything. Be sure to try the naan, Indian bread brushed with butter and cooked in a tandoor oven until it bubbles. Naan is perfect for sopping up every last drop of delicious sauce. Some exciting additions include tandoori rack of lamb and goat in many versions including curry. Indian desserts provide a perfect ending to an already decadent meal. The chai tea is special and simply a must. India's continues to please loyal fans – and after one visit, you will be one too. Plus it's open on holidays, which makes for some interesting celebrations. When it comes to gourmet Indian cuisine, the new India's remains a favorite, and Chris and company are simply the best.

India's Castle

Cuisine: Indian
Open: L: Mon-Sat D: Daily
Indiascastle.com

9555 E Arapahoe Rd   303-782-9700
Greenwood Village, 80112
Boston & Arapahoe

Price: $$ **Patio:** No
Reservations: Yes   **Brunch:** No
Location: Greenwood Village

India's Castle tucked into a strip mall in Greenwood Village exudes the charm of India with its lovely décor, accompanied by the aromas that make this country's cuisine so special. Start with poppadums and dipping sauce as you wait for your favorite appetizer. Choose from onion bhaji, samosas, pakoras, and kabobs – all available vegetarian if you prefer. Tandoori chicken marinated in yogurt, fish, ground lamb or shrimp are prepared in the super-heated tandoor oven. Traditional curries are served, as are masala, korma, saag, bhoona, vindaloo and coconut versions. Chicken saag with creamed spinach is terrific, as is the lamb curry. Indulge in the terrific breads that include naan, plain or with garlic, and whole wheat paratha with spices, cheese or lamb. Rice accompanies all, along with raita sauce and mango chutney. Vegetarians will appreciate the many options here. End with rice pudding, kulfi or gulab jamun. There is a nice beer and wine list plus a full bar and excellent service to make your visit even more special.

Indulge Wine Bar

Cuisine: American, Tapas
Open: L: Mon-Sat D: Daily
Indulgewinebar.com

1601 Mayberry Drive   303-991-1994
Highlands Ranch, 80129
Lucent & Highlands Ranch

1299 Washington Ave.   303-277-9991
Golden, 80401
13th & Washington

Price: $$ **Patio:** Yes
Reservations: Yes   **Brunch:** No
Location: Highlands Ranch, Golden

Indulge Wine Bar in suburban Highlands Ranch brings a great concept to the area. The space is beautiful with great décor. Enter the bar area with lots of seating, a terrific back bar and fabulous lighting. Big windows show off patio fire pits and comfortable furniture with a view of the foothills. The dining area is friendly and charming with a private glassed in room perfect for small parties. The central point is the ceiling where artwork from precious wine bottles is recreated in full color. Michelangelo would be impressed. The wine list offers many options from half and full glasses to flights and bottles. The menu is tapas, small portions for sharing. Start with hummus, guacamole, bruschetta and more. Pork ravioli, petite tenderloin and flat bread pizzas are appetizing options. Decadent desserts are perfect for pairing with sweet wines. Service is attentive. Indulge offers the neighborhood a great option for a pleasurable night out.

Izakaya Den, The Sake House with Tapas

Cuisine: Japanese, Sushi
Open: L: Sat D: Tues- Sat
Izakayaden.net

1487 S Pearl St.   303-777-0691
Denver, 80210
Pearl & Florida

Price: $$$$ **Patio:** Yes
Reservations: Yes   **Brunch:** No
Location: Old South Pearl, Denver

Izakaya Den has relocated next door to its sister restaurant Sushi Den. It is totally gorgeous in design. Lots of wood, a stunning sushi bar, beautiful open kitchen, fabulous seating and an upstairs bar with retractable ceiling for outdoor dining during good weather. Beautiful objects of art, plants and numerous nice touches set the scene. Enjoy excellent tapas appetizers, sushi, sashimi and the Japanese menu. Start with edamame, mussels, rolls and more. The ginger sashimi with bincho and jalapeño sashimi with hibachi are special. The list of sushi rolls is long and delicious. The fire roll, dragon roll and all the favorites and specials are delicious. There is a huge list of vegetarian options as well. The Japanese menu offers soups, salads, and entrées from beef to fish. Every presentation is as impressive to see as it is to eat. End with desserts if you have room. The cocktail and wine lists are a bit pricey but lovely choices. Izakaya Den remains tops in Asian dining in Denver.

Japango

Cuisine: Japanese
Open: L-D: Daily
Boulderjapango.com

1136 Pearl St.   303-938-0330
Boulder, 80302
Pearl & 12th

Price: $$-$$$ **Patio:** Yes
Reservations: Yes   **Brunch:** No
Location: Boulder

For a modern casual ambience and delectable melt-in-your-mouth sushi, Japango is one of the most popular destinations in Boulder. Sit at the long sushi bar near the entrance, or relax with friends in the comfortable dining room. Choose from a long list of traditional appetizers such as beef gyoza, edamame and lobster steeped in dynamite sauce. Order a plate of sushi and be sure to include the daily specials and tasty caterpillar roll when you do. Happy hour and lunch specials provide excellent value on a daily basis.

Jax Fish House & Oyster Bar

Cuisine: Seafood
Open: D: Daily
Jaxfishhouse.com

1539 17th St.   303-292-5767
Denver, 80202
17th & Wazee

Price: $$$$ **Patio:** Yes
Reservations: Yes   **Brunch:** No
Location: LoDo, Boulder, Fort Collins, Glendale

The wildly popular Jax is an amazing fish house in the Mile High City. Enter the bar area that stretches along the entire restaurant where crowds gather to visit, dine and imbibe their favorite spirits. The raw bar is incredible with the best oysters anywhere and fabulous shrimp, crab trio and more. From the counter, select cold plates of salt cured foie gras, seafood salad, big eye tuna, scallop ceviche and cured salmon. Hot dishes from the bar include mussels or clam steamers, the best ever made to order clam chowder (worth the trip) and chili crab. Whatever you order, make sure to try the house made epi bread, it is awesome. Try a martini made with fruit-infused vodka or a spicy bloody mary with shrimp hooked on the rim of the glass. The beer and wine list is sensational and watching the chefs cook is a real treat. The kitchen in the rear turns out some sumptuous dishes as well. Booths and tables are spaced along the wall for those not wanting to dine at the bar. Begin with gulf shrimp remoulade, roasted beets and endive and local greens for salads. The Jax lobster BLT with house made chips and a tasty burger with fries is astounding. Clams and spaghetti, sea scallops, sturgeon, calamari and a pork steak start the list of entrées. Oysters Rockefeller, atlantic salmon and fish of the season are more options. Gumbo, a grilled artichoke with crawfish hollandaise, and kedgeree make decisions close to impossible. Talented chefs entice diners with so many creative dishes. The lobster roll is by far the best in the city and totally addictive. Dessert is a must, whether it's rich sticky chocolate cake, key lime pie or the habit-forming butterscotch pudding. Add some of the best service in town and you have Jax. The Jax in Glendale is equally exciting with the same great food and service.

Jelly

Cuisine: Breakfast, Lunch
Open: B-L: Daily
Eatmorejelly.com

600 E 13th Ave.   303-831-6301
Denver, 80203
13th & Pearl

Price: $-$$ **Patio:** Yes
Reservations: No   **Brunch:** No
Location: Capitol Hill

Get up and get moving and head for the hot new breakfast and lunch spot in Capitol Hill called Jelly. The one-room eatery is bright and playful with lots of sunny colors, large windows and a bar where you can peek into the busy kitchen. Start with coffee or tea and then go for your favorites. Pancakes are a must with buttermilk, buckwheat, bacon, fruit, frosted flakes and banana or candied pecan sweet potato flavors. French toast is another treat with bhakti chai and stuffed as options. There are scrambles, Benedicts of salmon, crab, turkey and more, and several versions of biscuits and gravy. Don't miss the breakfast sliders and donut bites. If you prefer lunch, choose from a menu of sandwiches, salads and burgers. Be tempted with the deviled egg salad, curry chicken, Reuben and salmon BLT. Lots of variety in salads and burgers, and you can order breakfast items anytime. The staff is casual and friendly. Jelly brings just what the neighborhood wants – breakfast and enjoyment in a young upbeat atmosphere.

Jim 'N Nick's Community Bar-B-Q

Cuisine: Barbeque
Open: L-D: Daily
Jimnnicks.com

8264 E 49th Ave
Denver, 80238
Northfield & 49th

303-371-1566

Price: $$
Reservations: Yes
Location: Northfield, Aurora, Hampden, Southfield

Patio: No
Brunch: No

Enter this huge space to a terrific staff there to please from the first hello until farewell. This casual bar-b-q joint features booths in the front and tables in the rear. Everything on the menu is prepared in house. Start with pork nachos, a barbecue quesadilla, riblets, pork hot links, chicken tenders and creamy spinach and artichoke dip. Classic greek, the company salad, or the chopped southern with grilled veggies, pecans and bacon are all good. Spare ribs or baby back choices, or the combo where you pick two or three mains and two sides, are favorites. Plates of pulled pork, chicken, brisket, pork hot links, ham and a special turkey breast round out the menu. For a fun southern kitchen treat try the smokehouse pork chop, rib-eye, chicken tender or catfish. There are many sandwich selections as well. Decide on sides to complement your meal and do not miss the cheese biscuits – nobody can eat just one. Save room for homemade pies – chocolate or coconut cream are outstanding. There's beer, wine and cocktails to go with the grub. Service is top notch, kids are warmly welcomed and the prices are affordable. Jim 'N Nick's is fun.

Jing

Cuisine: Asian
Open: L-D: Daily
Jingrestaurant.com

5370 9Greenwood Plaza Blvd
Greenwood Village, 80111
Landmark Village of Shops

303-779-6888

Price: $$$-$$$$
Reservations: Yes
Location: Greenwood Village

Patio: Yes
Brunch: No

Jing at the Landmark showcases a dramatic Las Vegas-style ambience, wows with a large bar/lounge in black and white, with a fireplace spectacularly placed high on the wall, black chairs for comfort, black leather booths for privacy and a beautiful central bar. The main dining room shows off its white accents with gorgeous wood panels, leather booths, beautiful tables and chairs and marvelous china and accents. The semi-open kitchen lets diners view the chefs at work. Owner Charlie Huong of Little Ollie's and Asie (Aspen) fame lifts his creative cuisine to a new level at Jing. The sushi menu is amazing and the dim sum is a real treat. Appetizers include pan-seared pork dumplings, crispy calamari, spring rolls, lettuce wraps and the divine ahi Napoleon with mango pico de gallo. Mango lemon chicken and miso sea bass arrive picture-perfect with fabulous flavors in every bite. Ginger prawns are outrageous and the peppercorn tenderloin special. Thai basil chicken, pork tenderloin, salmon, peking duck, lamb and whole fish round out this fabulous menu. Fried rice, pad Thai and pan-fried noodles are a few of the sides that accompany entrées. Desserts keep pace with a molten chocolate cake, banana cream spring rolls, cheesecake and divine gelato. The wine list is excellent, the service perfect. Jing is unique in the area and brings a new element to the Denver Tech Center dining scene.

John Holly's Asian Bistro

Cuisine: Asian
Open: L-D: Daily
Johnhollysasianbistro.com

9232 Park Meadows Drive   303-768-9088
Lone Tree, 80124
Park Meadows & Yosemite

Price: $$ **Patio:** No
Reservations: Yes   **Brunch:** No
Location: Park Meadows

John Holly's brings something special to the Park Meadows area with his bistro which combines fantastic sushi with Asian specials that shine. The place is beautiful with the sushi bar as the center of attention. Soft purples accent the walls, there are great-looking chairs and the well-trained, friendly staff is perfectly dressed. Start with sushi. Try the eel, soft-shell crab, tuna and salmon rolls, all deliciously fresh and tasty. Entrées are Asian favorites prepared in unique ways. Gyoza, lobster roll, baked green mussels and lettuce-wrapped chicken are good choices. Enjoy soups and tempura served by the piece. The whole red snapper in szechuan sauce is amazing, combining sweet and spicy in a sauce that is irresistible. Another outstanding dish is chicken with eggplant and green beans, which offers a balance of brown and oyster sauces. Additional entrées include peking duck, ahi tuna tataki, kung pao chicken, orange beef and Thai honey pork. The noodle dishes, vegetarian choices and steamed entrées are also options. End your feast with a sweet and chilly mango sorbet. With reasonable prices and good food, John Holly's Asian Bistro is a winner.

Junz

Cuisine: Japanese, French
Open: L-D: Daily
Junzrestaurant.com

11211 S Dransfeldt Rd   720-851-1005
Parker, 80134
Dransfeldt & Twenty Mile

Price: $$$ **Patio:** No
Reservations: Yes   **Brunch:** No
Location: Parker

Junz puts Parker on the Japanese-French fusion dining map. Enter the lovely space to find a sushi bar displaying the most gorgeous array of rolls. The room is upscale but casual, with warm colors and comfortable seating. Servers are dressed beautifully, echoing the art of the food. No detail is overlooked, including an excellent and affordable wine list. Start with sushi. Each platter is breathtaking to see, better to eat. In the dining room start with soft-shell crab salad, a marvelous tuna tartare or a lobster salad. The calamari is some of the best in town. King salmon and the chilean sea bass with lobster bouillabaisse sauce are delicious. Tempura, chicken teriyaki and steak are other choices. End with tiramisù or a divine crème brûlée. If you don't live in Parker, Junz is well worth the trip, and if you do you're already there!

Kabob Station

Cuisine: Greek
Open: L-D: Daily

12041 Pecos St.   303-451-1595
Denver, 80234
120th & Pecos

Price: $ **Patio:** No
Reservations: No   **Brunch:** No
Location: Westminster

Hidden inconspicuously in a strip mall north of Denver, this small restaurant attracts droves of workers looking for a satisfying and affordable lunch. The décor is simple, and the plentiful and authentic middle eastern food is a bargain. Feast on traditional dips served with the best warm pitas that are made in-house daily. Follow with your choice of falafel, lamb, beef or gyro on rice served with pitas. Another tasty option is the divinely spiced shawarma served over rice or as a sandwich with beef, lamb or chicken. The daily lunch specials come with a light baklava. The knowledgeable and excellent staff will explain any dish and assure that you enjoy your meal. This is definitely a hidden gem and worth the trip.

Kachina Southwestern Grill

Cuisine: Mexican
Open: B/L/D: Daily Brunch: Sat-Sun
Kachinagrill.com

10600 Westminster Blvd   303-410-5813
Westminster, 80020
Promenade & Westminster

Price: $$$ **Patio:** Yes
Reservations: Yes   **Brunch:** Yes
Location: Westminster

Inside the Westin Westminster Hotel, Kachina Southwestern Grill is one terrific looking restaurant. As you enter the bar area and move into the main dining room, the feel is totally reminiscent of Santa Fe. White stucco, booths with logs under beige and white fabric, high ceilings and subdued lighting help create a serene place to dine. The menu offers something for everyone with tapas, plates to share and entrees. Start with shrimp and avocado tostado, scallop ceviche, fried oysters, green or red chile, corn chowder and greens. Share guacamole, a bison empanada, huitlacoche tamales or a blue corn dog. Navajo tacos include pork, chicken, lamb, duck and shrimp in any number you desire. Main dishes include bison meatloaf, striped bass, chicken enchilada and shrimp and waffles all with sides included. The grill on the ala carte section includes pork tenderloin, hanger steak, shrimp, chicken, quail and trout. For dessert try the beignets, gelato and other decadent choices. The wine list is adequate with lots of signature cocktails to choose from. Open for breakfast, lunch and dinner, Kachina Southwestern Grill offers an enticing menu in a fantastic setting.

Karma Asian Cuisine

Cuisine: Asian
Open: L-D: Daily
Karmaasian.com

22 S Broadway   303-871-0167
Denver, 80209
Broadway & Ellsworth

Price: $$ **Patio:** No
Reservations: No   **Brunch:** No
Location: Baker, S. Broadway

Karma Asian Cuisine is a wonderful fusion of Thai, Korean, Chinese and Vietnamese food. The soothing sound of a water fountain greets as you enter. The intimate dining room is surrounded by Buddhas of all styles offset against darkly painted walls. The menu starts off with a selection of Asian tapas, plus spicy edamame and pineapple cheese wontons with a pineapple mint sauce. Korean, Thai and Chinese soups are offered along with several wraps and salads. They have an ample selection of noodle dishes and house specialties along with the traditional pho noodle soup native to Vietnam. If you're in the mood for Thai curry, the mango curry served in a pot with a warming candle underneath is delicious. A unique feature of the menu is the Karma Wok. Choose from more than a dozen preparations and sauces, stir-fried with a choice of meat, seafood or tofu. To complement your meal, Karma offers several house specialty Asian cocktails, sake, beer and wine along with Thai iced coffee and tea. Try the daily happy hour with sake and food specials. Karma offers catering for your next party. You know you've done something right when you experience the cuisine of Karma.

Katsu Ramen

Cuisine: Ramen
Open: L-D: Daily
Ramendenver.com

1930 S Havana   303-751-2222
Aurora, 80014
S. Havana and Jewell

Price: $ **Patio:** No
Res: No   **Brunch:** No
Location: Aurora

On S. Havana and Jewell, Katsu Ramen is the place for perfect ramen. There are places all over town but this one is very special. The place is small, one room, and nothing fancy. You can see the open kitchen working very hard to keep up with all the orders. The staff is very friendly and helpful, and nothing is pretentious here. The appetizers include gyozo, edamame, tuna tartar, and miso soup. Next comes the rice bowls of every kind, so if prefer rice to noodles, this is the way to go. They even offer combos of rice and ramen. Now to the best part, the ramen bowls. Huge portions are served and no matter how full, it is hard to leave even a bite. The Tonkotsu is pork, the Shoyu a combination of pork, chicken, and soy, a chilled option, and the best spicy chicken ever. It is very spicy but delicious with an amazing broth and all sorts of goodies—and those thin divine noodles. As you drive up, look in the window as all the dishes are there in plastic-and named—so you will know when you get a seat, you'll be ready to order. And when you get your meal, one digs in very fast. Katsu Ramen is a perfect place for fabulous ramen at prices you can afford. And it is so worth the wait.

Keg Steakhouse +Bar

Cuisine: Steakhouse
Open: D: Daily
Kegsteakhouse.com

1890 Wynkoop St.   303-296-0023
Denver, 80202
19th & Wynkoop

Price: $$$ **Patio:** Yes
Reservations: Yes   **Brunch:** No
Location: LoDo

Big and beautiful, the Keg Steakhouse emits such an alluring aura that it attracts diners from far beyond its downtown LoDo location. Numerous tables situated throughout the attractive bar/lounge area are ideal for dining or just sipping cocktails, while comfortable booths in the dining room offer great views of the open kitchen. Opt to dine on the outdoor patio for a front-row seat watching Denverites pass by. Start with warm goat cheese and tomato salsa bruschetta, onion soup, crab cakes, chicken strips or one of several salads. For dinner the prime rib is tender and delicious as is the New York strip. Other entrées include fish, poultry, lamb and ribs. Dessert is always a good choice with a totally sinful seven-layer chocolate cake with ganache, hot fudge and ice cream, apple crumble, ice cream pie and carrot cake. As part of a successful national chain, Keg in LoDo is sure to please.

King's Land Chinese Seafood

Cuisine: Dim Sum
Open: L-D: Daily
2200 W Alameda Ave   303-975-2399
Denver, 80223
Zuni & Alameda

Price: $$ **Patio:** No
Reservations: Yes   **Brunch:** No
Location: Southwest

Rather than the traditional brunch spread of belgian waffles and eggs washed down with a bloody mary, go out for dim sum and try something totally different. Wash it down with green tea and go home happy and enlivened! Dim sum is the Chinese afternoon combination of breakfast, lunch and tea time. Light tea is enjoyed with many different small plates including dumplings, rolls, meats and vegetables. The dining room is large and there's a good chance a table can be found amidst the afternoon lunch crowd. Once a pot of tea has been set and poured for the table, sit back and let the ceremony begin. Like a mobile marketplace, servers stroll the dining room with small carts carrying an assortment of dishes. You'll see pork or shrimp-leek dumplings, bok choy and rape plants with oyster sauce, barbecued chicken feet, sliced crispy duck breast with fried buns, tripe and other traditional fare. A word of advice for the dim sum amateur – gather a big group of friends and try all of it. At an inexpensive restaurant, plates can range from $2.15 to $5.50 and can be split nicely between friends. Dim sum isn't about fancy art work on the walls or fine dining service. Rather, it's about making mealtime memories with other diners. Bring your friends to experience an exotic array of spicy tastes along with a bottomless pot of tea and you will have an evening to remember.

The Kitchen

Cuisine: American
Open: L-D: Daily
Thekitchen.com
1039 Pearl St   303-544-5973
Location: Boulder, 80302
11th & Pearl

Price: $$$-$$$$ **Patio:** Yes
Reservations: Yes   **Brunch:** No
Location: Boulder

The Kitchen in Boulder opens into a large room with a bar in the front for casual dining. The back of this room houses linen-covered tables with original brick walls, distressed wood floors and crystal chandeliers. A large wooden community table stands as the centerpiece and provides a voyeuristic view into the bustling open kitchen. The dinner menu is lined with small nibbles, charcuterie and cheeses. Dishes range from a classic panzanella salad to a comforting grilled chicken with mashed potatoes and sautéed greens. Signature dishes are tomato soup, garlic fries, mussels and the lamb burger. Save room for dessert which includes pot de crème, and sticky toffee pudding which is irresistible. The beer and wine list is excellent as is the service. A soothing Sunday brunch adds to the popularity of the restaurant. If you didn't get enough, head to the Kitchen's sister establishments, Upstairs and Next Door. Upstairs is a casual lounge featuring carefully selected wine, beer, crafted cocktails and simple rustic food. Next Door is a simple pub where bar-height tables and seats line the walls and community seating covers the center of the space. The menu is a casual interpretation of the dishes at The Kitchen—shared plates, sandwiches, salads, and soups, all less than $9. Whichever spot you choose you will be delighted.

The Kitchen

Cuisine: American
Open: L-D: Daily
Thekitchen.com

1530 16th St   303-623-3127
Denver, 80202
16th & Wazee

Price: $$$$ **Patio:** Yes
Reservations: Yes   **Brunch:** No
Location: LoDo

The Kitchen in LoDo brings great excitement. The space is beautiful with large windows, interesting unfinished walls, fabulous chandeliers and lighting and comfortable seating. The bar is a great option on the first level for gathering. The giant kitchen and a terrific community table are totally enticing and fun. The menu is the same as the upstairs dining area and features the same options as in Boulder. Start with the seafood bar or nibbles of garlic fries, hummus, beets and chevre, pork terrine or yellow fin tuna conserve. There are more options in olives, almonds, chicken liver pâté, sec and greens. Starters include divine tomato soup, bone marrow, mussels, escarole salad and grilled sausage. There are several pastas and entrées that include grilled chicken with cumin yogurt, a substantial pork chop, hake with clams and chorizo, lamb, and steak frites. End with lemon tart, pot au chocolate, apple cobbler, sticky toffee pudding or gelato. The wines are lovely with terrific selections from the keg, several beers, and of course cocktails. Service is casual, friendly and with a delightful staff to make dining a treat. The Kitchen serves lunch as well, and is a most welcome addition to Lower Downtown Denver.

The Kitchen Next Door Glendale

Cuisine: American
Open: L-D: Daily
Thekitchen.com

658 S Colorado Blvd   303-757-0878
Glendale, 80246
Colorado & Cherry Creek

Price: $$-$$$ **Patio:** Yes
Reservations: No   **Brunch:** No
Location: Southeast, Union Station

In the popular Glendale complex of restaurants, the Kitchen Next Door is one of several high demand choices. The space is contemporary, very loud with high ceilings and industrial design, fun lighting, a super focal bar with high tops and seating throughout. The menu is all day and night and starts with bacon wrapped dates, kale chips, calamari, hummus and terrific chicken wings. There are sandwiches of marinated chicken, pulled pork, a burger, a cuban and salmon salad all with a side of coleslaw. Plates range from fish & chips, veggie mushroom loaf, banger and mash and beef meatballs to mussels and hangar steak. There are salads, sides, soups and specials each night. Get there on Wednesday for the chicken. End with chocolate chip cookies, ice cream sandwiches, mousse or cake. There is a nice wine, cocktail and beer list to complement the food. The Kitchen Next Door brings a casual dining choice to Glendale.

KT'S Real Good BBQ

Cuisine: Barbeque
Open: L-D: Mon-Sat
Ktsbbq.com

4030 N Colorado Blvd   303-355-5483
Denver, 80216
Colorado & Albion

2675 13th St   303-442-3717
Boulder, 80304
13th & Alpine

Price: $	**Patio:** Yes
Reservations: No	**Brunch:** No
Location: Park Hill, Boulder	

Savor the taste of Memphis-style barbecue in north Denver and Boulder as you enjoy tender, slow-cooked meats smothered in house made sauces at KT's named for founders Kirk and Tricia Jamison. Order ribs, sausage links in spicy sauce, a massive pulled pork sandwich or a smaller sandwich for lighter eaters. Once you have ordered at the counter and are seated, pour on the heat with KT's double-diamond sauce or choose the sweeter Tricia's texas sauce. Chunky, buttery mashed potatoes, tasty beans and coleslaw are sides. Chocolatey brownies make a delectable dessert.

L'Atelier

Cuisine: French
Open: L : Tues-Fri D: Tues-Sat
Latelierboulder.com

1739 Pearl St   303-442-7233
Boulder, 80302
Pearl & 17th

Price: $$$-$$$$	**Patio:** Yes
Reservations: Yes	**Brunch:** No
Location: Boulder	

Boulder's L'Atelier is the place for a guaranteed special dining experience. Upscale and gorgeous, the food, wine and service is first class. The restaurant's interior boasts soft colors, magnificent china figurines and beautiful pieces of art. Tables are nicely spaced and adorned with elegant china, gorgeous silver settings and attention to every detail. Radek Cerny is an amazing chef, innovative both in his use of ingredients and with presentation. Add a significant selection of wines which cannot be topped in choice for a nearly unbeatable combination. The food is incredible and priced right – this is Boulder after all. Come in jeans or dressed up and start with bread and appetizers that include crab salad, tuna tartare, ravioli and beet salad. Indulge in mussels, lobster ravioli, shrimp dishes and all the specialties featured on any given day. No way to describe these dishes other than "divine." Entrées are even more so. The tuna with black rice and pickled vegetables, the outrageous veal chop and even more outrageous veal oscar with a side of lobster pasta start the list. Pastas, chicken preparations, fish entrées and vegetarian offerings make you second guess your decisions. Anything on the menu is a winner. End with the best cheesecake On A Shoe, a chocolate bag with fruit or and a chocolate foam dessert. If you have not been, you must get there and if you have, I know you are picking up the phone for a reservation.

La Cave

Cuisine: American
Open: B-L-D: Daily
Lacave5280.com

360 Union Blvd   720-963-2055
Lakewood, 80228
4th & Union

Price: $$$ **Patio:** No
Reservations: Yes   **Brunch:** No
Location: Lakewood

Inside the Sheraton Denver West in Lakewood, take the separate entrance into this stylish independently owned restaurant for an experience that will exceed your expectations. La Cave makes a great statement with artistic décor and soothing colors that welcome and create an air of casual luxury. The lounge is beautiful with a great circular bar, fabulous chandelier, walls of terrific wines, a special fireplace and plenty of seating. Enjoy a drink, dinner or the bar menu in this cozy area. Dining rooms are lovely with white wood floors, elegant gray carpets, spacious tables and chairs and spectacular views of the mountains from large picture windows. Owner Youssef Chihab, his partner Elizabeth and staff come from an impressive background and bring contemporary american cuisine to the table. Start with bread and olive oil as you peruse the menu. Appetizers include blue crab croquette, Mediterranean pizzette on gluten free crust, mussels, Korean bbq beef skewers and a sublime cheese tart with apple compote. The salads are a must, choose either the Caesar, La Cave salad or spinach and goat cheese. The lamb shank and eggplant ragout, grilled salmon and Mel's chicken (from Mel's restaurant) start the entrée list. Add ahi tuna, pork loin chop, steaks, hamachi or Tuscan pumpkin ravioli. Accompaniments with each dish add to the flavors and textures. Portions are generous. Desserts are decadent and the chocolate mousse cake tops all. The wine list is fabulous with offerings by half or full glass and bottle at reasonable prices. Breakfast, lunch and a great tapas menu add to the fun. Service is par excellence. La Cave is a great choice on Union Boulevard.

La Cour Bistro & Art Bar

Cuisine: Bar, French
Open: D: Tue- Sun
Denversartbar.com

1643 S Broadway   303-777-5000
Denver, 80210
Iowa & Broadway

Price: $$ **Patio:** Yes
Reservations: No   **Brunch:** No
Location: S. Broadway

You can't miss this bright blue two-story brick building on South Broadway! The main floor is small with a focal bar and view of the small kitchen. Bartenders are charming, the space is fun with lots of interesting art on the walls that changes often. Upstairs there is more space and more art to enjoy along with a fireplace, eye-catching chandelier and room for private dining. Wines are terrific and affordable, the menu has something for everyone. Share charcuterie plates of cheese or meat and pick your own. Shrimp cocktail, pâté and escargot are favorites. The onion soup is terrific and salads are lovely. Quiche is a signature with lorraine, veggie and green chili options that come with a side salad, soup or tartine, an open faced sandwich. The prosciutto, smoked salmon and tuna all rock. Desserts make a perfect ending with sorbets, ice creams and chocolate. La Cour is a super casual and friendly bistro that showcases good live music and art exhibits. With all the choices, this is a spot to stop in often and enjoy a treat for all the senses.

La Cueva Mexican Restaurant & Tequila Bar

Cuisine: Mexican
Open: L-D: Mon-Sat
Lacueva.net

9742 E Colfax Ave   303-367-1422
Aurora, 80010
Colfax & Emporia

Price: $$ **Patio:** No
Reservations: Yes   **Brunch:** No
Location: Aurora

For nearly 40 years, this East Colfax restaurant has proudly served some of Denver's best authentic Mexican food. Sit on tall wrought-iron stools in the colorful bar or settle into one of the pretty dining rooms for a grand meal. Warm chips and spicy salsa arrive complimentary at the table, but don't pass up the fresh and delicious guacamole. La Cueva's tortilla soup also makes a great appetizer, full of cheese, onions, jalapeños and crunchy corn strips. For dinner try a plate of deep-fried chicken taquitos served with beans, guacamole and sour cream. The divine mole, made from a creamy combination of several chilies, vanilla wafers, cinnamon graham crackers, garlic, marjoram and Mexican chocolate is terrific smothered over chicken breast or enchiladas. Short ribs or halibut Mexican-style when available as specials are a must. Other entrée possibilities include burritos, tacos, shrimp covered with ranchero sauce and burgers with green chile. La Cueva is family-owned and run, and the warmth shows in every visit.

La Loma

Cuisine: Mexican
Open: L-D: Daily
Lalomamexican.com

2527 W 26th Ave   303-433-8300
Denver, 80211
26th & Alcott

Price: $$ **Patio:** Yes
Reservations: Yes   **Brunch:** No
Location: Jefferson Park

When you walk into La Loma, you feel like you are part of the family. This restaurant located in a historic home built in 1887 is beautiful both inside and out. If you are with a large group ask for the round table in the dining room which is ideal for sharing food and conversation. If the weather is agreeable, grab a seat outside on the wonderful wrap-around patio. Servers will greet you promptly with water and complimentary chips and salsa. The chips are thin and salty and so delicious you will want to order guacamole or queso and continue eating them. The menu here is large and takes time to navigate. The first two pages are focused on margaritas and tequila. Order a fresco margarita while you continue debating about the food. The fresco has fresh squeezed lime juice, agave nectar and tequila and is just the right combination of sweet and sour. For dinner, choose fajitas, chili rellenos, flautas or stuffed sopapillas. There are also sample platters, which is a wonderful way to try several items. Make sure you try the green chili. La Loma is the perfect place to unwind after a long week and enjoy dinner with friends or family over delicious Mexican food.

La Merise French Cuisine

Cuisine: French
Open: L-D: Daily BR: Sat-Sun
Lamerisedenver.com

2700 E 3rd Ave   720-596-4360
Denver, 80206
3rd & Clayton

Price: $$$ **Patio:** Yes
Reservations: Yes   **Brunch:** Yes
Location: Cherry Creek

La Merise brings a touch of France to Cherry Creek North. Located in the former Argyll Pub space, walk down the few steps and enter a lovely bar, warm and welcoming for a drink or a meal. In the same room find banquettes and tables for dining, while a second room to the left of entry handles more guests or offers an option for semi-private parties. The menu offers French favorites in style. Baskets of bread and butter make a great beginning as you scan the menu and terrific wine list. The majority of wines are interesting French choices and wines from around the world. Appetizers of escargot, smoked salmon, oysters, foie gras, pâté and fabulous mussels are perfect for sharing. The onion soup, Caesar, niçoise and a terrific avocado crab salad make a great second course. For your entrée choose trout or salmon from the sea, or beef, pork medallions, lamb chops provençal, or steak au poivre from the land. Add chicken croquettes and a great burger to the list of options and decisions become formidable. End with the best chocolate mousse or one of several other decadent desserts. Enjoy lunch and brunch as well. Service is lovely as owners Elena and Baibo charm their guests and do much of the serving themselves. Le Merise is a delightful bistro and a wonderful addition to Cherry Creek.

La Sandía

Cuisine: Mexican
Open: L-D: Daily
Richardsandoval.com

8340 Northfield Blvd   303-373-9100
Denver, 80238
Northfield & 47th   Northfield and Park Meadows

Price: $$ **Patio:** Yes
Reservations: Yes   **Brunch:** No
Location: Park Meadows

Richard Sandoval (of Tamayo and Zengo fame) continues to share his signature décor and food around Denver with La Sandía. Color is everywhere in this spacious restaurant with the basics of blue, dark red and sand. Multi-colored accents are featured in acrylic panels that re-create mystical and magical Mexican folklore stories. A bar/lounge area and a lively patio add to the vibe. Start with salsa and chips. Guacamole is served to allow guests to "make their own." Try the queso fundido, chicken tamale, ceviche or beef sopes. Tacos come in many forms: Baja with battered tilapia, chicken, carne asada, pork and vegetarian. You might opt for chicken pibil, mole, enchiladas or milanese. Seafood choices include snapper veracruz, seafood mariscada and shrimp skewers. Don't miss dessert! Crêpes with cajeta, a brownie sundae with cinnamon ice cream, churros and tres leches cake are too good to pass up. Along with wine selections are the tasty lime, mango or hibiscus margaritas. La Sandía brings Mexican flare to Denver in the Park Meadows part of Lone Tree.

Lala's Wine Bar + Pizzeria

Cuisine: Pizza
Open: L-D: Daily BR: Sat-Sun
Lalaswinebar.com

410 E 7th Ave   303-861-9463
Denver, 80203
7th & Logan

Price: $$ **Patio:** Yes
Reservations: Yes   **Brunch:** Yes
Location: Capitol Hill

Enter this delightful space and enjoy a casual, friendly restaurant that welcomes all for wine and food. It is a favorite for happy hour. Warm woods, big windows, a large bar, comfortable seating and an open kitchen set the scene. Start with flat bread topped with a choice of roasted garlic, olive spread, eggplant, tomatoes and basil and more. The antipasto platter of meats

and cheeses, fried artichokes, meatballs, prosciutto and melon, frito misto and house made burritos get you going. Flat bread open-faced sandwich choices are excellent with salad toppings and more. Try the tuna, portobello mushroom with fontina and Caesar dressing, mozzarella with basil pesto, grilled chicken with beets and goat cheese, or the popular meatballs, provolone, parmesan and mozzarella. Pizza is another star with a thin, crispy but chewy crust and delicious toppings. The marguerite pizza with clam sauce, a simple pie with cheese, prosciutto and parmesan, or one with mushrooms, artichokes and cheese are all hits. There are pasta specials daily to round out the menu. Desserts are scrumptious, the wine list is terrific, and service shines. Open from lunch to late night, Lala's is a perfect place for gathering to enjoy good food and fun. Welcome to the neighborhood near 7th and Logan.

Lansdowne Arms

Cuisine: Irish
Open: L-D: Daily
Landsdownearmsbistroandpub.com

9352 Dorchester St   303-346-9136
Highlands Ranch, 80129
Mayberry & Dorchester

Price: $$ **Patio:** Yes
Reservations: Yes   **Brunch:** No
Location: Highlands Ranch

Lansdowne Arms brings great energy to Highlands Ranch in the form of an Irish bistro and pub. Although large with seating for more than 150 people, the ambience is so warm that one hardly notices. The first floor features a bar that is sensational in design with high tables for gathering to chat and drink. There are several dining areas, including a warm library space with red walls, black trim, a fireplace and comfortable seating. Upstairs, an australian bar room with a great atmosphere opens to an amazing patio with a fireplace and more seating. Owner Rob Dawe created this terrific space and added food, beer and wine that complement this architectural delight. Start with onion rings, baked artichoke dip, smoked salmon, mussels, prawns or chicken wings. For Irish fans, the ale-battered fish & chips dish is tasty. Corned beef and cabbage, and guinness shepherd's pie hit the spot. Other entrées include grilled half chicken, pork tenderloin and steaks with delicious sauces. Other options include salmon and pepper-crusted ahi tuna. Enjoy the steak and cheddar sandwich, the Reuben, a paddy melt or burgers with a variety of toppings. Leave room for kahlúa chocolate mousse cake, guinness chocolate-chip ice cream, cheesecake, or sticky-toffee pudding. Service is prompt and friendly and the wine list is great.

Le Central

Cuisine: French
Open: L-D: Daily BR : Sat-Sun
Lecentral.com

112 E 8th Ave   303-863-8094
Denver, 80203
8th & Lincoln

Price: $$ **Patio:** Yes
Reservations: Yes   **Brunch:** Yes
Location: Capitol Hill

Looking for a traditional French restaurant with affordable prices? Le Central fits the bill. The décor is simple and the helpful staff provides excellent service. Lunch includes salad niçoise, crêpe de pullet, grilled salmon and the quiche du jour, all served with soup or salad. Start dinner with utterly addictive loaves of house-made French bread. Onion soup, goat cheese fondue and any of the salads make great appetizers, but the signature mussels served several different ways in a large bowl with French fries are a must. Entrées include strip steak, medallions of chicken breast, veal scaloppini and sole. The half maine lobster in sweet butter with chanterelle mushrooms also makes a nice choice. Everyone raves about the cassoulet, so be sure to visit on days when it's available. Indulge in authentic French sweet endings. After more than 30 years in business, Le Central is as popular as ever.

Lee Yuan Chinese Cuisine

Cuisine: Chinese
Open: L: Mon-Sat D: Daily
Leeyuanchinesecuisine.com

4800 Baseline Rd   303-494-4210
Boulder, 80303
Baseline & Mohawk

Price: $ **Patio:** No
Reservations: Yes   **Brunch:** No
Location: Boulder

Need some quick Chinese food in Boulder? This tiny, inexpensive eatery draws crowds for dining in and taking out. Start with fantail shrimp, barbecue spareribs, crispy vegetarian egg rolls or hot-and-sour soup. For your entrée try the szechwan double delight with shrimp and chicken, steamed whole trout or spicy orange beef. All of the classic options are also available, including a delicious crispy duck.

Leña

Cuisine: Latin American
Open: D: Daily BR: Sat-Sun
Lenadenver.com

24 Broadway   720-550-7267
Denver, 80203
Broadway & 1st

Price: $$ **Patio:** No
Reservations: Yes   **Brunch:** Yes
Location: Baker, S. Broadway

Leña (pronounced LEN-ya) brings new excitement to popular
South Broadway as a hot spot for dining. Leña wows with
great Mexican and Argentinian food served on small plates.
The space is fabulous with a bar that covers one side of the
inviting room, perfect for dining or gathering. Booths and
tables are set throughout the other side with brick walls,
wood, huge windows and flattering lighting. There is dining
upstairs and a special banquet room is on the lower level. It is
casual, comfortable and feels like the place to be. Owner Jimmy
Callahan and his chefs have created a welcoming and charming
place where the food is the star. Begin with ceviche offered
many ways: octopus, tender and delicious, tuna with orange
or shrimp delight. Another feature is a Latin American wood
fire grill bringing super flavors to blood sausage with grilled
tomato, short rib served Korean style, flat and yummy bison
skirt steak, rib-eye, a pork chop, shrimp, chicken or vegetarian
options. The "Caliente" list starts with a potato cake, plantains,
empanadas and tacos. Bison short ribs, sea bass and pork belly
are the toppings for the homemade corn tortillas. Chuck
meatballs, sea bass, and awesome chiliquiles with chicken
bring more choices while chicken, mushrooms and divine
tamales with pork make decisions so hard to make. There are
sides, but do not miss the yucca cheese bread. Also be sure to
try the tres leches, buñuelos, flan, and the ice cream sandwich
for dessert. The cocktail, wine, and beer list complement the
food perfectly. Weekend brunch makes for a great hang out.
With wonderful food and service, reasonable prices and the
most welcoming hosts, Leña is on the list of spots to visit often.
It is addictive.

Linger

Cuisine: American
Open: L-D: Daily BR: Sat-Sun
Lingerdenver.com

2030 W 30th Ave   303-993-3120
Denver, 80211
30th & Umatilla

Price: $$-$$$ **Patio:** Yes
Reservations: Yes   **Brunch:** Yes
Location: Highlands

Hip and memorable describes the look at Linger. The name taken from the original building, Olinger Mortuary, shows the humor of owner Justin Cucci. The contemporary design charms throughout the restaurant. You'll find high tech décor, high ceilings, exposed pipes and fabulous walls with garage door windows that open and close weather permitting. Booths are covered in gray leather and seating is inviting and comfortable. The large open kitchen gives diners a chance to watch the chefs turn out all kinds of menu items. But do not forget the upstairs bar/lounge with fabulous community tables and a knockout rooftop patio. You will be entranced by the feel, and more by the food. It is street food from around the world and the chefs put their play and creativity into every dish. Start with popcorn and continue snacking with the raw trio of samosas, crab cake and mandarin-fennel lasagna. The plate is amazing and Chef Daniel Asher does raw food like no one in this area. Continue with crispy lentil salad with gala apple, sorrel, butter lettuce, goat cheese, pistachios and cumin-sumac vin and give the duck buns, chicken b'stilla, lamb belly tagine and mussels a shot. Goat tacos, puree of eggplant, chicken skewers done cobb salad style, and mussels to die for amaze, and every bite is totally awesome. It is impossible to pick a single dish as best. Save room for dessert – the salted caramel ice cream is a hit but the devilishly delicious doughnuts served in a paper bag are the way to go. Linger also has a fabulous wine, beer and cocktail list, and great, friendly service. From popcorn to pudding, you will linger at Linger. It is just the best.

Little Holly's Asian Café

Cuisine: Sushi, Chinese, Asian
Open: L-D: Daily
Littlehollysasiancafe.com

2223 W Wildcat Reserve Parkway 303-683-5558
Littleton, 80129
Wildcat Reserve & Highlands Ranch

Price: $$	**Patio:** Yes
Reservations: Yes	**Brunch:** No
Location: Littleton	

Serving delicious Asian food, Little Holly's draws big crowds to its Highlands Ranch dining room. Warm wonderful colors, eye-catching art and flowering plants create a wonderful haven for diners inside, while the covered patio makes a nice outdoor dining option for any season. Start with steamed chicken dumplings served with ginger-soy dipping sauce, or lettuce wraps filled with diced chicken and vegetables. You can't stop after the first mouthful of crispy, whole sea bass topped with sweet-and-sour sauce. Dig into spicy Hunan duck or try moo shoo chicken wrapped in soft pancakes. The basil platter with spicy beef, shrimp, chicken and a brown garlic sauce, maine lobster with ginger and scallions, salt-and-pepper shrimp, lo mein and rice dishes are more options. The innovative variety of choices and pleasant service make Little Holly's a top neighborhood restaurant choice.

Little India Restaurant & Bar

Cuisine: Indian
Open: L-D: Daily
Littleindiaofdenver.com

2390 S Downing St   303-298-1939
Denver, 80210
Wesley & Downing

Price: $$	**Patio:** Yes
Reservations: Yes	**Brunch:** No
Location: S. University	

Enter this restaurant and a wonderful aroma will make you anxious to be seated and start the feast. Cinnamon-colored walls, a trellis ceiling and murals invite you to try some great Indian fare. Black granite tables and comfortable seating add to the ambience. Start with poppadoms, vegetable samosas and onion strings, both seasoned with cumin and flavorful spices. The lamb vindaloo is spicy and delicious and the chicken saag a favorite. The tandoori chicken and fish masala tempt. Don't miss the naan bread- the fragrant garlic, the flavorful onion, delicious lamb and more. There is a large variety of dishes, each with special spices which makes for an exciting dining experience. End with typical Indian desserts and extraordinary chai tea. Service is wonderful, prices are reasonable and the wine and beer lists are nice. This welcoming restaurant, along with the original Little India on East 6th Avenue and two others in the metro area make good choices for Indian cuisine.

Little Ollie's

Cuisine: Chinese
Open: L-D: Daily
Littleolliescherrycreek.com

2364 E 3rd Ave   303-316-8888
Denver, 80206
3rd & Josephine

Price: $$ **Patio:** Yes
Reservations: Yes   **Brunch:** No
Location: Cherry Creek

Little Ollie's, the popular Chinese restaurant in Cherry Creek, continues to bring in fans who enjoy both the food and atmosphere. The beautiful patio sports a Chinese motif that adds a new dimension to Chinese dining. Inside, the bright, black-accented décor is a winner. Daily lunch specials bring in crowds for a quality, reasonably-priced meal. Indulge in lettuce-wrapped chicken and sweet barbecued spareribs for starters. For your entrée try Ollie's steamed sea bass prepared in a light ginger sauce or tasty black-bean sauce. Other entrées range from moo shoo pork, mongolian beef and curry chicken to crispy duck and fresh maine lobster stir fry. All items can be prepared hot and spicy or a little less fiery depending on your preference. Wines are exceptional for a Chinese restaurant. It is no wonder there is never an empty table at Little Ollie's. And as is the wish of those who love traditional Chinese food, Ollie's "delivers."

Little Man Ice Cream

Cuisine: Ice Cream
Open: Daily
Littlemanicecream.com

2620 16th St   303-455-3811
Denver, 80211
16th & Tejon

Price: $ **Patio:** Yes
Reservations: No   **Brunch:** No
Location: Highlands

In the energetic neighborhood of LoHi stands an independent storefront shaped like old-fashioned milk can. This 28' tall structure is a local landmark that encourages neighbors to stroll over for an evening scoop and tourists to stop by for a treat between destinations. During summer nights, families line up around the block discussing which of the numerous flavors they will order. Be prepared to change your mind multiple times before choosing, as every flavor is intriguing and mouthwatering. Little Man has not only mastered the customer experience, they have mastered ice-cream as well as gelato. The flavor combinations range from unique, like salted caramel peanut butter cup, to traditional. The chocolate is one of the best in town. Decisions are painful to make, so order a double scoop and try two flavors. The salted Oreo is not to be missed as it takes the traditional cookies and crème to an entire new level. Little Man Ice Cream not only lights up the skyline of LoHi, it will also light up your evening. Your taste buds will thank you for making the trip and remind you to return soon.

Locanda Del Borgo

Cuisine: Italian
Open: L: Tue- Fri D: Tue-Sun
Locanda-del-borgo.com

5575 E 3rd Ave   303-388-0282
Denver, 80220
3rd & Holly

Price: $$$ **Patio:** Yes
Reservations: Yes   **Brunch:** No
Location: Hilltop

Enter this Italian trattoria where the first thing you see is the beautiful bar area where you can enjoy drinks or dinner. Tables are nicely spaced throughout and the open kitchen is a great place to watch the chefs at work. Warm and comfortable with terra cotta, brick, big windows and lovely lighting, the atmosphere is welcoming. Pizzas are a special feature with the pizza oven as a showpiece. There are several varieties as well as appetizers of rolled pizza dough filled with arugula and mozzarella, and thin pizza dough with rosemary and garlic. There is much more to enjoy here. Other starters include fresh mussels steamed in white wine and garlic, fritto misto, bruschetta, small meatballs, and cheese and meat platters. All are great, as are the Caesar, seafood and beet salads. Pastas star with rigatoni Bolognese, penne with mozzarella and eggplant, gnocchi, ravioli and risotto with seafood. Oven-roasted chicken, veal scaloppini, ahi, rack of lamb and grilled flat iron steak show the variety of entrées. Add pork chops, a mixed grill of lamb, beef and sausage, a whole fish that is outstanding, cioppino and decisions are grueling. Desserts of chocolate hazelnut tart and apple tart are perfect endings. Homemade gelato is definitely the star. The wine list is excellent, and the service keeps pace with the rest of the experience. Locanda Del Borgo brings a contemporary Italian dining choice to the neighborhood and is well worth the drive from anywhere.

LoHi SteakBar

Cuisine: Steakhouse
Open: L-D: Daily BR: Sat-Sun
Lohisteakbar.com

3200 Tejon St   303-927-6334
Denver, 80211
Tejon & 32nd

Price: $$-$$$ **Patio:** Yes
Reservations: Yes   **Brunch:** Yes
Location: Highlands

It's fun in the Lower Highland area and LoHi SteakBar fits right in. The place is enticing as you enter the bar area with lots of seating and a handsome bar with large red shades over the area to accent the look. The dining area has great lights hanging from the high ceilings with amber colored faux-painted walls, comfortable booths and tables. Start with marinated olives and rosemary almonds, blue cheese fondue, hummus, ricotta spinach dumplings, buffalo chicken wings or meatballs in red gravy. The onion soup and the Caesar salad are favorites. Steaks are priced so one can enjoy them often: flat iron, strip, rib-eye or filet all come with steak frites that are hand-cut along with your choice of toppings. Hamburgers offer fried egg, chili and cheddar, onion, bacon and blue, or mushroom, Swiss and béarnaise. On the sandwich list the salmon BLT, chicken club and Portobello mushroom burger are good choices. If you want a big plate choose roasted half chicken, mussels, salmon or steak and eggs. End with the signature dessert of chocolate pudding, a banana split or cheese plate. The wine, cocktail and beer lists are well-priced. LoHi SteakBar is a neighborhood pick in this very popular hood.

Lola Mexican Fish House

Cuisine: Mexican
Open: D: Daily BR: Sat-Sun
Loladenver.com

1575 Boulder St   720-570-8686
Denver, 80211
Boulder & 16th

Price: $$-$$$ **Patio:** Yes
Reservations: Yes   **Brunch:** Yes
Location: Highlands

You can't miss Lola. It's the place where people are hanging out on the patio enjoying drinks with more happy fans gathered in the bar area imbibing on a favorite beverage. You will also find people waiting for a seat at the raw bar. The dining room features an open kitchen with comfortable seating at booths and wooden tables. Bright colors and artifacts on the walls remind you that you are in a Mexican restaurant. Menu items are beyond creative and bring Mexican fare to a new level. Start with guacamole, prepared table side with a margarita, sangria or wine. Avocado fondue is mandatory, and duck carnitas, pickled shrimp, dumplings and lobster quesadillas shine. Tomato soup with asadero cheese grilled tortillas and the silky corn soup with fried avocado and red chile bring new interest to the soup course. Grouper, whole golden trout, whole fried fish, and a stew with monkfish, shrimp and scallops in spicy lobster-mushroom broth start the list of seafood specials. Mexican pot roast of lamb, grilled strip steak with mole, and black plum chipotle barbecued short ribs bring more imaginative creations to the palate. Decadent desserts include a dense chocolate mud cake, flan and Key lime pie. Service shines and the specialty drink and wine lists are excellent. The noise level is high but the spirit and fun that diners experience make Lola the place to be. Their weekend brunch is one of the most popular in town.

Los Dos Potrillos

Cuisine: Mexican
Open: B-L-D: Daily
los2potrillos.com

8251 S Holly St
Centennial, 80122
County Line & Holly

720-529-0299

10065 W San Juan Way
Littleton, 80127
San Juan & Kipling

303-948-1552

Price: $$
Reservations: Yes
Location: Littleton, Centennial

Patio: Yes
Brunch: No

When you enter either location of this family-owned restaurant you will be greeted with great warmth. The exteriors of both locations are somewhat plain, but the food inside is exciting. The staff is hospitable and the menu includes an extensive list of Mexican favorites. Start with the delicious complimentary chips and salsa. Order plates to share like guacamole, chile rellenos, nachos and quesos. Entrées offer burritos, seafood dishes, stews, salads and combination plates. There are carnitas on the weekends, chicken dishes, enchiladas, tacos, tostadas, menudo and tamales. The fajitas are delicious with a nicely charred and smoky flavor. For dessert treat yourself to the sopapillas with ice cream and chocolate or strawberry topping. There is a full-service bar with a wide selection of Mexican beers and margaritas. On Wednesday nights at County Line and Holly and Thursday nights at C-470 and Kipling enjoy live mariachi music. When you want great Mexican food with hospitality try either location of Los Dos Potrillos.

Lou's Food Bar

Cuisine: American
Open: L-D: Daily BR: Sat-Sun
Lousfoodbar.com

1851 W 38th Ave
Denver, 80211
38th & Shoshone

303-458-0336

Price: $$
Reservations: No
Location: Northwest, Sunnyside

Patio: Yes
Brunch: Yes

Chef/Owner Frank Bonanno and crew do it again with Lou's Food Bar. The free-standing building is bright and décor is simple with a great bar, comfortable banquette seating, booths, and tables throughout the room. The lighting is terrific and a

salumi bar a central point. The food has a French accent but is designed for all palates. Start with the charcuterie: salumi plate with house-cured meats, cheese plate of homemade cheeses and pâtés. "Just for the fun of it," boasts house smoked salmon with homemade cream cheese, escargot, French onion soup, Carpaccio and shrimp cocktail. The grilled artichoke with madras curry aioli and the crab cakes with remoulade are popular choices. For the salad course go for niçoise, duck leg confit, shrimp and beet or white bean and haricots verts. The blackened fish sandwich, French dip and Angus burger are some main courses, as are the house made selections of sausage. Other mains include fried or roasted chicken, salmon, hanger steak, ribs and carnitas enchiladas. A favorite on the menu is the spaghetti and mozzarella-stuffed meatballs. And the fries go with anything. Enjoy desserts, a nice wine, beer and drink list and excellent service in this welcoming spot. Lou's Food Bar is a fun place in this ever growing neighborhood.

Lo Stella Ristorante

Cuisine: Italian
Open: L-D: Tue-Sun
Lostelladenver.com

1135 Bannock St   303-825-1995
Denver, 80204
12th & Bannock

Price: $$$-$$$$ **Patio:** Yes
Reservations: Yes   **Brunch:** No
Location: Golden Triangle

Italian is the theme of the new Lo Stella located in the Golden Triangle. Owners welcome you with Italian accents and heaps of charm with proud family recipes brought to Denver. The place copies the décor from previous restaurants with an open kitchen, huge pizza oven, nice bar and seating throughout. It is casual and comfortable and a place for families, dates and more to gather. Start with the grilled vegetable or caprese salad, mussels, prosciutto and cantaloupe, octopus and Carpaccio of salmon. The pasta list includes marinara, pesto, Bolognese, seafood and ravioli with wild herbs or with fish and shrimp sauce. There is a long list of pizza. Entrees include grilled filet, steak on the grill, rack of lamb, chicken Milanese, veal scaloppini, salmon trout and branzino. Of course all are infused with the Italian accents of their roots. Sides of potatoes, porcini mushrooms or vegetables come with entrees. Desserts include tiramisu, panna cotta and Italian apple pie. The Italian wine list complements the food nicely. They serve lunch as well as dinner. Lo Stella Ristorante brings another good dining choice to the neighborhood.

Lower 48 Kitchen

Cuisine: Contemporary
Open: D: Mon-Sat
Lower48kitchen.comL

2020 Lawrence St A   303-942-0262
Denver, 80205
21st & Lawrence

Price: $$$$ **Patio:** Yes
Reservations: Yes   **Brunch:** No
Location: LoDo

Lower 48 brings Mario Nocifera and Chef Alex Figura partner together in Lower 48. Both come from great backgrounds and are now delighting diners in their own space. The place is big, open, and has an industrial look with high ceilings, huge windows, great lighting, an open kitchen, and focal bar. The wood tables are accented with red chairs and staff is nattily dressed with great aprons. Touches of Americana continue with a private dining area with railroad ties and even a train door bringing the railroad theme-and crossing the country. In the rear is a bar area that will feature wines and specials. The menu starts with bites. These really are one taste and $2 and range from a grain crisp with pickled fruit, Johnny cake, chickpea fry, fritter, smoked chicken wing and a hoecake. All are tasty. Small plates from Brussels and squash, roasted beets, savory pancakes, and braised squid with lima beans are some options. Entrees include a pasta, scallops, chicken leg and breast, and braised brisket. The main course for two offers a 32 oz. ribeye. Desserts are amazing with an inverted caramel tart, grit custard, and the best citrus and meringues. The wine list is excellent and service is nice. Lower 48 brings many dishes in small portions to tempt foodies to enjoy here.

Luca D'Italia

Cuisine: Italian
Open: D: Tue-Sat
Lucadenver.com

711 Grant St   303-832-660
Denver, 80203
7th & Grant

Price: $$$$ **Patio:** No
Reservations: Yes   **Brunch:** No
Location: Capitol Hill

Luca D'Italia brings great excitement to the Denver dining scene. The space is inviting with wonderful art accenting soft gray walls. Modern tables and chairs and a separate hammered-aluminum bar add a contemporary feel. A table of wines makes a great focal point in the dining area, while the bar attracts diners and those who just want to stop by for a drink. The terrific staff provides amazing hospitality along with excellent, knowledgeable service. Chef/Owner Frank Bonanno brings his style and knowledge of Italian food to the menu. Complimentary crostini change nightly and wonderful homemade Grateful Breads start the meal. Appetizers include house-made mozzarella with fried baby artichokes, sweetbreads, grilled octopus and burrata. Lovely salad choices change often. Every good Italian loves pasta and Frank really knows his noodles. Lobster fra diavolo, linguine vongole and pappardelle Bolognese with wild boar are all wonderful. Don't miss the ricotta ravioli, squash agnolotti or gnocchi. Entrées include grilled prawns, sole and black cod. Try veal saltimbocca, rack of lamb, pork and the popular rabbit three ways. End the meal with decadent desserts. There is an extensive wine list to complement your meal. Luca makes for a special night out.

Lucile's

Cuisine: Cajun, Breakfast
Open: B-L: Daily
Luciles.com

2124 14th St.   303-442-4743
Boulder, 80302

Price: $$ **Patio:** Yes
Reservations: No   **Brunch:** No
Location: Boulder, Denver, Fort Collins, Longmont, Littleton

Lucile's, the quintessential breakfast and lunch spot in Boulder for more than 20 years, has locations in Denver, Longmont, Fort Collins and Littleton. You'll be greeted with a smile and a "hi y'all." Featuring Cajun/Creole fare, the décor is warm and friendly. At the Denver location you will find a large bar complete with wine and beer, a sitting room for those waiting for a table, and simple tables and chairs throughout the small dining room. Weather permitting, seating on the front patio is lovely. Start with fresh juices, not-to-be-missed beignets and a cup of chicory coffee as you decide on your entrée. Eggs Benedict, Rockefeller, New Orleans and Jennifer bring many versions of the standard – all with terrific hollandaise and your choice of grits or potatoes. Several omelets, pain perdu (French toast), delicious granola, oatmeal and rice pudding porridge make decisions difficult. Don't miss the biscuits with homemade jams. If you are in the mood for lunch enjoy homemade soup, grilled chicken salad, muffaletta, or po'boys of sausage or fried oysters. Choose entrées such as gumbo, shrimp Creole, crawfish étouffée, or shrimp and grits. No Southerner would miss dessert, and the decadent chocolate pecan truffle torte, bread pudding and banana beignets make for perfect endings. Lucile's is a welcome addition to the breakfast scene wherever they are located.

Lucky Pie Pizza & Tap House

Cuisine: Italian, Pizza
Open: L-D: Daily
Luckypiepizza.com

1610 16th St   303-825-1021
Denver, 80202
16th & Wazee

Price: $$ **Patio:** Yes
Reservations: Yes   **Brunch:** No
Location: LoDo

Lucky Pie is located in the former Dixons space and ready for games and guests. A second location can be found in Louisville. Both places look great with a casual but clean and interesting interior. The LoDo outdoor patio is a perfect people watching spot in warm weather. The menu at both locations has many options with a nice selection of house-made cheeses: fresh mozzarella, ricotta, stracciatella,and meats that include smoked ham, prosciutto, and deviled ham with grilled bread and fig preserves, perfect to complement the 17 craft beers and varied wines offered here. Braised lamb meatballs, spreads, chicken liver mousse and mussels make up the appetizers while the spicy Caesar, beet, apple, kale, and chopped salad are a great second course. Pizza is the specialty with cheese, prosciutto, Popeye of spinach and cheeses with and an add-on of bacon, pepperoni, Napolitano, wild mushroom and puttanesca. There are other main course such as fried chicken, lamb ribs, trout, duck breast, hanger steak and a burger. The chocolate mousse with beer is a fun dessert choice. Service is casual and friendly, the food very good and the drinks great.

J:

K:

Luke's, A Steak Place

Cuisine: Steakhouse
Open: D: Daily BR: Sun
Lukesasteakplace.com

4990 Kipling St   303-422-3300
Wheat Ridge, 80033
50th & Kipling

Price: $$$ **Patio:** Yes
Reservations: Yes   **Brunch:** Yes
Location: Wheat Ridge

Take the whole family for a steak dinner at this casual, western-style restaurant in Wheat Ridge. Your meal comes with salad, bread and a side of potatoes or spaghetti. Lobster tail and tasty fish dishes will please non meat eaters. Great service and prices make Luke's an excellent alternative to the high-end steakhouses. The space is large and welcoming and nicely done. White linens on the tables dress up the casual feel and service is terrific with the warm, efficient staff poised to help every patron. Owner Bob Mayer does a great job on the food and stops by to check on all diners. The bread is warm and comes with both an oil and vinegar dipping sauce and butter. The salad served family style is full of goodies with a really delicious dressing. There are several steaks from strip and rib-eye to filet. Lobster tail and tasty fish dishes are great alternatives. The sides range from potato skins sliced and fried with onions, sweet potatoes, baked potatoes and rice to an array of veggies. End with bread pudding, pecan tart or yummy cheesecake. The wine and drink options are a thoughtful list to complement the food. Prices are affordable to make this a real treat.

Maggiano's Little Italy

Cuisine: Italian
Open: L-D: Daily
Maggianos.com

500 16th St   303-260-7707
Denver, 80202
16th & Tremont

7401 South Clinton St.   303-858-1405
Englewood, 80112
Denver Tech Center

Price: $$ **Patio:** Yes
Reservations: Yes   **Brunch:** No
Location: Englewood, Downtown

Both the freestanding DTC Maggiano's and the Denver Pavilions location draw large crowds of people hungry for traditional family-style Italian prepared with style and love. Red-checkered tablecloths, Sinatra crooning in the background, family photos on the walls and lots of wood create the appropriate atmosphere and mood. A staff of amazing cooks and servers dish up family-sized portions to share. Start with mussels in marinara, fried calamari and the spinach and artichoke dip. Maggiano's salad has everything to make lettuce exciting, or go for the Caesar. Any of the pastas are good choices but a favorite is the Rigatoni D; rigatoni with chicken in a Marsala cream sauce. The spaghetti with meat sauce, lasagna with meat sauce and eggplant parmesan are all so good. Veal parmesan, chicken piccata, balsamic salmon and the several renditions of your favorite entrées are ample enough to share. Decadent desserts please, particularly the apple crostada, chocolate cake and spumoni ice cream. Do not miss the Classic Pastas. This is a terrific feature worth the trip. Order one of many pasta selections and after you dine the kitchen prepares another and packs it up for you to take home for seconds. The price is $12.95- one great deal for some mighty fine eating. The special family-style meals are another fun option for the group at affordable prices, and doggy bags arrive free of charge. A nice wine list complements the food. Maggiano's remains a Denver favorite.

Mangiamo Pronto!

Cuisine: Italian
Open: B-L-D: Mon-Sat
Denveritalianrestaurants.net

1601 17th St   303-297-1229
Denver 80202
17th and Wazee

Price: $$ **Patio:** Yes
Reservations: Yes   **Brunch:** No
Location: LoDo

Mangiamo Pronto! occupies a prime LoDo location on the corner of 17th and Wazee and is open for breakfast, lunch and dinner. The space is a large room with fantastic colors, interesting art, a high open ceiling and big picture windows. A large counter shows some of the dishes available and affords a glimpse into the kitchen. Order here and the wait staff will deliver your meal to your table. Start with breakfast goodies and then stay for lunch. Try the tapas of olives, fresh anchovies, and white bean purée with chicken cracklings or Italian cured meats. Salads include caprese, arugula with roasted pears and Caesar. Paninis are sure to please and are generously sized with turkey cranberry, shredded pork loin, grilled zucchini and peppers or chicken breast. Presentation is pleasing with a side of balsamic chips or garbanzo bean salad bringing an exciting combination of flavors and textures. There's more with thin-crust pizzas. Dinner forgoes the paninis and switches to appetizers, salads and pasta. There's a nice wine list to complement your meal and terrific coffees and desserts too. Do not leave without the decadent gelato. Mangiamo Pronto! is a simple, casual and inviting LoDo dining option.

Marco's Coal-Fired Pizzeria

Cuisine: Italian
Open: L-D: Daily
Marcoscoalfiredpizza.com

2129 Larimer St. Denver, 80205 Larimer & 22nd	303-296-7000
10111 Inverness Main St. Englewood, 80112 Inverness & Dry Creek	303-790-9000

Price: $$ **Patio:** Yes
Reservations: Yes   **Brunch:** No
Location: LoDo, Ballpark, Englewood

Enter this terrific space and feel transported to an Italian trattoria or pizzeria! The restaurant is bright and casual with a bar for gathering or dining, tables and booths throughout the single room and a wonderful exposed brick wall with murals. The show stopper is the pizza kitchen visible to all. Start with an appetizer of their signature lemon coal-fired chicken wings as you decide on the rest of your meal. Salads make a great second course or starter. Everything from a rich prosciutto with greens and gorgonzola to a simple arugula with parmesan are fresh and fabulous. The star is definitely the pizza- Napoletana or New York-style, both are cooked in the Italian imported wood-burning oven. Flour, tomatoes and several other ingredients are imported. Nothing but the best is the theory, and it works. Thin crust pizzas are crispy but still tender and chewy topped with extraordinary choices. Toppings include prosciutto, mozzarella and tomatoes, Abruzzi and the divine white pizza, Calabria. The oven is so hot pizzas cook in just under two minutes. The New York pizzas include Brooklyn, Bronx, Manhattan, Queens and Staten Island. Then there are "assemble your own" pizzas and calzones. The many topping/filling choices include sausage, meatballs, salami and veggies. Several enticing sandwiches round out the menu from pollo to prosciutto and mozzarella. Meatball sliders are well worth the trip! Don't miss the Nutella pizza for dessert or go for tiramisù or cannoli. There is a terrific wine list along with beer and daily specials. Enjoy the back patio when weather permits, it is enclosed with heat lamps to keep you comfortable. Marco's Coal-Fired Pizzeria is offering catering- what a great treat with their portable fabulous pizza oven. And they deliver. Add friendly service, and Marco's brings a great adventure in pizza to Denver.

Maria Empanada

Cuisine: Latin American
Open: B-L: Daily D: Mon-Sat
Mariaempanada.com

1298 S Broadway Ave   303-934-2221
Denver, 80210
Louisiana & Broadway

Price: $ **Patio:** Yes
Reservations: No   **Brunch:** No
Location: S. Broadway

Maria Empanada is a tasty concept on South Broadway. The space is bright and much larger than its previous location with plenty of seating to enjoy the great fare. Lorena brings Argentina to Denver with all her goodies. Start with breakfast empanadas of eggs. The torta of eggs, potatoes and onions is traditional in Spain. Empanadas come savory and sweet with many vegetarian options. Tortas are awesome with veggie, mushrooms and the spinach and cheese quiche. Pastries filled with ham, cheese and more make decisions hard. Do not miss the Empanada Gallega- a huge rectangle of dough filled with tuna, eggs and red peppers. Then there are the sweet empanadas, cookies, brioche and muffins to please all ages. You must see the coffee service using a special machine that is one of only four in the United States. Add the orange juice squeezer that presses fast and fresh on request, and the special hot milk with chocolate and your beverage choice will be something to brag about. Maria Empanada is a delight and perfect in this fast growing part of Denver.

Marczyk Fine Foods

Cuisine: Grocery
Open: Daily
Marczyckfinefoods.com

770 E 17th Ave	303-894-9499
Denver, 80203	
17th & Clarkson	
5100 East Colfax	303-243-3355
Denver, 80220	
Colfax & Filbert	

Price: $$ **Patio:** No
Reservations: No   **Brunch:** No
Location: Uptown, Park Hill

Pete and Barbara Marczyk's dream has come true. Located on the corner of 17th and Clarkson, Marczyk Fine Foods provides thrilled crowds with tempting choices from cases full of all things delicious. Fresh one-of-a-kind items make you want to start cooking at home. A variety of meats, fish, poultry, divine cheeses and entire sections of coffee and tea are just a sampling of what is available. The produce is awesome and tastes as good as it looks. Breads from Denver's top bakers, tempting pastries, various prepared foods and carryout sandwiches are all delightful. The attentive and caring staff will happily make sure your orders are ready to go and ready to serve. Many top shelf oils, vinegars and canned items are available here and nearly impossible to find elsewhere. They have an outstanding deli section where you can pick up lunch or dinner, and don't forget Friday night burger night from April till October. They grill them on the spot-you just sit, eat, and enjoy. The wine shop next door will help you pair the perfect vintage with your meal. A second location on East Colfax provides a second chance to stock up on amazing products you will absolutely love.

Marg's World Taco Bistro

Cuisine: Mexican
Open: L-D: Daily BR: Sat- Sun
Margstacobistro.com

200 Fillmore	303-321-6274
Denver 80209	

Price: $$ **Patio:** Yes
Reservations: Yes   **Brunch:** Yes
Location: LoDo, Cherry Creek, Uptown

Three Denver locations make great spots for people watching as well as enjoying sensational tacos and more. With bright decor featuring lime-green accents, large windows and nice lighting,

Marg's is casual and fun. The varied cocktail and drink menu brings in thirsty crowds. Start with chips and salsa, guacamole, a beanless bean dip, grilled taquitos or shrimp ceviche. There are soups and salads as well. The tacos come either two or three to a platter in many creative combinations such as caprese, Asian with seasoned chicken and peanut sauce, Banh Mi, Moroccan, Korean, French and Pacific. Proteins range from pork, beef and chicken to shrimp, fish and tofu. Additional specialties include carnitas, a club, chicken vindaloo and tilapia. All come with rice and beans. This is a fun spot with good food and drinks whether you are in Cherry Creek, LoDo, Uptown.

The Market at Larimer Square

Cuisine: Sandwiches, Bakery
Open: B-L-D: Daily
Themarketatlarimer.com

1455 Larimer St   303-534-5140
Denver, 80202
15th & Larimer

Price: $$ **Patio:** Yes
Reservations: No   **Brunch:** No
Location: Larimer Square, Downtown

An essential part of Larimer Square, it is impossible to think of this block without The Market. The place feels like a European coffeehouse bustling with folks from early morning until late at night. Tables are crowded into every corner and the selection of gourmet grocery items on the shelves supply you with the ingredients to make your own feast at home. Bakery cases beckon with sweet rolls, muffins, cookies and other desserts. For a decadent treat try the old-fashioned chocolate cake or the spring fling filled with cream cheese, butter cream and fruit- simply amazing! Start early with coffee, pastries and breakfast specials. At lunch and dinner choose from a variety of soups, salads and entrées from the hot and cold cases, or order a freshly made sandwich. Try the sweet chicken curry sandwich with raisins and walnuts on marbled rye, runza, lentils and Greek salad. In the late evening, sit on the patio with a latte or ice cream and enjoy people watching in Larimer Square.

Masterpiece Delicatessen

Cuisine: Deli
Open: Daily
Masterpiecedeli.com

1575 Central St	303-561-3354
Denver, 80211	
16th & Central	
1710 Sherman St	303-832-6732
Denver, 80203	
17th& Sherman	

Price: $$ **Patio:** Yes
Reservations: No   **Brunch:** No
Location: Uptown, Highlands

Who would think a deli could bring so much fanfare and fun to Denver diners? It's true if you head over to Masterpiece Delicatessen in either of its two locations in LoHi and Uptown. You'll find cases of food from which to choose with the kitchen in full view in LoHi. Justin Brunson and Steve Allee aim for casual fare with outstanding sandwiches, salads and desserts. Just try to choose between the gourmet grilled cheese, white truffle egg salad, smoked turkey with pears and arugula, Reuben with house-made corned beef, the Italian, the Cubano, 12-hour braised beef brisket, wild ahi tuna or roasted vegetable. Pick your bread and add sides of pasta salad or potato or veggie chips. Don't miss a cup of soup or the array of salads from arugula, spinach and Cobb to Greek. At breakfast indulge in house-cured gravlox, egg sandwiches, pork roll with eggs, oatmeal, muffins and yogurt. Delicious coffee drinks, smoothies, juice and wine complement the food. Masterpiece Delicatessen is a treat with patio dining available at both locations.

Mateo Restaurant Provençal

Cuisine: French
Open: L: Mon-Fri D: Mon-Sat BR: Sun-Sat
Mateorestaurant.com

1837 Pearl St	303-443-7766
Boulder, 80302	
19th & Pearl	

Price: $$$ **Patio:** Yes
Reservations: Yes   **Brunch:** Yes
Location: Boulder

Mateo serves up excellent bistro fare in a casual, warm setting accentuated with soft gold's, oranges and reds. The central bar sitting atop a concrete floor adds life to the space. Dinner entrées range from a traditional croque monsieur sandwich to

pappardelle with mushrooms, thyme and cream. Start with mussels, oysters, shrimp, clams, crab or an onion and goat cheese tartlette. Salads include duck confit and frisée, tuna niçoise, and beef Carpaccio with arugula. Main courses of salmon with English peas, Alaskan halibut and grilled Niman Ranch pork loin are real crowd pleasers. End with sumptuous desserts. The staff is energetic and eager to help explain the menu and offer suggestions. Located at the eastern end of the Pearl Street Mall in Boulder, Mateo is a Flatirons favorite.

Max Gill & Grill

Cuisine: Seafood, American
Open: D: Daily BR: Sat- Sun
Maxgillandgrill.com

1052 S Gaylord St   303-722-7456
Denver, 80209
Gaylord & Mississippi

Price: $$-$$$ **Patio:** Yes
Reservations: Yes   **Brunch:** Yes
Location: Southeast-Washington Park

Max Gill & Grill brings seafood and more to the old South Gaylord area. The space resembles a New England coastal retreat with several areas for dining, a focal bar, lots of wood and exposed brick and a casual, friendly feel. Start with the raw bar and enjoy oysters, clams, shrimp and lobster. Jalapeño cornbread whets the appetite for choices of seafood, and spit-roasted and grilled entrées. Appetizers include fried green tomatoes, crab cakes, calamari, empanadas and a walnut-crusted goat cheese plate. Seafood entrées include cioppino, swordfish, salmon and fish & chips. The grill features items first smoked on the premises then grilled, including pork chops, ribs, prime rib and chicken. Other options include a burger, burrito and steak Oscar. The lobster roll with parmesan truffle fries is a favorite. End with Key lime pie or chocolate cake. The wine list features an excellent selection by bottle or glass. Beer, margaritas and specialty drinks add to your enjoyment. Max Gill & Grill welcomes all in this popular Denver neighborhood.

Max's Wine Dive – Denver

Cuisine: American
Open: D: Daily BR: Sat-Mon
Maxswinedive.com

696 Sherman St   303-593-2554
Denver, 80203
7th & Sherman

Price: $$-$$$ **Patio:** Yes
Reservations: Yes   **Brunch:** Yes
Location: Capitol Hill

Fried chicken and champagne?... why not?! The menu says they pride themselves on bringing gourmet comfort food in an exciting and unique atmosphere. And it's true, the food is comforting. Southern fried chicken, mashed potatoes and collard greens are at the top of the list followed by shrimp and grits and short-ribs. If comfort food isn't what you're looking for, they have small plates like a charcuterie board or baked oysters. This fun and funky place with a top-notch wine list is a complete contrast in a casual industrial atmosphere. Located in Denver's Governor's Park neighborhood, this new spot brings a different experience to the area.

McCormick & Schmick's Seafood & Steaks

Cuisine: Seafood, Steakhouse
Open: L: Mon-Fri D: Daily
Mccormickandschmicks.com

8100 E Union Ave   720-200-9339
Denver, 80237
Denver Tech Center

Price: $$$-$$$$ **Patio:** Yes
Reservations: Yes   **Brunch:** No
Location: Southeast-DTC

This surf and turf spot in the DTC has great ambience. Enter the restaurant located in the Penterra Plaza building and the first thing you encounter is a beautiful lounge. Tiffany inspired stained glass chandeliers designed with the logos of Colorado sports teams catch your eye. Comfortable seating and a large bar create an inviting space for gathering and dining, and to enjoy the specials during specific hours. Dining rooms are large with etched glass and an open kitchen as the focal point. Order fish grilled plain or try the specials. Start with oysters, crab cakes or an ahi tuna martini. Fried oysters, mussels and crispy calamari are more options. Soups, salads and sandwiches are available for lighter dining in the evening. Entrées include seafood stew, mahi-mahi or striped bass. For land lovers, chicken, steak and prime rib fit the bill. End with desserts such as pecan pie, a chocolate bag filled with white chocolate mousse and fruit, flourless chocolate cake and tiramisù. McCormick & Schmick's provides an upscale experience in the DTC area.

McCormick's Fish House & Bar

Cuisine: Seafood, Steakhouse
Open: B-L-D: Daily
Mccormickandschmicks.com

1659 Wazee St   303-825-1107
Denver, 80202
17th & Wazee

Price: $$$-$$$$ **Patio:** Yes
Reservations: Yes   **Brunch:** No
Location: LoDo

McCormick's, adjacent to the historic Oxford Hotel just one block from Union Station has been updated. The menu is the same as McCormick and Schmick's.

The Mediterranean Restaurant

Cuisine: Greek, Mediterranean
Open: L-D: Daily
Themedboulder.com

1002 Walnut St   303-444-5335
Boulder, 80302
Walnut & 10th

Price: $$-$$$ **Patio:** Yes
Reservations: Yes   **Brunch:** No
Location: Boulder

This colorful eatery is spacious, stretching several rooms wide with sunlight pouring through all windows. Imported tiles splash color on the white walls and fresh flowers are arranged on every table. Outside a decorative sun smiles over thriving potted plants on the comfortable enclosed patio. Almost everyone in Boulder drops by for a visit at some point looking for delicious Mediterranean fare prepared by the talented chef. Start with tapas such as grilled strip steak with blue cheese, Brie with roasted garlic, black bean and garbanzo hummus, tomato bruschetta, fried calamari, chicken satay and several daily specials. Share several of these for a meal. Don't miss the mushroom bisque if it's the soup of the day. For your entrée try coq au vin, a juicy roasted chicken served on a bed of whipped potatoes. Other options include terrific wood-fired pizza, fish grilled with garlic and lemon and several versions of paella. Order dessert- the pastry chef consistently changes the possibilities and all are terrific. The wine list is great and service shines. The Med continues to wow crowds in Boulder.

The Melting Pot

K: Great atmosphere! Cheese + chocolate courses are the best! Main entré is a little plain, but comes with great dressings!

3

J: Always fun to cook your own "food" and enjoy company. Super tasty!

Cuisine: Fondue
Open: L-D: Daily
Meltingpot.com

2707 W Main St
Littleton, 80120
Santa Fe & Main

303-794-5666

Price: $$$-$$$$ **Patio:** Yes
Reservations: Yes   **Brunch:** No
Location: Littleton, Louisville

When it comes to fondue, the Melting Pot has cornered the market on cool locations. The downtown Littleton restaurant is housed in the former Littleton Library, a quaint brick building that dates to around 1916. Louisville's Melting Pot is in the Old Mine Shaft Building and features photography and images from long before Main Street was paved. Both locations are perfect for couples and groups looking for a good time. In addition to the basic cheese, meat and lobster, you can try teriyaki sirloin, vegetarian or Cajun-spiced andouille sausage fondues. For dessert, skip plain-old chocolate in favor of the gourmet flaming turtle or the cookies-and-cream marshmallow dream. Try mixing your chocolate with several suggested liqueurs for a more flavorful, heady experience. Get creative and happy dipping!

Mercantile dining & provision

Cuisine: American
Open: B-L-D: Daily
Mercantiledenver.com

1701 Wynkoop St
Denver, 80202
Wynkoop & 17th

720-460-3733

Price: $$$$ **Patio:** Yes
Reservations: Yes   **Brunch:** No
Location: LoDo, Union Station

Mercantile dining & provision brings a fabulous concept to both locals and travelers at the historic Denver Union Station. The space is awesome and the largest in the development with an interior that lives up to the name. A huge bar winds around the entire front space. Market items are displayed along the walls around the showcase open kitchen complete with a chef's table. Warm woods, an awesome tile floor and bar seating greet you. In the dining room, feast your eyes on the turquoise upholstered chairs situated around lovely tables and banquettes. The dining room is dinner only while the market opens early morning. Breakfast and lunch are available and you can grab a seat, but it is serve yourself until dinner service begins. Chef/proprietor Alex Seidel has earned numerous national awards and also owns the popular Fruition. His great talent and touches are apparent here. With Executive Chef Matt Vawter at the helm, the menu is extraordinary in choices and tastes. Start with grilled naan and lamb rillettes, chickpea soup, green strawberry and rhubarb salad. More amazing choices include shishito peppers, carbonara with faro and marrow bone with carrot pancakes, mussels, and halibut cheeks. The Market Provisions platter of cured meats, cheeses, rillettes, pickles, jardinière and Grateful Bread is the most popular dish for good reason. All are great for sharing. Divine pasta might be your next course. Do not miss the caramelized gnocchi with pancetta, ricotta and sun dried tomato jus or tagliatelle with razor clams and shrimp. Vegetables take on new meaning with the best broccoli a la plancha in the universe, spinach and goat tortellini and spring garlic budino. Seafood entrées bring scallops and Spanish octopus while the meat and poultry list includes chicken, duck breast and short ribs. End with decadent desserts. There is an excellent wine list and service shines with staff nattily dressed and exuding friendly, helpful attitudes. Mercantile reflects Alex's warm, caring personality and his extraordinary talent. Union Station is a Denver star and Mercantile the perfect complement to this amazing space.

Meritage Restaurant

Cuisine: American
Open: B-L-D: Daily, BR: Sun
omnihotels.com

500 Interlocken Blvd   303-438-6600
Broomfield, 80021
Omni Interlocken Hotel

Price: $$$$	**Patio:** No
Reservations: Yes	**Brunch:** Yes
Location: Broomfield	

Inside the upscale Omni Interlocken Hotel in Broomfield, Meritage is a delightful dining spot. The room is beautiful with a great bar, terrific tables and booths in an elegant and welcoming setting. Extensive windows offer terrific views of the Flatirons as you sit in comfort and enjoy the evening and conversation. Start with wine from the marvelous Sommelier who fascinates guests with his descriptions of wines and stories behind the wineries. Start with excellent breads as you look over the menu. An additional menu featuring the flavors of France paired with regional cuisine may be the way to go. Start with flatbread and pears, caramelized onions and cheese that is a must. Appetizers include seared scallops, cheese puffs with zucchini and mint, a charcuterie and cheese platter and wild mushroom ragout. Beef Carpaccio, crab cakes and foie gras are other choices. French entrées of duck breast, sea bass with black currant vinaigrette, chicken grilled with fruit, beef with short rib ravioli and steak and frites are served with a French accent in the sauces and sides. End with apple tart tatin, divine macaroons, ice cream or pot de crème. With perfect service, great wines and terrific food, Meritage steps away from the usual hotel dining experience and is a perfect choice for a great night out.

Mizuna

Cuisine: French
Open: D: Tue- Sat
Mizunadenver.com

225 E 7th Ave   303-832-4778
Denver, 80203
7th & Grant

Price: $$$$ **Patio:** Yes
Reservations: Yes   **Brunch:** No
Location: Capitol Hill

Diners flock to Mizuna so they can feast on some of the city's most amazing award-winning cuisine. The incredibly talented Chef/Owner Frank Bonanno has created a restaurant that brings a perfect night of dining. The room is not large but it's very comfortable with table and banquette seating and a private dining area that can accommodate up to 15 people. The bar draws you in with a copper front, wood and seating for eight to enjoy drinks and dining. The copper look is echoed in the open kitchen. The front of the house runs with grace and charm, with Frank and his wife/partner Jacqueline bringing a caring touch to each and every diner. The lobster macaroni and cheese appetizer is essential, or try Hudson valley foie gras torchon, escargot, Wagyu beef pastrami, hamachi or spring garlic bisque to start. Spring pea agnotlotti, asparagus salad and frisée with serrano jamon make a great second course. Striped bass, ostrich loin, monkfish and lamb cassoulet grace the list of entrées. Veal tenderloin, salmon, halibut or duck breast arrive with beautiful presentations and great flavor. The menu changes monthly. The wine list is excellent, and every element right down to the warm chocolate chip cookies showcases Bonanno's talent.

Moe's Original Bar B Que

Cuisine: Barbeque
Open: L-D: Daily
Moesoriginalbbq.com

530 Broadway   303-630-1980
Denver 80203
Broadway off of 6th Avenue

Price: $$ **Patio:** Yes
Reservations: No   **Brunch:** No
Location: Aurora, Boulder, Denver, Lakewood, Englewood

When one is craving barbecue in Denver there is no better place to venture. Moe's keeps the menu simple with standard entrées and a list of rotating sides and desserts. Some staples never change, and for good reason. All of the meats are seasoned and cooked to perfection and the ratio of barbecue sauce to meat could not be better. Sides are just as much a highlight as the barbecue itself. Whichever protein you select, do yourself a favor and pair it with the homemade cornbread. The mac n cheese will melt in your mouth and the green beans make you want to eat your greens. Wash your meal down with one of the local beers and indulge in the banana pudding. If you are in the mood for bowling, live music or arcade games, the South Broadway location is ideal. If cozying up to the bar, playing trivia or just sitting at a quiet table is more your preference, check out the North Broadway location. You can also find Moe's food truck roaming around Denver with barbecue delights on the go.

Moongate Asian Grill

Cuisine: Chinese
Open: L-D: Daily
Moongateasiangrill.com

745 Quebec St   303-329-2921
Denver, 80220
Severn & Quebec

Price: $$ **Patio:** No
Reservations: Yes   **Brunch:** No
Location: Southeast, Lowry

There are more Asian eateries than one can count in Denver but Moongate stands out among them. With only 26 seats, the bright colors, umbrellas, fish on the walls and a palm tree make the space feel open and welcoming. Vietnamese, Chinese and Thai dishes arrive in substantial portions at reasonable prices. Start with crispy spring rolls wrapped in thin pancakes and fried. Other appetizers include edamame, chicken satay and crab Rangoon. Pineapple, vegetables, eggs, cashews, chicken and shrimp combine to bring great flavor to the Thai fried rice. Lightly battered and fried whitefish fillets with black bean sauce make a great Chinese entrée. You'll find lo mein, beef, seafood and vegetarian dishes as well, all served beautifully and with a smile from the friendly staff.

Moonlight Diner

Cuisine: Diner
Open: B-L-D: Daily
Moonlightdinerdenver.com

6250 Tower Rd   303-307-1750
Denver, 80249
Tower & 64th

Price: $$ **Patio:** Yes
Reservations: No   **Brunch:** No
Location: DIA

Stop by the Moonlight Diner near DIA for great food day or night. This spot caters to locals, visitors and hotel guests. Order a classic breakfast of biscuits and gravy with sausage patties or corned beef hash, banana bread French toast, omelets or huevos rancheros. At lunch and dinner enjoy chicken wings, nachos, or jalapeño poppers. Try the Aussie burger topped with bacon, cheese, red beets, pineapple and a fried egg or just go for an all-American cheeseburger. Other sandwiches include meatloaf, cheese steak, grilled cheese, BLTs and clubs. If you're really hungry get the chicken-fried steak, spaghetti and meatballs or fish & chips and don't miss the prime rib dinner. A great kids' menu features favorites for the youngsters. Desserts include German chocolate cake, fruit pies, brownies and old-fashioned malts in a fun diner setting.

Moontower Tacos

Cuisine: American, Mexican
Open: B-L-D: Daily
Moontowertacos.com

609 Grant St   303-832-1107
Denver, 80203
6th & Grant

Price: $-$$ **Patio:** Yes
Reservations: No   **Brunch:** No
Location: Capitol Hill

What fun to have some really delicious tacos near all the TV stations. It is right behind Wendy's on 6th and Grant and the place to go. Enter the bright, spacious spot with big picture windows, bold colors and a counter for ordering. Staff delivers your order. Start with breakfast tacos with scrambled eggs, avocado and pico de gallo. Or add beef brisket and smashed potatoes or fajita beef and roasted corn and peppers. There are more build your own optoins. The main menu features super roasted or fried chicken, beef brisket, spicy chicken, beer-infused brat, pork belly and shrimp. Start with those main proteins and dig into so many different combinations. There are several vegetarian options too in quesadillas, chimichangas, chips and queso, guacamole or salsa. Don't forget the tres leches and Oreo cake balls. Lots of sauces to choose from as well as your choice of corn or flour tortillas. The concept was developed in Austin bringing this super style of Mexican delights to Denver. Prices are so affordable at this fun spot for a snack or carryout.

Morton's The Steakhouse

Cuisine: Steakhouse
Open: D: Daily
Mortons.com

1710 Wynkoop   303-825-3353
Denver, 80202
17th and Wynkoop

Price: $$$$ **Patio:** No
Reservations: Yes   **Brunch:** No
Location: LoDo

Morton's remains a popular steakhouse in Lower Downtown Denver. With a classic steakhouse menu and a rather masculine feel, guests are pampered during the dinner experience. The sophisticated atmosphere blends the elegance of wood with lovely linens and pictures of celebrities and customers on the walls. Your server arrives with a cartful of large raw steaks, veal, fish and chicken. Salads, vegetables, appetizers and tomatoes are piled on too. Choose your cut and get on with the show! Appetizers include oysters, scallops wrapped in bacon, smoked salmon, crab cakes and lobster or shrimp cocktail. Salads shine with the wedge, house and the best chop salad. Steaks arrive cooked as ordered. You may want to reserve a slice of prime rib when you make your reservation. Don't miss the luscious live Maine lobster or lobster tail. Shrimp Alexander is a house specialty. Sides for sharing complement your entrée. Big, glorious desserts end the meal. Enjoy the made-to-order warm chocolate cake, apple upside-down tart or soufflé for two as a special treat. The excellent wine list features many exceptional reds. Be sure to stop in for fabulous happy hour dishes in the bar. Morton's does a great job in LoDo and is a smart choice for dining.

My Brother's Bar

Cuisine: Pub
Open: L-D: Mon-Sat
Mybrothersbar.com

2376 15th St
Denver, 80202
Platte & 15th

303-455-9991

Price: $ **Patio:** Yes
Reservations: No   **Brunch:** No
Location: Highlands - Platte Valley

Denver's oldest bar continues to survive the renovation of downtown Denver serving old and new customers just like they always have with friendly hospitality. You'll rub shoulders with business people, road workers, college folks and old hipsters as you listen to classical music playing in the background. Shielded from the street by a fence and some greenery, the back patio is perfect for long hours of relaxation and impromptu parties. Drink a beer or two before your burger arrives. These thin patties hold a legendary place among fans and late-night diners (food 'till 1:30 a.m.). The reason for special raves is the fact they are cooked on a flat griddle leaving big flavor in the meat. Other choices include a spicy Cajun tuna sandwich or a bowl of chili. During Girl Scout Cookie season, Brother's buys hundreds of cases to help the cause. Look for boxes stacked to the ceiling!

Natural Grocers by Vitamin Cottage

Cuisine: Market
Open: B-L-D: Daily
naturalgrocers.com

2375 15th St.
Denver, 80202
15th & Platte

303-458-5300

Price: N/A   Patio: No
Reservations: No   **Brunch:** No
Location: Arvada, Aurora, Belmar, Boulder, Fort Collins, Glendale, Lakewood, Longmont, Louisville, Platte Valley

Natural Grocers by Vitamin Cottage (formerly "Vitamin Cottage") is more than just vitamins! Although carrying a comprehensive selection of vitamins and more - with the well-educated staff to help, there is another exciting aspect to a stop at one of their many locations: groceries and fine food, all organic, displayed beautifully, and with so many choices. The produce is marvelous, and when possible, purchased from the green farmers in the state and ready to eat. There is a great selection of fish, chicken, and Maverick Ranch beef. The shelves are lined with dry items from cereals and nuts to pasta, sauces, and more. Even pets eat well from here with the selection of dog and cat food. You can pick up some prepared items as well. With the friendly staff and great selections, Natural Grocers by Vitamin Cottage is "naturally" the place to be.

Neighbors

Cuisine: Wine Bar, Cocktails, & Tapas
Open: D: Tues-Sat
Neighborswinebar.com

2202 Kearney   303-333-1149
Denver, 80207
22nd & Kearney

Price: $$ **Patio:** Yes
Reservations: No   **Brunch:** No
Location: Park Hill

This is a terrific wine bar with tapas and Panini set in the Park Hill neighborhood. The décor is inviting as you find one room with warm wood, green walls and art from neighborhood artists, wood tables and chairs and a great bar for dining or enjoying a drink. A wall of wine is a classic addition as is the patio for warm summer nights. The wine list is awesome by glass or bottle and there are cocktails as well—and beer. First there is an entire menu of cheeses and meats from which to choose and enjoy with complementary wines. Start with hummus with mixed veggies and blue cheese, Asian crab dip, jalapeño peppers, a divine hot artichoke and feta dip, garlic shrimp, seared tuna tostados, Portobello mushrooms with crab, and olives. That is just the beginning as there are some terrific salads as well, the classic wedge with divine blue cheese, arugula with artichoke hearts, and heirloom caprese bring great salads to diners. Don't miss the Panini: classic Italian, ham, turkey, beef, or an amazing eggplant grilled with peppers, Fontina and mayo. Leave room for decadent desserts of tart, cakes, gelato, and the best chocolate cake. The service is friendly and with nice wines at good prices, Neighborhood totally lives up to a name being everything a wine bar with good food should be.

New Saigon

Cuisine: Vietnamese
Open: L-D: Tues-Sun
newsaigon.com

630 S. Federal Blvd.   303-936-4954
Denver, 80219
Federal & Exposition

Price: $-$$ **Patio:** No
Reservations: Yes   **Brunch:** No
Location: Denver - South West

Vietnamese cuisine has established a vast following in Denver capturing the taste buds of residents from all over the city. New Saigon was one of the first serving food so delicious that fans don't mind the wait for a table. You can't go wrong with anything from the vast menu. Every dish boasts fresh ingredients and a distinctive taste. Be sure to order the spring rolls, vegetables, and shrimp rolled in a soft wrapper. Try a random chef's special if you can't decide, or follow the suggestion of your server. Vegetarians delight in dining here, as numerous selections fit their needs. New Saigon continues to attract the crowds.

New York Deli News

Cuisine: American, Breakfast, Deli
Open: B-L-D: Daily
nydndenver.com

7105 E. Hampden Ave.   303-759-4741
Denver, 80224
Hampden & Poplar

$-$$ **Patio:** No
Reservations: Yes   **Brunch:** No
Location: Denver - South East

Leaving Denver well welcome to New York. You'll know it's true as soon as you enter. This Jewish deli boasts matzo balls, hot pastrami, potato pancakes, cheese blintzes, and lox and bagels. For breakfast, try steak and eggs, blintzes or a fish platter. At lunch, dig into a hearty meat sandwich, grilled frankfurters or stuffed cabbage. Triple-decker combo sandwiches will satisfy the Dagwood in you. Dinner features roasted half chicken, liver and onions, and spaghetti and meatballs. You can even order chicken soup by the quart for medical and culinary emergencies. Don't miss this taste of New York City.

Nile Ethiopian Restaurant

Cuisine: Ethiopian
Open: L-D: Daily
nileethiorestaurant.com

1951 S. Havana St.   720-748-0239
Aurora, 80014
S. Havana & Jewell

Price: $$ **Patio:** No
Reservations: Yes   **Brunch:** No
Location: Aurora

Nile Ethiopian restaurant has a delightful atmosphere with supremely friendly wait staff. Choose from the standard table with chairs to an authentic Ethiopian table specially built to accommodate platters of injera. It is alleged that Nile is owned and operated by a woman who was a famous singer and dancer in Ethiopia. As in all Ethiopian restaurants the meal is served on a big round of injera with extra injera served in a basket on the side. The injera is a sour tortilla or pancake that is used as a plate and utensils. The dishes are heaped on the main platter and you eat by tearing a piece of injera and using it to pick up the food. Almost all Ethiopian food is savory, so the combination creates a perfectly balanced bite every time. While there are many delicious meat dishes, Nile is a vegetarian paradise. Many varieties of lentils are available along with collard greens, cabbage, potatoes, and carrots. The meat dishes are plentiful with an array of traditional beef, lamb, and chicken to choose from. Don't miss the vegetarian combo or the doro wat (chicken prepared with the famous berbere sauce—an Ethiopian magic sauce that makes everything taste fantastic). Whatever you order, you simply can't go wrong here. A note: Ethiopian food is not for the faint of palate. The flavors are bold and the communal plate might frighten those afraid of sharing. But if you are looking for a mouth-watering excuse to eat great food with your hands, rejoice!

The Nickel

Cuisine: American
Open: B-L-D: Daily, BR: Sat-Sun
thenickeldenver.com

1100 14th St   720-889-2128
Denver, 80202
At the Hotel Teatro

Price: $$$$ **Patio:** Yes
Reservations: Yes   **Brunch:** Yes
Location: Denver - Downtown

The Teatro Hotel has done a total revamp on the lobby floor and it is great. To the right as you enter is a divine lobby-called the study. Comfortable seating, warm and friendly and attached to a super bar area where breakfast is served along with an all day, all night menu, and charcuterie too. The Nickel takes over the former Prima space and looks wow. It is somewhat larger with a bar that wraps around the entire space and fabulous banquette seating with comfortable beautiful chairs and fabric on the back of the booths. Great lighting, bright windows, and warm colors complete the scene. Share warm Parkerhouse rolls, hummus, pickles, olives, cheeses and meats. Or go for chicken liver mousse, kampachi crudo or smoked salmon rillette. The TO START course is corn bisque, house made ricotta with squash blossoms, squid bruschetta, pork belly, lamb ribs and Wagyu beef skewers. Salads of tuna nicoise, heirloom tomato burrata, Caesar, and feta and watermelon make a next course. Entrees range from scallops, half chicken, roasted leg of lamb and grilled Wagyu coulotte to short ribs, salmon, and a burger. Sides of veggies, grilled peaches, corn, and potatoes round out the menu. End with chocolate mousse, panna cotta, and more. The cocktails and wine list complements the menu. There is also an all-day/all night menu available here. Service is nice, and Nickel a great choice before theater, and the valet service is a big plus too.

The 9th Door

Cuisine: Tapas
Open: D: Daily
the9thdoor.com

1808 Blake St.	303-292-2229
Denver, 80202	
18th & Blake	
925 Lincoln St	303-832-7027
Denver, 80203	
9th & Lincoln	

Price: $$-$$$ **Patio:** No
Reservations: Yes **Brunch:** No
Location: LoDo, Capitol Hill

LoDo is home to an authentic tapas bar, The 9th Door. The décor is terrific with Spanish and Moroccan influences, and the paprika-red color gives a warm feeling to the long room. The bar is gorgeous, perfect for enjoying drinks with the featured small dishes. Paisley-printed banquettes and booths set the tone for those who want a more traditional dining setting. The menu offers a nice variety of tapas but the "small" plates are definitely sized for sharing. Cold dishes start with green and black Spanish olives and toasted Marcona almonds to enjoy while nibbling on very fresh bread with olive oil. Or try the chilled tomato salad with Cabrales blue cheese, the very traditional potato and egg omelet, or the grilled asparagus wrapped with cured salmon. For hot choices, try fried calamari, fried artichokes, and shrimp marinated in olive oil, garlic, and chile piquin. End with flan, chocolate cake or ice cream. A nice wine list and several Sherries complement the food. Service is excellent and the prices are reasonable. The 9th Door brings something different and exciting to the area. There is a second location on 9th and Lincoln.

Nocturne Jazz Club

Cuisine: Contemporary, American , Jazz club
Open: L-D, Mon-Sat
nocturnejazz.com

1330 27th St	303-295-3333
Denver, 80205	
Between Larimer and Walnut on 27th	

Price: $$$ **Patio:** No
Reservations: Yes **Brunch:** No
Location: Curtis Park, RiNo

Nocturne Jazz Club brings a new element to the wildly popular area called Rino. The décor is very clubby as you enter with dark

drapes and walls, a great looking bar and a glance at a winding staircase. The dining area shows off the stage where live music is played nightly. Both local and national performers will grace the stage. Owners Scott and Nicole Mattson are beyond excited with their new concept. The food is small plates with gnocchi fritto, oysters, a cheese plate, a Cubano slider, and cabbage and arugula salad on the menu. Add farmhouse riffs of olives, crispy beans, pickles and Grateful Bread, apricot glazed lamb belly, squid and octopus, and African grain risotto for all to share. End with sweets, ice cream, and cannoli in a jar. The wine and cocktail list is, of course, a main feature of Nocturne. With a new and different concept and lovely staff, Nocturne Jazz Club is a great option for jazz lovers in the area.

NoNo's Café

Cuisine: Cajun, Creole
Open: B: Mon-Fri, L-D: Daily, BR: Sat-Sun
nonoscafe.com

3005 W. County Line Rd.   303-738-8330
Littleton, 80129
County Line east of Santa Fe

Price: $-$$ **Patio:** Yes
Reservations: Yes   **Brunch:** Yes
Location: Littleton

Look for the charming yellow house and the full parking lot and you have found NoNo's Café. Brian and Sondra Brewster have created a lovely atmosphere in this sunny, large space. A porch around the exterior makes for comfortable waiting or dining, while the interior is bright with high ceilings, quilts hanging from rafters, and antique and sports memorabilia on the walls. Families delight in the warm welcome, friendly service, and Louisiana-style food. Start with crabmeat au gratin, alligator pears (avocados filled with special dressing), burgundy mushrooms or grilled shrimp skewers. For soups, don't miss chicken and sausage gumbo or shrimp bisque. Southern cooking reigns here, with jambalaya, blackened catfish, pork chop, rib-eye, and crawfish pasta. Home-style entrées include pasta, ham, beef stroganoff, and delicious mac and cheese. If sandwiches are your thing do not miss the incredible kickin' chicken or blackened catfish. Save room for decadent desserts of flan, cake, bread pudding, and the signature sweet potato crumble. Nice drink, beer and wine lists are available to complement your meal. NoNo's Café is truly Southern comfort and a place for all to savor the South. Y'all come!

NoRTH Italia

Cuisine: Contemporary, Italian
Open: L-D: Daily, BR: Sat-Sun
northitaliarestaurant.com

190 Clayton Lane
Denver, 80206
2nd & Clayton

720-941-7700

Price: $$-$$$ **Patio:** Yes
Reservations: Yes   **Brunch:** Yes
Location: Cherry Creek

NoRTH brings a great dining experience to Cherry Creek North combining old and new—"old" brick walls, expansive windows, and corrugated ceiling, but "new" wood floors, sleek white and light green furniture with chrome, a great bar and an open kitchen. The cuisine is modern Italian. Start with zucca (fried zucchini) chips that are seriously addictive, crisp calamari or grilled artichokes. Grilled bread, chopped salad, and romaine hearts are other starters. The flat-crust pizza from the wood-burning oven boasts a crust that is chewy, not crisp, with several topping choices. Pastas include strozzapreti with mushrooms, spinach, pine nuts and parmesan cream and risotto. There are many options for entrées. Short-rib osso buco, salmon with roasted squash, Delmonico steak, rosemary chicken, duck breast, and veal chop are a few of the choices. Each plate delivers excellent presentation. Don't leave without desserts of tiramisù and warm Nutella chocolate cake. The upbeat crowd enjoys the bar scene, where seats are at a premium. NoRTH is a popular spot in Cherry Creek North for food and fun.

The Noshery

Cuisine: Bakery, Contemporary
Open: B-L: Daily
nosherycafe.com

4994 Lowell Blvd
Denver, 80221
50th & Lowell

720-524-3893

Price: $$ **Patio:** Yes
Reservations: No   **Brunch:** No
Location: Berkeley

The area near Regis is getting busier by the minute, and The Noshery is a perfect neighborhood spot for breakfast and lunch. The place is charming with a simple interior, cheery and bright with a counter for ordering and then staff serves your food. Andrea Knight who was the former sous chef at D-Bar and Nikki Whitehair, who was making pastry at D-Bar and Strings, bring great food at affordable prices. Start with egg sammi with sausage, cheese, bacon, ham, tomato, arugula, mushrooms-you pick it and the result is divine. There's biscuits and gravy, potato waffles with smoked salmon or home-style waffles with seasonal fruit compote, and yogurt and granola. At lunch pick a sandwich on amazing homemade rolls and filled with chicken salad, flank steak, prosciutto, turkey (fresh made there), and veggie. Antipasta, arugula and grain salad, mac n cheese, and the soup of the day round out the menu. There is a list of daily specials as well. And the muffins, squares, and pastries are to die for. Huge and delicious, go for salted caramel, lemon meringue or peanut butter and chocolate tarts, or whatever chefs prepare. The coffee is great and the staff the friendliest ever. They plan on opening for small plates until 8pm and a wine selection soon. The Noshery is a great neighborhood place—no matter what your hood, it is worth the drive.

Oak at Fourteenth

Cuisine: Contemporary
Open: L-Mon-Sat D: Daily
oakatfourteenth.com

1400 Pearl Street   (303) 444-3622
Boulder, 80302
14th & Pearl

Price: $$$$ **Patio:** Yes
Reservations: Yes   **Brunch:** No
Location: Boulder - Downtown

Oak at Fourteenth is fabulous dining at its best in Boulder. The décor is incredible. Enter to the open kitchen and spy the wood-burning oven, or head for the great looking bar and enjoy drinks or your meal. Great tile behind the bar, super colors, huge windows and comfortable seating make it hard to pass up. It is totally upbeat and casual--it is Boulder after all. The menu is so exciting that it is impossible to decide on what to order. Enjoy a glass or bottle of wine with great bread as you try to choose. Shared plates include tomato braised meatballs, beef marrow, burrata cheese with ramps, shrimp with gnocchi, and calamari. Add the best pork belly, hamachi, foie gras, amazing sea scallops with artichokes, salmon tartare and outrageous steamed clams with harissa and now try to decide. The crispy farm egg, wild mushroom and asparagus is a must. Small plates amaze with clam chowder, Asian pear salad, and the best shaved apple and kale salad with parmesan, togasahi, and candied almonds. Kale is finally on the really good list with a bite of this. Large plates delight with ricotta cheese and spring pea ravioli with grilled lamb belly, salmon, grilled duck breast with forbidden black rice, and chicken with asparagus. Add oak-grilled Tender Belly pork loin or chipotle chili-rubbed beef short ribs that come from the wood burning oven and you have an unbelievable choice of dishes. Each has complementary accompaniments that change with the season, add to the taste and presentation, and are just awesome. Outstanding dessert choices make it hard to decide: dark chocolate and olive oil cake with peanut butter ice cream, lemon and ricotta cheesecake, root beer float, salted caramel budino, honey cake and the best lemon mousse with pistachio cookies imaginable. The wine list is excellent and service is as perfect as the food. Oak on Fourteenth is one very special place. After dining here you will be wishing to return as soon as you can. It is just the best!! What a great place. Acorn, a sister restaurant rocks in Denver.

O Bar

Cuisine: Tapas, Asian, Wine bar
Open: L-D: Daily
littleolliescherrycreek.com/obar.html

2364 E 3rd Ave   303-316-8888
Denver, 80206
3rd & Josephine

Price: $$-$$$ **Patio:** Yes
Reservations: Yes   **Brunch:** No
Location: Cherry Creek

Little Ollie's has grown-in a great way!!!! The super Little Ollie's has another option with O Bar attached with a different concept next door to this favorite place. It's really the same space but two very different restaurants. O Bar is light on the Chinese cuisine but includes tapas and some different items than featured at Little Ollie's. The bar is awesome with huge windows, interesting textures, comfortable seating and lighting. It's a special place for lunch, cocktails, and dinner. Start with sushi rolls and sashimi. Both are delicious and presented beautifully. The small plates are extraordinary with bacon wrapped dates, divine Thai mussels, salt and pepper ribs, ahi tartar, jalapeno calamari and mac and cheese. Then add baby back ribs, hanger steak, seared tenderloin, and Kobe on the rock and be thrilled. The truffle edamame dumplings and Chilean seabass are the best. Just go to order these and indulge in amazing treats with super flavors. Street tacos of short ribs, chicken, or seabass are terrific and a must try are sliders of Kobe beef, duck confit, pork belly, and tuna. For those who want more American fare go for the cheese or veggie burger, the addictive tuna burger, club, seabass, chicken, and lobster sandwiches. Whatever you choose, get the kale salad— well maybe the sweet potato or truffle fries are more your style. You'll love them all. The cocktails and wines are a great complement to the food. The service is excellent, and the place is a perfect hangout for all. O Bar is just what Cherry Creek needs and is a perfect spot for dining and fun.

Ocean Prime

Cuisine: Seafood, Steakhouse
Open: L: Mon-Fri, D: Daily
oceanprimedenver.com

1465 Larimer St.   303-825-3663
Denver, 80202
15th & Larimer

Price: $$$$ **Patio:** Yes
Reservations: Yes   **Brunch:** No
Location: Larimer Square

Ocean Prime takes up a huge corner on Larimer Square. It's a multi-million dollar restaurant with a fabulous first-floor bar/lounge and dining upstairs. The decor is beautiful with comfortable seating, good lighting, wonderful private rooms, and an upstairs bar area that charms. It even features a fire pit, sofas, and blankets. The first-floor lounge is a natural stopping place for all. A seafood and steakhouse, à la carte offerings are on the menu with many options. Some highlights are tuna tartare, oysters, a crab cake, Caesar salad, a wedge, and French onion soup. The seafood selection includes a great sea bass, scallops, grouper, salmon, and crab, lobster, and shrimp. Pork, lamb and chicken are also offered. Pick your steak and sauce (additional charge) with all the usual cuts available. Add sides to complement your entrée. The 10-layer carrot cake is a must for dessert. Or go for chocolate peanut butter mousse. The wine list is extensive and the service top notch.

Odyssey

Cuisine: Italian
Open: D: Wed=Mon
odyssey-italian-restaurant.com

603 E. 6th Avenue   303-318-0102
Denver, 80203
6th & Pearl

Price: $$ **Patio:** Yes
Reservations: Yes   **Brunch:** No
Location: North Cherry Creek

Enter this charming house and on the main level find a focal bar, a comfortable room and nice seating. Look out onto 6th Avenue from the big picture windows, or weather permitting, dine outside. Lovely linens and table settings and interesting art add to the scene. Upstairs is more dining with an intimate feel and smaller rooms are available as well. The cuisine brings Italian fare with an emphasis on steak and seafood. Start with homemade bread with oil and vinegar as you decide on dinner. Go for fried calamari, mussels, ravioli, sausage peppers and onions, aroncini, fried eggplant or zucchini. The pastas are many: clams with linguini, lobster ravioli, lasagna, and shrimp. The eggplant rollantini is a favorite. All entrees are served with bread and a Caesar salad. Seafood entrees include red snapper, salmon, trout and sea bass with seasonal veggies and pasta. Veal dishes include parmesan, marsala, and piccata. Chicken is offered in the same style as well. Steaks and lamb chops please, and shrimp skewers or combos with the meats round out the choieces. There are several vegetarian entrees too. End with cheesecake, chocolate cake, or tiramisu. There are cocktails, beers and wines, and super service. With affordable prices and a friendly welcome, Odyssey is a place to visit in the very popular neighborhood.

Okinawa Sushi

Cuisine: Sushi, Japanese
Open: L-D: Daily
okinawalittleton.com

12652 W. Ken Caryl Ave #E   720-981-9088
Littleton, 80127
Ken Caryl & C-470

Price: $$-$$$ **Patio:** Yes
Reservations: No   **Brunch:** No
Location: Ken Caryl - Littleton

What a treat to enjoy amazing sushi in the Littleton area. Okinawa Sushi brings a real treat to the area. Enter the delightful space where the sushi bar is stunning and the perfect place to watch the chefs prepare the rolls. The décor of white, a stone wall behind the bar, burnt orange walls, banquette seating and beautiful tables set the scene. The lighting adds to the scene and fish on the wall a great final touch. Start with gyoza, grilled squid, divine baked green mussels with mayonnaise sauce, hamachi with ponzu sauce, and crispy, lightly battered tempura. The sushi and sashimi are fresh and marvelous in presentation. All the favorites are there with the best quality in all the fish. The shrimp sushi with mango and California rolls shine. Order a la carte or special dinners of sushi or sashimi that are served with soup and salad. The bento box with tempura fish, chicken, or pork is outstanding in size and taste: the teriyaki salmon, California roll, tempura, sticky rice, and veggies is truly wonderful. There are noodle and rice bowls as well. End with cheesecake, mochi and red bean ice cream. The wine and beer list are outstanding. Service shines and prices are affordable. With excellent food and super service, Okinawa Sushi is a special place, no matter where you live and worth the drive.

Old Blinking Light

Cuisine: Southwestern
Open: L-D: Daily, BR: Sun
oldblinkinglight.com

9344 Dorchester St.   303-346-9797
Highlands Ranch, 80129
Highlands Ranch Town Center

Price: $$	**Patio:** Yes
Reservations: Yes	**Brunch:** Yes
Location: Highlands Ranch	

Old Blinking Light is a terrific looking space, hip, and just a touch upscale. Comfortable seating, big windows, brick, funky chandeliers, interesting lighting, and an open kitchen greet diners in this wonderful restaurant. The patio, complete with a charcoal pit and heat lamps when needed is a real treat. The food is seasonal American with a southwestern soul. Start with chicken queso nachos, a flash-fried avocado that rocks, cheesy grit-stuffed jalapeños, tuna sashimi, and prawn tapas. Lighter items such as the warm beet salad, Caesar, or tortilla soup Taos style make great second courses, or enjoy Nat's salad with rich bacon. Indulge in great burgers: plain, cheese burger, green chile cheese burger, smoked pork or sloppy duck. All come with divine sweet potato fries. Specialties include honey-smoked chicken, cowboy steak, baby back ribs, and halibut, salmon, and beef fajitas. Other favorites include fish tacos, beef red chile corn enchiladas, a vegetarian burrito, a combo plate, and chile cheese rellenos. End with great desserts. Margaritas are a specialty but there are also wines and beers along with other specialty drinks.

Old Major

Cuisine: Contemporary
Open: D: Daily, BR: Sat-Sun
oldmajordenver.com
3316 Tejon St.
Denver, 80211
33rd and Tejon

720-420-0622

Price: $$$$
Reservations: Yes
Location: Highlands

Patio: Yes
Brunch: Yes

Old Major is very unique. Enter to the bar area with garage doors that open, indoor outdoor bar service, great reclaimed wood, a fabulous bar and seating and the place to gather at any time. Every detail in each area is awesome with the lighting of old water buckets, air filters, and more. The dining room with its reclaimed woods and white accents, and the wall décor with light bricks of aerial film photos of Colorado stunning, and the meat curing room and open kitchen something not to miss. A table in the center is available for a special kitchen dining experience. Chef/Partner Justin Brunson shows his incredible talent with swine, seafood, and more. Start with house made pretzel rolls served with mustard butter. Oysters, a lobster hot plate, smoked fish, lemongrass sausage with a fried egg, lamb orecchette, mussels, and foie gras with a rhubarb bar are wonderful in presentation and taste. The soups, grilled Caesar and spring salad rock. "The Butcher" brings whole spring chicken with veggies, Nose to tail with confit, rib, pork belly, ham, ear and vinaigrette, rabbit, pork schnitzel, and a 24 oz rib eye with blue cheese, wine, foie gras butter and duck fat fries. The entrée list continues with seared scallops, striped bass, and halibut. Sides of duck fat fries, Brussels sprouts, French lentils and mustard greens complete the choices. Decisions are impossible. There are vegetarian options that please as well. Justin is so creative and the attention to detail makes each dish exciting. The menu changes often. End with melted chocolate tart, bacon crème brûlée, and macaroons. The cocktails, beer, and wine list are excellent as is the service. Old Major is a major treat and special in Denver dining.

Olive and Finch

Cuisine: Breakfast, deli, contemporary, wine
bar and coffee shop

Open: B-L-D: Daily

Oliveandfincheatery.com

1552 E 17th Ave
Denver, 80218
17th and Franklin

303-832-8663

Price: $$
Reservations: No
Location: Uptown

Patio: Yes
Brunch: No

Mary Nguyen has done it again with Olive & Finch. Start with a bright space with big windows and nice seating throughout though the eye candy is the case of goodies as you enter and then sneak a peek at the open kitchen. Tile walls, wood, and a coffee service that begins at 7am makes this a place to go. Place your order at the counter and staff delivers your meal. There is an abundant array of drinks, coffee, tea and liquor and wine. Eating in, silver and linen are provided as well. Breakfast all day is always a treat. Eggs your way, yummy scrambles, French toast and more along with gorgeous pastries in the case delight. Sandwiches include house roasted turkey, tongue, homemade corned beef, pastrami, ham and chicken to start. These just begin the fillings that are piled with so many great options that it is hard to choose. The Reuben, Cubano, and Woody are a few. All come on great bread with homemade chips and pickle. The soups change daily. Get a bowl or order it with half a sandwich or one of the salads in a smaller size. Those include quinoa, beets, turkey, and bacon, Caesar and specials. You will be full but leave room for the sweets. Brownies, cookies, muffins, chocolate cakes, carrot cakes, cheesecake, and super delicious options take away any thought of watching what you eat. At dinner, there are entrees and reservations are accepted. It's a fun choice on 17th Ave.

Ophelia's Electric Soapbox

Cuisine: American, Bar

Open: BR: Sat-Sun, D:Tue-Sun
opheliasdenver.com

1215 29t St.   303-993-8023
Denver, 80202
20th between Lawrence and Larimer

Price: $$-$$$ **Patio:** Yes
Reservations: Yes   **Brunch:** Yes
Location: LoDo

Ophelia's brings excitement to Denver with a third brilliant concept of Justin Cucci. The place is massive and creates an ambience of combining a night club with a restaurant and wow! Once a brothel and then a peep show house, the sensual feel continues throughout the place. Enter and walk into a sexy, funky, area with romantic velvet couches on one corner next to the bar that takes a huge space in the main room, done with pinball machines as the top. It is awesome. The art on the walls and poster-like pictures are totally seductive, particularly the gorgeous lady who inspired the boudoir theme and stirred Justin to choose the name, Ophelia. Tables and booths surround the area with an atrium that overlooks the lower level where a huge old movie screen, (visible from upstairs), a stage, seating for live music, disc jockeys, and private events fill the room. The downstairs Jägermeister bar made of 4,000 bottles is a show stopper. Low seating in this area can be changed if the event warrants. It has to be seen to appreciate the details including the lighting, yard sticks made into bathroom doors and more. The food, wine, and service match the ambience in quality and excitement. Start with divine cornbread served in an iron skillet and from the brothel boards choose the cheese incident, divine scallops with house hot sauce served in a dropper, and wild boar sausages in a blanket. The chilled spring pea soup is worth the trip as are the crispy Brussels sprouts and kale salad with chicken, avocado, bacon, egg, and dates. Still in the soup and salad section enjoy lamb gyro or roasted baby carrots to die for. Small plates bring mussels, duck wings and ribs. More to come with burgers of ostrich, veggie or bison and arepas or Monte Cristo remix. Entrees of NY strip and frites, salmon, and a perfect roasted half chicken make decisions impossible. Sweets if you dare include vanilla bean cheesecake, s'more cake, and smoked salt caramel. The wine, cocktail and beer list complement the food perfectly. And as no detail is overlooked, there is valet parking available for guests. Ophelia's is totally unique in Denver and it will tantalize you in décor and food from beginning to end.

Original Pancake House

Cuisine: American, Breakfast
Open: B-L: Daily
originalpancakehouse.com

8000 E Belleview Ave	303-224-0093
Greenwood Village, 80111	
Belleview & Ulster (DTC)	
5900 S. University Blvd.	303-795-0573
Greenwood Village, 80121	
University & Orchard	

Price: $$ **Patio:** No
Reservations: No   **Brunch:** No
Location: Denver Tech Center, Greenwood Village

When you're wondering where to go for breakfast one answer is the Original Pancake House. It serves fantastic breakfasts every day in two locations. You'll know you're there when you see the line waiting for a table. Fifteen varieties of pancakes are available, including pecan, wheat germ, blueberry, and chocolate chip—all are delicious! Try the Dutch baby (apple pancake) that covers the whole plate. The menu also features waffles, crêpes, eggs, omelets, and cereals. The egg-white omelet arrives like a giant soufflé. The quality of the food is worth slightly higher prices. It is a Denver favorite.

Osaka Ramen

Cuisine: Noodles, Japanese
Open: L-D: Daily Mon-Fri Dinner: Daily
Osakaramendenver.com

2611 Walnut	303-995-7938
Denver	
26th and Walnut	

Price: $$ **Patio:** No
Reservations: No   **Brunch:** No
Location: RiNo, Cherry Creek, multiple locations

Osaka Ramen is the first of many places open by Jeff Osaka. Formerly doing upscale food, the theme is casual, and in this case ramen noodles and complementary dishes. The place is small with a huge open kitchen than spans the room, seating along the wall with the white paint accented in a blue city scene-and dragon. Tables and chairs are simple in design. The focal bar for dining is a perfect seat to watch the chefs at work. The menu starts with ramen: Shio-chicken both with pork shoulder, Shoyu, spicy miso, and tonkotsu. All are excellent with noodles cooked perfectly and the broth spicy and delicious. The vegetable is the only choice without pork

but features green-coconut curry, tofu and more. All have interesting broths, ingredients, and of course that soft egg. Bento boxes include steamed rice, pickles and salad and use chicken, beef, tofu or bass as the protein. Fun to see and to eat if you do not opt for ramen. There are small plates of salad, green beans, tofu, peppers, curry, oysters, and fried rice. Enjoy and share for starters as all are delicious. For dessert go for the tea cake, panna cotta, donuts, and tambo tambo. There are a wonderful selection of wines, sake, and more to go with the food and service is top notc. It's simple fun and the start of many by the terrific Jeff Osaka.

Osteria Marco

4½

Cuisine: Italian, Pizza
Open: L-D: Daily
osteriamarco.com

1453 Larimer St.   303-534-5855
Denver, 80202
Larimer Square

Price: $$ **Patio:** Yes
Reservations: Yes   **Brunch:** No
Location: Larimer Square

The Bonnanos have a terrific hit with Osteria Marco. Located in Larimer Square it's open for lunch and dinner daily. The scene is fantastic starting with a salumi stand on the street level for folks to stop by for a snack. Down the stairway enter the big room with a large bar area and lots of comfortable seating. From the salumi and formaggi list you will find a large selection of hand-crafted cheeses and imported meats. Antipasti include meatball sliders, mozzarella en carozza, crochette, and fonduta. The excellent salads are perfect for entrées or to share. Paninis are a dream come true in taste and presentation. Rotisserie chicken, tomato and parmesan fonduta, wild mushroom with cheese, mozzarella and basil with pesto, and lamb with goat cheese are examples of the perfectly grilled sandwiches. Pizzas are amazing with marguerite, sausage, meatball and pepperoni, wild mushroom, four cheese, prosciutto with asparagus, and sausage with house ricotta. The pies have a thin crust with just the right amount of texture and wonderful cheese toppings. If you are looking for entrées, choose pork, chicken, prime rib or leg of lamb from the rotisserie. Leave room for decadent desserts. The wine list works well with the food in both affordability and selections. Service is excellent, prices reasonable, and the whole experience a treat. Osteria Marco is a Larimer Square favorite for all.

The Palace Arms

Cuisine: Contemporary
Open: D: Tues-Sat
brownpalace.com

321 17th St.　　　　　　303-297-3111
Denver, 80202
The Brown Palace Hotel

Price: $$$$　　　　　**Patio:** No
Reservations: Yes　　**Brunch:** No
Location: Denver - Downtown

The royal grandeur of the Brown Palace Hotel flows into the Palace Arms restaurant. After just one step into this 19th century restaurant, immaculately detailed with Napoleonic-era décor, you instantly feel like royalty. From the wait staff donned in tuxedos to the elegantly appointed room with red booths, luxurious seating, beautiful china, and shiny silverware you quickly realize you are in for an awesome experience. As you begin to munch on an assortment of rolls, Melba toast, and crackers you peruse a menu designed to please all diners. While enjoying an amuse bouche, take a few minutes to study the wine list with over 900 selections that earned them the Wine Spectator's Award of Excellence. Indulge with appetizers of octopus, short ribs, and foie gras. Soups and salads are wonderful but order the tableside Caesar salad. Entrées include salmon, halibut, Colorado lamb, and pork. Day boat scallops and Kobe or Wagyu Japanese beef are more temptations. Finish off with a composed cheese course or choose from one of the sweet finales like the favorite chocolate soup. Take a pocketful of chewy macaroons to savor on the way home. The Palace Arms is the ultimate extravagance.

Palettes

Cuisine: Contemporary
Open: L: Tues-Sun, D: Fri
ktrg.net/palettes

100 W. 14th Avenue Pkwy.　　303-534-1455
Denver, 80204
Denver Art Museum

Price: $$$　　　　　**Patio:** Yes
Reservations: Yes　　**Brunch:** No
Location: Denver - Downtown

Palettes at the Denver Art Museum offers an exciting contemporary feel with white walls, a black unfinished ceiling, open kitchen, and gorgeous art. The main dining area is bright with floor to ceiling windows and private dining spaces offering opportunities for meetings and parties. Owner Kevin Taylor delights diners with gourmet dishes presented beautifully. Lunch options include excellent sandwiches, salads, appetizers, and entrées. Fried calamari, Cobb salad, grilled salmon salad, burger, chicken with pancetta club sandwich, and a BLT with avocado entice guests. Dinner entrées include seared sushi-grade tuna, grilled salmon, pork schnitzel, potato-crusted veal porterhouse, risotto, and crispy chicken. An artful wine list adds wonderful choices. Denise Taylor does a wonderful job at the front of the house. What a treat to enjoy lovely food and surroundings—and the incredible museum.

The Palm

Cuisine: Steakhouse
Open: L: Mon-Fri, D: Daily
thepalm.com/Denver

1672 Lawrence St.   303-825-7256
Denver, 80202
Westin Tabor Center

Price: $$$$ **Patio:** Yes
Reservations: Yes   **Brunch:** No
Location: Denver - Downtown

The Palm is an American steakhouse located at the rear of the Downtown Westin Hotel. Not just for out-of-towners this restaurant brings in a mix of local high-powered business people and a loyal group of regulars. As you enter catch a glimpse of the framed caricatures of local celebrities. The large wooden pillars give the room an intimate feel; while the picture windows add great light give it a cozy look. Begin with a cocktail at the bar. Appetizers include fresh seafood selections of jumbo shrimp cocktail, clams, oysters on the half shell, and lobster bisque. The crab cakes are excellent either as an appetizer or your main course. Entrées consist of steakhouse classics with a large selection of fish, pasta and Italian favorites. Try the chicken Parmigiana for a treat. Lunch brings locals who arrive for business or fun. The lunch menu is much the same as dinner, with the addition of salad choices, a Philly cheese steak and a corned beef Reuben. The Palm is well known restaurant not just in Denver but throughout the country.

Panzano

Cuisine: Italian
Open: B-L: Mon-Fri, D-Daily, BR: Sat-Sun
panzano-denver.com

909 17th St.   303-296-3525
Denver, 80202
17th & Champa

Price: $$$$ **Patio:** Yes
Reservations: Yes   **Brunch:** Yes
Location: Denver - Downtown

Panzano, a revered downtown restaurant, resides in the Hotel Monaco. The upscale but casual décor accents a wonderful open kitchen, bar and several private rooms. Soft grays, with red throughout the space, provide a warm modern look which is a perfect backdrop for the excellent food served here. Snag a seat at the food bar to chat with the chefs as they go about their preparations. Service is superb, the wine list excellent, and the food special. Executive Chef Elise Wiggins brings excitement and is known to charm guests at their table or at the bar. Happy Hour in the bar/lounge area is a great time to try out the delightful appetizers coming from the kitchen. Several dishes make a perfect complement to drinks. Enjoy an array of wonderful homemade breads with an extraordinary sun-dried tomato dipping sauce as you decide on your meal. Start with crêpes filled with mushrooms, pancetta-wrapped grilled shrimp, duck-liver mousse, crispy calamari, and Brussels sprouts. Greens with gorgonzola or the grilled Caesar salad make a great second course. Pizzas are freshly made and always a great shared item. Pastas are a special feature here and Elise puts her original flair on each dish. Entrées of fresh fish, chicken Marsala, seared sea-scallops, and grilled ranch steak make decisions impossible. You'll find veal choices, chicken, and something for every taste. Fish specials change often and there are always vegetarian options. Eggplant parmesan is a real treat. End with fantastic desserts. The wine list complements the food and front of the house service is excellent. Panzano continues to be a favorite dining spot in Denver.

Papa Mazzotti's

Cuisine: Italian
Open: L: Daily
papamazzottis.com

2252 Lake Ave.   303-255-8612
Thornton, 80229
SE Corner of 104th & Colorado Boulevard

Price: $$ **Patio:** No
Reservations: No   **Brunch:** No
Location: Thornton

If you don't look carefully you'll miss this locally owned Italian restaurant. Located in Thornton for a decade or so, the restaurant continues to expand with the addition of new dining rooms. Teri, cook, owner, and caterer is either operating in the kitchen or catering an event. Service at Papa Mazzotti's is warm and friendly, making each customer feel a part of the family. The menu includes salads, soups, and breads for starters, plus sandwiches, cannoli, pasta and specialty dishes. The wedding soup with mini meatballs is included with your meal. Homemade spaghetti is the reason to dine here. Choose Alfredo or marinara and add a meatball for a real treat. Other choices include ravioli, lasagna and sausage. Traditional Italian desserts round out the menu. The sundae topped with imported Italian wine sauce is a favorite. This neighborhood spot offers a fantastic night out.

Pappadeaux

Cuisine: Cajun, Seafood
Open: L-D: Daily, BR: Sun
pappas.com

7520 E. Progress Pl.   303-740-9449
Greenwood Village, 80111
Quebec & Belleview

Price: $$$ **Patio:** Yes
Reservations: Yes   **Brunch:** Yes
Location: Greenwood Village

This Cajun fish house continues to capture the taste buds of diners with crowds waiting to get a table. The massive main dining area becomes quite noisy when full. Whet your appetite with a crabmeat cocktail, deep-fried frog legs, oysters with hollandaise sauce, boiled crawfish or a bowl of seafood gumbo. Have a tasty po' boy sandwich or deep-fried seafood for your entrée. Enjoy the fish specials, pepper shrimp, rib eye and mashed potatoes, or shrimp étouffée. Complement your meal with a generous side of dirty rice or French fries. Finish with a slice of sweet potato pecan pie or a brownie smothered in ice cream. The Sunday brunch buffet is popular too.

Parisi

Cuisine: Deli, Italian, Pizza
Open: L-D: Mon-Sat
parisidenver.com

4401 Tennyson St.
Denver, 80212
44th & Tennyson

303-561-0234

Price: $$
Reservations: No
Location: Berkeley

Patio: Yes
Brunch: No

Parisi, a terrific pizzeria/deli/trattoria is truly a taste of Italy. Enter the well-designed space reminiscent of Italian gardens with brick, wrought iron, lights strung across the ceiling and chandeliers. Family pictures lining the walls add to the atmosphere. Place your order at the counter and the warm and friendly staff takes over and serves your meal. Amazingly perfect timing allows guests to be seated as soon as their order is taken. Enjoy remarkable Italian food with delicious plates of pasta, gigantic focaccia sandwiches and specials that change frequently. The pizzas are delightful with both traditional and pizza Bianca choices. The white pizza, with mozzarella, tomato, basil and olive oil, is ethereal. Try the roasted chicken, spicy ribs, tender veal, and flavorful lamb chops, and don't miss the pasta with pesto, or Panini vegetarian with tomatoes, zucchini, eggplant, pesto, and cheese. A trip to the dessert counter is mandatory with great gelato and cannoli. Take home olives, cannoli shells, fresh mozzarella, imported olive oils, and prepared foods for lunch, dinner or entertaining. After just one visit you'll become a regular and part of the family at this sensational restaurant. For a true taste of Florence, delight in the full-service dining experience downstairs in lovely surroundings. Read about it under Firenze a Tavola. Whether dining at Parisi or Firenze a Tavola, for extraordinary Italian fare you will be thrilled.

Park & Co.

Cuisine: American
Open: L-D: Daily, BR: Sat-Sun
parkandcodenver.com

439 E. 17th Ave.   720-328-6732
Denver, 80203
17th Ave. & Pennsylvania

Price: $-$$ **Patio:** Yes
Reservations: No   **Brunch:** Yes
Location: Uptown

Park & Co., the sister restaurant of Park Burger, brings the hamburger craze to East 17th Avenue. The décor is simple with high ceilings, large windows in front, and a cool bar that circles the restaurant with dozens of seats. Banquette seating helps set the mood and gets you in the mood for an entertaining evening. Enjoy foosball or shuffle board or head out to a terrific patio weather permitting. Jean-Philippe Failyau expands his list of eateries with this latest addition. Start with a warm soft pretzel cooked to order and served with sharp cheddar fondue, stuffed dates with bacon, deviled eggs, baked brie, and crispy buffalo chicken wings. The sweet potato fries are not to be missed as an appetizer or with your burger. Salads include a great chopped salad, the wedge or warm spinach. Indulge in a Croque Monsieur or Madame, Cordon Bleu, or Chivito rib eye with ham, fried egg, slaw and provolone from the sandwich list. The burgers are top notch - the royal with bleu cheese and caramelized onions, el chilango with guacamole, cheddar and jalapeño, the croquet with fried egg, ham and Swiss, and the New Yorker with corned beef, sauerkraut, Swiss and 1,000 Island. The veggie burger is great and specials abound. The wine and drink list is substantial and service shines. Park & Co. is a great option for that casual meal in the neighborhood.

Park Burger

Cuisine: American
Open: L-D: Daily
parkburger.com

1890 S. Pearl St.   720-242-9951
Denver, 80210
South Pearl & Jewel

Price: $-$$ **Patio:** Yes
Reservations: No   **Brunch:** No
Location: Platte Park, Highlands, Uptown, RiNo

Jean-Philippe Failyau's Park Burger is a hit in the Platte Park neighborhood. Long and narrow with brick halls, high ceilings, colors of turquoise and coral, banquette seating, and an entertaining bar and kitchen, this is the spot to get a really great burger and perfect accompaniments. Burgers are made of beef, buffalo or veggies. Build your own or go for the Royal with caramelized onions, bleu cheese and bacon, the Croque with ham, fried egg and Swiss, or the barbecue with cheddar, barbecue sauce and onions. The add-ons include cheese, guacamole, fried egg, mushrooms, caramelized onions and jalapeños. Don't forget sweet potato or hand-cut fries to add to the meal. Now for the really good part: indulge in a milkshake, root beer float, lemonade or soda. There is a short but terrific beer and wine. Sit down service and affordable prices make this a treat. Failyau is a chef/partner at Osteria Marco in Larimer Square and proves that something simple, but simply terrific, can win fans and repeat customers. Park Burger should be part of your neighborhood wherever you live.

Parsley

Cuisine: Sandwich Shop, Juice Bar
Open: L: Daily
parsleyandbailey.com

303 W. 11th Ave.   303-893-7914
Denver, 80204
11th & Cherokee

Price: $$ **Patio:** No
Reservations: No   **Brunch:** No
Location: Central - Denver

Nestled in the Golden Triangle neighborhood in an older brick building, Parsley is a breath of organic fresh air. There is a cozy seating area and a comforting menu that combines a good variety of organic and very fresh vegetable juices and fruit smoothies and a nice selection of healthy sandwiches. Get your energy boost with the parsley mix juice—a blend of organic parsley, beet, and celery or Kate's kiss a mouthwatering combo of organic parsley, spinach, celery, and carrot. Or sample the unique smoothies like the chai tea banana—a mix of organic chai tea, banana, soy milk, and agave served with or without almonds. If you are up for a sandwich follow your mood and pick favorites like the roast beef with cream cheese, the lox and guacamole or the fig and brie. Soups bring more comfort to this neighborhood gem with offerings like carrot curry, potato leek, or pinto bean.

Pasta, Pasta, Pasta

Cuisine: Italian, Market
Open: L: Mon-Sat

2800 E. 2nd Avenue #108.   303-377-2782
Denver, 80206
2nd & Fillmore in Fillmore Plaza

Price: $$-$$$ **Patio:** Yes
Reservations: No   **Brunch:** No
Location: Cherry Creek

Definitely a Cherry Creek hot spot for everything from lunch
to catering and carryout, Pasta, Pasta, Pasta continues to wow
fans year after year. After many years, they have moved to new
digs and now are using china, serving wine, and offering more
space for seating to complement the food. It is still counter
service but that is part of the charm. If you dine in you'll see
lots of Denver celebs among those who gather several times a
week for Italian food and more. Enjoy wonderful salads and
sandwiches as well as terrific favorites like pasta dishes made
with homemade noodles, plus Italian-style veal and chicken.
But don't stop there. Roasted or fried chicken, brisket, gefilte
fish, prakes, kugel, latkes, schnecken, and desserts please those
who don't feel like cooking or want to host catered parties.
The meal you receive from an order here is the most awesome
possible. Just do it for yourself for the ultimate pampering.
Pasta, Pasta, Pasta remains a Cherry Creek favorite because
they are the best at what they do.

Patio Mediterranean Grill and Bar

Cuisine: Cuisine: Mediterranean
Open: L: Daily D: Tues-Sat
Patiomed.com

11075 Airport Way   720-887-1004
Broomfield, 80021
Jefferson Airport

Price: $$ **Patio:** Yes
Reservations: Yes   **Brunch:** No
Location: Jefferson Airport Broomfield

Patio Mediterranean Grill and Bar brings a great treat to
the Broomfield area. The space is simple, one room, and not
fancy at all. There is a nice bar to gather for drinks, beer, and
wine, and the dining room features nicely spaced tables and
huge windows to watch the planes take off and land and enjoy
the spectacular view. The patio is a perfect spot for watching
the scene. The view is great but go for the food that is so
extraordinary. Partners Aharon Brudner and Yehoda Eli bring

their foods of Israel and all the Mediterranean to all here. The flavors, presentations, portions, and prices rock. Start with perfect hummus with pita, the best falafel this side of Israel, baked cauliflower topped with tahini that makes this the dish of the year, and fire roasted eggplant with summer gazpacho. Soups and salads are divine but the daytime wraps might make you think you could fly with the spicing to add to the taste/ Moroccan fish, salmon with eggplant cream sauce, rib eye skewers, and an outrageous burger round out the choices. Don't miss the fries too. Desserts are a must, all decadent and a perfect ending. Although very casual at first glance, your eyes will be wide open visually to all, and you leave very full and more than thrilled that you came. Service and caring makes it all even better. Patio Mediterranean Grill is one terrific choice and being new meaning to airport dining.

Patxi's Pizza Uptown

Cuisine: Pizza
Open: L-D: Daily
patxispizza.com

1598 E. 17th Avenue   303-832-8000
Denver, 80218

Price: $$ **Patio:** Yes
Reservations: No   **Brunch:** No
Location: Uptown, Cherry Creek, Cherry Hills

Patxi's on 17th joins the pizza craze in Denver and has some really good pizza. Pronounced, potshe, this restaurant takes up the corner and lots of space with casual décor. Enter to a huge bar, lots of dining space, private rooms, and a super patio. The folks are very friendly and service is efficient and friendly. There are several styles of pizza here. The Chicago stuffed features a yummy bottom crust, lots of filling and a crust mixed in on top. There is the Neapolitan or thin crust type, and even a specialty of gluten free. The gluten free crust comes out cracker like but it much better than most and fun for folks that want to enjoy a pie within limits. Order with red sauce, margarita, sausage, pepper, the works, veggie and more or white pizzas too. You can choose from the specialty pie list or build your own. Nice salads accompany the pies as well. Wine, beer, and cocktails complement your choices. Dine in or order to go. Deliveries are special as the staff gets your order correctly and delivers on time. If you like, they offer half-baked pizza with instructions to finish baking at home, a nice option. 17th Avenue gets busier and busier, and Patxi's is a fun choice for dining.

Patzcuaro's

Cuisine: Cuisine: Mexican
Open: L-D: Daily
patzcuaros.com
2616 W. 32nd Ave.   303-455-4389
Denver, 80211
32nd & Bryant

Price: $-$$ **Patio:** Yes
Reservations: No   **Brunch:** No
Location: Highlands

Mexican soap operas blare from the TV in the corner and portraits of revolutionary characters line the walls of this Mexican eatery. Chips and spicy salsa arrive immediately. Cool your palate with a giant glass of horchata or with liquado de fruita in strawberry, cantaloupe or pineapple. Forget the basics and order something different such as pork chops smothered in spicy sauce with potatoes and jalapeños, shrimp sautéed with hot peppers or Mexican-style beefsteak. If you're looking to order a classic dish, cheese enchiladas, smothered burritos and sizzling fajitas all get rave reviews from diners. For a sweet finish, try a sopapillas.

Paxia

Cuisine: Modern Mexican
Open: L-D: Daily BR: Sat-Sun
paxiadenver.com
4001 Tejon   720-583-6860
Denver, 80211
40th & Tejon

Price: $$-$$$$ **Patio:** Yes
Reservations: Yes   **Brunch:** Yes
Location: Sunnyside - Denver Northwest

Paxia is a unique Mexican restaurant. The décor is warm and friendly with bright colors, comfortable seating, and a room for large parties available for guests. Start with margaritas, wine, and beer served with salsa and chips. There are three degrees of heat to please all tastes from mild to hot hot. The food does not have the heavy handed use of cheese, rice and beans which are a staple in too many Mexican restaurants. Start with ceviche three ways—white fish, shrimp, and octopus, tostadas de tingas—mini tostados with chipotle marinated beef with queso fresco, and tlacoyos which translates to masa and black bean cakes topped with grilled pear cactus, jalapeño, tomato, onion and chicken. Chiles en Nogada: read white and green with a poblano pepper stuffed with pine nuts, almonds, raisins, and seasoned beef covered with walnut cream and pomegranates. The molcajetes: a broth of stewed tomatoes, garlic, jalapeños, and onions served in a mortar and pestle and filled with shrimp, fish, seafood, and cheese is another unique dish. Sides include rice, terrific guacamole, salsa and house made corn tortillas. Dessert is fun with a tower of sorbets over fresh fruit and spun sugar. With good food, exceptional service this is a popular stop for Mexican food.

Pepper Asian Bistro

Cuisine: Asian Fusion
Open: L-D: Daily
pepperasianbistro.com

2831 E. Colfax   303-388-8377
Denver, 80202
Colfax & Detroit

Price: $$ **Patio:** No
Reservations: Yes   **Brunch:** No
Location: East Colfax

This is a delightful bistro in an area quickly becoming very popular on East Colfax. The space is very pretty, inviting and modern with a super bar, and two rooms of seating. Windows open to the street creating a patio ambience. Black, tangerine, and soft colors make an interesting   background. The food is excellent. Start with spring roll, pot stickers, edamame, chicken satay, gyoza, and dumplings. There are several soups and salads including a great seaweed salad and hot and sour soup. Beef brings pepper steak, Hunan, Szechuan and Mongolian beef to name a few. The mango sesame, Hunan, orange, and Kung Pao chicken are great but the chicken with eggplant the best (order it spicy!). You can order any dish to the heat of your choice which is great. There are many seafood options including salmon or shrimp teriyaki, and yummy vegetable dishes too. If pork is your thing, there are many options along with rice and noodle dishes that include a very good pad Thai. Enjoy dessert, a full bar, cocktail, and wine and sake list too. Service is very pleasant, prices great. And they deliver.

Perry's Steakhouse

Cuisine: Steakhouse
Open: L: Fri, D: Daily
perryssteakhouse.com

8433 Park Meadows Center Dr.   Lone Tree, 80124
D154   303-792-2571

Price: $$$$ **Patio:** No
Reservations: Yes   **Brunch:** No
Location: Lone Tree

Perry's is the newest steakhouse in Park Meadows. It's a remarkable looking space with some of the best staff ranging from hostesses to managers. It is huge with a separate bar lounge where one can meet with friends or enjoy your dinner. The dining room is stunning with comfortable upscale seating. Add terrific food and you are set. Start with great wine, bread and a huge list of appetizers to choose from. The fried asparagus with crab is unique and delicious. The chop salad with bacon is just one of several options here. Entrees bring all the cuts of steak, fish and more. The pork chop is the signature here—and should be. It is a giant, so large it has to be roasted in the oven. One is enough for 4 but the brave manage the entire chop on their own. It is carved tableside and served with applesauce. Sides are very good as well. End with decadent desserts. Perry's is a great addition to this area and a real treat.

The Perfect Landing

Cuisine: American, Breakfast
Open: B-L-D: Daily
theperfectlanding.com

7625 S. Peoria St.   303-649-4478
Englewood, 80112
Arapahoe & Peoria

Price: $$-$$$ **Patio:** No
Reservations: Yes   **Brunch:** No
Location: Centennial

To find The Perfect Landing drive to the terminal at Centennial Airport. Enjoy an incredible view of the entire Front Range while watching planes take off and land while you dine. The walls are lined with photographs of pilots with their planes both big and small. Breakfast, lunch, and dinner are served. Omelets are made with four eggs, and come with potatoes plus a choice of breads—Danish, sweet breakfast bread, muffin, biscuit, bagel, English muffin or croissant. If you prefer pancakes, choose from plain, pecan, walnut, blueberry, and chocolate chip. Three different Benedicts give guests a myriad of choices. Sandwiches and salads are good options for lunch. Dinner brings a different feel with an upscale menu to accompany the view. Start with calamari, escargot or Southwestern-style lobster cakes. Entrées include many choices from fish to steak, and a Kobe beef burger, cowboy rib-eye, strip, and filet. Other options include pork, chicken, and veal selections. Atlantic salmon, halibut, sea bass, and monkfish are a sampling of the seafood dishes. End with homemade desserts. Excellent service, a nice wine list, and no "security lines" make this a fun spot for airport dining.

Pete's Kitchen

Cuisine: American, Greek, Breakfast
Open: B-L-D: Daily
petesrestaurants.com

1962 E. Colfax Ave.   303-321-3139
Denver, 80206
Colfax & Race

Price: $ **Patio:** No
Reservations: No   **Brunch:** No
Location: East Colfax

Pete's Kitchen, open 24 hours a day, and is a household name for after hours or early morning dining. You will find workers from the night shift, policemen on duty and maybe even a limo waiting while a celeb stops by after a performance. Enjoy breakfast fare such as pancakes dripping with syrup, pork chops and eggs, or gyro meat with potatoes. Burgers, Mexican dishes and Greek specialties satisfy lunch and dinner cravings. For dessert, indulge in a slice of homemade pie with ice cream, yum.

Pho 888 Vietnamese Noodle and Grill

Cuisine: Vietnamese
Open: L-D: Daily
lovepho888.com

539 Sable Blvd   303-367-4180
Aurora, 80011
Sable & E 6th

Price: $ **Patio:** No
Reservations: No   **Brunch:** No
Location: Aurora

You will have to figure out your directions to Pho 888 but once you find this spot you will be hooked for life. And so are the people who keep this one room place filled. It's nothing fancy-simple tables and chairs, linoleum and some pictures on the wall where you will see three bowls filled with plants. Those are the sizes of Pho. All very generous dependent on the size of your appetite. Start with delicious goi cuon spring rolls, egg roll, wontons or a salad of chicken, or shrimp and pork, or grilled combo. There are noodle bowls, fried rice, rice plate options, but the pho is awesome and the reason to come. The list begins with rare steak, rare steak and tripe, rare steak and tendon, or more steak choices. Then there are bowls with a meat ball, chicken, vegetarian, or shrimp. The accompaniments with cilantro, lime, veggie, and all the regular goodies are so fresh and complement the huge bowl. The broth is outrageous and rice noodles cooked perfectly. There are smoothies, jelly pearl drinks, Vietnamese coffee, tea, and mocha too. It's very inexpensive and very delicious, and a terrific staff makes it even better. It's a go!

Piatti

Cuisine: Italian
Open: L: Mon-Sat, D: Daily
piatti.com

190 St. Paul St.   303-321-1919
Denver, 80206
2nd & St. Paul

Price: $$$-$$$$ **Patio:** Yes
Reservations: Yes   **Brunch:** No
Location: Cherry Creek

If you want terrific Italian food in a wonderful atmosphere, Cherry Creek's Piatti fits the bill. The warm and bright room features an open kitchen, cozy fireplaces, a bar, and covered patios. Baskets of bread arrive with an addictive balsamic, olive oil, and garlic dip. The focus of the food is on fresh, local ingredients. Start with fried calamari, bruschetta or cozze-steamed mussels. Soups that change daily, mozzarella and tomato salad, or a perfect Caesar could be your next course. The grilled Caesar with prosciutto is worth a visit. Pizzas straight from the wood-burning oven make a nice appetizer or entrée. Dinner entrées feature a chicken breast with risotto, veal dishes, fish, and beef. Veal saltimbocca is a fan favorite. The outstanding seafood stew is packed with goodies, while buffalo osso buco draws in many diners. It is worth checking out the pastas that include their signature Bolognese, ravioli in lemon cream, rigatoni, risotto and capellini. Leave room for sweet endings of tiramisù, chocolate cake, panna cotta or gelato. The children's menu is terrific, drawing top ratings with good reason. The staff caters to even the youngest diners and pays attention to the smallest details. General Manager Susan Klos and Executive Chef Mario Godoy make this restaurant very special. A terrific lunch menu, great service, and complimentary valet parking keep guests coming back to Piatti.

Pinche Tacos Tequila & Whiskey

Cuisine: Mexican, Tacos
Open: L: Tues-Sun, D: Daily, BR: Sat-Sun
tacostequilawhiskey.com

1514 York St.   720- 502-4608
Denver, 80206
E. Colfax & York

3300 W. 32nd Ave   720-502-4608
Denver, 80211
32nd & Irving

Price: $$	**Patio:** Yes
Reservations: No	**Brunch:** Yes
Location: Denver - Central, Highlands	

One of Denver's hottest trucks, Pinche Tacos, finally opened a brick and mortar space and the fans flooded the doors from day one and never stopped. In a quaint and fun space at Colfax and York, Pinche Taqueria Tequila & Whiskey Bar brings diners the simple and traditional menu that the truck offered in a sushi-style ordering format. There are musts on the menu: queso a la plancha, the pork belly and the lengua. The queso a la plancha is a meatless surprising delight topped with roasted tomatillo salsa and fresh guacamole. The pork belly is always cooked to perfect crispness and accompanied by a charming tangy agridolce. The lengua is the ever-winning wildcard, a beef tongue taco that blends sweet, sour, and salty in a combination of flavors and textures that can make even the shyest of eaters love offal. There are so many great choices here that decisions are impossible. On some nights they do entrée specials, a real treat. Pinche offers great specialty cocktails and an extensive list of reserve tequilas as well as quality whiskeys. Don't miss the churros with hot chocolate for dessert- they are the cherry on this Mexican cake. The second location in the Highlands is a bit bigger-with the same awesome food. Everyone loves Pinche Taco.

Pizzeria Basta

Cuisine: Contemporary, Pizza
Open: L: Fri, D: Daily
pizzeriabasta.com

3601 Arapahoe Blvd   303-997-8775
Boulder, 80303
36th & Arapahoe, in the Peloton

Price: $$$-$$$$ **Patio:** Yes
Reservations: Yes   **Brunch:** No
Location: Boulder

Located in part of a housing project, the Peloton, you will find a gem of a restaurant that is tops in every detail. Enter this modern/rustic spot—one room with stone, wood, a tech unfinished black ceiling, nice lighting, comfortable seating and a bar where you can watch the wood-burning pizza oven produce the best pies. Chef/Owner Kelly Whitaker shows his amazing talent in every bite. Start with domestic charcuterie and cheese, chicken liver mousse housemaid baked ricotta with wild boar salami, or burrata with house cured pork belly. The wood-fired vegetable salad is worth the visit. Pizza stars and there is none better. The crust has romance and character—if that is how you could describe a crust. It's chewy but thin, crusty enough with marks from the oven, but just right in texture and a perfect fit for toppings of tomato sauce with mozzarella, crushed tomato with garlic, arugula and prosciutto, white sauce, or sausage and rapini. The market menu changes often and features a salad, polenta, pasta, and pizza each day. Do not miss the short rib with smoked potato, the half chicken, and several options for sides. More raves for the sandwiches and calzone. The sous-vide shaved pork or vegetarian fillings on pizza-baked bread are served with the best potato salad with bacon. Desserts are beyond incredible: wood-grilled vanilla, chocolate hazelnut, burnt caramel with salt and maple-candied speck homemade gelatos are beyond heavenly, and the warm chocolate tart, tiramisù, and gianduja dipped biscotti are pretty darn wonderful too. The wine list and service are excellent. Kelly and staff make dining memorable. Try Pizzeria Basta once and you will be hooked.

Pizzeria Locale

Cuisine: Italian, Pizza
Open: L-D: Daily
pizzerialocale.com

1730 Pearl St.
Boulder, 80302
18th & Pearl

303-442-3003

Price: $$-$$$
Reservations: Yes
Location: Boulder

Patio: Yes
Brunch: No

Pizzeria Locale brings great pizza and more to Boulder. Next door to its sister restaurant, the fabulous Frasca, this place is a perfect complement to the more formal dining experience. The space is stunning yet casual and welcoming. A large bar is on the left as you enter and catch your first glimpse of the pizza oven which is fabulous. The big steel oven is surrounded by a pizza bar that curves around the restaurant. Comfortable seating throughout the one room creates comfort. Nab a seat at the pizza bar and enjoy an up close look as the fantastic chefs and friendly staff work. Bobby Stuckey and Lachlan MacKinnon-Patterson do it right as they focus on doing one thing well and being what they set out to be—in this case, creators of great pizza. Start with salads of arugula with parmesan, seafood, and tuna with white beans, tomato mozzarella or prosciutto with greens. The appetizers include grilled veggies, rice balls and mini veal meatballs. Pizzas are stupendous, marguerite, marinara, white with four cheeses and sausage, a pie with cheeses, prosciutto and arugula, anchovy and caper, creamed corn, and many more. The crust is thin but perfectly cooked, the toppings sublime. Don't leave without dessert. They include a Nutella pizza, cassata cake, and lemon tart with meringue, ice creams and butterscotch pudding. The wine list is terrific with choices by the glass or bottle, and service shines. One expects the best from the folks at Frasca, and they deliver. Pizzeria Locale is a total treat and a place to visit often.

Pizzeria Locale, Denver

Cuisine: Pizza
Open: L-D: Daily
pizzerialocale.com

550 Broadway St.   720-508-8828
Denver, 80203
Broadway & W 6th

Price: $$ **Patio:** Yes
Reservations: No   **Brunch:** No
Location: Denver - Central

The first Pizzeria Locale in the gourmet fast food chain hits Denver with a big bang. Owned by the folks at Frasca--and a sister to the one in Boulder--this spot has no table service and you order, go through the line and the pizza cooks in two minutes. The space is knockout with white tile, high open ceilings, huge windows and some super pictures to brighten up the stark black and white. The staff wears red and white and big smiles as you order. Pick one of the specialty pies or create your own. The crust is thin and fabulous and after you choose, the pizza is put in a wood-burning oven and is ready in 120 seconds. Salads come in small or large sizes and range from simple arugula to tuna or capanata. Add your beverage choice that includes a delicious red or white wine and you are ready to take a seat at one of the many tables and enjoy. The food is terrific and the prices reasonable. Frasca and company have done it again with this super upscale fast food place. More locations are opening throughout the area.

The Plimoth

Cuisine: Contemporary
Open: D: Tue-Sat
theplimoth.com

2335 28th Ave   303-297-1215
Denver, CO 80205
28th between York & Josephine

Price: $$$-$$$$ **Patio:** Yes
Reservations: Yes   **Brunch:** No
Location: North City Park

The Plimoth calls itself a neighborhood eatery, and indeed it is a special one. Located in a house in the City Park North hood, it is charming with a fun patio as you enter while inside the one room space features a focal bar, seating along the window, an open kitchen and warm feel. Brick, big windows, green flock-like wallpaper and modern lighting set the scene for some terrific food. The crowd comes and happily waits as there is seating for about 40 throughout the room. Start with totally divine potato chips—yes-can we please have more! The small menu changes constantly but starters include roasted sugar-pie pumpkin soup, a decadent cauliflower turnip gratinee smothered in mornay sauce and cheese, a terrine with warm apple and cabbage salad, and grilled flatbread chowdah. Entrees include a delicious hanger steak, bone in pork chop with an apple and leek smash, crispy chicken thighs with spaetzle, scallops with an oyster-pumpernickel stuffing, and a vegetarian option. All are beautiful to see, better to eat. Chef/owner Peter Ryan shows his creativity and talent with each dish. End with chocolate truffles, divine lemon meringue tart, clafoutis, a tart, or cheese platter. The wine list is very nice to complement the food. Service shines and prices are reasonable. With the combination of excellent food, wine, service, and price, the Plimoth is a treat in the neighborhood.

The Populist

Cuisine: Contemporary
Open: D: Tues-Sat
thepopulistdenver.com

3163 Larimer   720-432-3163
Denver, 80205
Corner of 32nd and Larimer

Price: $$$ **Patio:** Yes
Reservations: Yes   **Brunch:** No
Location: RiNo

The Populist, from the duo of the wildly popular Crema, is one treat. Noah Price and Jonathan Power have created the most inviting spot in town. The look is post-Victorian with washed-down elegant wallpaper that is copied on the seat backs of banquettes that line one wall of the room. Tables throughout the rest of the area feature ice cream chairs while the bar built from rough-cut patinated copper and burnt pine is the focal point. The outside area is terrific as well. The food is designed to be affordable, but eclectic and creative, and the results are inspiring. The wine, beer, and cocktail list complement the food and are priced to bring people back. The menu is designed for sharing and offers unique one of a kind items... A great example of the creativity and eclectic style is the tasting menu for two. The dishes are all served for sharing. Start with the bar mix of popcorn and more as you begin. The apple and parsnip soup, curried chickpea salad, carrots three ways, and lettuce and pear salad might be your terrific courses to share. Smoked trout rillettes, a bacon and egg, chicken liver pate and kale and quinoa delight. Outstanding describes the beet and pea agnolotti, awesome tandoori chicken, fish, and beef round out the feast. That is until dessert: chocolate ganache and roasted pumpkin flan make for a happy ending. Each dish has combinations of spices and sauces that bring out every flavor that combine for the final dish. The six course dinner for two is $65. All the items are available a la carte as well. It's fun, it's casual, it's awesome food, it's reasonably priced, and it's a must on places to go. The Populist is a huge hit in Denver dining.

The Post Brewing Company

Cuisine: Brewery, American
Open: L: Fri-Sat, D: Daily, BR: Sun
postbrewing.com

105 W. Emma St   303-593-2066
Lafayette, 80026
W Emma & S Public

Price: $$ **Patio:** Yes
Reservations: No   **Brunch:** Yes
Location: Lafayette

Two words: Mob scene. Three words: Worth the wait! Ever since early 2014 when The Post opened its doors in an empty remodeled VFW Post building, people have flocked for the delicious chicken and award-winning brews, turning the town of Lafayette into a destination for everyone from true foodies and hipsters to families of all types. Service is attentive and cheerful, whether you're parked in a booth, share table, bar or back patio. Some standout items on the menu include appetizers such as deviled eggs and hot chicken drumsticks. Warning: If you don't try the buttermilk cheddar biscuits, there's something wrong with you; they are addictive, especially slathered with honey butter. Go directly for the fried chicken – do not pass go. Order an individual plate, or share a bucket. The taste will take you back to your childhood. Oh, and it's gluten free too! Other menu stars include melt-in-your-mouth wood-fired pork shoulder, chicken and waffles and hand-carved roast beef. Choose a salad or sandwich and get some sides, such as broccoli pepper slaw, green chile mac & cheese or crispy Brussel sprouts to round out the meal. Imbibe options include a tasty variety of house brews along with a full bar. Oh and dessert, um, yum. Cherry pie, pecan pie, whoopee pie... all are sweet ways to end a fantastic time at The Post.

J: Amazing food and I love the atmosphere. Can't wait to go back and sit on the patio.

K: Love it! Delicious food, good beer, though a bit pricey.

219

Potager

Cuisine: Contemporary
Open: D: Tues-Sat
potagerrestaurant.com

1109 Ogden St.   303-832-5788
Denver, 80218
11th & Ogden

Price: $$$$ **Patio:** Yes
Reservations: No   **Brunch:** No
Location: Capitol Hill

Strolling into Potager you will find a really "cool" restaurant. Ceilings cluttered with steel and duct work soar to warehouse height. Giant windows light the room and the open kitchen sets the scene while the beautiful back garden provides a treat, weather permitting. A small lounge lined with couches offers comfort to those waiting for a table. Enjoy a glass of wine from the eclectic, well-crafted wine list. A real attraction is the selection of wines by the glass or half glass. Potager's menu changes monthly. Start with bread and appetizers that might include mussels with garlic, or a cheddar cheese soufflé. Other options include shredded pork on bread, and gnocchi. Main courses range from duck confit, and pan-roasted monkfish to a barbecued pork chop. More choices include steak, chicken, and always a pizza. Each presentation brings a picture of colors. Finish with chocolate pudding, rich and dark as Christmas fudge, but as smooth as silk. Service is friendly and efficient. Potager is a fun neighborhood spot with really imaginative food.

Prohibition

Cuisine: American, Pub
Open: L: Wed-Sun, D: Daily, BR: Sat-Sun
prohibitiondenver.com

504 E. Colfax   303-832-4840
Denver, 80203
Pennsylvania & E Colfax

Price: $-$$ **Patio:** Yes
Reservations: No   **Brunch:** Yes
Location: Denver - Central

No Prohibition at this place. You enter a really fun bar and pub with décor of the time and great food. The mahogany bar that spans most of the room is terrific in design and perfect for gathering, watching the games on TV, and enjoying a meal. High ceilings, big windows in front, and formidable doors create the ambience. Booths and high-top seating around the room make for enjoyable viewing. The food is way above your average bar with the chef coming from a high-end background in cuisine. Start with elk jalapeño mini sausage sandwiches, braised short rib sliders with homemade BBQ sauce, fries, or hot nuts. Salads are so good with mixed greens or the kitchen sink. Both shine as does the nightly soup. Mains of short ribs, a tasty chicken pot pie with biscuit top, BLTCA, and a variety of burgers from beef and chicken to veggie and short rib arrive on yummy buns giving a variety of options. Add French fries, sweet potato fries and veggies for $2 each and you are set. Do not leave without trying the strudel served warm in an iron skillet a la mode. There is a nice cocktail, beer, and wine list to complement the extraordinary food. Service is casual but knowledgeable and the prices are affordable, Prohibition went out a while ago but this "Prohibition" is one that everyone wants to keep.

Proto's Pizzeria Napoletana

Cuisine: Pizza
Open: L-D: Daily
protospizza.com

2401 15th St.   720-855-9400
Denver, 80202
15th & Platte

Price: $-$$ **Patio:** Yes
Reservations: No   **Brunch:** No
Location: Multiple locations throughout the metro area.

Proto's is all about pizza. Attractive, simple surroundings, a nice bar and a great patio please fans of every age. Good wines and friendly efficient service keep people smiling and coming back for more. Napoletana-style pizzas are irregularly shaped works of art that eschew cracker texture in favor of great taste. A combination of pesto, mozzarella, feta, kalamata olives and artichoke hearts nicely accents the blistered, charred crust. Select another tasty combination—sun-dried tomatoes, basil and mozzarella, or build your own pie from the broad list of ingredients. A variety of salads is offered to accompany your pizza selection. Try them all, but save room for a tartufo or cannoli. You'll leave stuffed but ready to return on Friday night since it is clam pizza night. Get there early while there is space available.

Punch Bowl Social

3

Cuisine: Bowling alley, American
Open: L-D-Daily, BR: Sat-Sun
punchbowlsocial.com

65 Broadway   303-765-BOWL (2695)
Denver, 80203
Near 1st & Broadway

Price: $$ **Patio:** Yes
Reservations: Yes   **Brunch:** Yes
Location: Baker

The Punch Bowl Social is open at 1st and Broadway. The place is cavernous—wow. Enter into a dining room on one side, a living room setting on the other complete with dart boards. Move into the next room and find a second set of bars and yes your eyes did not deceive you—a bowling alley! There is ping pong, shuffle board and more—a Disneyland for diners. The fare is diner food served for breakfast, lunch, dinner, and late night. Start with popcorn, deviled eggs, fried okra, and chicken wings. The soups include green chile and chicken and dumplings, while salads feature a Waldorf and chefs. Build your own burger of beef, elk, buffalo, salmon or veggie; add rubs and cheeses and your choice of extras. For sandwiches choose pastrami, cheese steak, a hot dog, tuna melt, and Thanksgiving choices. Entrees bring smashed chicken fried chicken, mac and cheese, ham, pad Thai, tacos, meatloaf, fish and chips, salmon, and spaghetti and meatballs. There's something for everyone. This is casual fun and a place to let go and bring out your inner child.

P17

3½

Cuisine: French/American
Open: L: Mon-Fri, D: Mon-Fri, Sun, BR: Sat-Sun
p17denver.com

1600 E. 17th Avenue   303-399-0988
Denver, 80218
17th & Franklin

Price: $$$ **Patio:** Yes
Reservations: Yes   **Brunch:** Yes
Location: Uptown

P 17 on Franklin and 17th Ave. is where Mary goes French Bistro instead of Vietnamese Asian. There are some Vietnamese dishes remaining from the old menu like the Pho but the emphasis has changed. There is gougere, mussels, divine grilled squid with pesto and tomatoes, beets, frisée and watermelon salad, and onion soup with a grilled cheese sandwich. Lamb burger, a country French sandwich, fried chicken sandwich, Monte Cristo, and a giant BALT with a fried egg that is a challenge in its enormity. More cheese at an added price is worth it for the salad. The vanilla cake with caramel corn for dessert is great. There are many dinner options too such a beef cheeks, roasted chicken, pappardelle, pork, gnocchi, and sea bass. Wines are served half or full glass as well as bottle. With nice prices P17 brings different dining option to the avenue.

Que Bueno!

Cuisine: Mexican
Open: D: Daily, BR: Sat-Sun
quebuenomexicangrill.com

10633 Westminster Blvd. #600   303-464-1171
Westminster, 80031
Westminster Promenade

Price: $-$$ **Patio:** Yes
Reservations: No   **Brunch:** Yes
Location: Westminster

Enter the space and look forward to upscale Mexican dining. The bar/lounge area is large and inviting with a view of the open upstairs dining area. The dining rooms are comfortable and beautiful. The use of brass, iron, color-changing glass paintings of Mayan scenes, and other details in the design reflect the caring detail of Owner Rod Tafoya. Mark Schafer, who designs all the food and with the chef prepares traditional dishes as well as a terrific selection of specials, And they are extraordinary. Start with chips and dips. Guacamole, empanadas, ceviche and marvelous sopes of chicken, pork, guacamole or vegetarian are a few of the appetizers. Spicy gazpacho with shrimp is a must. Entrée choices include tacos, fajitas, and enchiladas. The fish tacos are delicious and the classic Mexican plates shine. Salmon in a spicy-yet-sweet sauce with asparagus and chiles, a marvelous chicken mole full of flavor, and the chiles rellenos oozing with cheese are not only great to eat, but great-looking as well. Do not miss the paella. Desserts are a must with decadent bread pudding with cajeta, a Mexican chocolate brownie à la mode, and sopapillas with chocolate sauce and piñon nuts. The beer, margarita, wine and special drink selections complement the food. The patio is terrific and live entertainment, terrific service, and reasonable prices make Que Bueno! a top choice for ethnic dining.

Racines

Cuisine: American, Mexican
Open: B-L-D: Daily, BR: Sat-Sun
racinesrestaurant.com

650 Sherman St.   303-595-0418
Denver, 80203
6th & Sherman

Price: $$ **Patio:** Yes
Reservations: Yes   **Brunch:** Yes
Location: Governor's Park

Racine's is one of Denver's oldest standbys for food and fun. The space offers hip, modern décor while the large room boasts a bright interior, center bar and roominess between the tables for comfortable dining. Bright colors, vibrant paintings, and great lighting mark a quirky spot. The menu is full of choices. Start with guacamole, a creamy artichoke dip, nachos or smoked salmon. Salads include a great salmon salad, ahi niçoise, Cobb, and nutty cheese with greens. Pastas range from chicken gorgonzola to lasagna, ziti, and shrimp scampi. If sandwiches are your gig go for the club, French dip, Reuben or one of the burgers. The turkey is roasted daily for the sandwiches and taste terrific. Did you say you want Mexican? Tortilla wraps, enchiladas, rellenos, burritos, and fajitas will fill the bill. Don't miss the fish and chips, steaks, coconut shrimp, and salmon entrées. No one should leave without a dessert such as brownies, ice cream pies, fruit cobblers, and more to end the meal. Breakfast is a treat with eggs, oatmeal, pancakes, and Benedicts. And a favorite extra is that breakfast is available all day! The wine list is excellent and margaritas are a signature. Hefty portions, welcoming ambience, and reasonable prices are what continues to make Racine's a popular choice with all.

Range

Cuisine: American
Open: B-L-D: Daily
rangedowntown.com

918 17th St.   720-726-4800
Denver, 80202
17th & Champa At the new Renaissance Hotel

Price: $$-$$$ **Patio:** No
Reservatioons: Yes   **Brunch:** No
Location: Downtown

The hotel Renaissance is absolutely fabulous. It was a former bank and they have kept the integrity of the 75 year old building with its great columns, murals, high ceilings, marble, and

even the doors to the vault and added art/deco contemporary furniture and accompaniments to the sensational lobby. The Teller bar is awesome, fireplaces around for guests to enjoy, and a welcome feel. The restaurant, Range, continues to bring a feel of the west with its décor. Enter to an open kitchen, a fabulous bar, wines on display, and comfortable seating with views of downtown and you are set for your dining experience. The cocktail, wine, and beer list rock. They have local wine in the keg, and special beers made just for them that continue with the theme. The menu created by Chef Paul Nagan is contemporary American. Start with bbq'd oysters with hot sauce, blistered peppers, and carrot hummus to share. The flatbreads are designed for sharing. Salads of fried green tomatoes and burrata, kale Caesar, and farm greens please or try crispy duck egg and the grilled albacore tuna with quinoa. Add smoked trout cakes, rabbit croquetas, and steak tartar tostadas to complete this section. Striped bass, scallops, chicken, Tender Belly pork, lamb and steak arrive with great sides. End with decadent desserts. The breakfast and lunch menu are terrific. Service is extraordinary under the direction of Tommy Lloyd. Range is not a typical hotel restaurant and is a place for gathering downtown.

Rialto Café

Cuisine: Breakfast, Contemporary
Open: B-L: Mon-Fri, D: Daily, BR: Sat-Sun
rialtocafe.com

934 16th St.   303-893-2233
Denver, 80202
16th & Curtis

Price: $$$ **Patio:** Yes
Reservations: Yes   **Brunch:** Yes
Location: Denver - Downtown

The Rialto Café, located in the Marriott Courtyard Hotel on the 16th Street Mall, feels like a freestanding restaurant with large picture windows, lots of wood and a terrific bar that accents the art deco décor. Enjoy drinks or dinner in the bar or dining room. If you choose opt for the appetizers during happy hour. For dinner start with appetizers of artichoke hearts and green beans, bruschetta and empanadas. Several soups and salads are available for lighter meals. The burgers are very popular or go for one of the pasta dishes. The list of favorites includes roast chicken, petit filet, grilled ahi, a pork chop, short ribs, a Tuscan country casserole and chicken pot pie. End with apple cobbler, molten chocolate cupcakes, and bread pudding. The weekend brunch brings in fans before theater. Rialto is a nice choice for downtown dining before a Denver Center for the Performing Arts event or anytime.

The Rib House

Cuisine: Barbecue
Open: L-D: Daily
theribhouse.com

1920 S. Coffman St.   303-485-6988
Longmont, 80504
The Prospect shopping area

Price: $$ **Patio:** Yes
Reservations: No   **Brunch:** No
Location: Longmont, Boulder

Located in Prospect, one of the funkier areas of Longmont, the Rib House is authentic Kansas City barbecue. Tracy and Merry Ann Webb both Kansas City natives, founded the Rib House in 2001. Bob's sampler platter with brisket, pork and baby back ribs provides a great introduction to K.C. cooking. Sauces range from mild, medium and hot to Jessica's fire sauce. The medium has great flavor with the right amount of spice. All of the barbecued meats are excellent and are melt-in-your mouth tender. Sides include spicy chipotle potato salad and a delicious cheesy corn bake. Other choices for entrées include a turkey leg, and a hickory-smoked turkey sandwich with French fries. Last, but certainly not least, the carrot cake is extraordinary! The menu claims it to be the best on the planet. The Rib House offers plenty of combo platters that can be shared by the whole family. It's a fun spot for all and a great choice for dining in South Longmont. They now have a location in Boulder.

Rioja

Cuisine: Contemporary
Open: L: Wed-Fri, D: Daily, BR: Sat-Sun
riojadenver.com

1431 Larimer St.   303-820-2282
Denver, 80202
14th & 15th on Larimer

Price: $$$$ **Patio:** Yes
Reservations: Yes   **Brunch:** Yes
Location: Denver-Larimer Square. Downtown

Rioja ranks among Denver's best restaurants for good reason. Chef/Owner Jennifer Jasinski, winner of a James Beard Award 2013, and her partner and front of the house, Beth Gruitch who is equally fabulous, create a special restaurant with the best food, wine and service. The totally new look is spectacular and brings the ambience to a new level of excitement. Contemporary, with shades of green, crushed velvet fabrics, comfortable seating and an outstanding additional dining space that is equally

alluring are complemented with comfortable seating and divine booths. The two dining spaces are separated by a wall of wine—wow. The copper topped bar in front and eating bars in the rear remain a big hit. Lighting, contrasting wall design rocks and mirrors strategically placed set the scene. The food and wine remains the same. Start with great wines, a huge selection of breads, and a nightly special as you decide on dinner. Appetizers include gazpacho soup, duck confit, fresh bacon, salmon crudo, raclette, and the signature picnic plate laden with meats, cheeses, olives, jams, and great parmesan crackers. Salads include Rioja house salad and avocado citrus with trumpet mushrooms, goat cheese, and more. The chicken arrives with cauliflower gratin, poached pork tenderloin with divine ricotta tart, and lamb with braised belly. Salmon, scallops, and octopus are offerings from the sea, and divine pastas include artichoke tortellini, black truffle gnocchi, and butternut squash fettuccini with short rib. A special vegetarian feature appears on all menus. End with decadent desserts. The wine and cocktail list are very special under Beth's direction. With phenomenal service every guest knows they are the most special of the night and want to hurry back. Rioja is definitely a top Denver restaurant and a dining must.

Root Down

Cuisine: Contemporary
Open: D: Daily, BR: Fri-Sat-Sun
rootdowndenver.com

1600 W. 33rd Ave.   303-993-4200
Denver, 80211
33rd Ave. & Osage

Price: $$$-$$$$ **Patio:** Yes
Reservations: Yes   **Brunch:** Yes
Location: LoHi - Highlands

Root Down is awesome, heavenly, and just perfect. Built in a 1950s service station, Chef/Owner Justin Cucci has created mid-century modern décor including a bowling alley lane as his bar, 50's Knoll chairs and a phone collection on the walls. A refinished basketball court floor adds to the fun. The bar area is fabulous for gathering with friends for a meal, while the main dining area has booths, banquette seating, and an upbeat feel with an open kitchen for customer sightseeing. The globally influenced seasonal cuisine includes vegetarian and vegan offerings along with fish, poultry and beef. Small plates are outstanding and perfect to share or for dinner. Start with the outrageous carrot and red curry soup or the soup of the moment as all are amazing, including the vegan cold pea soup. Salad presentations change often and are always innovative in presentation and use of ingredients, all showing the creativity of the chefs. Veggie burger sliders on "nun buns," buffalo sliders and duck confit sliders compete for popularity while the risotto with fava beans, peas, and candied walnuts, sweet potato falafel, beet gnocchi, and arepas with mozzarella bring vegetarian dishes to new heights of taste. Seared diver scallops with plantain hash, mussels, and an amazing tuna bring raves. Entrées are offered in full or half portions and include halibut, beef tenderloin, chili chicken, and a to die for pork chop. Decadent desserts include chocolate cake with marshmallow, croissant bread pudding with bourbon butter sauce, fabulous fruit cobbler with lemon grass sorbet, Key lime pie with avocado, and goat milk panna cotta. The wine list is terrific and cocktails reflect attention to detail. Service is outstanding. Weather permitting the garage doors open and the patio is not only the place to hang out but also the place to enjoy the spectacular view of the city. The weekend brunch is extraordinary. Root Down rates as one of the best restaurants in Denver's dining scene and brings fun and excitement to this popular area. The place offers a unique and exciting ambience and a perfect experience from greeting through leaving-with fabulous service, food and wine. They do everything right.

Rosenberg's Bagels and Deli

Cuisine: Deli & Bagels
Open: B-L: Tues-Sun
rosenbergsbagels.com

725 E. 26th Avenue   720-440-9880
Denver, 80205
26th & Clarkson

Price: $$ **Patio:** No
Reservations: No   **Brunch:** No
Location: Curtis Park or Five Points

Oh how everyone longs for that New York bagel in its glory.- crispy outside and soft and perfect in. And that is what Josh Pollack has done in this wildly popular location. Walk in and find comfortable seating and head upstairs to the line where you can look at the goodies in the glass cases. Keep moving and admire the look and take in the aroma of hot out of the oven bagels, and when its your turn, place your order. Bagels of every kind: plain, egg, pumpernickel, poppy, onion, whole wheat, and everything. Fill them with a huge range of cream cheese, plain and flavored, or go for tuna, egg, chicken, or whitefish salad. Or choose the club, the beef, the Reuben, or any combo or protein you are craving. The bagels come with a side of potato salad, slaw, chips, or cookie. The array of desserts is awesome, and soft drinks and super coffee and espresso options add to the fun. Rosenberg's Bagel brings New York at its best to Denver.

Russell's Smokehouse

Cuisine: Barbecue
Open: L: Mon-Sat, D: Daily
russellssmokehouse.com

1422 Larimer St.   720-524-8050
Denver, 80202
14th & Larimer

Price: $$-$$$ **Patio:** No
Reservations: Yes   **Brunch:** No
Location: Downtown - Larimer Square

Head on down the stairs and enter through the bar area and settle down for down-home, smoking-good barbecue. The décor is simple and fun with some great art on the wall, but it's about the barbecue. Start with cornbread, warm from the oven. Go for smoked potted trout, BBQ rabbit sliders, pigs in a blanket, chicken wings, shrimp in bbq sauce, or crab cocktail. The salad list includes iceberg wedge, greens with smoked tomato dressing, cucumber and beets, salmon and romaine, and smoked preserved tuna. Here come the goodies from the smoker: the combo, baby back ribs, beef ribs, bacon wrapped trout, and salmon. The smoked half chicken falls off the bone or enjoy sausage or brisket. There's more with fried chicken, blackened catfish and prime rib. A list of sandwiches made from the smoked items is another option. Russell's offers three distinctive barbecue sauces to add to the fun: sweet, vinegar, and spicy—or some of each! Sides of mashed potatoes, spiced corn, collard greens, fries and mac and cheese are yummy but remember beans and slaw come with the entrées. Don't leave without the pie of the day or an old fashioned banana split. A terrific list of beer, wine, drinks and coffee complement the food. Russell's Smokehouse is a touch of fun in Larimer Square.

SALT

Cuisine: American
Open: L-D: Daily, BR: Sat-Sun
saltboulderbistro.com

1047 Pearl St.   303-444-7258
Boulder, 80302
Pearl Street Mall

Price: $$$ **Patio:** Yes
Reservations: Yes   **Brunch:** Yes
Location: Boulder

SALT brings fabulous design and enticing food and wine to Boulder. The 100-year-old building formerly Tom's Tavern has been totally redone exposing beautiful brick walls, incredible ceilings and woods that create a "new" look with splendid lighting, an open kitchen, and seating both upstairs and in the garden-level space that features an awesome bar. Every detail shows interesting features that bring the design to a new level. Talented Chef/Owner Bradford Heap brings a menu that matches the fun and innovation of the building. Outstanding flat bread from the wood-burning oven, pear with crispy polenta and gorgonzola sauce, cheese platters, an amazing roasted winter squash salad, and wood-fired Manila clams are some of the small plates. Entrées include rotisserie half chicken, a wood-grilled pork chop, New York strip steak, a big burger, and prosciutto-wrapped Alaskan cod. Add a roasted vegetable tatin and a vegetable tasting to please all. The braised Colorado lamb shank is a favorite. End with decadent desserts: beignets with lemon curd and fresh berries, dark chocolate caramel tart, quince tart, and deconstructed chai. The wine and beer lists complement the food and the service shines. SALT, with or without pepper, is the place to be in Boulder

Salt & Grinder

Cuisine: Sandwiches, Deli
Open: B-L-D: Daily
Saltandgrinder.com

3609 W. 32nd Ave   303-945-4200
Denver, 80211

Price: $$ **Patio:** Yes
Reservations: No   **Brunch:** No
Location: Highlands

Salt & grinder takes W. 32nd by storm with a menu of terrific "Jersey" sandwiches and more. The ambience is fun with exposed brick walls, a counter in front to order and an open kitchen in the rear. It's one room full of happy diners-and a super patio too. Comfort and casual, the food is truly comfort. Start at breakfast with a burrito, Italian sandwich on Kaiser roll, The Jersey of ham, cheese and fried egg, the Philly pork roll, Luca with fried egg and bacon while Marco gets the egg with sasuage. Smoked salmon and French toast with PBJ round out that morning yum. The rest of the day and night bring sandwiches and salads galore. Served with matching sides that add to the fun and taste, go for rare roast beef, tuna, chicken, or egg salad, BLTH, Frankie with prosciutto, coppa, ham and burrata, or the Tuscan with mozz, basil pesto, roasted peppers and more. The sausage or meatball sub is a huge hit as are all the variations of turkey, Reuben, and even minis. All come full (huge) or double (huger). The salads of chef, chopped, quinoa, Caesar, and wedge are very good and add salmon or chicken if you like. Grateful Bread gets credit for the fabulous breads on all the dishes. There are cocktails, draft beer, and wine to go with the selection of soft drinks too. Open all the time with the delightful servers who bring your order, Salt & Grinder is the place to be in the hood.

Sarto's

Cuisine: Italian
Open: D: Mon-Sat, BR: Sat-Sun
Sartos.com

2900 W 25h Ave   303-455-1400
Denver, 80211
25th & Elliot

Price: $$$-$$$$ **Patio:** Yes
Reservations: Yes   **Brunch:** Yes
Location: Jefferson Park

Sarto's is one fabulous spot in Denver. Start with the design. White marble meets soft gray and awesome and stunning describes the effect. Enter to a cichetti bar where Chef prepares tastes of his choice to excited diners lucky enough to nab a seat here. The regular bar is just as spectacular with its marble top, comfortable seating and great fun for a drink or for dinner. The room is filled with booths and tables with gray fabric on the upholstery, super lighting, and a wow! In Italian, Sarto's means tailor—so Sarto's brings the perfect outfit. Start with the pattern-great Italian food with a modern twist designed for every type. The fabric translates to everything fresh, prepared on premise from pasta and bread through dessert. Start with appetizers of antipasti, carpaccio, crudo of scallops, fritto that is lightly breaded and so delicious and the pizzette. Textures include arugula romaine with sherry vinaigrette and goat cheese, beet, and awesome salads. Pastas are awesome with ravioli stuffed with ricotta, tagliatelle, Bolognese, and a perfect carbonara a few choices. The section of entrée proteins from the wood burning oven include salmon, brick chicken, lamb, beef, and more. Don't miss the accessories of risotto, gnocchi, cauliflower, pasta, asparagus, and artichoke that are available to complement your meal. Of course you will find parmesan, piccata, marsala, and other favorites with chicken, veal, or vegetarian. Decadent desserts of semifreddo, panna cotta, crème brulee, chocolate tart and gelato end this Italian feast. The pantry next door (actually attached) is a great addition with sandwiches, salads, panini, wine and more along with all to take home including pasta and sauces from the restaurant. The "tailor" has to put on a finishing touch and the wine and cocktail list and great service make it exceptional. The bill is on an alteration slip but do not worries, as there are no alterations needed—and no Valentino prices either. OwnersTaylor and Kajsa Swallow charm all and make Sarto's the place to be.

Sassafras American Eatery

Cuisine: Breakfast, Southern
Open: B-L: Daily
Sassafrasamericaneatery.com

2637 W. 26th Ave.   303-433-0080
Denver, 80211
26th & Clay

Price: $$ **Patio:** Yes
Reservations: Yes   **Brunch:** No
Location: Jefferson Park, Uptown

Sassafras is the breakfast destination on the north side of Denver which has been longing for a great restaurant for years. You'll feel at home with the friendly staff and authentic Southern charm. Beach attire-themed salt and pepper shakers, adorable cloth napkins, and thick wood-paneled floor makes you want to sit in the wooden booths for hours. Once seated, start with the house-made biscuits and gravies (all three flavors) as an appetizer for a ravenous group. It is debatable if the country sausage, duck, or local mushroom gravy is the highlight, but one thing is for sure the biscuits are some of the best in town. The piglets and pancakes are a delightful and spicy spin on the breakfast tradition, while the eggs Sardou has fried oysters you won't want to miss. Sassafras takes their grits seriously and they should. The New Orleans Style BBQ shrimp and grits comes with plump, flavorful shrimp and is a sweet, yet hearty breakfast option, and the Southern Sunrise grits spices it up with zesty green chili. Don't miss the homemade jams, pickled green chilies and peppers, all unique in flavor. During the summer save room for one of their creamy milkshakes. No matter what time of year you visit, Sassafras will make you feel at home and enjoy some southern hospitality during your stay. There is a second location on E, Colfax now.

Savory Spice Shop

Cuisine: Spice Shop/Gourmet Market
Open: Daily
savoryspiceshop.com

2041 Broadway   303-444 0668
Boulder, 80302
Multiple locations throughout the metro area

Price: N/A   **Patio:** No
Reservations: No   **Brunch:** No
Location: Boulder, Littleton, Lowry, Aurora, Southlands,
Colorado Springs, Ft. Collins

Started in 2004 by the incredible couple, Mike and Janet
Johnston, Savory Spice Shop (savoryspiceshop.com) has
locations in Denver, Littleton, Boulder and Colorado Springs -
and is growing across the country too. Savory Spice Shop offers
a large variety of freshly ground seasonings, spices, extracts and
gift sets. The spices are ground in small weekly batches, so you
know they're fresh and amazing. They will happily sell you
small amounts so those big jars do not have to sit in the cabinet
and you can go back as needed. There are sweet spices as well
as savory from which to choose. Ask about the differences in
all and you will get a full explanation, a taste, and even a recipe
if you like. Just walk through the front door and in one whiff
you'll be hooked. Choose from 140 original recipe seasonings,
all hand blended. If you want something special, they can do
it—and do it with style and just as you dreamed that spice
would be. Savory Spice is the place for every herb!

Scalzotto Italian Cuisine from Vicenza, Italy

Cuisine: Italian
Open: L-D: Mon-Sat D: Sun
scalzottoitalianrestaurant.com

88 Lamar St, Unit 110   303-465-6196
Broomfield, 80020

Price: $$ **Patio:** No
Reservations: Yes   **Brunch:** No
Location: Broomfield

It may be located in the corner of an unsuspecting Broomfield
strip mall, but it'll be tough to find a more authentic Italian
restaurant than Scalzotto. The owners and chef are direct from
Vincenzo, a city outside of Venice. They serve up wonderful fare
with quality and passion that has been sorely missed in these
parts. All their pasta are made fresh in-house and the menu
is designed with authentic and innovative ingredients. Try

the Fagottini pasta stuffed with prosciutto and pear covered with a mascarpone cheese sauce, or Bigoli all'Anitra con Spinaci e Mandorle (pasta served with a duck sauce, spinach and almonds). Main entrees are mouthwatering, including Spezzatino di maiale con polenta, which is stewed pork with polenta, or Vitello Ossobuco con Verdure Grigliate (veal shank served with grilled vegetables). And do not leave without dessert. Our favorite was the Meringata, a parfait of mixed berries served with fresh whipped cream and sugar meringue... simply divine. Scalzotto is perfect for a date night, or a night out with the kids. Service is friendly and attentive. The owner's wife is a Colorado lady who convinced these Italians all to come here, and quite frankly, we're glad she did.

School House Kitchen & Libations

Cuisine: American
Open: L-D: Daily
Schoolhousearvada.com

5660 Olde Wadsworth Blvd   720-639-4213
Arvada, 80002
57th & Olde Wadsworth

Price: $$ **Patio:** Yes
Reservations: Yes   **Brunch:** No
Location: Arvada

The School House is one incredibly designed space. It really was a school and they have kept the history and charm. Enter and the host stand is a card catalogue. There are gym floors and basketball floor wood on the tables in the huge rooms with high ceilings while the huge focal bar is filled with so many of their specialty whiskeys that is seems unreal. There is a huge selection of cocktails, wines, and beer as well. TVs surround the room-bet they were not there when it was school, but the sound is turned down. Tables and banquette seating surround the bar room. There are other dining spaces, an upstairs, and patios both up top and on the sidewalk. The menu starts with mussels, queso, pork belly buns, shishito peppers, chicken wings, and more. Salads range from chopped. Grilled romaine with bacon, and Greek to pear and kale. Then come sandwiches with turkey, BLT, shrimp po'boys, prime rib, lamb, and chicken and waffle. The longest list is build your own with flatbread, burger, and mac n cheese or poutine. The list is very long with sauces, cheeses, protein, fruit and veggie. Entrees of ribs, prime rib, salmon, meatloaf, lasagnetti, and spanakopita end the list. The service is very good, and prices are reasonable. The School House brings childhood memories.

Season's 52

Cuisine: American
Open: L-D: Daily
Seasons52.com

8325 Park Meadows Center   Lone Tree, 80124
Drive   303-799-0252
Park Meadows & County Line

Price: $$-$$$ **Patio:** Yes
Reservations: Yes   **Brunch:** No
Location: Lone Tree

In a freestanding building in Park Meadows complex, this new restaurant brings in the crowd. It is very pretty, Mediterranean in feel with an open kitchen, stunning bar area, and private wine and dining rooms as well. High ceilings, booths done in colorful fabric, and nicely spaced tables throughout create the ambience. The menu features seasons with a standard menu and then the seasonal additions. The big thing here—nothing has more than 495 calories—and more important, the food tastes good. Start with flatbreads from blackened steak and blue cheese to roma tomatoes. Appetizers include cider glazed grilled chicken skewers, hummus, edamame, stuffed mushrooms, and tuna tartare. There are many small salads along with entrée size of tuna crunch, chicken, grilled salmon, lump crab wedge, and flat iron steak. The presentation is original and shows attention to detail. There are tacos and lettuce wraps as well as sandwich choices from Banh mi to a burger. Entrée options include half chicken, turkey skewer, steak, scallops, trout, salmon, and branzino. There are pastas and vegetarian items as well. Desserts bring a blue ribbon production with every favorite combo done in small bites and are awesome. Priced at $2.75 for one and $28.00 for the entire array. It's big, it's fun, and really delicious, and a welcome addition to the Park Meadows complex.

Second Home Kitchen and Bar

Cuisine: American
Open: B-L-D: Daily, BR: Sat-Sun
secondhomedenver.com

150 Clayton Lane   303-253-3000
Denver, 80206
In the J.W. Marriott

Price: $$-$$$	**Patio:** Yes
Reservations: Yes	**Brunch:** Yes
Location: Cherry Creek	

Second Home is the restaurant in the JW Marriott in Cherry Creek North, and the décor is stunning. The bar/lounge area has cowhide panels in the walls, a fabulous bar with Colorado wood; fabulous lighting, and terrific furniture in black, white, red, browns and tones that say welcome and enjoy the scene. The main dining room features large windows that open as an entrance to the patio, an open kitchen and the same warm tones. Fabrics are lovely, a wall of bark is the star in the private dining area, and the wine wall is spectacular. The fare is definitely comfort food. Start with the array of pizzas with a thin crust and many different toppings. Appetizers include tuna tartare, barbecue pork sliders, crab cakes, and beer-battered baby artichokes. For choices from the rotisserie, try chicken, leg of lamb, hanger steak or filet. Sandwiches of roasted chicken, olive oil-poached tuna salad, grilled veggies and lamb French dip, and the burger are more options. End with desserts of crème brûlée, molten chocolate cake, Snicker's fudge candy bars with gelato, and oatmeal chocolate cookie baked to order. The wine list is nice and prices reasonable. The lovely patio features an open-pit fire to add to the scene. The bar area is wildly popular. Second Home is a nice option in Cherry Creek.

Seoul Korean BBQ

Cuisine: Korean
Open: L: Mon-Fri, D: Daily
seoulkoreanbbq.com

2080 South Havana St.   303-632-7576
Aurora, 80014
Havana & Evans

311 W. 104th Ave.   303-280-3888
Northglenn, 80234
104th Ave. & I-25

Price: $$ **Patio:** No
Reservations: Yes   **Brunch:** No
Location: Aurora - Northglenn

Walking into Seoul Korean BBQ on Havana at Evans in Aurora is a bit of an Alice-in-Wonderland experience. As you enter the restaurant you have no idea that inside you will find an upscale ambience that sets the scene for dining. For a good time ask for a barbecue table. This is the spot to experience authentic Korean barbecue. If you are a novice, try the combination appropriate for the size of your party along with any substitutions the waiter suggests. Served first is "Punchon," traditional Korean side dishes. The wait staff then will serve a leek pancake that is delicious by itself and exquisite with the accompanying sauce. Next is a spicy seafood and tofu soup. The main event takes place in the center of your table with the friendly and efficient staff grilling your selection of meats. The tables are equipped with unobtrusive ventilation to make this possible without excessive smokiness. As the meat is grilled, place it into lettuce leaves, topping it with a delicious, spicy bean paste and any of the previously served side dishes, and then dip the lettuce wraps in the accompanying sauce. It's a fun introduction to Korean barbecue! While you're there, try the frozen sake. When you want Korean food in an upscale environment, this is the place to go.

Seven 30 South

Cuisine: American
Open: L-D: Daily, BR: Sat-Sun
730southbarngrill.com

730 S. University Blvd.   303-744-1888
Denver, 80209
S. University & Exposition

Price: $$ **Patio:** Yes
Reservations: Yes   **Brunch:** Yes
Location: Bonnie Brae

Seven 30 South is a real neighborhood restaurant that draws fans from around the corner and around the city. Head to the bar if you want to watch sports, have a drink or eat a full meal. Or, have a seat in the dining room and enjoy the bright windows and wood décor. The patio is covered and enclosed with nice large windows which can be enjoyed year-round. Seven 30 South offers a variety of dishes to please everyone. Dip your bread into the pesto olive oil mixture as you peruse the menu. Start with calamari, sourdough bread pizza, soups or other appetizers. Entrées include roasted chicken, veal, pasta and beef. Enchiladas and salmon are musts. Day or night, dig into terrific sandwiches such as the chicken club, Portobello on focaccia, turkey and bacon, and an outstanding hamburger with fries. Salads are generous here. Try the grilled spicy salmon over greens, southwestern chicken, Mediterranean or Caesar. Specials are exciting and vary daily. The weekend brunch is remarkable, with eggs Benedict on croissants, frittatas, omelets, waffles and burritos served along with several lunch items. Excellent desserts make a perfect ending. The wine list offers first-rate buys by the glass or bottle, and service is knowledgeable and friendly. At Seven 30 South, you'll become a regular after just one visit.

Shanahan's

Cuisine: Steakhouse
Open: D: Daily
shanahanssteakhouse.com

5085 S. Syracuse St.   303-770-7300
Denver, 80237
Off Belleview & I-25

Price: $$$$ **Patio:** Yes
Reservations: Yes   **Brunch:** No
Location: Denver Tech Center

Shanahan's is wow! The building is spectacular with Shanahan's spelled out in neon. Enter and be awed by the magnificent lounge with a large bar, well-selected paintings, high ceilings and a display of Super Bowl and Championship rings plus Super Bowl trophies that will knock your socks off! So will the walls of wine with more than 4,000 red wines on one and 3,000 whites on another. More "wow" comes from the stunning dining room which features high ceilings, a wonderful fireplace, white brick, and comfortable seating with booths and tables. You can see the three private dining rooms and an amazing patio from here. The food shines with a menu that satisfies meat lovers as well as those who prefer fish or poultry. Start with awesome oysters, tuna tartare, crab cakes, Kobe beef carpaccio, fried calamari, prawns and Dungeness crab cocktail, or onion rings. Do not miss the burrata or the beet and house salads. The chop salad is worth the trip, heavenly. Classic cuts of filet, strip, rib eye, and pepper steak start the list of entrées. Add porterhouse, cowboy, and lamb chops, the outrageous veal chop, duck and chicken roasted in an iron skillet with veggies. The option of special sauces is a real treat. Seafood lovers delight in salmon, halibut, sushi style ahi tuna, diver scallops, mahi mahi, lobster tail and Alaskan king crab legs. All portions are à la carte, arriving cooked to order. Some entrees include special sides that complement the dish perfectly. Sides for sharing include a must-have mac and cheese, baked sweet potato, Lyonnais potatoes and savory vegetables. Decadent desserts end the feast with must-have fruit cobbler, chocolate cake and the signature ten layer lemon cake. The wine list brings not only fabulous wines but offers excellent selections by the glass or bottle. Service is perfect. Dining in the bar area is the biggest treat where you can indulge in the dining room menu or excellent bar menu for a casual night out. The dynamic and charming Marc Steron, along with his partners do it all right. And Shanahan's wins a championship ring for Denver dining!

Shells and Sauce

Cuisine: Italian
Open: D: Tues-Sun, BR: Sat-Sun
shellsandsauce.net

2600 E. 12th Ave.   303-377-2091
Denver, 80206
12th & Elizabeth

Price: $$ **Patio:** Yes
Reservations: Yes   **Brunch:** Yes
Location: Congress Park

Enter this delightful spot and you know you are going to have a wonderful experience. This is what every neighborhood trattoria should be—warm, friendly and fun, with delicious food and wine. The restaurant is designed with colors of terra cotta and gold, tile floors, lovely oak tables and terrific tableware. Add an open kitchen, a bar with great lighting, and big windows, and the scene is set for the Italian-Californian food prepared to please the crowds. Start with homemade bread with terrific dipping sauce and peruse the wine list that offers many choices at great prices by the glass or bottle. Then pick your appetizer from calamari fritto, Brie bruschetta, sausage with peppers and onions, caprese salad and Sicilian mussels. Salads include arugula, spinach with nuts and berries, a terrific Caesar, or the best addictive chop salad. For pastas try shrimp scampi, linguine with clams, delicious stuffed shells, the best lasagna ever or baked cheese ravioli. The seafood cioppino pasta is a must. Entrées range from chicken, eggplant or veal parmesan, chicken or veal Marsala, an amazing balsamic-glazed salmon fillet and top sirloin. Specials are totally enticing and change nightly. Each dish comes with accompanying sides that add texture and flavor. For lighter fare don't miss the steak or salmon salads. Desserts are not-to-be-missed with chocolate ganache torte with chocolate mousse filling, crème brûlée, the best tiramisù in Denver and gelato. Weekend brunch is as exciting as dinner and a must on your list. The bar is lively and you will always find a crowd. Let Brady, Cole or whoever is at the bar pick your wine or cocktails. You will be delighted. The upstairs patio is awesome. Service is so friendly and excellent, and you will be known by all who work there soon. Add reasonable prices, and Shells and Sauce is a dream come true.

Ship Tavern

Cuisine: American
Open: D: Daily
Brownpalace.com

321 17th St   (303) 297-3111
Denver
Brown Palace Hotel

Price: $$$$ **Patio:** No
Reservations: Yes   **Brunch:** No
Location: Downtown - Denver

Located in the prestigious Brown Palace Hotel which has been open for over 100 years, The Ship Tavern is a mere child at 78! The décor has remained the same over the years, lots of wood, checkered table cloths, ship paraphernalia everywhere, and a staff that seems to have been there for many of those years. A huge bar is lined across one wall for guests to gather and seating is comfortable throughout the room. Start with warm Parker House rolls and signature Melba toast. There are so many appetizers from mussels and calamari to crab cakes and soup. The onion soup is very special. The wedge, Caesar, and house salads are some of the salad options. Entrees start with prime rib (always been there) and the trout. It too remains a classic.

There is a CAB steak, chicken, and some really down home fish and chips with crispy potatoes. There are many desserts but you have to end with black bottom pie! The staff is terrific and wine list excellent. It's a step into the past brought up to the present and a lot of fun with very good food and service.

The Silver Plume Tea Company

Cuisine: Café, Tearoom
Open: Seasonally for breakfast and lunch
silverplumetearoom.com

940 Main St.   303-569-2368
Silver Plume, 80476
I-70 exit 226

Price: $-$$ **Patio:** No
Reservations: Yes   **Brunch:** No
Location: Silver Plume

Driving to or from the mountains or just want to take a ride for a delightful experience without going too far from Denver, the place to go is the Silver Plume Tea Company. The town of Silver Plume is small, just turn off I-70 3 miles west of Georgetown and you are there. Silver Plume Tea Company is an antique shop as well as a tea room. There are old-fashioned hats, all sorts of tea accessories, some of which are old, jewelry, and all sorts of knickknacks. But the array of teas really star with so many fantastic loose leaf teas from which to choose, about seventy or more. Some favorites include Kinnel's Scottish, Genmai cha (green), jasmine, white, gunpowder green and on and on. And then Sarah cooks up a storm of wonderful dishes each day. Try waffles and breads, such as dill and whole wheat, chicken salad, baked chicken, egg salad, Cornish pasties, or whatever the day brings. The quiche is a must have. The pies are a specialty and wow--go for berry, peach, apple, buttermilk pecan, or add cookies, cinnamon rolls, muffins, brownies or cupcakes. All are wonderful. There is full service at fun tables and your tea is steeped to order. Plan high tea, a party, or order and they deliver. Silver Plume becomes a perfect destination with Silver Plume Tea Company.

Snooze, an A.M. Eatery

Cuisine: American, Breakfast
Open: B-L: Daily
snoozeeatery.com

2262 Larimer St.   303-297-0700
Denver, 80205

Corner of Park Ave. West & Larimer Multiple locations throughout the metro area.

Price: $$ **Patio:** No
Reservations: No   **Brunch:** No

Location: Ballpark, Centennial, Denver-East, Fort Collins, Southglenn, Boulder Union Station

If you're searching for a bit of breakfast bliss hit Snooze. Snooze proves that innovative décor and funky, delicious foods can go hand in hand. Exposed brick walls meet glossy wood floors and modern, almost whimsical, 1970s Jetsons-style booths and a stainless steel bar. Above the chatter and clanging silverware, Snooze is refreshing and comfortable. Sweet aromas drift through the air. You can get your normal breakfast fare of omelets and scramblers, but there are dishes beyond the old standards. Start with a wide selection of "bevies," including fresh juices, Snooze's own coffee blends, Numi teas, or a classic Bloody Mary. If you've got a sweet tooth, try the molten chocolate French toast—thick, buttery brioche filled with chocolate and topped with vanilla crème, chocolate sauce and banana-walnut compote. Don't miss steak and eggs Benedict, two delectable stacks of grilled beef tenderloins, caramelized onions, roasted poblanos, poached eggs, salsa fresca and smoked cheddar hollandaise. If you decide to sleep in, Snooze provides an excellent array of soups, salads and sandwiches for lunch, but the number one reason to hurry into Snooze is for pancakes. Try the sweet potato pancakes with bourbon-maple glaze and ginger butter or the pineapple upside-down cakes with sticky sweet chunks of caramelized pineapple, cinnamon butter and crème anglaise. Or, mix it up with the pancake flight, featuring three kinds of pancakes artfully arranged for a tasting extravaganza. And with a full liquor license, you can't go wrong. There are several locations that wow the fans.

Solera Restaurant & Wine Bar

Cuisine: Contemporary, Mediterranean
Open: D: Tues-Sun, BR: Sun
Solerarestaurant.com

5410 E. Colfax Ave.   303-388-8429
Denver, 80220
E. Colfax & Grape

Price: $$$$ **Patio:** Yes
Reservations: Yes   **Brunch:** Yes
Location: Park Hill

If you're in the mood for a sophisticated yet relaxed dining spot, Solera is an excellent choice. As you enter the softly lit bar is the spot to sit at one of the tables or nab a seat at the bar and sip a cocktail or stay for happy hour dining in this popular area. The dining room is totally redone with terrific colors, green walls, fabulous lighting and some terrific photographs to add to the ambience, all complementing the well-positioned tables. The enclosed, garden-like heated patio makes a perfect setting for dining al fresco. Chef/Owner Goose Sorenson presents an eclectic menu full of flavors from around the world. Start with to-die-for Thai-style calamari rings with spiced peanuts, mint and cilantro, or enjoy Hudson Valley foie gras, mussels, a cheese platter and ahi tuna. Exciting salads include butter leaf lettuce with Maytag blue cheese and Caesar. Entrées include salmon, risotto, paella of seafood or vegetables, scallops with mac and cheese, and the signature half chicken. Other options include a New York steak, shrimp with pasta, and lamb. Goose's accompaniments heighten the flavor of the main course. Excellent desserts, including a decadent chocolate cake with peanut butter ice cream, delicious butterscotch bread pudding, and tres leches cake complete your meal. The wine list is terrific with wonderful selections by glass and bottle. Special wine tastings take place every Wednesday for added appeal. Service is excellent. The patio is spectacular, weather permitting. Solera brings wonderful dining to Denver in a great neighborhood.

Solitaire

Cuisine: American
Open: Dinner: Daily
Solitairerestaurant.com

3927 W. 32nd Ave.   303-477-4732
Denver 80212
32nd & Perry

Price: $$$$ **Patio:** Yes
Reservations: Yes   **Brunch:** No
Location: Highlands

Solitaire opens in the Highlands Garden Café space. The new look is totally contemporary with a very different motif. Enter and find several dining areas on the main level and a huge room upstairs. The bar area is super looking and takes up an entire room. The colors of off white and gray are accented with the red aprons on the black of the staff's uniforms. Gray fabric chairs are so comfortable and conversation even happens in some of the areas. There is great art on the wall, and of course, there is patio dining weather permitting. Mark Ferguson has a great resume of his cooking talents and now has his own spot with his wife, Andrea. Start with uni shooter, scallops crudo, big eye tuna tartare, and oysters. Next come braised artichokes and beets, charred octopus with grapes and chorizo, smoked sturgeon, and a braised short rib slider. Ricotta agnolotti, duck breast, a lamb chop, hanger steak, and swordfish round out the choices. End with lemon "cheez" cake, butterscotch pudding, chocolate mousse or bruleed tapioca pearls. The wine and cocktail list are excellent, and service is outstanding. The menu changes daily so surprises await your every visit. All the choices here are small plate sized. Solitaire is a welcome choice for dining in this neighborhood.

Spice China

Cuisine: Chinese
Open: L-D: Daily
Spicechina.com

269 McCaslin Blvd.   720-890-0999
Louisville, 80027
McCaslin & Century

Price: $$ **Patio:** No
Reservations: Yes   **Brunch:** No
Location: Louisville

This large comfortable restaurant is a pleasant addition to the fast-growing Louisville-Superior area. Knowledgeable staff steer you toward wonderful house specialties or mainstays from the large menu. Start with scallion pancakes or calamari sprinkled with pepper and spices. Try the fishermen's feast (white sole, shrimp and scallops stir-fried with fresh vegetables in a flavorful white sauce). The ever-popular General Tsao chicken is paired with shrimp in Shaohsing wine sauce. Spice China is child-friendly and well worth the visit.

Spicy Basil, Asian Grill

Cuisine: Asian, Thai
Open: L-D: Daily
spicybasil.com

1 Broadway, Unit B-100   303-871-8828
Denver, 80203
1st & Broadway

Price: $-$$ **Patio:** Yes
Reservations: No   **Brunch:** No
Location: Baker

As you enter this delightful eatery enjoy the bright colors, tempered steel and whimsical artifacts scattered throughout the room. The menu combines flavors of Thai, Vietnamese and pan-Asian dishes. Start with summer rolls with tuna, spring rolls, satay, pot stickers or shrimp. All are wonderful, as are the salads of grilled duck, beef, and avocado and crab. Entrées arrive on gorgeous serving dishes and are picture-perfect in presentation. Thai-barbecue chicken, royal chicken and crispy duck are served with a pyramid of brown or white rice. The contrasting colors on the plates, placement of ingredients, and perfect spices and seasonings are a real treat. Other dishes include curries, tempura, rice and noodle bowls. Order any to your heat preference. End with fried ice cream or cheesecake. Service is friendly and efficient. A short wine list offers some good buys. Spicy Basil is a special place for Asian food and fun.

Spinelli's

Cuisine: Deli, Italian, Market
Open: B-L-D: Mon-Sat, B-L: Sun
spinellismarket.com

4621 E. 23rd Ave.   303-329-8143
Denver, 80207
23rd & Dexter

Price: $ **Patio:** No
Reservations: No   **Brunch:** No
Location: Park Hill

There's a great little spot nestled in Park Hill called Spinelli's Market. Extraordinarily well kept, Spinelli's is a sheer delight. Enter and gaze at the spectrum of imported meats, cheeses, pastas, spreads, sauces and vegetables. The meat-lover's sandwich competes with the classic Italian sandwich stacked with capicola, smoked ham, Genoa salami, provolone, roasted peppers, marinated onions, lettuce, tomato and house dressing on an Italian roll. On the lighter side the Tuscan is wonderfully satisfying with sliced chicken, Haystack Mountain goat cheese, pesto, Anjou pear slices and arugula served on a chewy baguette. Complete your meal with specialty Italian sodas. Don't forget to take some goodies home for later.

Spuntino

Cuisine: Contemporary, Italian
Open: L: Tues-Fri, D:Thurs-Sat, BR Sat-Sun
spuntinodenver.com

2639 West 32nd Ave.   303-433-0949
Denver, 80211
32nd & Clay

Price: $$-$$$ **Patio:** Yes
Reservations: Yes   **Brunch:** Yes
Location: Highlands

Spuntino is a delightful dining spot in the Highlands. The space is modest and quirky, with barn wood combines with traditional wallpaper and fabric backed banquettes as a background to the focal bar. It is a terrific choice for gathering or enjoying your meal. There are tables scattered about as well. The small open kitchen turns out interesting and creative food. There is a lovely wine list and bread offered if you but ask. Start with antipasti platters, vegetables presentations or warm olives. Then come broccoli rabe or gorgonzola dolce bruschetta, fungi with house made focaccia, or divine octopus with chorizo, and sweet peppers. The asparagus, bacon and pecorino, the burrata with pesto, and panzanella salads are all winners. The pastas are made in house and tagliatelle with mushrooms agnolotti, and gargati with goat are some choices. The main dishes range from eggplant with quinoa and raised rabbit to flat iron steak, chicken and the fish of the day. All come with lovely sides. Desserts are decadent and fun. There is a super wine, beer and cocktail list to complement the food. Service is excellent too. Spuntino is a nice choice for a great night out in the hood.

Squeaky Bean

Cuisine: American
Open: D: Tues-Sat BR: Sun
thesqueakybean.net

1500 Wynkoop St.   303-623-2665
Denver, 80202
15th & Wynkoop

Price: $$$$ **Patio:** Yes
Reservations: Yes   **Brunch:** Yes
Location: LoDo

The Squeaky Bean brings their concept to LoDo with its new space and menu. The new chef is creative and the food shows it. The décor features super woods, lighting, huge windows, and a great bar. The new menu is a great change although still complicated; the food is excellent in taste and presentation. Start with sweetbreads, octopus, chicken pate, or Bangkok TV dinner. The carrot soup is great and a weggie salad divine. On the menu is escarole, Brussels sprouts, beets, and cauliflower soup as well. Entrees of salmon and fried chicken are terrific, or go for bison short rib, rib eye, sturgeon, lamb shank, or meatball in a can. There are many vegetarian options as well. The brownie and meringue lemon desserts are worth the trip. The wine list is excellent and service is truly great. The new feel at Squeaky Bean is warm and welcoming, and lots of fun.

Star Kitchen

Cuisine: Chinese, Dim Sum
Open: L-D: Daily
starkitchendenver.com

2917 W. Mississippi   303-936-0089
Denver, 80219
Mississippi & Federal

Price: $$ **Patio:** No
Reservations: No   **Brunch:** No
Location: South Federal

Dim Sum is the tasty Chinese equivalent to the American brunch and can even be compared to the Spanish tapas of small plates. When served in the traditional Chinese manner in an authentic Chinese setting at the Star Kitchen in Denver, it is a not-to-be-missed experience. The Star Kitchen in south Denver is a veritable treasure house of the best of Chinese cuisine at any time of day. The restaurant offers dim sum on the weekend and a regular menu every day of the week, including hot pot, banquet and lunch specials. But don't deny yourself the pleasure of dim sum...you take your seat amid diners enjoying choosing among the plates as servers roam the restaurant in Chinese style, with carts of incredible gourmet temptations including more than 50 items to please your palate! Try the shrimp-stuffed eggplant, the crystal leek dumpling, the steamed BBQ pork bun, clams with black bean sauce, the cilantro dumpling and don't miss the sticky rice or the fried noodles with special sauce. If your taste runs to congee, you'll find it at Star Kitchen. Would you like dessert? Have the mango pudding or Chinese angel cake. And all of this at a price that delights the budget as well as the appetite, plates with four pieces run from $2.20 to $5.75, the variety changes on any given day and time. The regular menu is just as extensive and satisfying to consider. Seafood is a specialty here every time of day; shrimp, scallop, eel, clams and lobster abound in true Oriental dishes perfectly prepared by practiced chefs. This is the place to finally try those dishes that have always interested you but you could never find the time or place to indulge!

Star of India

Cuisine: Indian
Open: L-D: Daily
starofindiadenver.com

3102 South Parker Rd.   303-755-1921
Aurora, 80014
Dartmouth & Parker Rd.

Price: $$ **Patio:** No
Reservations: No   **Brunch:** No
Location: Aurora

Located in an unassuming strip shopping center, Star of India has been family owned and operated since 1996. The atmosphere is casual and welcoming. Appetizers include samosas and wonderful vegetable pakoras (fritters). For entrées, select terrific tandoori dishes, rice dishes or a nice variety of vegetarian dishes. There is an extensive selection of traditional Indian sauces such as masala, curry, vindaloo, korma and saag which can be prepared with chicken, lamb, fish or shrimp. The chicken makhani is outstanding. The naan and garlic naan are both wonderful, but don't miss the kabli naan made with nuts and raisins. For dessert, try kheer, or pistachio or mango kulfi. There is a full service bar that includes Indian beverages such as lassi and chai. The very reasonably priced lunch buffet is available daily and on Wednesday nights there is a special vegetarian buffet. They offer carryout, delivery and catering along with a private party room. The staff is eager to ensure that your meal is perfect and prices are reasonable. When you want Indian food in a welcoming casual environment Star of India is a perfect choice.

Steakhouse 10

Cuisine: Steakhouse
Open: L: Mon-Fri, D: Mon- Sat
Steakhouse10.com

3517 S. Elati St.   303-789-0911
Englewood, 80110
Hampden & Elati

Price: $$$$ **Patio:** No
Reservations: Yes   **Brunch:** No
Location: Englewood

Steakhouse 10, a warm and welcoming small restaurant, puts a different twist on steak in the Denver area. Pretty woodwork, a large bar, comfortable seating, nice lighting and lovely welcome diners daily. The feeling is totally upbeat. Warm bread is the perfect beginning to your meal. Start with saganaki, imported kasseri cheese, fried and flamed with brandy. As the terrific staff lights the fire, they give a choral "opa!" signaling that you are ready to enjoy this treat. You will be hooked the moment you taste it, and the scrumptious cheese disappears in seconds. There are other appetizers but a very special one is their presentation of buttery rich escargot. Soup or salad accompanies each entrée. The house salad, a wedge with blue cheese or a terrific Caesar are available. The Greek salad, done "island style," is incredible with feta, tomatoes, onions, peppers and olives, but no lettuce. Prime filet, New York strip, rib-eye and gangster steak are prepared exactly as ordered. Chicken, lamb, pork and fish including grilled salmon round out the menu. Seasonal vegetables and a choice of potatoes or rice complete the plate. For dessert don't miss rich decadent chocolate mousse, baklava or the amazing chocolate layer cake à la mode. A private dining area offers a great spot for parties. Dine at the bar for a different experience and wherever you choose, the wine list and service rock. You'll be delighted with the delicious food and the warm Greek hospitality at Steakhouse 10. The Kallas family, Costa and Pete, make you part of their family when you visit this charming restaurant.

Steuben's

Cuisine: American
Open: L-D: Daily, BR: Sat-Sun
steubens.com

523 E. 17th Ave.   303-830-1001
Denver, 80203
17th & Pearl

Price: $$ **Patio:** Yes
Reservations: No   **Brunch:** Yes
Location: Uptown, Arvada

Memories of comfort food return in grand style at Steuben's, owned by the charming Josh and Jen Wolkon, who also own Vesta Grill and Ace. The space is casual and fun with comfortable seating. Pick a table or grab a stool at the large friendly bar. Opt for outdoor seating in the front of the restaurant or at the big patio area on the side weather permitting. An entire section of the restaurant is devoted to take-out with a board listing all the dishes available. The menu is fun diner food with an upscale touch. Start with garlic shrimp, chile-soy chicken wings, baked clams, Chinese ribs, deviled eggs, mussels, meatballs or spicy hot green chili. Pick entrées like braised short ribs, Memphis barbecue ribs, cioppino and pan-roasted chicken as some choices. Fried chicken with mashed potatoes, biscuits and gravy is a favorite. Don't miss the grilled veggie, and the lime-chile chicken sandwiches. Diners love the Maine lobster roll, rich and chunky on a special roll. End with decadent desserts of chocolate cake, brownie à la mode, apple pie, butterscotch pudding, and ice cream. There are several fun drinks available, ranging from a milk shake to your choice of super cocktails and wine. Enjoy the wildly popular brunch on Saturday and Sunday. The staff is terrific which makes your visit complete. Steuben's is a perfect neighborhood hangout and just what a diner should be. Steuben's 2 is now open in Arvada.

Steve's Snappin' Dogs

Cuisine: American
Open: L-D: Daily
stevessnappindogs.com

3525 E. Colfax   303-333-7627
Denver, 80206
E. Colfax & Monroe

Price: $ **Patio:** Yes
Reservations: No   **Brunch:** No
Location: East Colfax

Drive up to the sleek, fun building and head on in. Order at the counter and grab a seat. The hot dogs come directly from New Jersey. There's the plain or the Chicago dog with spicy mustard, green relish, red onion, tomato, celery salt and a dill pickle. The Jersey is served with spicy mustard, green relish, caraway sauerkraut, red onions and sliced bacon. There are options for kosher dogs, low-carb dogs and vegetarian dogs. Other toppings include chili con carne, cheddar cheese, coleslaw and onions. If you aren't in the mood for a hot dog, order a smash burger, the gobbler (grilled turkey, Swiss and cranberry mayo on sourdough) or the garden burger. Sides of bacon, green chile, and deep-fried green beans and carrot sticks enhance the experience. Enjoy skin-on or chili-cheese fries or onion rings. While there, try the fresh-squeezed lemonade or limeade, or the decadent frozen hot chocolate. Other sweets include a frozen banana on a stick and Famous Amos cookies. Stop in for breakfast for the fried egg and cheddar-jack cheese burrito. Or try the fried egg on grilled sourdough with lots of add-ons. An enclosed heated patio provides additional seating for more fans. And don't forget ice cream! The root beer float is amazing—a large glass of vanilla ice cream served with a can of A&W root beer on the side. There's also a special Steve's beer and wine. Steve's Snappin' Dogs makes East Colfax the place to be. And Steve's is now at DIA too.

Stoic & Genuine

Cuisine: Seafood
Open: L-D: Daily
Stoicandgenuine.com

1701 Wynkoop   303-640-3474
Denver, 80202

Price: $$$$ **Patio:** Yes
Reservations: Yes   **Brunch:** No
Location: Union Station, LoDo

Stoic & Genuine hits Denver at the exciting Union Station bringing great seafood, ambience, and fun for Denver diners. Beth Gruitch and Jennifer Jasinski, owners of Rioja, Bistro Vendome, and Euclid Hall, hit the mark again with this amazing place. The ambience is awesome with its stunning look. Long and narrow, there are two focal bars; the drink area (where you can dine), and the long, sleek kitchen bar where one can watch the chefs and be part of the action. Booths and banquettes line the walls. The use of wood, steel, high ceilings, unique walls of fishnet and glass balls, and every detail down to the napkins and plates set the exciting scene. The cocktail list is outrageous, and wines and beer rock. Seafood is the star and the incredible food is created under direction of Chef Jorel Pierce. Start with raw oysters served with your choice of several granites, a house specialty that is addictive. Also available are broiled oysters, fried clams, lobster, crab, and soft shell crab and your feast begins. Mussels, corn masa soup, and amazing salads of watermelon with crispy ham, broccoli, avocado and sunflower seeds, and heirloom tomatoes might be your next choice. Indulge in sandwiches of fried oysters, fried clams, beet and ginger cured salmon, a Hangtown fry burger, and a mini lobster roll reminiscent of Cape Cod. "Main & Maines" reflect favorites of crab legs, whole lobster, redfish, and even a choice or two if you want to stray from the water. End with outrageous desserts of pie in a jar which translates to delicious strawberries and cream, rum banana Foster, and German chocolate. Service is excellent and caring. Stoic & Genuine is a treat and a great addition to Denver dining.

Sugarmill

Cuisine: Desserts, American
Open: B-L-D Mon-Sat Brunch: Sat-Sun
Sugarmilldesserts.com

2461 Larimer St, #101   303-297-3540
Denver, Co 80205
Larimer & 25th

Price: $$-$$$ **Patio:** Yes
Reservations: No   **Brunch:** Yes
Location: RiNo

What fun in the RiNo district as Noah French, along with Troy Guard open Sugarmill next door to Los Chingones (actually attached so you can go from one to the other without exiting). The place is delightful under leadership of Noah French whose pastries are amazing. So is the rest of the menu in this small, chic spot. The focal bar is the place to be along with seating along the walls but you want to watch the staff preparing the food. The wine list rocks, but the food is the star. Breakfast, lunch, and dinner are served here. At night choose the quiche of the day, cheese plate, and oven roasted sunchokes, mushroom toast, beet hummus, faro salad or escarole salads to start. Foie gras torchon with kumquat marmalade, a prosciutto baguette, short rib tortellini, and beef Wellington rock. Do not miss the roasted chicken and the best turkey pot pie. Desserts are the main attraction: Noahsphere, apple almond tart (to die for), chocolate hazelnut, a bunch of bananas, red velvet crème brulee, and pineapple upside down cake start the list. The citrus, Pavlova honeycomb, and chocolate jasmine bar make decisions impossible. No way to describe the details of each dish so one must try them. Service is lovely, the prices nice. The Sugarmill is upbeat, fun, delicious, and a must visit spot to visit any time of day.

Sushi Den

Cuisine: Japanese, Sushi
Open: L: Mon-Fri, D: Daily
sushiden.net

1487 S. Pearl St.   303-777-0826
Denver, 80210
S. Pearl & Florida

Price: $$$-$$$$ **Patio:** No
Reservations: Yes   **Brunch:** No
Location: Old South Pearl

Crowds often wait hours for a table at Sushi Den, one of Denver's most popular sushi spots. It's worth the wait. Once seated, you

won't be disappointed. For real sushi action, request a seat at the sushi bar where sushi chef's layer cut and roll rice and fish with amazing speed. Tables offer a slightly quieter spot to enjoy your meal. Every morsel is skillfully selected to bring you the best possible flavor. Daily specials offer the latest catches from Japan. Try the monkfish liver for something really exotic. In addition to sushi try appetizers of mussels, mushrooms, soups, salads or shrimp. Entrée specialties include teriyaki, tempura, and baskets of steamed fish or vegetables. Complete dinners include soup and salad. For dessert try a slice of tiramisù or a dish of green tea ice cream. Sushi Den remains tops for sushi in Denver.

Sushi Sasa

Cuisine: Japanese, Sushi
Open: L: Mon-Sat, D: Daily
sushisasadenver.com

2401 15th St.   303-433-7272
Denver, 80202
15th & Platte

Price: $$$$ **Patio:** Yes
Reservations: Yes   **Brunch:** No
Location: Platte Valley

At Sushi Sasa prepare to indulge in an amazing experience. The contemporary décor offers a simple but upscale feel with white walls, hanging lights, beautiful wood tables, and a sushi bar as the main focal point. There is a beautiful room with space for large groups and parties. Chef/Owner Wayne Conwell serves the most delicious Japanese dishes, ranging from sushi to cooked dishes that show his finesse and creativity. Start with amazing sushi rolls, sashimi, tempura or a salads, soup, and delicious appetizers. Pick your favorite sushi rolls or enjoy a terrific selection of tapas that are fabulous in presentation and taste. Some of the great dishes include grilled calamari with Korean seasonings and vegetables, mussels, sea bass with spicy ginger sauce, soft shell crab salad, tuna tataki and duck breast. There is a selection of vegetarian dishes, tempura and noodles to please all. Every sushi roll is a work of art to see and better to the taste. They are perfect. Don't leave without dessert, especially the molten-chocolate cake and wasabi tiramisù. The wine and sake list pairs well with the meal, and service is excellent. Sushi Sasa is one of the most exciting restaurants in the Denver dining scene.

Sushi Tazu

Cuisine: Japanese, Sushi
Open: L-D: Daily
denver-sushi.net

300 Fillmore St.   303-320-1672
Denver, 80206
3rd & Fillmore

Price: $$$-$$$$ **Patio:** Yes
Reservations: Yes   **Brunch:** No
Location: Cherry Creek

With a steady stream of loyal customers, Sushi Tazu continues
to charm in the ever-changing Cherry Creek area. Enjoy all your
favorites, including a variety of delicious specialty rolls. Starters
such as miso soup, salads, shrimp dumplings, edamame,
tempura and grilled squid make a great first course. For your
entrée, try teriyaki salmon, ginger calamari or a tasty noodle
bowl. Accompany your meal with beer, wine or sake.

Sushi Zanmai

Cuisine: Japanese, Sushi
Open: L: Mon-Fri, D: Daily
sushizanmai.com

1221 Spruce St.   303-440-0733
Boulder, 80302
Broadway & Spruce

Price: $$$ **Patio:** No
Reservations: Yes   **Brunch:** No
Location: Boulder

Totally different from most sushi establishments, Sushi
Zanmai offers customers a rowdy, exciting evening. Hang out
with wannabe rock stars as they sing their hearts out into a
karaoke machine. Sushi Zanmai was the first restaurant in
Colorado to institute "sushi happy hour," where sushi is value
priced by the single piece, and the tradition continues. A full
Japanese menu keeps everyone happy. Kids will love the special
menu designed just for them. Sit back with your sake (also
known as bravery juice) and have a rowdy good time.

Sweet Ginger

Cuisine: Chinese, Japanese, Sushi, Thai,
Vietnamese, Asian Fusion
Open: L-D: Daily
sweetgingerdenver.com

2710 E. 3rd Avenue   303-996-7270
Denver, 80206
3rd & Clayton

Price: $$-$$$ **Patio:** Yes
Reservations: Yes   **Brunch:** No
Location: Cherry Creek North

Sweet Ginger is one sweet spot to enjoy Asian cuisine. The place
is beautiful with a terrific tile sushi bar where guests can enjoy
the fare and watch the chefs prepare fabulous platters of sushi.
The dining room is bright and warm with purple print fabric
on the chairs and banquettes, a beautiful floor, and black and
white colors throughout that create a stunning setting. The
food shines with choices of Thai, Chinese, Vietnamese and
Japanese dishes. Start with pot stickers, gyoza, spring roll, satay
chicken and edamame. A selection of soups and salads from all
the regions of Asia make a great second course. Then the fun
begins as you try to decide on entrées. The selection of wraps
includes a terrific mu shu. Thai curries range from spicy green
and red to panang for those who prefer less spice. Chicken
pleases with BBQ half-chicken, sesame, basil, Royal, Kung Pao,
lemon grass, and teriyaki preparations. Beef options include
Sriracha, basil, whiskey, jalapeño and Hunan. There are several
shrimp and vegetable dishes as well. Sweet Ginger specials
are a must with crispy duck, soft shell crab, and crazy curry.
Sushi comes with your choice of rolls or full dinners. Service
is friendly and there is a full bar to complement the food. With
affordable prices, exceptional food, and delightful ambience,
Sweet Ginger is a welcome addition to Cherry Creek North.

Swing Thai

Cuisine: Thai
Open: L-D: Daily
swingthai.com

301 S. Pennsylvania St.   303-777-1777
Denver, 80209
Pennsylvania & Alameda and Multiple locations throughout
the metro area.

Price: $$ **Patio:** Yes
Reservations: No   **Brunch:** No
Location: Wash Park, LoDo, Denver-East, Highlands

Swing Thai is much more than a quick stop for Thai food.
You will find some of the best Thai food in the city at all
locations, with great dishes full of flavors that are delicious.
Start with spring rolls, a green papaya salad, or the outrageous
lemongrass soup. Pad Thai, drunken noodles, and curries start
the list of traditional dishes prepared perfectly and spiced
mild, medium or hot as you wish. The very fresh ingredients in
each dish complement the authentically spiced items. The stir-
fries bring many choices from shrimp, chicken and beef to tofu
and veggies. Do not miss the barbecue Thai herb chicken with
rice, the sweet and sour shrimp, and the red curry. There are
several choices of sides and sauces as well as mango sticky rice,
and ice cream for dessert. Add wine, beer or sake to make your
meal even more enjoyable. Service is terrific, prices affordable,
and the food just what Thai food should be. Eat in, carry out,
catering and delivery add to the fun. After one visit, you will be
one of the many fans.

Syrup

Cuisine: Breakfast, Café
Open: B-L: Daily
breakfastdenver.net

300 Josephine, #2.   720-945-1111
Denver, 80206
3rd & Columbine

Price: $-$$ **Patio:** No
Reservations: No   **Brunch:** No
Location: Cherry Creek-Downtown

Walk down a few steps and enter the bright, cheery room in
Cherry Creek North. Touches of green, white chairs, and
comfortable tables with a big window opening to the street
set the scene. The fare is breakfast and lunch, and of course
features many items with syrup. There are several waffle dishes
from traditional to chocolate or apple. The pancakes are so

good and you can get them silver dollar size or traditional with your choice of regular, gluten-free, or buckwheat flour. Eggs Benedict come in many forms, and there are numerous omelets from which to choose. Enjoy a breakfast sandwich, Boulder and yogurt, oatmeal, eggs your way and a burrito. Lunch features burgers, a Thanksgiving sandwich with turkey and stuffing, a French toast sandwich stuffed with ham, cheese, tomato and bacon, and a Cobb club. There are salads as well as baskets of muffins, and beignets. It's simple and fun and a good way to start the day. There is a second location downtown.

Table 6

Cuisine: American
Open: D: Daily, BR: Sun
table6denver.com

609 Corona St.   303-831-8800
Denver, 80218
6th Ave. & Corona

Price: $$$-$$$$	**Patio:** Yes
Reservations: Yes	**Brunch:** Yes

Location: North Cherry Creek, Capitol Hill

Table 6 is one of the most exciting restaurants in Denver and a plus for the popular East 6th Avenue dining scene. Seating only 42 people the interior features hardwood floors, exposed brick walls, a kitchen with copper trim, and a small bar area for gathering. Bistro chalkboards with dessert and wine lists, beautiful wood tables and black leather chairs set the scene. The overall atmosphere is charming and upbeat. Chef Mike Winston is extremely creative and brings exciting options with the ever-changing menu. Start with fried Brussels sprouts salad, tater tots "Table 6 style," chicken Schwarma, pigs in a brick, and roasted bone marrow. Grateful Bread is the bread of choice and it is delicious. Entrée choices change continually. The imaginative menu includes steelhead trout, short ribs with black pepper noodles, duck confit, shrimp, ham and black eyed peas, ricotta gnudi, lemongrass chicken scaloppini with candied yams, and divine lamb burnt ends with fig bbq. Presentation and accompaniments are not only eye catching but delectable. Desserts aim to whet the appetite with a fresh fruit tart of the moment, gelato, special cakes and the signature chocolate beignets. The generous wine list complements the food. Owner Aaron Forman heads the front of the house and entertains and charms his guests. Service shines with an informative, friendly staff. Sunday brunch is one of the best in town. Table 6 does a remarkable job in every way and is top-notch Denver dining.

Tables

Cuisine: Contemporary
Open: D: Tues-Sat
tablesonkearney.com

2267 Kearney St.   303-388-0299
Denver, 80207
23rd & Kearney

Price: $$$ **Patio:** No
Reservations: Yes   **Brunch:** No
Location: Park Hill

Enter this enchanting, funky restaurant in the Park Hill area and get ready for a wonderful dining experience. The space has been redone and is much bigger and beautiful but keeps the casual charm that we remember. A great bar, huge kitchen, soft walls and several dining spaces are all part of the restaurant. Terrific barn doors separate a private dining room or space for private parties. The artsy doors, high chrome ceilings and mismatched, but interesting, tables give Tables a creative look. Amy Vitale and her husband, Dustin Barrett, bring delightful meals to diners searching for a special neighborhood spot to spend the evening. Enjoy fabulous fresh bread and a glass of wine as you peruse the ever-changing menu. Start with appetizers of tuna tartare, crispy sweetbreads, lump crab cakes, and a soup of the day. Try the excellent Caesar salad, a baby spinach salad, beets with goat cheese, or heirloom tomatoes and peach over greens. Main courses include trout with panzanella salad, halibut in broth, amazing scallops and other fish specials that are fabulous in presentation, creativity and taste. Grilled New York steak with gorgonzola mashers and a marvelous grilled pork chop with green chile and cornbread are worth the trip. Half chicken is always on the menu and changes seasonally plus an exciting vegetarian option adds to the choices of great meals. Imaginative desserts such as s'mores with homemade marshmallows and chocolate sauce, ricotta cheesecake, the best carrot cake and lemon cake filled with rhubarb puree and topped with meringue are the perfect ending to any meal, especially with their homemade ice cream. Add a wonderful selection of wines by the glass or bottle, perfect knowledgeable service and a very warm welcome for a truly special experience. This spot is definitely a favorite in Denver for good reason. Amy and Dustin wow the fans making Tables your favorite neighborhood restaurant no matter where you live. It is Denver's tops.

Tacos Jalisco

Cuisine: Mexican
Open: B-L-D: Tues-Sun
Original-tacosjalisco.com

4309 W. 38th Ave.   303-458-1437
Denver, 80212
Tennyson & 38th

Price: $-$$ **Patio:** No
Reservations: Yes   **Brunch:** No
Location: Denver - North

This unpretentious Mexican eatery continues to garner awards and gain fans for great tacos in North Denver. Start with an order of chips and three salsas of varying flavors and degrees of heat. Balance the heat with horchata, a sweet rice, sugar and cinnamon drink. The soup of the day features one of many tasty traditional possibilities. Soft tacos arrive four to an order, stuffed with your choice of pork, beef tongue, lamb, shredded beef, chicken or sausage. Other choices include burritos, enchiladas, tacos, rellenos and chimichangas. Desserts include sopapillas and fried ice cream.

TAG

Cuisine: Contemporary/Fusion
Open: L: Mon-Fri, D: Daily
Tag-restaurant.com

1441 Larimer St.   303-996-9985
Denver, 80202
Larimer Square

Price: $$$$ **Patio:** Yes
Reservations: Yes   **Brunch:** No
Location: Larimer Square

TAG in Larimer Square is a favorite hot spot in Denver dining. Chef/Owner Troy Guard wows the crowds in his restaurant. The space is great-looking, modern with high ceilings, wood floors, lots of browns, red leather booths, banquettes and an open kitchen. Every element in design is well thought out with contemporary chandeliers and a fabulous wine adega that goes from floor to ceiling in the middle of the room. An elevator takes diners downstairs to enjoy the large bar and additional seating. Troy's tenure at restaurants around the globe is reflected in the menu he presents. He has an array of contemporary cuisine with touches from around the world. Start with appetizers of flash-seared Kona kampachi, taco sushi, roasted bone marrow and pork belly buns. Crisped seafood pot stickers, veal cheeks and oxtail sopes are more choices. Big salads are great for sharing, and sushi selections are another option. Hawaiian snapper with Peking duck salad, mahi mahi, miso black cod and roasted halibut show the talent of the chef as he lightly accents each with great sauces. Szechuan Colorado lamb, rabbit loin, lemon grass chicken and hanger tenderloin please meat lovers. And everyone loves to indulge in Kobe beef with Asian pear watercress salad or Kobe beef sliders with duck-fat fries. End with totally decadent desserts of chocolate, gelato and pineapple. A nice wine list complements the food. With mouthwatering food, an upbeat feel, and terrific service, TAG in Larimer Square is a special treat.

Tag Burger Bar

Cuisine: Burgers, Pub
Open: L-D-: Daily BR Sat-Sun
tagburgerbar.com

1222 Madison   303-736-2260
Denver, 80206
12th and Madison

Price: $$ **Patio:** Yes
Reservations: Yes   **Brunch:** Yes
Location: Congress Park

Tag Burger is a fun addition to 12th Avenue. The place looks great and it's hard to miss – the building sports a bulldog mural on the outside but once indoors you will encounter a cozy space with a popular bar, community table, open kitchen and comfortable seating. There are more murals on the walls plus garage doors that open wide and plenty of booths. Choose from a great selection of wine, beer or signature cocktails list as you look over a simple menu. Start with deep-fried pickles, brisket nachos, chicken wings, mac and cheese, Brussels sprouts, onion rings, potato bites or baked potato. Fries have a special section with old school, sweet potato (divine), fries with cheese whiz, duck fat, or truffle aioli on those spuds. The salads are terrific and nicely priced. Burgers rule and the basics are classic, lamb, bison, turkey, veggie and salmon. Add-ons range in price and ingredients and include spicy ranch, potato chips, avocado, grilled onions, cheeses, and a fried egg. There is a bistro menu for every day. On Sundays fried chicken is the order of the day, crispy and fork tender and perfect with mashed potatoes and veggies. End with deep fried Oreos or a milkshake. Service is timely and the place is always busy with young families to senior citizens. Owner Troy Guard has a real winner with this fun spot, perfect for this neighborhood area. The hood welcomes Tag Burger Bar.

Taki Sushi

Cuisine: Japanese, Sushi
Open: D: Daily
Takisushi.com

420 East Bayaud Ave.   303-282-0111
Denver, 80209
Bayaud at Logan

Price: $$-$$$ **Patio:** No
Reservations: Yes   **Brunch:** No
Location: Wash Park

Don't let the unassuming exterior of this cozy little sushi spot fool you. Step inside for some of the most unique sushi in West Washington Park. Take a seat at the sushi bar or enjoy dinner in their intimate contemporary dining room. Beer, wine and sake are available to accompany your dinner along with happy hour drink specials. The sushi bar and kitchen appetizer selections are varied and plentiful. Sweet potato tempura and gyoza are terrific appetizers to start your meal. Taki Sushi offers noodle bowls and a varied selection of hibachi and teriyaki entrées from the kitchen. Thirty types of sushi and sashimi are available, but the real specialty is Taki Sushi's unique specialty rolls. More than 50 rolls are on the menu allowing the fusion talents of the sushi chefs to shine. Don't miss the Mayflower roll with spicy crabmeat and mango inside and seared tuna outside. The red dragon roll has spicy tuna and crunch topped with pepper tuna and avocado. If an intimate Japanese fusion dining experience with attentive friendly service is what you crave, then Taki Sushi is your place!

Tamales by La Casita

Cuisine: Mexican
Open: B-D: Daily
Tamalesbycasita.com

3561 Tejon St   (303) 477-2899
Denver, CO 80211

Price: $ **Patio:** Yes
Reservations: No   **Brunch:** No
Location: Highlands

Tamales by La Casita is a family owned restaurant that serves the best tamales in town. In fact, they often sell out. Go for lunch and grab a table on the patio or in the open and bright dining room. Servers are friendly and hustle around to appease the lunch rush. Order your tamales 'Christmas style', meaning they are covered in both red and green chili. The menu does not stop with tamales they also serve delightful breakfast burritos, spicy huevos rancheros, soft chili rellenos, frito pies and enchiladas. There is also an entire gluten free menu with lots of delicious options. The beer list is short and affordable and the margaritas are made in house. This place is a real crowd pleaser, and one that you will be excited to return to.

Tamayo

Cuisine: Contemporary, Mexican
Open: L: Mon-Fri, D: Daily BR: Sat-Sun
Modernmexican.com

1400 Larimer St.
Denver, 80202

720-946-1433
14th & Larimer

Price: $$$$
Reservations: Yes
Location: Larimer Square

Patio: Yes
Brunch: Yes

Tamayo is a very popular space on Larimer Square. Start with the tile bar lined with great bottles of tequila and an inviting space to gather for a drink. The dining room has brown leather fabric on the booths, fabulous wood chairs with comfortable table seating and super lighting. Upstairs the patio is arguably the best in town and private dining rooms offer party space for larger groups. The food is the star here and owner Richard Sandoval continues to impress with his upscale creative Mexican cuisine. Start with four variations on their guacamole: traditional, spicy crab, tuna tartare, and bacon. All are winners. Enjoy the tortilla or corn soup and several salads and then the selection of tortas. Smoked brisket, mahi mahi, chicken and pork make decisions difficult. But ceviche, queso fundido (sizzling cheese that arrives in a pan over a flame), flatbread and a squash blossom quesadilla are perfect for sharing. Specialties of the house are just that with a filet with poblano chile potato gratin, chicken adobada, carne asada, pork carnitas, and the best halibut with adobo. Cazuelas of braised chicken with mole and plantain, pork shoulder with mole verde, and short ribs are a must. End with divine desserts that range from bread pudding to chocolate tart with peanut butter and a terrific date cake. Presentation of each dish is special as well. The wines, beer, and cocktails are a perfect complement to the food. Service is excellent with the well-informed staff able to help with selections that cater to every need. Tamayo brings top notch food and fun dining to Larimer Square.

Telegraph

Cuisine: Small Plates, Contemporary
Open: L-D: Daily BR: Sat Sun
Telegraph.com

295 S. Pennsylvania
Denver, 80209
Alameda and Pennsylvania

Price: $$ **Patio:** Yes
Reservations: Yes   **Brunch:** Yes
Location: Denver - South Central

Telegraph, sister restaurant of Brazen, brings just what this neighborhood has been longing for. Enter to a super bar with seating all through this part of the bright dining room. The room beyond shows off a huge, divine focal open kitchen with much seating so guests can watch the chefs prepare the terrific dishes. The menu will be much like Brazen with small plates, fancy tastes, pasta, veggies, and special items along with a few entrees that feed two or more. The ramen which is the best anywhere will be available for lunch all the time, and there will be no late night here. That means some who retire on real time can enjoy the homemade noodles and spicy broth that combines for their ramen. The patio is awesome as well. Enjoy being part of this funky, fun scene where fans gather to eat, drink, and play.

Thai Basil

Cuisine: Asian, Thai
Open: L-D: Daily
Thaibasil.com

1422 East 18th Avenue   303-861-1226
Denver, 80218
Multiple locations throughout the metro area.

Price: $$ **Patio:** Yes
Reservations: Yes   **Brunch:** No
Location: Aurora, Highlands, Littleton, Uptown, Wash Park

The small dining room is full of bright colors, big windows and funky fusion collectibles. Every plate is an artistic creation full of superb food, and the friendly staff is prompt, informative and friendly. Begin with chicken satay with Thai peanut sauce or pot stickers filled with pork and veggies. Soups like wonton, sizzling rice and hot-and-sour create unforgettable tastes and aromas and could easily serve as a meal. Thai basil chicken with water chestnuts, bok choy and ginger is spicy and flavorful. Crispy fillets of fish arrive in an oblong bowl filled with peppers, vegetables and a fragrant black bean sauce. Don't miss the crispy golden-fried soft-shell crab served with Asian guacamole. Other entrées include duck, beef and vegetarian choices. With reasonable prices and a nice beer and wine list, Thai Basil has it all.

Thai Kitchen

Cuisine: Thai
Open: L: Mon-Sat, D: Daily
ufeedme.com/thaikitchen

2130 N. Main St., Unit 5   303-772-7800
Longmont, 80501
21st & N. Main

Price: $$ **Patio:** No
Reservations: Yes   **Brunch:** No
Location: Longmont

Longmont is lucky to have this gem of a restaurant tucked into a strip mall on the north side of town. You may not go for the atmosphere, but it is well worth the drive to experience the truly authentic Thai food. Spring rolls are a must to start your meal. They are served with a homemade sweet sauce that is delicious but has a bite. Another great way to start your meal is with the chicken satay. Entrées include a traditional pad Thai with pork, lamb with beef, and Kang Massaman with chicken. All are deliciously fresh and enjoyable. Entrées are served with jasmine rice and can be spiced up or down to your personal preference. This delightful restaurant does not have a liquor license, but be sure to try the Thai iced coffee and tea. Both are an excellent alternative to alcoholic beverages. Friendly service, good food and affordable pricing will bring you back time and time again.

Tocabe

Cuisine: American, Indian
Open: L-D: Daily
tocabe.com

8181 E. Arapahoe Rd.   720-485-6738
Greenwood Village, 80112
Greenwood Plaza Blvd

Price: $-$$ **Patio:** No
Reservations: No   **Brunch:** No
Location: Greenwood Village

Tocabe brings a unique concept to Denver with American Indian cuisine that is delicious and certainly out of the ordinary. Walk in and place your order at the counter and enjoy. There are traditional dishes, all made with the award-winning Navajo fry bread. Order the "American Indian tacos" with choice of meat, choice of beans, lettuce, cheese, tomatoes, purple onions, sour cream and choice of salsa. Or order the "stuffed Indian tacos" with choice of meat, choice of beans, cheese, tomatoes, purple onions, Hatch green chile and choice of salsa. For meat, try the ground buffalo, or the shredded beef which is marinated in chiles, pepper and cinnamon. Salsa choices include corn salsa, mild salsa and white hominy salsa. There are a myriad of possible combinations. End with dessert tacos with hot apples or cherries, or fry bread with honey, cinnamon or powdered sugar. With a wonderful family there to care for you, some terrific food and affordable prices, Tocabe is a big hit.

Tokio

Cuisine: Sushi, Japanese
Open: D: Daily
Mytokio.com

2907 Huron   720-639-2811
Denver
One block W. of Coors Field

Price: $$$ **Patio:** No
Reservations: Yes   **Brunch:** No
Location: Prospect

Located in a newly developing area, Prospect, Chef/Owner Miki Hashimoto has created a unique and exciting concept. Start with décor, designed to resemble a typical Japanese house; intimate and warm with fabulous decor. This unique cuisine is served in the dining room which seats 60 and has a 25 ft. ceiling. A magnificent community table made of ash wood matches the sushi bar where your dishes are created. There is a loft for private dining which includes a sake bar. Lighting, color, and every detail is awesome. Miki adds new ideas to the menu starting with the binco-tan charcoal grill with very high heat resulting in delicious skewers of chicken, asparagus wrapped in bacon, pork, squid, and more. Small plates range from shishito peppers, edamame, gyoza, tataki, divine pot sticks, and mushrooms. One of main features is Ramen. Miki brings Japanese noodles and presents bowls with pork, chicken, vegetables, and tofu with the noodles and broth with a variety of seasoning. And of course the sushi shines as rolls of many favorites and specialties are presented. And the sashimi, chef's choice is a must. End with green tea or the regular version of tiramisu, ice creams and more. The sake, wine, beer, and drink list is excellent and servers add to the experience. Tokio is a welcome addition to the dining scene and worth the trip.

Tommy's Thai

Cuisine: Thai
Open: L-D: Mon-Sat
tommysthaidenver.com

3410 E. Colfax Ave.   303-377-4244
Denver, 80206
Colfax & Cook

Price: $-$$ **Patio:** Yes
Reservations: Yes   **Brunch:** No
Location: East Colfax

Tommy's Thai, a favorite spot for Capitol Hill and Congress Park residents, has re-created itself with a renovated building and new décor. The dining room is modern and upbeat, and the entire place has a fresh, bright and comfortable feel. Royal chicken curry, a stir-fry with chicken, onions, bell peppers, carrots and cashews, is a real crowd pleaser. Pad Thai, the national dish of Thailand, is another very popular item. Rice noodle soup with chicken and the chicken-coconut soup with galangal, lime leaves and fresh sliced mushrooms are just two of the outstanding soup choices. All lunches and dinners come with steamed or fried rice and can be ordered mild, medium, hot or Thai hot. Be sure to try the homemade coconut ice cream for dessert. Delivery is offered in a limited area. If you're looking for good Thai food at affordable prices, this is the place for you.

Tom's Home Cookin'

Cuisine: American, Southern
Open: L: Mon-Fri

800 E. 26th Ave.   303-388-8035
Denver, 80205
26th Ave. & Clarkson

Price: $ **Patio:** Yes
Reservations: No   **Brunch:** No
Location: Five Points

Tom's Home Cookin' is the place to soothe that Southern food craving and it begins with just a little soul. Appropriately positioned in the center of Five Points, this eatery is immersed within one of Denver's richest cultural communities. It is open Monday through Friday from 11 a.m. until 2:30 p.m., or until the food runs out. Be prepared to wait in a line. The décor features Deep South paraphernalia ranging from old bottles of hot sauce and 1950's-era baseball posters to swampland travel brochures. The ambience or lack thereof, fits. Checkered apron-festooned owners, Tom Unterwagner and Steve Jankousky quickly fill the orders. If there's an open seat, a rare commodity, eat on the outdoor patio or in the sun-drenched, covered porch. Or take your grub with you, as everything's served in a box ready for transport. The menu changes daily. For less than $10, you can get a main item, two heaping sides, bread and a drink. Menu choices include slow-cooked pot roast; country-fried steak smothered in thick, peppery gravy, tasty meatloaf, and "lick your fingers" barbecued ribs. Don't forget about sides that include delicious options of buttered corn, glazed yams, squash casserole, macaroni and cheese worth dreaming about, cornbread studded with jalapenos, green beans, chunky mashers and collard greens. You can even order a smorgasbord sampler of four sides, bread and a drink. Wash it all down with some authentic sweet tea and finish off the feast with a hearty piece of Coca Cola chocolate cake, sweet potato pie or juicy fruit cobbler. Leave the credit cards and checks at home, they only accept cash. Guests from all backgrounds are bound to one another, linked at the soul, after a meal at Tom's Home Cookin'.

Tom's Urban 24

Cuisine: American, Breakfast
Open: B-L-D: Daily
Tomsurban24.com

1460 Larimer   720-214-0515
Denver
Corner of 15th and Larimer, Downtown

Price: $$-$$$ **Patio:** Yes
Reservations: Yes   **Brunch:** No
Location: Downtown

Tom's Urban 24 in Larimer Square, takes a great corner space and does food 24 hours a day—thus the 24! The space is bright with clean, modern design featuring huge windows, orange and beige curved leather booths, a super chandelier of turquoise, orange and clear lights and a focal bar. Go up the staircase to more dining upstairs with a view of the lower level and the happenings outside. Tom Ryan, creator of Smashburger, keeps to the theme with many options. Breakfast brings omelets, pancakes, eggs, burritos, pop tarts and more. At lunch go for pho, salads, a list of chicken or beef burgers with special preparations or design your own, and specialty sandwiches. There are many specialties, sides from which to choose, and salsas and chile. Dinner offers the same as lunch with more items. In the appetizers, find deviled eggs, a white bean dip and calamari. Urban pho comes in several forms. Enjoy a filet or shrimp and lobster pot pie, steak and eggs, an egg bake, barbeque ribs, and chickenlooper, a special fried chicken with corn pancakes. Tacos, pizza, burritos, and mac' n' cheese bring more choices. The drinks, wine and beer complement the food. There's late night, off hours, early morning all available for guests. It's a different option in the Larimer Square restaurant scene.

Tony's Market

Cuisine: Deli, Market
Open: B-L-D: Daily
Tonysmarket.com

4991 E. Dry Creek Rd.   303-770-7024
Centennial, 80122
Holly & Dry Creek Rd. and Multiple locations throughout the metro area.

Price: N/A	**Patio:** Yes
Reservations: No	**Brunch:** No

Location: Bowles Village, Castle Rock, Centennial, Denver-South of Downtown

This boutique gourmet market is a dream come true for home chefs. Enter the incredibly well-laid-out market and shop to your heart's content. You'll find everything at Tony's, from wonderful produce to the perfect meat, but the taste test goes to the prepared foods. Try a turkey sandwich, piled high with spicy guacamole, lettuce, tomato and bacon on a croissant. The $7.99 price tag includes a cookie, chips and a pickle. It's one of the best buys in town. Pasta salads range from Oriental chicken to a Greek with spinach, penne, olives, feta and pesto dressing. Moist salmon en croute, stuffed with spinach and red peppers in a flaky crust, reheats beautifully. Frozen appetizers such as escargot, spanakopita, miniature hot dogs and more make entertaining easy. Other ready-to-cook foods like chicken Marsala, veal saltimbocca, stuffed cabbage, fried chicken and sliced beef brisket are available. Don't miss the ciabatta bread, chocolate chip cookies and fudge brownies. Desserts, breakfast rolls and ice creams are more choices. At the Broadway location, enjoy the bistro for dining on premise.

Tortuga's

Cuisine: Cajun, Caribbean
Open: D: Tues-Sat
Tortugaslongmont.com

218 Coffman St.   303-772-6954
Longmont, 80501
Across from Post Office

Price: $$ **Patio:** Yes
Reservations: Yes   **Brunch:** No
Location: Longmont

Don't think Denver is your only option for unique dining. Tortuga's brings the fresh, flavorful taste of the Caribbean to a vintage brick house located in Longmont's Old West Side. The focus is on seafood, but there are numerous dishes that combine the fruit-of-the-sea along with the fruit-of-the-land. Rock shrimp ceviche, served with crispy corn tortilla chips, is a treat. Seared halibut is served with a fresh mango salsa, black beans, rice and crispy fried plantains. Mojo served with either the catch of the day or chicken is another classic Caribbean flavor that Tortuga's creates with sage, cumin and olive oil. If you like your food hot, a few dashes of Pete's Heat, Tortuga's own bottled hot sauce, combines both hot and sweet, fruity flavors to satisfy the brave and tempt the meek. The rocking jambalaya has so many flavors that your taste buds will go wild. Don't forget dessert; you have never tasted chocolate bread pudding better than this, and the cool, creamy Key lime pie leaves you longing for tropical trade winds. This is a definite Longmont treat.

Trapper's Chop House

Cuisine: Steakhouse
Open: D: Daily
trapperschophouse.com

19308 E. Cottonwood Drive   303-248-2132
Parker, 80138
Atop the Holiday Inn

Price: $$$$ **Patio:** No
Reservations: Yes   **Brunch:** No
Location: Parker

Parker can brag about being the location for one great steak house when it comes to Trapper's. Located on the top floor of the Holiday Inn, the space is beautiful. Enter to a fabulous bar that circles around a large area to gather for drinks, dinner, or goodies from the bar menu. The dining room is upscale and welcoming with comfy booths, nicely spaced tables with white linen and a spectacular view from the picture windows. Pick the spot near the fireplace for a special treat. Peruse the extensive wine list as you decide on your meal. Start with mussels, baby back ribs, shrimp Romesco, sesame seared tuna or a spectacular stacked Portobello mushroom on puff pastry. The house Caesar, wedge, caprese, and tomato, cucumber and onion salads can be a second course or add a protein for an entrée. Romancing the Stone" is the signature here that sets Trapper's apart from other steakhouses. It is a volcanic hot rock that sears your meat at 450 degrees. Cook it at the table or the kitchen will take over if you prefer. Select the sirloin, filet, buffalo strip loin, game tasting, tuna, scallops, or build your own combo if you prefer. The dishes come with the best chipotle sweet mashers, jalapeno cheddar mashed, baked or roasted potatoes. The sauces are delightful as well: red wine, béarnaise, basil aioli, or chipotle remoulade. Other entrées include steak Oscar, bone-in rib eye, pork tenderloin, salmon, lamb chops, and stuffed chicken breast. Don't leave until you indulge in the chocolate cake à la mode or apple strudel with cinnamon ice cream. The wine list is excellent and service shines. Trapper's is a hidden gem in Parker.

Trattoria Stella

Cuisine: Italian
Open: L: Mon, Wed-Sat, D: Wed-Mon, BR: Sun
trattoriastella.squarespace.com

3470 W. 32nd Ave.   303-458-1128
Denver, 80211
Lowell & 32nd

Price: $$ **Patio:** Yes
Reservations: No   **Brunch:** Yes
Location: Highlands

Enjoy the tradition of an Italian trattoria in this cozy West Highland restaurant. In warm weather, the terraced front patio allows you to watch the neighborhood folks stroll the sidewalk. Pastas dominate the menu with eggplant fettuccine, creamy sausage and tomato with rigate, fettuccine arrabbiata, and Alfredo or aglio olio topping the list. Choose from a nice dessert selection including tiramisù, crème brûlée, espresso pound cake and apple pie. Don't miss the Sunday brunch. A specials board details the frittata and omelet of the day, as well as the fruit selection for the addictive crepes. Other choices include an Italian version of French toast, piled high with whipped cream and fruit or the Brie and grape omelet, a delightful mixture of savory and sweet. It's a happening place on West 32nd in Highland.

Trattoria Stella East

Cuisine: Italian
Open: L-D:Mon-Fri Br-D: Sat, Sun
trattoriastella.squarespace.com

3201 E. Colfax   303-320-8635
Denver, 80206
Colfax & Steele

Price: $$ **Patio:** Yes
Reservations: Yes   **Brunch:** Yes
Location: East Colfax

Fun and bright best describe Trattoria Stella on East Colfax where fans congregate for casual dining. One room with large windows that open when the weather permits, bright colored chairs around the tables, booths, and a small open kitchen set the scene. The bar area is separate but attached to the restaurant. Start with homemade bread as you look over the menu. Appetizers include calamari, baked Brie, whipped gorgonzola spread, and shrimp fra diavola. The salad list includes the cherry house salad, carrot house salad, arugula salad, and an outstanding 32nd Street salad. The pasta list includes crispy gnocchi, chicken fettuccini, and spaghetti Bolognese. Grilled beef tenderloin, scallop risotto, and lasagna are more options for entrées. Pizzas are fun with margarita, grilled vegetable, Alfredo chicken, arugula, classic, and hot pepper. If you prefer, build your own. The decadent dessert list brings chocolate pot de crème, chocolate pie, Key lime pie, and fruit pies. The wine list is good, and service shines. Trattoria Stella East is a pleasant choice on E. Colfax.

Treppeda's Gourmet Market

Cuisine: Deli, Italian, Market
Open: L-D: Mon-Sat
treppedas.com

300 2nd Ave., #105   303-652-1606
Niwot, 80544
2nd & Franklin

Price: N/A   **Patio:** Yes
Reservations: Yes   **Brunch:** No
Location: Niwot

Niwot has graduated from its farm town days to a pleasant bedroom community for the high-tech industry. Residents have sophisticated tastes, and Treppeda's meets the demand with an exceptional catering service and tasty food reminiscent of East Coast delis. Choose among family-style platters laid out on the countertop or order from a daily-changing à la carte menu. Wonderful deli sandwiches with Italian salami or fresh roast beef are served on a rustic roll, French baguette or focaccia. Fresh green salads make a terrific side with your meal. Finish with a brownie or a slice of carrot cake. Now open for dinner, enjoy the terrific cheeses and meats, seared shrimp, calamari, or faro risotto with mushrooms for appetizers. There are several pastas ranging from gnocchi and carbonara to orecchettte Bolognese and sausage al forno. Entrées include rabbit, lamb, Kobe sirloin, fish and pork shoulder. And there is pizza to please as well. This is a nice addition for Niwot diners.

Trillium

Cuisine: Scandinavian, Contemporary
Open: D: Tues-Sun
trilliumdenver.com

2134 Larimer St.   303-379-9759
Denver, 80205
21st & Larimer

Price: $$$$ **Patio:** Yes
Reservations: Yes   **Brunch:** No
Location: LoDo

Trillium has elevated the food offerings for the fast-growing LoDo area of North Larimer Street in Denver. Trillium sits in a modern space with exposed ceilings, one brick wall, large windows, and a focal bar of black and white tile. A semi-open kitchen finishes the room where pscale wood tables and chairs are spaced for comfortable dining. With a lovely background, Chef/Owner Ryan Leinonen brings a creative menu with touches of Scandinavia to the food. Start with the best rolls, a recipe of his mom—and nobody beats mom's cooking, and a selection of smorgasbord. Choose Aquavit cured salmon, ham mousse, pickled shrimp, and maple cured trout. Add truffled tater tots, Portobello fries, cauliflower soup, and oysters, but don't stop until you taste the cheese, or splurge on caviar. Smaller plates include a winter salad, apple, potato and beet salad, foie gras mousse, trout raaka, fried smelts, and brioche topped with poached shrimp and more. Bigger plates shine in taste and presentation: steelhead trout over a rich mussel dill cream broth, duck breast, open ravioli of grilled prawns in mushroom bisque, chicken breast with Brussels sprouts, egg noodles and bacon mustard vinaigrette. Arctic char and Lake Superior whitefish round out the very interesting and enticing menu. Leave room for desserts that range from carrot cake and fried apple strudel to lemon buttermilk pudding cake, panna cotta, and warm chocolate fallen cake. All are totally decadent and worth the indulgence. The wine list is excellent and the friendly staff complements the food.

Trinity Grille

Cuisine: American
Open: L: Mon-Fri, D: Mon-Sat
trinitygrille.com

1801 Broadway Blvd.   303-293-2288
Denver, 80202
Tremont Pl. & 18th

Price: $$$-$$$$ **Patio:** No
Reservations: Yes   **Brunch:** No
Location: Denver - Downtown

As you enter Trinity Grille, the feeling of an old San Francisco eatery comes to mind. Lots of wood, bare floors, colorful art and an excellent wait staff greet patrons. Start with a crab cake, definitely the signature here. If you prefer, two cakes come as an entrée with fries and slaw. Rich, gooey onion soup is another hit and reflects the tradition of the menu. For main courses, choose from schnitzel, pork or veal chops, a selection of steaks and French-fried lobster, a 14-ounce lobster, cut into chunks and deep-fried, that has pleased fans for years. Order the sinfully delicious chocolate soufflé with your meal so that it will be ready when you finish your entrée. Arrive early to get a seat at lunch. Reservations are accepted for dinner.

True Food

Cuisine: American/Healthy
Open: L-D- Daily BR Sat-Sun
Foxrc.com

2800 E. 2nd Avenue Suite 101   720-509-7661
Denver, 80206
2nd avenue and Detroit

Price: $$$ **Patio:** Yes
Reservations: No   **Brunch:** Yes
Location: Cherry Creek North

True Food brings a unique addition to Cherry Creek North. The place is good looking—huge, open with super big windows, beetle kill wood, high open ceilings and interesting lighting. The open kitchen is massive with side tables for preparations and a bird's eye view for diners. A focal bar welcomes seating. Dr. Andrew Weil, known for his healthy lifestyle regimen is the source of the menu items—with help from the chefs. Gluten free, vegetarian, vegan as well as regular food are on this menu. This is a perfect place for people who have diet issues but still want to dine out with friends. Start with miso soup, Thai shrimp dumplings, edamame dumplings, caramelized onion tart, vegetable crudités, and hummus. The salad list brings kale, albacore sashimi, the farmer's market, chopped, a harvest, and autumn ingredients and a protein can be added for an entrée. The pizzas are terrific: tomato and roasted kale, chicken sausage, wild mushroom, and squash. The options continue with a bison burger, tuna sliders, turkey burger, and a BLT. All are accompanied by kale and sweet potato hash. Entrees of chicken shrimp, curry, lasagna, salmon, and street tacos make decisions difficult. End with chocolate for any diet, apple tart, gelato and more. The wine and drink list is excellent to complement the food. If you are looking for a healthy alternative with plenty of choices, this is your place.

The Truffle Cheese Shop

Cuisine: Market
Open: Mon-Sat
Denvertruffle.com

2906 E. 6th Ave.   303-322-7363
Denver, 80206
6th & Fillmore

Price: NA   **Patio:** No
Reservations: No   **Brunch:** No
Location: Cherry Creek North

Step into The Truffle and enter gourmet heaven. Good things come in small packages and everything you ever wanted in the way of cheeses, and more, is available in this small shop. And if you can't find what you're looking for the delightful owners Karin and Rob Lawler will search worldwide to help you find it. They charm guests with an unbelievable knowledge of products and their hospitality makes you linger longer than you planned. Browse through counters, cases and cabinets filled with special imports. Sample over 35 cheeses from around the world, all aged with care and rotated until ripe and ready to be purchased. Buy elite caviar, special honeys, magnificent oils and vinegars, chocolates, fresh breads and olives not available in other markets. The meat selections are exceptional and add a perfect complement to the cheeses. You can also find imported pastas, jams, dried mushrooms and herbs. The Truffle offers picnic baskets for outdoor adventures, catering and special orders. The platters and catered trays are the hit of any party. After just one visit, you will want to become a regular. And yes, there are truffles available at the shop! There is now a second location in the Highland where you can also dine on their goodies—giving all another great choice!

Truffle Table

Cuisine: Wine bar, Tapas, Cheese
Open: D: Tues-Sun
Truffletable.com

2556 15th St
Denver, 80211
On the corner of Umatilla

303-455-9463

Price: $$$
Reservations: No
Location: LoHi

Patio: No
Brunch: No

This divine small plate wine bar is a special place. The setting is delightful with the focal bar with seating, tables around the room, huge picture windows, great art on the walls, and terrific lighting. The scene is set in this small charming spot for a delightful night. Start with snacks of pickled veggies, marinated olives, and artisan butter board. Black bean hummus, cauliflower and apple soup, and Brussels sprouts gratin make a perfect way to begin. The main menu features Artisan cheeses and cured meats—you choose or the staff will in different size plates. The cheeses are awesome, exciting, and addictive. Or, indulge in Chistorra sausage rolls, awesome kale and squash salad with wild rice, bagna cauda, the best grilled cheese sandwich, fondue, and mac and cheese. Musts also are Iberico ham and pumpkin pain d'epice with cheese, shaved Brussels sprouts and apple jam. Wednesday night is raclette night, always a treat. Decadent divine desserts include tea custard with brown sugar shortbread, fig and apple Newtons, panettone bread pudding, and caramel chocolate tart. Now to the just as important part—the wine!!!! The selections are incredible, tastes better, and prices reasonable. Go for flights if you like as well. Staff is so knowledgeable and talented to make your visit perfect. One visit to the Truffle Table and you will be a fan forever.

240 Union

Cuisine: Contemporary
Open: L: Mon-Fri, D: Daily
240union.com

240 Union Blvd.   303-989-3562
Lakewood, 80228
2nd & Union

Price: $$$ **Patio:** Yes
Reservations: Yes   **Brunch:** No
Location: Lakewood

Fans from all over come to enjoy cutting-edge cuisine in a comfortable atmosphere at this Lakewood gem. After 25 years, 240 Union remains tops in food, wine and service. Owner Michael Coughlin celebrates this milestone with an amazing new look. The décor is sophisticated and lively. An open kitchen spans the length of the room, and wood panels representing Colorado's mountains nicely divide the space. An elegant bar with granite, steel and great panels is the spot for gathering or dining. A private wine/dining room offers alternate seating options for parties or dining. There is a stunning private dining room in the rear. The colors of gray and charcoal with white, great art, and awesome lighting welcomes diners. Nicely spaced cloth-covered tables and chairs add to the comfort. Michael and his talented executive chef tie all the elements together to bring you an exceptional dining experience. The wine list is excellent, and the wait staff is well-trained, friendly, and informative. The homemade poppy seed focaccia is the best, warm from the oven. The rotating seasonal menu brings interesting delights at each change. Appetizers include amazing calamari tempura, deviled eggs, warm asparagus with poached egg, baby artichokes "Milanese".smoked salmon, crab and shrimp cocktail, and scallops. Add lamb sausage meatballs, and a must have short rib taco and share to enjoy tastes of all. Salads and soups change often and are intriguing. Pasta dishes shine: linguini with clams, capellini with shrimp and spicy tomato sauce, and conchiglie with chicken, along with several choices of pizza. Entrées bring a whole fish roasted in the pizza oven, the signature spit-roasted half chicken, salmon, halibut, and cioppino. Other options include chicken-fried lobster tail, a bone in rib eye, lamb duo, and the favorite pistachio-crusted pork chop with risotto. The list makes decisions impossible. End with glorious desserts such as sticky toffee pudding, chocolate silk or Key lime pie and crème brûlée. Lunch and Sunday night prime rib specials are more temptations. With excellent food presented beautifully with exciting sides, great wine and cocktails, and delightful hospitality, 240 Union is the top choice for dining on the west side.

The Uber Sausage

Cuisine: Deli/American
Open: L-D: Daily
Theubersausage.com

2730 E. Colfax
Denver, 80206

303-862-7894

1535 Central St
Denver, 80211

303-433-4575

Price: $-$$
Reservations: No
Location: East Colfax, Denver - LoHi

Patio: Yes
Brunch: No

"With a truly great sausage, one can do great things." If this sounds like a quote by a wise American president, it's not. This is The Über Sausage motto. Operating in one small room with just a few seats and a patio, the wait is worth it and the food travels well. Place your order and get ready to chow down on a tasty Über Sausage sandwich, and you will be glad you came. Each one a study in tastes and textures that is always hearty and downright delicious. The Über Sausage serves a selection of homemade links using premium ingredients such as naturally raised beef, bison, chicken, lamb, veal and pork combined with just the right sweet, savory or spicy homemade condiments and crunchy veggie and fruit combinations tucked inside a baked French baguette supplied by City Bakery. Some favorites include the chicken rosemary sausage club sandwich, the lamb sausage, Greek style with tzatziki sauce, cucumber and the flavors of Greece, the lemongrass pork sausage done banh mi style with all the trimmings and the most popular green chile sausage with the fixin's and a side of the best green chile, or try the super veggie sausage. For a hint of nostalgia, try the tater tots or the house made chips spiked with seven do-it-yourself seasonings. They also have an Über truck for sausages out and about. The second Uber is bigger and has a large patio to enjoy your meal.

Uncle

Cuisine: Noodles
Open: D: Mon-Sat
Uncleramen.com

2215W. 32nd Avenue   303-433-3263
Denver, 80211
32nd between Zuni and Tejon

Price: $$ **Patio:** Yes
Reservations: no   **Brunch:** No
Location: Highlands

Uncle is a delightful noodle restaurant next door to Highland Tap and Burger. This space brings great ambience to the neighborhood with black slate, white tiles, stainless and wood treatments creating a contemporary slick look that is totally inviting. Grab a spot at the bar or get comfortable at one of the tables in the small seating area. Start with fabulous oysters, crab tots with harissa mayo or Olathe corn. Steamed buns are terrific. The bread is homemade and filled with pork belly, shrimp, tofu and a delicious crispy bass filled with old bay, mayo and romaine. Sesame pancakes with different fillings are another yummy option. Duck arrives with plum, cucumber and scallion, chicken is seasoned with ginger, scallion and carrot and shiitake arrives with hoisin, cucumber, and scallion. The main bowls are a treat: ramen with pork ribs, corn and an egg or cold sesame noodles with chicken, chili, apple, udon and mushrooms. An amazing rice bowl with fried Brussels sprouts and pork belly, spicy lamb ramen and Bibimbap that features rice, hanger steak, spicy cucumber, trumpet mushrooms and egg. Portions are generous and the food so tasty. An excellent wine, beer, and sake list complements the food. Prices are reasonable, service timely and Uncle is a favorite in the popular Highland neighborhood. After one visit you will be a regular.

Undici

Cuisine: Italian
Open: L-D: Mon-Fri   D: Sat
Undicidenver.com

1200 E. Hampden Ave.   303-761-2828
Englewood, 80113
Old Hampden and Downing

Price: $$-$$$ **Patio:** Yes
Reservations: Yes   **Brunch:** No
Location: Englewood

Undici translates to "eleven" in Italian, as this is the latest restaurant of the Kallas family, owners of Steakhouse 10. The space is gorgeous with high ceilings, a granite and stone bar, expansive windows and beautiful art. The lounge is designed for comfort and the social atmosphere is perfect for drinks and enjoying appetizers. Dining is divided into two rooms on the first level with more seating upstairs. Olive-green, mustard and French-roast colored walls are accented with Italian mosaic tile, a waterfall and Venetian plaster. Owners Alex and Dina are your hosts and bring charm and attention to every guest interaction. The cuisine is Italian in every way. Start with bread and dipping sauce, fried calamari, carpaccio, the antipasto platter, bruschetta or a cheese platter. Salads bring choices of caprese, Caesar, tricolore and Greek. The pasta list starts with gnocchi, risotto, ravioli with lobster pâté, and cannelloni with cheese. Rigatoni, linguine with clams and spaghetti with shrimp are more offerings. Chicken parmesan covered with mozzarella and a rich tomato sauce, veal Marsala and cioppino as well as duck, veal, fish and sirloin are entrée choices. All are served with vegetables or pasta. Don't miss the decadent tiramisù for dessert. The wine list is terrific, with reasonable prices by the glass or bottle. The Kallas family will make you part of their family from the first hello until the last goodbye.

Union, an American Bistro

Cuisine: American
Open: L-D: Tues-Sat
Unionamericanbistro.com

1 Wilcox St.   303-688-8159
Castle Rock, 80104
South Street and Wilcox

Price: $$ **Patio:** Yes
Reservations: Yes   **Brunch:** No
Location: Castle Rock

Union is a spot for casual dining in Castle Rock. As you enter, view the open kitchen featuring a pizza oven and stainless trim, a beautiful bar and a community table in the first room. The main dining area features warmly lit red brick and stucco walls, high wood ceilings and cozy seating. The nattily dressed staff is friendly and efficient. Start with an array of appetizers that include Thai flat bread with grilled chicken and spicy peanut sauce, mussels and a cheese platter. Salads and sandwiches are available for lighter fare. Entrées include double bone-in pork chops, grilled salmon and beef tenderloin. Do not leave without dessert. The decadent chocolate chip cookie tart with ice cream and caramel, chocolate-espresso cupcake and cheesecake bring a perfect ending to the meal. Union is a place for good food and a fine time.

United Chinese Restaurant & Sushi

Cuisine: Chinese
Open: L-D: Daily
Unitedchineserestaurant.com

12161 Sheridan Blvd.   303-469-2230
Broomfield, 80020
120th & Sheridan

4150 E. 128th Ave   720-977-8888
Thornton, 80241
Thornton

Price: $$ **Patio:** No
Reservations: Yes   **Brunch:** No
Location: Thornton

Thornton can boast a special restaurant in United Chinese. As you enter the beautiful large dining area, a waterfall and a scene of China are visible. The room is soft with burgundy wood tones and light walls. Seating is comfortable with large tables and lovely booths. Start with crispy noodles, hot-and-sour soup, crab cream cheese won tons or scallion pancakes. More great starters include egg rolls, fried shrimp and dumplings. The entrée list is long making decisions a challenge. Orange beef arrives crispy with a tangy orange-peel sauce while the mu shoo pancakes bring nicely cooked veggies, chicken or pork wrapped in a delicious pancake. Chicken satay with peanut sauce, steamed fish in ginger sauce, shrimp with crispy green beans and a terrific version of lo mein are a few other options. Combination dinners are offered if you can't decide on just one item. Presentation of each dish is beautiful. Enjoy chocolate cake, red-bean or green-tea ice cream for dessert. Nice wine and beer lists give great options as well as a beautifully served green tea. Service is excellent and prices are affordable.

The Universal

Cuisine: Breakfast/American
Open: B-L: Tues-Sun
Theuniversaldenver.blogspot.com

2911 W. 38th Ave.   303-955-0815
Denver, 80211
38th and Elliot

Price: $-$$ **Patio:** No
Reservations: No   **Brunch:** No
Location: Northwest - Sunnyside

The Universal has earned a spot on the list of terrific lunch and breakfast restaurants in this popular North Denver neighborhood. Enter to a great bar, walls of stucco, barn wood, big windows, comfortable seating and an inviting feel. Start your day with The Universal classics: two eggs with the trimmings, biscuits and gravy, eggs Benedict or a seasonal veggie Benedict. All entrées arrive with eggs cooked to order and plates looking as great as they taste. Cornbread rancheros start with a piece of cornbread layered with black beans, roasted tomato salsa, two fried eggs, pico fresco, cheese, sour cream and avocado all adding up to yum. The grills are a signature and bring raves from all. They are available in some dishes and always as a side. Don't miss the fried egg sandwich with bacon, sausage or ham with tomato and gruyère on croissant. Add pancakes, custard toast, oats or yogurt and granola and the sun is shining. The coffees and loose leaf teas are also awesome. At lunch there are more choices with several sandwiches like the house smoked pulled pork, classic BLT, apple and brie, tempeh, turkey melt, a burger and the best egg salad. Several side options complement the food. Don't miss chicken leg confit with collard greens and cornbread, the extraordinary chop salad or spinach salad. And remember those grits of the day with two eggs. Prices are reasonable, the staff friendly and informative and you feel totally welcome here. The Universal is just what the neighborhood needs to make everyone happy at breakfast and lunch.

US Thai Café

Cuisine: Thai
Open: L-D: Tues-Sun

5228 W. 25th Avenue
Edgewater, 80215   303-233-3345
Ames and 26th

Price: $$ **Patio:** No
Reservations: No   **Brunch:** No
Location: Edgewater

It is a common debate—Is it U.S. Thai or US Thai? You can debate the pronunciation of this Thai restaurant tucked off the main street of Edgewater, but one thing everyone in your party will agree on is how remarkable the food is. While the restaurant does most of its business as take-out orders, if you select to stay you will be impressed with the friendliness of the servers and the promptness of your order. Every meal at US Thai should begin with their signature spring rolls and peanut sauce. Two come per order, so share with a friend and save room for your main dish. It is hard to pick a favorite dish, but depending on your mood you cannot go wrong with the green curry, pad Thai or drunken noodles. One word of caution— their heat ranking scale is unique. Thai Medium is extremely spicy, even for those of us who adore some extra kick. My recommendation for first timers, order Mild and get extra spice on the side. Whatever you choose, US Thai is great fun.

Venice Ristorante

Cuisine: Italian, Steakhouse
Open: L: Mon-Fri, D: Daily
veniceristorante.com

5946 S. Holly St.   720-482-9191
Greenwood Village, 80111
Orchard & Holly

Price: $$$$ **Patio:** No
Reservations: Yes   **Brunch:** No
Location: Greenwood Village

Venice hits the spot and fills the bill for great Italian dining in the suburbs. Alessandro and Sara Carollo have created an upscale restaurant with wonderful high ceilings, wood floors, faux-painted gold walls, beautiful murals of Venice and lovely table settings. Ceiling drapes add a dimension that lessens the noise level. It's warm and comfortable, the perfect spot to meet friends. The efficient staff adds to the personal feel. Appetizers include perfectly fried calamari, delicious tomato bruschetta, and mouthwatering mozzarella and tomatoes. Enjoy mussels or an antipasto platter as well. Pastas are delicious, from ravioli, penne, and linguine with clams to spaghetti Parmigiano. The luscious melt-in-your-mouth gnocchi is the best. For entrées, Colorado lamb chops, chicken or veal piccata, veal scaloppini, or salmon. The fish specials are outrageous, including whole grouper, pan-seared monkfish, cioppino, and salmon. Perfectly cooked vegetables and sides of pasta come with the entrées. There are prime steaks for the meat lovers in your group. End with tiramisù, profiterole or cannoli. All of this adds up to a wonderful spot for dining.

Venice Ristorante & Wine Bar

Cuisine: Italian
Open: L: Mon-Fri, D: Daily
veniceristorante.com

1700 Wynkoop St.　　　　　303-534-2222
Denver, 80202
17th & Wynkoop

Price: $$$$　　　　　　**Patio:** Yes
Reservations: Yes　　　　**Brunch:** No
Location: LoDo

Allessandro and Sara Carollo have created a fabulous Italian restaurant in LoDo with stunning design, food and service. The bar/lounge is very large and comfortable, a perfect area for casual dining and drinks. A mural of Venice covers the back wall while the gorgeous glass adega can be seen behind the bar. The adega is the focal point of the dining room as well. Housing hundreds of bottles of wine, guests are welcome to wander through the room. The extensive choice of wines includes many by the glass or bottle. Big picture windows, soft lighting, and beautiful china and glassware add to the ambience. Start with great bread and appetizers of fried calamari, mozzarella wrapped in prosciutto, bruschetta, and grilled artichokes. Carpaccio, prepared several different ways, is a treat. The Caesar served in a parmesan bowl is a must and other salad options round out the selection of greens. Pastas include ravioli, linguine with clams, penne, and several vegetarian options. Risotto is another favorite and preparations vary. Fish is listed on the specials page, offering the freshest available sea bass, halibut, whole branzini, cioppino, salmon and more. The seafood linguini is a signature. Chicken favorites include Marsala, parmesan, and sausage with peppers. Veal fans delight in the many options, but the most spectacular dishes are the veal chop and the rack of veal. Prime steaks and rack of lamb please those who want simpler preparations. Wonderful vegetables, sauces and sides of pasta accompany each dish. End with tiramisù, profiteroles or the decadent Nutella crêpe à la mode. Service is excellent with the knowledgeable and charming staff adding to the pleasure of dining. Venice is a big hit in the LoDo dining area for good reason.

Vert Kitchen

Cuisine: Café, Deli, French
Open: B-L: Daily
vertkitchen.com

704 S. Pearl St.   303-997-5941
Denver, 80209
S. Pearl & Exposition

Price: $-$$ **Patio:** Yes
Reservations: No   **Brunch:** No
Location: Old South Pearl

Vert Kitchen brings a classic, all-organic, French-style deli to South Pearl. This modern, clean and well-organized boutique restaurant seats 18 people (including the front and back patio). Vert, meaning "green," is the vision of French-trained chefs, Noah Stevens and Emily Welch. The menu, short but sweet, is a clear representation of their talent and vision. The restaurant offers a selection of sandwiches and choice of side salad that are amazing. The house-roasted turkey is deliciously inventive with chèvre, pine nuts, greens, tomatoes and a balsamic-fig spread. The hearty pork shoulder with peppers, roasted cabbage and sweet paprika is another fantastic choice. For lighter fare, try the lemon tuna "confit" with fresh albacore, chervil, cucumbers and Greek yogurt. House made soup of the day and perfectly prepared coffee selections are also available. You may choose to stay or "take away," as they offer box lunches which include a sandwich of your choice, side of seasonal salad and a bottled beverage. Vert Kitchen is a refreshing and delightful addition to the West Wash Park neighborhood.

Vesta Dipping Grill

Cuisine: Contemporary
Open: D: Daily
vestagrill.com

1822 Blake St.   303-296-1970
Denver, 80202
18th & Blake

Price: $$$-$$$$ **Patio:** Yes
Reservations: Yes   **Brunch:** No
Location: LoDo

Vesta continues to be a top spot in Denver. As one of the most innovative and popular restaurants, it has it all. The architecture includes curves of copper, exposed brick and cloth-shrouded light fixtures, but the food and impeccable service are what keep people coming back again and again to this popular LoDo dining spot. Owners Josh and Jen Wolkon are incredible folks. Enjoy people-watching at the bar that stretches most of the length of the restaurant, or grab a seat on the patio to watch the crowds outside. Start the night with a glass of homemade sangria or sample a wine from the creative and unique wine list served at reasonable prices. More than 30 sauces are available to accompany your entrée, ranging from sweet to savory to hot or Vesta-hot. Use the chef's choice on the menu or choose your own. Bites include BBQ pork belly and salmon tartare. Appetizers of Vesta roll, ponzu shrimp, duck pot stickers, venison kielbasa and tagliatelle delight. Add a chaucterie plate and salads of tomato and avocado and heirloom spinach with feta and enjoy the flavors of each. The main courses bring many choices: venison, salmon, striped bass with maitake mushrooms, and scallops start the list. Grilled beef tenderloin, venison, duck breast, and masala half chicken show the creativity of the chefs as each accompaniment adds to the flavor and taste of each dish. Presentation is very special. The dessert list is decadent: flourless dark-chocolate cake with coffee ice cream, daily bread pudding, or the Wacky Apple. The "candy bar" is a must, and the ice cream sandwich is awesome. Be sure to ask about their special menus for those with food allergies. Executive chef Brandon Foster, has added great new dishes to the menu that bring his special touch to Vesta. The staff is among the best in town. Vesta is totally upbeat place with great energy in every aspect.

Vine Street Pub

Cuisine: American, Brewpub
Open: L: Tues-Sun, D: Daily
mountainsunpub.com

1700 Vine St.   303-388-2337
Denver, 80206   1
7th & Vine

Price: $$ **Patio:** Yes
Reservations: No   **Brunch:** No
Location: Uptown

Vine Street Pub is a Boulder favorite with a location in Denver. The space features wooden picnic tables, booths, a great bar, large windows and eclectic décor. Casual and friendly, this is a place to relax. The beers are outstanding with several boutique selections and a short but nice wine list complements the brews, along with a selection of non-alcoholic beverages. The staff is friendly and helpful making guests feel comfortable. Start with a plate of nachos, or hummus with chips and bread. The pub's famous fries can be ordered as an appetizer or as a side and while you wait for a table baskets of the goodies are put out for noshing. House specialties include a huge burrito, quesadillas and fish and chips. Enjoy sandwiches for your main course:

burgers of every kind including vegetarian, turkey and pesto, grilled chicken, a fabulous Monterey chicken, tuna and a BLT. Choose your bread, add a side, and you'll be totally satisfied. The wrap special each day is a must as well. Enjoy cheesecake for dessert. Kids are treated well with a menu of their own. With its staff and affordable prices, you won't mind cash only. Vine Street Pub is the perfect casual spot to the popular 17th Avenue dining scene.

Virgilio's Pizzeria

Cuisine: Italian, Pizza
Open: L: Mon-Fri, D: Daily, BR: Sat-Sun
virgiliospizzeria.com

10025 W. San Juan Way   303-985-2777
Littleton, 80127
C-470 & Kipling

Price: $$ **Patio:** No
Reservations: No   **Brunch:** Yes
Location: Littleton

Enter this small pizzeria and know you are in for one terrific pizza. The décor is simple and the open kitchen is the focal point as the chefs toss the dough and pile on fresh ingredients. With some seats at the counter, the room can seat about 40 people. Settle down for a big treat. Start with garlic knots, totally addictive, warm from the oven and served with marinara sauce for dipping. No one can eat just one. The Caesar, house and Greek salads are exceptional with terrific dressings. Pizza is the star. The crust is thin, perfectly cooked, and the toppings feature freshly grated cheeses and all your favorite ingredients. House specials include white pizza, marguerite, veggie, pepperoni and sausage, Greek, puttanesca, bacon and sausage, or pick your own toppings. Calzones, along with hero sandwiches, are other options. Looking for pasta? There are stuffed shells, meatballs and spaghetti, ravioli, ziti and eggplant parmesan. If you have room, end with delicious gelato, cannoli, tiramisù or sorbet. The wine and beer list complement your pie. Service is terrific, and Virgilio is there to charm every guest. After one visit, no matter where you live, you'll know it's worth the drive, and Virgilio's will be a favorite "neighborhood" pizzeria.

Vita

Cuisine: Contemporary
Open: L-D: Daily, BR: Sat-Sun
vitadenver.com

1575 Boulder St.   303-477-4600
Denver, 80211
15th & Boulder

Price: $$-$$$ **Patio:** Yes
Reservations: Yes   **Brunch:** Yes
Location: Highlands

The dining picture in the Lower Highland continues to grow and Vita brings fun with its knockout décor and patios. Diners delight in exposed ceilings, large picture windows that open onto the patio when weather permits, merlot-colored accents and brick walls. Seating is comfortable. The bar is the place to meet inside or wander outside when the windows are open. The rooftop patio is the place to meet. Start with gnocchi, fried calamari, marinated ahi tuna, braised pork belly, flat bread pizza or risotto fritters. The list of entrées includes ravioli, lasagna, chicken rolletini, and several fish options from salmon and tuna to scallops. The beef short rib, pork tenderloin, and lamb rack are more options. Desserts include "almost" flourless chocolate cake with espresso gelato, a coffee toffee pot de crème, gelatos and more. The wine and martini lists are excellent and service shines. There is a fabulous happy hour for drinks, wines and appetizers. It's casual, friendly and upbeat.

Walnut Brewery

Cuisine: Brewpub
Open: L-D: Daily, BR: Sat-Sun
walnutbrewery.com

1123 Walnut St.   303-447-1345
Boulder, 80302
11th & Walnut

Price: $-$$ **Patio:** Yes
Reservations: Yes   **Brunch:** Yes
Location: Boulder

Walnut Brewery was the first brewpub to open in Boulder and remains a wonderful spot to enjoy fresh beer and tasty fare. An extensive appetizer list boasts pan-seared Brie, Asiago cheese dip, spicy Buffalo wings and grilled Portobello. Soup lovers can make a full meal out of the beer-onion soup. Brewery favorites include fish and chips made with salmon, barbecue ribs in stout sauce, fried chicken, and a long list of burgers and sandwiches. For dessert, enjoy a slice of chocolate derby pie, or carrot cake with caramel sauce.

Walnut Café

Cuisine: American, Café
Open: B-L: Daily
walnutcafe.com

3073 Walnut St.   303-447-2315
Boulder, 80301
Walnut Gardens Shopping Center

Walnut Café South Side   Boulder, 80305
673 S. Broadway   720-304-8118
Table Mesa & Broadway

2770 Arapahoe Rd   720-328-9208
Lafayette
Atlas Valley Shopping Center

Price: $ **Patio-Yes**
Reservations: No   **Brunch:** No
Location: Boulder

Imagine the quintessential country diner. Now make it healthy, fresh and hip--not wannabe hip--just savvy enough. That's the Walnut Café. Choose from the main location on Walnut Street, the South Side Walnut in South Boulder or the newer Super Mini Walnut Café in Lafayette. The environment at the Walnut Café is always light and cheery. There are outdoor patios at all locations and they even provide light fleece blankets to keep you comfy on crisp Colorado mornings. The wait staff is friendly, and the breakfast and lunch items are delicious and reasonably priced–as little as $3. There are plenty of healthy (OK, maybe not-so-healthy- but-delicious) choices for both meat eaters and vegetarians alike. Locals migrate on a regular basis for espresso drinks, waffles, pancakes, eggs, omelets and homemade quiches, specials ones most days. Of course, don't miss desserts, which include a selection of award-winning pies and mini cupcakes made fresh each day! Favorite menu items include blueberry cornbread, fluffy pancakes, Belgian waffles, French toast, vegetarian Sloppy Joes, huevos rancheros, Boulder scramble, big dill eggs, quiche of the day and pie for dessert. Seriously, don't skip the pie. The Walnut Café is a must, but do expect a bit of a wait for a table during peak hours on weekends. It's worth the wait.

Washington Park Grille

Cuisine: American, Italian
Open: L: Mon-Fri, D: Daily, BR: Sat-Sun
washparkgrille.com

1096 S. Gaylord St.   303-777-0707
Denver, 80209
So. Gaylord & Mississippi

Price: $$-$$$ **Patio:** Yes
Reservations: Yes   **Brunch:** Yes
Location: Washington Park

Wash Park Grille has offered tasty cuisine in a casual atmosphere for years. Crowds from the surrounding neighborhood drop in to play a free game of pool, hang out on the patio or have a drink in the bar. Start with a white-port mojito for a great twist on the popular drink. Settle down and indulge in one of the reasonably priced wines as you nibble on homemade bread. Start your meal with wild boar baby back ribs, calamari, crab cakes or grilled skewers of mozzarella, basil and Roma tomatoes. Pasta possibilities include Tuscan lasagna, fettuccine Alfredo, angel hair pasta with sun-dried tomatoes, and lobster tail pappardelle. Order seared ahi, rib-eye, pork chops or lemon chicken from the grill. Finish with death-by-raspberry crème brûlée or chocolate ecstasy. On Sundays, stop in for a casual, delicious buffet brunch that will make your day.

WaterCourse Foods

Cuisine: Breakfast, Natural Foods
Open: L-D: Daily BR: Sat-Sun
watercoursefoods.com

837 E. 17th Ave.   303-832-7313
Denver, 80218
Emerson & 17th Ave.

Price: $$ **Patio:** Yes
Reservations: Yes   **Brunch:** Yes
Location: Uptown

One of Denver's few vegetarian/vegan restaurants, WaterCourse Foods is part of the popular 17th Avenue area. The space is bright and cheery with big windows, a case displaying pastries and muffins, a carryout station and lots of seating. Open for breakfast, lunch and dinner daily, crowds come to enjoy their favorites. Breakfast until 5 p.m. is always a treat, where you can enjoy scrambles, biscuits and gravy, tamales, burritos, pancakes, French toast and granola. Lunch and dinner feature appetizers of baked Brie with toasts, nachos, French fries and seitan Buffalo wings. Sandwiches and wraps include a po' boy of polenta and Portobello mushrooms, buffalo tofu, eggplant parmesan and a tempeh burger. "Build your own" salad offers an entire salad bar menu but you pick the items and the kitchen takes charge and brings it to your table. There are several pastas, stir-fries, and tofu dinners to round out the menu. Some of the favorites include pasta puttanesca, fettuccini with sweet marinara, a terrific giant veggie burrito, and a tempeh chorizo and fried potato taco plate. End with dessert selections that change often. A wide range of beverages include smoothies, juices, coffee and tea, along with wine and beer. Service is casual and friendly. Totally organic and green, WaterCourse fills a niche for vegetarian dining and pleases carnivores as well.

Waterloo

Cuisine: American
Open: L-D: Daily
watercoursefoods.com

809 S. Main St.   303-993-2094
Louisville, 80027
Main & Spruce

Price: $$ **Patio:** Yes
Reservations: No   **Brunch:** No
Location: Louisville

Quickly becoming a favorite spot in Louisville, Waterloo offers tasty fare in a warm and lively atmosphere. The name pays homage to a record store in Austin, Texas. Images of music greats don the walls and the sound track is a total feel good. Waterloo serves a handsome variety of burgers, salads, salads and appetizers. The menu specialty is the signature potato burger and not to be missed. This is Coleman beef with shredded potatoes kneaded in to absorb the flavor and moisturize each mouthful. With live music on many nights and a back patio for chillin', Waterloo is a great spot for a great time.

J:

K:

Wazee Supper Club

Cuisine: Pizza
Open: L-D: Daily
wazeesupperclub.com

1600 15th St.   303-623-9518
Denver, 80202
15th & Wazee

Price: $$ **Patio:** No
Reservations: No   **Brunch:** No
Location: LoDo

The Wazee Supper Club bills itself as "The Granddaddy of LoDo" and lives up to its name for casual atmosphere and unfussy food. Enter and find a cheerful setting with a large bar, terrific windows to catch the crowd and comfortable seating with booths and nicely spaced tables. The place has been renovated and great exposed pipes and urban lighting add to the scene. Start with appetizers perfect to share such as Italian breadsticks, chicken skewers with Thai dipping sauce, crispy mozzarella sticks, chicken wings and crab cakes. The artichoke dip and bruschetta with hummus, tapenade and tomato relish are ore choices. Caesar, Greek, house, Cobb or blackened salmon salads make filling entrées. Chili and soups round out the first course selections. There are burgers and sandwiches from a turkey melt and Reuben to a gyro and French dip. The pizza is a big hit with its thin crust with the right amount of crunch and with an endless list of toppings to build your own. A good choice is a Stromboli for your main dish. End with decadent desserts as you enjoy the crowd. With live music on select nights this is a fun choice in LoDo.

Welton Street Café

Cuisine: Caribbean, Southern
Open: L-D: Daily

2736 Welton St., Suite 107   303-296-6602
Denver, 80205
27th & Welton

Price: $-$$ **Patio:** No
Reservations: No   **Brunch:** No
Location: Curtis Park, 5 Points

Welton Street Café is a bright and cheery family restaurant serving Southern and Caribbean-style cooking in the Five Points redevelopment. The staff is friendly, and the food is delicious. Start with their specialty wings, available plain, hot, honey-hot or barbecue-style. Then move on to why you really came here: the meals of fried chicken, fried fish. Caribbean

"jerk" chicken, and pork. The fried chicken is stellar—seasoned perfectly, hot, crispy and delicious. It takes a while to come out, but that's a sign of properly prepared fried chicken. Fried fish options are catfish, whiting and perch. There's fried shrimp as well. Smothered pork chops, sandwiches and burgers round out the menu. The cornbread accompanying the meals is excellent, and don't forget the homey and comforting sides. For dessert, try the peach cobbler, sweet potato pie or rum cake. They also do a brisk carryout business; call in your order to reduce wait time. When you want a fix of good Southern comfort food, check out Welton Street Café. You'll be satisfied until the next time you're hungry and crave more of that fried chicken!

West End Tavern

Cuisine: American
Open: L-D: Daily, BR: Sun
thewestendtavern.com

926 Pearl St.   303-444-3535
Boulder, 80302
9th & Pearl

Price: $$ **Patio:** Yes
Reservations: No   **Brunch:** Yes
Location: Boulder

Boulder's most successful restaurateur, David Query, has revitalized the original West End Tavern to a bustling hot spot in town. The space is primarily a bar scene, but families can comfortably enjoy the festivities too. The menu features American comfort food with new twists on old classics. Start with deep-fried pickles and Buffalo wings. Other popular dishes include burgers, mac and cheese, sandwiches and salads. At dinner, entrées range from pecan-blackened catfish and fried chicken to steak specials. West End's big draw is its rooftop patio which offers views of the Flatirons.

West 29th St. Restaurant and Bar

Cuisine: American
Open: L-Mon-Fri, D Daily-BR Sat-Sun
West29th.com

5560 E. 29th Avenue   303-233-3377
Wheat Ridge, 80214
29th between Sheridan and Wadsworth

Price: $$-$$$ **Patio:** Yes
Reservations: Yes   **Brunch:** Yes
Location: Wheat Ridge

West 29th Restaurant and Bar is a fun spot located near Sloans Lake. The free standing house is charming. As you enter to a super bar area, enjoy drinks or dinner or move into the dining area with nicely spaced tables amid colorful Indian rugs on the wall. The patios are the place to be weather permitting. There is an open kitchen as well. Start with lovely wines and beer at affordable prices as you peruse the menu. Appetizers include a crab cake, beet tartar, calamari, meat and cheese plates and potato croquettes. The Caesar, soups, and the mixed greens with grilled asparagus, eggs, and bacon and lemon vinaigrette delight. Entrees of roasted chicken, fish and chips, a filet, and peppercorn seared flatiron start the list of main course options. Add trout, halibut, wild salmon, and double cut pork chop and you are in for treats. There are pastas and a burger as well. All come with complementary sides that add to the taste of each dish. End with crème brûlée, lemon bar or tiramisu. Service is friendly and hospitable and prices are reasonable. The staff makes an extra effort to entertain the youngsters. West 29th Restaurant and Bar is a delightful addition to this neighborhood.

The White Chocolate Grill

Cuisine: American
Open: L-D: Daily, BR: Sat-Sun
whitechocolategrill.com

8421 Park Meadows Center Dr.   303-799-4841
Lone Tree, 80124
Vistas at Park Meadows

Price: $$$ **Patio:** Yes
Reservations: Yes   **Brunch:** Yes
Location: Park Meadows, Lone Tree

The White Chocolate Grill is a part of "restaurant row" in the Vistas at Park Meadows. The first thing you see as you enter the building is a fabulous outdoor fireplace. Contemporary in design, the large space is warm and comfortable with an open kitchen and bar that features a wall of colored tequila bottles—not to be opened! This is not a dessert-only spot although they feature white chocolate desserts at the top of the menu, along with chocolate and apple pie. Eat dessert first or start with a fresh artichoke, egg rolls, tomato gin soup or sesame-crusted tuna. There are several salads offered, and of course a section of burgers and sandwiches. Entrées start with barbecued baby back ribs, blue cheese-crusted filet, prime rib and pork. Fish options include blackened mahi mahi, trout and salmon. Sides include couscous, fries, potatoes, honey-roasted carrots and steamed broccoli. The wine list is nice, the service great. White Chocolate Grill is a nice choice for dining in the Vistas.

White Fence Farm

Cuisine: American
Open: D: Tues-Sun: L: Sat-Sun
Whitefencefarm.com

6265 W. Jewell Avenue.   303-935-5945
Lakewood, 80232
Between Sheridan and Wadsworth on Jewell

Price: $$ **Patio:** No
Reservations: No   **Brunch:** No
Location: Lakewood

White Fence Farm is an adventure. It's far more than just dining. Drive into the huge property and be delighted with its charm. The main building is huge. Start with 7 dining rooms designed for large parties, small or intimate meals, spots for kids and even a room where no children are allowed. It's all very casual and done in that country feel. Keep walking and find the sweet bar—stop here for malts, milkshakes, candies, homemade pies, brownies, and cookies-yum. Then there's a gift shop with all sorts of mementos, gifts, and even special bottles of salad dressing, spices, salsas, and jellies. Next visit the bar lounge where a very nice list of cocktails, wines, and beer make this the place to enjoy live entertainment nightly. We are not done yet as there is music during weekend lunch in the gazebo, and the live animal farm to enjoy and interact with the animals. Now it's time for food. Dinner at the White Fence Farm is served family style. All meals come with addictive hot corn fritters, pickled red beets, creamy coleslaw, kidney bean salad, and special blend cottage cheese along with a choice of baked, mashed or fried potato. This all goes with their famous chicken that is steamed and then fried in very hot oil when ordered to crisp and brown. There are other options of a delicious pork chop, steak, turkey while available, shrimp and fish. Seconds of sides come at no extra charge. Do not leave without decadent desserts of house made pies, cheesecake, sundaes, ice creams and more. When you dine here take the kids and enjoy the farm or be sophisticated and stay for an adult night of drinks and entertainment. Either way, or in between, White Fence Farm is a special place to visit and brings super service, affordable prices, and a very different and unique dining experience.

Wild Basil

Cuisine: Chinese, Sushi, Thai, Vietnamese
Open: L-D: Daily
wildbasil.com

8247 S. Holly   303-779-8889
Littleton, 80122
S. Holly & County Line

Price: $$	**Patio:** No
Reservations: No	**Brunch:** No
Location: Littleton	

Enter this delightful spot and find a welcoming restaurant with shades of green and tan, a brick wall, and comfortable seating with booths and tables. Service is excellent with a friendly staff to assist you. Start with spring rolls, steamed dumplings, egg rolls, calamari, chicken lettuce wraps or excellent soft-shell crab. Entrées start with chicken prepared in several ways: lemon grass, Thai basil with vegetables, royal and spicy garlic. The crispy duck is a must, or enjoy the Peking duck. The beef selection ranges from curry lime, black pepper and Mongolian to Sriracha and orange. Shrimp and pork dishes are excellent, or delight in scallops, mussels or tofu. There are curries and noodle bowls, a wonderfully flavored pad Thai, drunken noodles and fried rice. Presentation is beautiful, flavors terrific and portions substantial so sharing is a great way to enjoy many dishes. There is beer and wine to complement your dinner. With affordable prices, wonderful food and families welcome, Wild Basil is a perfect neighborhood spot for special Thai cuisine.

Wild Eggs

Cuisine: Breakfast/Lunch
Open: B-L: Daily
wildeggs.com

300 E. Alameda   303-744-3447
Denver, 80209
Alameda & Logan

Price: $-$$ **Patio:** Yes
Reservations: No   **Brunch:** No
Location: South Central

Enter this bright spot and get ready for a happy day. The décor is lively with vibrant colors, fabulous pictures of eggs (from their kitchen) and egg dishes, great lighting, a bar, and comfortable seating. Start with excellent coffee and tea or a bar drink if you like. Then try to figure out what to order. Crêpes with berries, French toast, a terrific list of pancakes that include one with bananas, peanut butter, syrup and chocolate chips, or waffles from a plain Belgian to bananas Foster. The egg options include a burrito, enchilada, a BLT with eggs, avocado, cheddar, a Greek frittata, huevos, scrambles, and skillets. The "benes" rock with veggie, wild mushroom, and lox and bagel along with traditional. If omelets are your thing there is a big selection here too. Lunch brings soups, salads and sandwiches with Reuben, a burger, and grilled cheese between the bread and salads of chicken, taco, and smoked salmon. Don't forget the "everything" muffin, their rendition of an 'everything' bagel, and several sides as well as oatmeal and granola. Potato latkes are exceptional. The staff is excellent, and you'll find this "eggceptional" restaurant on your list of breakfast options.

Williams & Graham

Cuisine: Bar, GastroPub
Open: D: Daily
williamsandgraham.com

3160 Tejon St.   303-997-8886
Denver, 80211
32nd & Tejon

Price: $$-$$$ **Patio:** No
Reservations: Yes   **Brunch:** No
Location: Highlands

The trend of the Prohibition-era secret bar has swept the country from coast to coast the last few years and Williams & Graham brought that trend to the Mile High City. A speakeasy-styled bar in the hot LoHi neighborhood, Williams & Graham looks like an old bookstore, dark and packed with floor to ceiling bookshelves. One of those bookshelves opens as a large door and takes you back in time to the 1920 into a beautiful bar and comfortable dining area filled with cozy booths and soft dark furniture. The bar is certainly the main attraction--this is where widely recognized bar wiz Sean Kenyon can be found most nights mixing up carefully crafted cocktails for very appreciative customers. Kenyon is an artist and a craftsman with his bar program but he keeps things approachable and his customer service commitment is very strong. The food menu at Williams & Graham is petite but offers a mighty complement to the cocktails. The ham and gruyère cheese sandwich is explosively rich and satisfying, the deviled eggs are a fun staple and the Boar Ham with mushrooms and mashed potatoes is a delight. The experience that Williams & Graham offers is magical in many ways--and the top notch quality of the service, food, and cocktails make this place a well-loved Denver establishment.

The Wooden Spoon

Cuisine: Bakery, Café
Open: B-L: Tues-Sun
woodenspoondenver.com

2418 W. 32nd Avenue   303-999-0327
Denver, 80211
32nd & Zuni

Price: $-$$ **Patio:** Yes
Reservations: No   **Brunch:** No
Location: Highlands

The Wooden Spoon is one cute place---and the food is excellent. Enter this small one room café with limited seating, and be greeted by a friendly smiling person behind the counter where you order your meal. Look at the fabulous pastries and muffins on display in the display counter. The soft yellows, high exposed ceiling, and fun pictures of chickens and spoons set the scene. Owners Jeannette and Jason prepare everything on site and the result is some exceptional sandwiches, salads, and more. Start with breakfast where the egg sandwiches served on toasted brioche can be had with many extras at little cost. Or get Noosa yogurt with house made granola and fruit or choose from the daily baked scones, muffins, quiche, turnovers, croissants, sticky buns and more. For lunch be thrilled with the best turkey, roasted here, with tomato, salsa verde, Swiss and spinach, BLT, ham and swiss, roast beef, mozzarella and arugula, or herb goat cheese on the sandwich list. The bread is remarkable with fillings and flavorful toppings on all, and they are served with homemade coleslaw or chips. Salads include quinoa with candied pecans and cranberries, butter lettuce with walnuts, apple and cheese, or the daily soup. Desserts are a must: cookies, chocolate, amazing lemon meringue tart, brownies, along with major cakes and many other luscious sweets. They cater and have a great carry out.

The Wooden Table

Cuisine: Italian
Open: L: Mon-Fri, D: Mon-Sat
thewoodentablerestaurant.com

2500 E. Orchard Rd.   303-730-2152
Greenwood Village, 80121
Orchard & University

Price: $$$$ **Patio:** Yes
Reservations: Yes   **Brunch:** No
Location: Greenwood Village

The Wooden Table brings an upscale treat to the neighborhood. Start with a stunning ambience--large windows, a sensational bar of cherry wood, a community table and lovely tables of beautiful woods. Comfortable seating, large windows, and soft lighting add to the scene. Chef/Owner Brett Shaheen and front of the house/partner Jane Knauf are the most delightful team setting the tone along with a friendly staff. The food is Italian and delicious. Start with addictive bread, the best mussels with sausage, house made mozzarella with panzanella salad, frutti de mare crudo, and chicken liver mousse. You must have the eggplant parmesan rollotini and the mussels are worth the trip. The arugula salad with deep fried oyster mushroom, pecorino, and truffled vinaigrette, prosciutto di parma, spinach and Caesar salads rock.. Brett makes all the pasta and this course amazes: ravioli, tortellini with shrimp, pappardelle with duck, gnocchi with lobster, and agnolotti with house-made sausage. All come in half orders as well. Monkfish with bay scallops, duck with duck confit and foie gras, veal cheeks, and divine pork are marvelous options not to be missed. House made sausage with chicken cacciatore, beef tenderloin with braised short rib, and outstanding lamb loin with a zucchini goat cheese fritter are more of the exciting entrées. Each presentation is as lovely to see as it is to enjoy with complementary flavors. The newest feature, a fabulous cheese cart makes for a fabulous course. The wines that pair are special as well. End with decadent desserts of tres leche cake, tarts, cheesecake, and more. A terrific wine list and thoughtful service are a plus. The bar offerings delights guests who gather for drinks or to enjoy dinner. The Wooden Table brings something special to the Denver dining scene and is a favorite locale for Italian dining.

Work & Class

Cuisine: American: Latino
Open: D:-Tues-Sun
Workandclassdenver.com

2500 Larimer
Denver
25th & Larimer

303-342-3490

Price: $$
Reservations: No
Location: RiNo

Patio: Yes
Brunch: No

The most exciting place to open in Denver is this fabulous restaurant owned by Chef Dana Rodriguez, front of the house Delores Tronco, and Tony Maciag, longtime bartender, who make one fantastic team. Together they are bringing awesome "Latino" inspired food and drinks with unbelievable vision to the masses in Denver. The space is small with a super bar, community table, comfortable seating, huge windows, fun lighting, woods, a super photograph that covers a wall and the focal kitchen. The place rocks with totally upbeat feel, and the food and service are divine. The talents of Rodriguez are showcased as she combines exceptional flavors and tastes in each dish. Although portions are certainly adequate for sharing, no one wants to give up a bite. Start with red chile goat stew-worth the trip-but so are the blue corn empanadas, salmon fritters, and meatballs. And that is only a start. Tempura broccoli with asparagus, avocado, spinach, cucumbers and pecorino, mixed greens with cheese and candied pecans, and peppers five ways are awesome. The meat section is another unique treat. Order lamb, pork, goat, short ribs, catfish, and chicken in portions of small, medium, and large and pair the list of accompaniments that are available in two sizes as well. The goat cheese corn tortillas, awesome cornbread, asparagus, green chili beans, sweet potato and bacon hash, and cheddar mashers are just some of the possibilities. It's impossible to choose. Decadent desserts include butterscotch pudding, stuffed doughnuts, apple bread pudding, sundae, and cranberry and orange cobbler. The cocktail and wine list is incredible, and priced reasonably. The cucumber pomegranate whiskey cocktail is addictive. Service brings another round of raves with friendly, informative, and efficient staff and pricing that is affordable. It's a joy to rave about a restaurant that is firing on all cylinders. The owners deserve much success in this venture. Work and Class has won well-deserved national awards and is tops in Denver.

Wynkoop Brewing Company

Cuisine: Brewpub
Open: L-D: Daily, BR: Sat-Sun
wynkoop.com

1634 18th St.   303-297-2700
Denver, 80202
18th & Wynkoop

Price: $$ **Patio:** Yes
Reservations: Yes   **Brunch:** Yes
Location: LoDo

The former J.S. Brown Mercantile Building in LoDo now
houses Denver's oldest brewpub, Wynkoop Brewery. Hardwood
floors, thick timber pillars and the pressed-tin ceiling remain
from the original structure—a place where ranchers, miners
and city folks shopped for dry goods. Upstairs, 22 pool tables,
two private poolrooms, several dart lanes and a bar serving
microbrews make this one of the city's finest billiard halls. The
Wynkoop is well known for Railyard Ale, terrific India pale ale,
Sagebrush Stout, and Denver's favorite, once brewery owner
and now governor, John Hickenlooper. The LoDo mainstay
also boasts seasonal specials like the raspberry ale and chile
beer. Hard cider makes a great autumn treat, but you can avoid
the alcohol altogether with an ice-cold root beer. Their beers are
now popular throughout the U.S. The restaurant is changing
with the times and a new updated menu theme is terrific. Small
plates include spicy sausage flat bread, mussels, fried calamari,
queso and a hummus dip. Salads include the pub, spinach
with dried cranberries and blue cheese, Caesar, ahi tuna, and
the best Thai Cobb with chicken, avocado, bacon, cucumber,
rice noodles and peanut dressing. Sandwiches include a super
burger, beef or buffalo, a Dagwood, French dip, Monterey
chicken, Reuben, grilled cheese and pulled pork. There are large
plates of Shepherd's pie with lamb, fish and chips, bangers and
mash, meatloaf, trout, and a pork porterhouse. Don't miss the
crunchy, crisp fried chicken with mashers and biscuit. There
are daily specials as well. For dessert, revel in the black-and-
tan cheesecake brownie served hot with vanilla ice cream, the
peach cobbler à la mode, apple tart, gingerbread or just a dish
of delicious caramel-cajeta ice cream. A terrific selection of
mixed drinks and wines are available as well as beer. This place
is home to the Denver chapter of the San Francisco 49'ers and
can be found rockin on select Sundays in the fall. Come for an
hour and stay for the day – you won't be sorry.

Ya Ya's

Cuisine: Mediterranean
Open: L-D: Daily, BR: Sun
yayasbistro.com

8310 E. Belleview Ave.   303-741-1110
Greenwood Village, 80111
E. Belleview & DTC Boulevard

Price: $$$ **Patio-Yes**
Reservations-Yes   **Brunch-Yes**
Location: Denver Tech Center

The attractive freestanding building boasts a fountain and pond, making patio dining feel elegant and refreshing. Tables go fast, as the ambience is perfect. The large friendly interior has a high-energy feel with dark woods and decor reminding one of a sophisticated club. The front of the restaurant has comfortable tables, while roomy booths in the rear make for more intimate dining. Start with homemade focaccia with baba ghanouj. Appetizers of bruschetta with oven-roasted cherry tomatoes, artichoke pizzetta, fried calamari, crab cakes and mussels are perfect for sharing. Add ravioli, squid-ink taglietelli, and a salumi plate or hamachi crudo for more choices. There are several salads and pasta dishes to entice. The kale salad is a must, along with Caesar and Greek, and pastas include lasagna and cavatelli. For your main course, choose pork tenderloin, hanger steak, and a selection of steaks and lamb chops, or enjoy grilled salmon, scallops and seared ahi. The trout is very special and a favorite of all. Presentation and flavors add to the appeal of the main protein. There is a selection of pizzas if you are in the mood. An ethereal hot chocolate soufflé tops the dessert list but crème brûlée, cheesecake and a phyllo-wrapped brownie also fill that sweet tooth. The kiddie menu is terrific with a "dirt pot" to please the younger set. The huge wine list offers an excellent selection by the bottle or glass at affordable prices. Ask your server and they will happily bring a selection to taste and then pour your choice at the table. Terrific and friendly service adds to the fun. Ya Ya's is a great choice in the area, or well worth the drive. And, valet parking is complimentary.

Yak and Yeti, Restaurant and Brewpub

Cuisine: Indian/Brewpub
Open: L-D: Daily
Theyakandyeti.com

7803 Ralston Rd. Arvada, 80002	303-431-9000
6385 Wadsworth Arvada	303-431-9000
9755 E. Hampden Denver	303-751-9443

Price: $$ **Patio:** No
Reservations: Yes   **Brunch:** No
Location: Arvada, Westminster, Denver

Yak and Yeti Restaurant & Brewpub in Arvada is a special treat set in a charming old mansion, rumored to be haunted. The food combines Indian, Nepalese and Tibetan influences to create exciting dishes. As you enter, the bar fills the entire first floor, complete with a view of the brewpub where the brew master makes several beers that change often. The dining room upstairs features a soft and welcoming ambience with warm colors and comfortable seating. Start with poppadums, the combination appetizer plate with samosas, pakoras, and the best onion fritters. Tandoori chicken is perfect served on a sizzling plate, the chicken tiki masala, sang paneer, lamb kabobs and lentils are some of the many entrées. Spicy potatoes in curry, lamb korma and a great selection of vegetarian dishes make decisions impossible. There are rice dishes, noodle bowls and a variety of naan breads as well. End with galob jammon, carrot pudding, rice pudding and kheer. There is a nice list of wines and lassis to complement the meal. Portions are large, prices reasonable, and service friendly. Yak and Yeti brings the best of Indian/Nepalese food to the area.

Yanni's

Cuisine: Greek
Open: L: Tues-Sat, D: Tues-Sun
yannisdenver.com

5425 Landmark Pl. Greenwood Village, 80111 Landmark Center	303-692-0404

Price: $$-$$$ **Patio:** Yes
Reservations: Yes   **Brunch:** No
Location: Denver Tech Center

Yanni's brings fun in the Landmark area. It's casual with a large bar, comfortable seating and a private dining room. Bright colors and blue tabletops set the scene for some good Greek food. Munch on appetizers, drink beer, wine and ouzo, and let your troubles melt away. Start with homemade bread warm from the oven, crispy outside and soft inside. You must have Saganaki that arrives with an "Opa!" It is melted kasseri cheese soaked with brandy, flamed and doused with lemon juice. Nibble on dolmades, feta with olives, grilled octopus, or fried potatoes and cheese baked in phyllo as you contemplate your next course. Don't miss the Greek salad or the Greek chicken soup. For entrées, try roasted leg of lamb, eggplant casserole, spanakopita or tasty kabobs. Seafood lovers will enjoy red snapper or salmon prepared Greek-style. Desserts include baklava, crème caramel and homemade rice pudding. Yanni is there to greet you and make your experience even more fun.

Yard House

Cuisine: American
Open: L-D: Daily
yardhouse.com

14500 W. Colfax Ave.	303-278-9273
Golden, 80401	
Colorado Mills	

1555 Court Place	303-572-9273
Denver, 80202	
16th Street Mall	

Price: $$-$$$ **Patio:** Yes
Reservations: No   **Brunch:** No
Location: Colorado Mills Golden, Downtown

Enter the Yard House and move into a large space with sleek stainless steel and get a good view of the kegs that line the walls. Pipes across the high ceiling deliver some of the more than 150 beers to taps at the focal bar. Seating is comfortable and the modern look continues throughout the restaurant. Although the menu has familiar bar dishes, there are gourmet items as well. Start with tasty chicken lettuce wraps, crab cakes, spicy tuna roll, nachos, ribs or onion rings. The turkey club is delicious, and burgers come in all forms. Enjoy pizza or pasta dishes such as penne with chicken or seafood linguine. House favorites include fish and chips, turkey potpie and excellent steaks. The sea bass and lamb chops are other options. End with decadent chocolate soufflé cake, crème brûlée or a killer Kona-coffee ice cream sundae. The wine list offers several excellent choices. Service keeps pace with friendly, efficient staff adding to the fun. There are now two locations.

Yura's Modern Asian Kitchen

Cuisine: Asian
Open: L-D: Mon-Sat D: Daily
Yurasdenver.com

955 Lincoln St.   303-813-9000
Denver, 80203
9th and 10th and Lincoln

Price: $$-$$$ **Patio:** No
Reservations: Yes   **Brunch:** No
Location: Denver - Central

This Asian restaurant deserves raves. The décor is lovely with a huge bar in the front area, lovely plants, wallpaper and seating in the main dining room, and most of all excellent food. The owner Tae is Korean, his wife and chef Vietnamese and together they bring a fusion of flavors and taste. Start with appetizers of spring rolls, dumplings, Thai char-grilled pork sausage, Thai chicken meat ball, sliders, and mussels. There are salads and soups and then the real fun begins. Noodle bowls and rice plates with a Vietnamese noodle bowl, bimibiap, and rice plate, pho, stews of duck or beef, fried rice, stir fry noodles with garlic noodles, Pad Thai, and drunken noodles are favorites. There's a pork chop with lemongrass, the divine curry chicken and Thai basil chicken. Beef and seafood dishes, lamb shank or chops. And tofu options round out the list. Do not miss the family hot pot and the awesome garlic ginger king crab legs with noodles.! There's a nice cocktail, beer, and wine list, excellent service, and great prices to add to the appeal. Get to Yura's once and you will be making plans for your next visit.

Z Cuisine A Cote

Cuisine: French
Open: D: Wed-Sat
Zcuisineonline.com

2239 W. 30th Ave.   303-477-1111
Denver, 80211
30th & Wyandot

Price: $$$-$$$$ **Patio:** Yes
Reservations: No   **Brunch:** No
Location: Highlands

Funky, charismatic, delightful and very French describe this tiny bistro. The one-room location exudes charm as the wood tables and chairs are accented by a terrific bar and vintage décor and a very jazzy chandelier. Mirrors and paintings round out the French feel. Chef/Owner Patrick Dupays and his wife Lynnde, wander through this cozy room and make guests feel at home. The restaurant has moved its main area to the A Cote space and now Z Cuisine space is for special nights, etc. Fresh French bread from Grateful Bread arrives at your table in a little brown paper back to accompany all the dishes. Start with the charcuterie plate to share with pork rillettes, pate, and cheese with fun accompaniments. The onion soup is outstanding as the cheese oozes over the top. Sardines, a terrine of foie gras, and fondue are other interesting dishes. The chevre log on crostini and lettueces and a tartine of ham and behamel appeal to all. Cod brandade, quiche, and cassoulet make exciting entrees when on the menu.End with rhubarb ice cream, choux with cream, crème brulee and a divine pot de crème. The wine list and cocktails complement the food and service is efficient and friendly. From "A" to "Z," Patrick and Lynnde bring a touch of France to Denver.

Zaidy's

Cuisine: Deli, Breakfast
Open: B-L-D: Daily
zaidysdeli.com

121 Adams St.   303-333-5336
Denver, 80206
1st & Adams

Price: $$ **Patio:** Yes
Reervations: Yes   **Brunch:** No
Location: Cherry Creek

In Yiddish, Zaidy means grandpa, and you'd be proud to take your Zaidy to Zaidy's for a treat. As you are seated, a plate of dill pickles and sauerkraut is delivered to your table--you can purchase a jar of the crisp dills at the deli counter as you leave. Breakfast on the weekends is popular, so expect a wait. Egg dishes and waffles are the standards along with beautiful smoked sturgeon or lox and cream cheese and, of course, bagels. A longtime favorite is the latke-Reuben sandwich, two delicious golden brown potato pancakes stuffed with lean corned beef, sauerkraut, Swiss cheese and Russian dressing. You won't find better matzo ball soup this side of your favorite Jewish grandma's house. Matzo Brie, a traditional Passover dish, is served year-round. Order early for holiday takeout as supplies are limited. Zaidy's is one of Denver's most popular delis.

Zengo

Cuisine: South American, Sushi, Asian Fusion
Open: D: Daily, BR: Sat-Sun
Richardsandoval.com/zengodenver

1610 Little Raven St.   720-904-0965
Denver, 80202
Riverfront

Price: $$$$ **Patio:** Yes
Reservations: Yes   **Brunch:** Yes
Location: Riverfront Park

Zengo translates as "give and take," and Chef/Owner Richard Sandoval has created an exciting spot that gives a fascinating combination of Latin and Asian cuisine, taking the best of both in presentation and preparation. The design brings a retro look with lots of red Jetsons-like Plexiglas lights and big, white 1970's ball chandeliers, stone walls, and an orangey-red ceramic tiled bar merging all the elements together in this 150-seat restaurant. The focal point sushi and ceviche bar and open kitchen add great touches to the scene. A large lounge offers a comfortable place for meet and greet. Don't miss the cucumber mojito, specialty drinks and terrific wine list. Start with ceviche, sushi rolls, and tuna tataki. The selection of appetizers ranges from crunchy calamari and Thai chicken empanadas to Kobe beef gyoza and lobster pot stickers. The charbroiled black cod, wok-seared tuna and chile-grilled prawns bring selections from the sea but beef tenderloin, Kobe beef, braised short ribs, pork loin or chicken tandoori are also available. Desserts are decadent with chocolate tastings, churros with cold-hot chocolate mousse, pineapple upside-down cake and panna cotta. The well-informed staff offers friendly, excellent service. This upscale spot in Riverfront is the place to meet and share a fantastic evening of fun and good food. There is something new and exciting at Zengo. It is their test kitchen menu which changes every few months. It is a fun option in dining. Zengo certainly keeps up with the latest and brings a real treat to this popular area.

Zolo Grill

Cuisine: American, Southwestern
Open: L: Mon-Sat, D: Daily, BR: Sun
bigredf.com

2525 Arapahoe Ave.   303-449-0444
Boulder, 80302
28th & Arapahoe

Price: $$ **Patio:** Yes
Reservations: Yes   **Brunch:** Yes
Location: Boulder

Boulder wouldn't be the same without Zolo Grill, a popular spot year after year. Zolo offers impressive Southwestern food with an upbeat ambience that packs the place every lunch, dinner and late evening. A small patio offers a great view of the Flatirons. Very casual, the informative and friendly staff keeps things moving as crowds gather to dine. Start with the Zolo salsa sampler--three different dips served with colored corn chips. Other possibilities include seafood rellenos, fresh guacamole, empanadas and queso. Pork ribs over frisée and marinated onion and peppers are a must. The Caesar or smoked chicken salad and the tortilla soup bring more choices. Entrées include the red chili, barbecue duck tacos, pork chops, enchiladas, and tasty spinach and vegetable tamales. Several fish selections include catfish and sea bass served with complementary sides to accompany the protein. Dessert lovers will be hard pressed to turn down any of the fantastic treats, but the grilled banana cream pie topped with coconut and caramel is the best. Zolo remains a stellar option for dining in Boulder.

Lucy Lea Tucker

"Ask not what you can do for your country.
Ask what's for lunch."
Orson Welles

• •

Acquolina

Cuisine: Italian

Open: D: Daily

415 E. Main St.   970.925.8222
Aspen, 81611

Price: $$$$ **Patio:** Yes
Reservations: Yes   **Brunch:** No

Set on the bustling Main Street of Aspen and brought to
you from the owners of Campo de Fiori, Acquolina has the
largest selection of spirits in the valley - set in a sophisticated,
clean atmosphere with a beautiful interior. The romantic
and modern-chic space boasts comfortable seating, a large
bar area and big picture windows for people watching. Start
with calamari with grilled shrimp and a chorizo "soria," cherry
tomatoes and baby arugula or delight in the unique branzino
aromatizzato, striped bass fillet with garlic spinach, sweet
pepper confetti with a red curry sauce. For your dinner, enjoy
classic Italian favorite pastas, Milanese pounded breaded veal,
wild salmon with grilled vegetables or the Colorado lamb
sirloin with roasted garlic jus or the lighter option of mixed
seafood with a white wine and tomato broth. No one goes
thirsty with the impressive 20 page wine list. Acquolina is
unique Italian fare with an emphasis on flavor.

Ajax Tavern

Cuisine: Contemporary

Open: L-D: Daily

thelittlenell.com/dining/ajax-tavern

685 E. Durant Ave.   970.920.6334
Aspen, 81611
Gondola Plaza; Hunter & E. Durant

Price: $$$ **Patio:** Yes
Reservations: Yes   **Brunch:** No

Ajax Tavern, just steps from the Silver Queen Gondola at
the base of Aspen Mountain serves American and French

dishes inspired by the bounty of Colorado. With an inviting bar area inside and an expansive deck and bar outside, the Tavern continues to serve après-ski favorites including the famous truffle fries tossed with Parmigiano-Reggiano, fresh parsley and truffle essence, and bottomless Rose on Tuesdays in the summer. Established as a top spot for incoming skiers, locals, tourists and celebrities alike, this hot spot is also a comfortable bistro for family and friends to gather any time. The patio is a highlight and draws you in at the base of iconic Ajax Mountain. A woodsy interior with comfortable booths, round tables and a casual atmosphere sets the tone. Attached to the five star, five diamond hotel, The Little Nell runs the management and food service - enough said. The lunch and dinner menus are dialed with a variety of dishes ranging from staples like the Colorado lamb Bolognese, the French onion soup - which is cooked for 48 hours to extract flavors or the chicken liver Bourbon pate. Don't forget the decadent Ajax Double burger – made with meat from Kurt Russell's Home Run Ranch - and the fresh raw bar selections with ice cold East and West Coast oysters king crab and other delicacies from the sea. Finish with seasonal cobblers or the interactive and fun chocolate fondue. The view alone is worth the price - then add in serious service, amazing cuisine and an extensive beer and wine list with something for everyone. The Ajax Tavern is, hands down, the place to eat well and 'see and be seen' among the Aspen crowd on the patio for lunch or dinner or as an après-ski destination during ski season.

Artisan Hand Crafted Cuisine

Cuisine: Global Contemporary
Open: D: Daily (Seasonal)

300 Carriage Way   970.923.2427
Snowmass Village, 81615
Stonebridge Hotel (December-April & June-September)

Price: $$$ **Patio:** Yes
Reservations: Yes. Recommended during high season
Brunch: No

Located in Snowmass' Stonebridge Inn, the Artisan implies specialization, mastery and unmatched craft. Chef Randall Baldwin runs the kitchen crafts with locally sourced cuisine from the best ingredients of the season and of the valley. Dine on bar favorites like the mouth-watering pastrami sandwich on a soft pretzel roll or take it up a notch in the dining room with pan seared scallops, sweet potato hash with bacon, shiitake and leek accented by chipotle aioli or the hazelnut crusted ruby red trout with brown sugar bourbon butter, grilled asparagus, and roasted fingerlings or delight in local, pan seared elk loin medallions with manchego cheese, scalloped sweet potatoes with roasted poblano pepper. The setting is beautiful with a huge lounge area featuring a welcoming bar, comfortable seating both inside and out onto the patio, weather permitting. The dining room in the back opens to a stunning view through panoramic windows, a bit more formal, but still comfortable. The wine list is great with several choices by the glass, all at very good prices. The service is excellent with affordable prices and the place just what every guest wishes for when away from home. The Artisan is Snowmass' best 'elegant' restaurant, but Colorado casual enough for a pint of beer on the patio.

Asie

Cuisine: Chinese

Open: L-D: Daily

413 E. Main Street   970.920.9988
Aspen, 81611
Main & Mill

Price: $$$ **Patio:** Yes
Reservations: Yes   **Brunch:** No

Set on Main Street in historic downtown Aspen, Asie is Aspen's answer to Asian fusion, featuring Chinese, Thai, and Japanese cuisines. The spacious outdoor patio and bar area add to the simple yet modern ambience. Kick off your dining experience with sushi rolls, sashimi tuna or Shanghai spring rolls, dumplings, fried rice, barbecued ribs or the house favorite 'chicken lettuce-wraps.' Everyone loves the Thai basil chicken sautéed with a savory jalapeño sauce; the red panang or green curry and the Peking duck are done to perfection. The plate presentation is simple and elegant. Asie is a great place to power through a business lunch, as there are great daily specials or just the place to fill your hankering for Chinese delivery on a Sunday night. Be sure to say "hi" to the man who runs the show, everyone's pal, Charlie Huang!

Aspen Art Museum

Cuisine: Café

Open: Tue – Sun 10:00 a.m. to 6:00 p.m.

aspenartmuseum.org

637 E. Hyman Ave.,   970.925.8050
Aspen 81611

Price: $$ **Patio:** Yes
Reservations: No/Yes during high ski season   **Brunch:** No

Enjoy a cultural coffee, lunch, snack or après ski (or apres hike or bike) with wine, cheese and art on the AAM's roof-deck at SO cafe. The fresh and thoughtful menu changes every Tuesday. With an airy ambience on the rooftop and unprecedented views of Aspen Mountain and Independence Pass, SO features an innovative, rotating menu prepared from fresh locally sourced ingredients by AAM culinary partners Julia and Allen Domingos. SO is named after a type of free-flowing Japanese brushstroke as well as, of course, an English expression of quantification and excitement. A non-collecting institution, the AAM presents the newest and most important evolutions in international contemporary art and provide audiences with thought-provoking experiences of art, culture and society. Admission is always free.

Bangkok Happy Bowl

Cuisine: Thai/Asian

Open: D: Daily, Days, Delivery Takeout: L-D

aspenthai.net

300 Puppy Smith Street   970.925.2527
Aspen, 81611

Price: $$ **Patio:** No
Reservations: No   **Brunch:** No

The only Thai food place in town is located "downtown" Aspen at the North Mill Station space by Clark's Market and the Post Office. Ready to serve you from 'the land of smiles,' Bangkok Happy Bowl serves up authentic Thai cuisine with an emphasis on take-out and delivery operations, as well as at a small, happy bar area and an intimate dining room with imported decor from Thailand. The Red Curry, Cashew Chicken and Pad Thai are great options.

bb's Kitchen

Cuisine: American-Bistro

Open: L - D: Daily

525 E. Cooper Avenue   970.429.8284
Aspen, 81611

Price: $$ **Patio:** Yes
Reservations: No   **Brunch:** Yes

bb's Kitchen serves up American comfort food with a view. With floor to ceiling windows, views of the surrounding mountains make this a popular spot. Longtime local and owner, Bruce Berger, describes bb's fare as "Grandma's recipes with a modern technique." Wood detailing, a fireplace and warm, red tones, bb's has that cozy yet sophisticated feeling. Totally different than most places in Aspen, this is a neighborhood retreat in bustling downtown Aspen. There is a great patio with red awnings, inviting bar-lounge, open kitchen, and a menu where you want one of everything. Enjoy anything from soups, salads and sandwiches to pizza, risotto and duck pate. Dinner spans the globe from Asian lettuce wraps to Colorado elk tenderloin to Tandoori Lamb chops. To complement the wide array of omelettes and breakfast classics with a contemporary twist, bb's is the one stop shop for bottomless mimosas and bloody Marys on a Sunday. Decadent desserts for breakfast are mandatory like the monkey bread and banana bread, after lunch or dinner indulge in the lemon meringue tart. Great wines, cocktails, and beer complement the food. bb's kitchen is just the place to be – better than your own kitchen and much more fun. Proudly serving modern American cuisine and offering rooftop views of the mountains.

Big Wrap

Cuisine: American, To Go

Open: Daily: Monday - Saturday

520 E. Durant Ave   970.544.1700
Aspen, 81611

Price: $ **Patio:** Yes
Reservations: No   **Brunch:** No
*Kid friendly

Every day around lunch there is a line that winds out the door – for a reason! A hungry crowd of devoted locals and tourists alike descend upon this lovely wrap, salad, soup and smoothie spot, set smack-dab in the heart of town. The best value in town with everything under $10, like the homemade vegan soups, fresh tacos and of course, the wraps! Favorites include the 'Pesto Wrapture' and the 'Thai Me Up' – delicious ingredients, seasoned well and wrapped up in a soft flour tortilla, or served in a bowl with lettuce. The 'Babs-E-Que' wrap named after proprietor, Babs, is also a favorite with BBQ sauce and mashed potatoes. The salads are fresh and unique. This is a great stop for 'to go' meals or stay and chat with the line of locals and ready the daily papers at the counter. The fresh, homemade chips are worth the line!

Brexi

Cuisine: French
Open: D: Daily
411 Monarch St.,   970.925.2838
Aspen, CO 81611

Price: $$$$ **Patio:** Yes
Reservations: Yes   **Brunch:** No

If you are in the mood for classic French brasserie fare - look no further! Located at the corner, street-level entrance of the exclusive Dancing Bear complex, the interior is impressive with black and white tiled floors, gorgeous, antique chandeliers and a cozy fireplace set inside the dining room. Run by Aspen power-house restaurateurs Craig and Samantha Cordts-Pearce, the sexy brasserie is a lifelong vision turned reality by the pair. Brexi's menu features local beef tartare with harissa aioli and quail egg and outstanding mussels. The delightful outside patio with flowers galore is something to behold. Brexi's enthusiastic sommelier will readily assist in pairing your food choices with wines and unique beer offerings. Classics like the charcuterie and cheese plates, steak au poivre, beef Bourgogne, bone marrow and foie gras hit the nail on the head for French cuisine. Surprisingly, their thick, juicy burger is a hit as well. The affordable, solid by-the-glass wine prices are inviting – swing by for a drink at the bar and you'll end up staying for dinner.

Cache Cache

Cuisine: French - American
Open: D: Daily (seasonal)
cachecache.com
205 S. Mill St.   970.925.3835
Aspen, 81611
S. Mill & Hopkins

Price: $$$$ **Patio:** Yes
Reservations: Yes   **Brunch:** No

Indulge in the flavors of American and classic French cuisine with touches from the Mediterranean. Always filled with the beautiful people, Cache Cache has established itself as an essential in this food-lovers town. Their wine program is pretty spectacular too! The fabulous wine list and top notch table service add to the overall dining experience. Al fresco dining in the courtyard is as comfortable as dining inside the energetic dining room. Start at the vibrant, pulsating bar with delectable black mussels, smoked Scottish salmon or King crab beignets and drink whatever the friendly bartenders are pouring by the glass. Coq au vin is done to the tee and presented beautifully in a black, cast iron pot. Marvelous entrées include pork tenderloin, osso buco and filet mignon. The Colorado rack of lamb is a signature dish that cannot be taken off the menu – cooked to perfection with a Dijon-herb crust, veal jus and potatoes au gratin. Finish with excellent desserts such as the apple crisp or the deliciously warm chocolate cake with caramel sauce. Put Cache Cache on the 'must' list when you visit Aspen.

Campo De Fiori

Cuisine: Italian
Open: D: Daily
campodefiori.net

205 S. Mill Street	970.920.7717
Aspen, 81611	
Mill & Hopkins	

Price: $$$	**Patio:** Yes
Reservations: Yes	**Brunch:** No

Campo, a place where dinner can easily turn into dancing at the bar. This sexy, subterranean restaurant is hopping with energy and activity any night of the week! Specializing in Northern Italian fare, Campo de Fiori maintains a busy and popular reputation with an always-crowded bar, dining room and outdoor courtyard. The small, lively Tuscan inspired trattoria know for its handsome servers and cozy tables, presents an inviting setting. Elbow your way through the bar to settle in with friends and vie for service from those good looking guys behind the bar. Appetizers include buffalo carpaccio, frutti de mare and a simple caprese plate of tomatoes, mozzarella and basil in olive oil. Dine on classic Bolognese pasta or the popular penne vodka. A nightcap espresso chocolate martini will hit the spot as a spontaneous dance party breaks out. Who said fun and food couldn't go hand in hand?

Caribou Club

Cuisine: Contemporary
Open: D: Daily from 6:30 PM
caribouclub.com

411 E. Hopkins Avenue   970.925.2929
Aspen, 81611

Price: $$$$ **Patio:** in the courtyard
Reservations: Yes   **Brunch:** No

This private club serves up Aspen's best food and drink to Aspen's elite and the visiting elite. Dining at the Club is legendary: the cuisine is Contemporary American, the Chef is Miles Angelo. Famous dishes that come out of the Caribou kitchen are: oysters poblano, New York bison and dry aged rib eye. The décor is described as 'English club with a western sensibility' a comfortable and elegant combination that makes you feel like you are sitting in Ralph Lauren's living room. This is the only place in Aspen that you can have dinner and stay to dance. The retro disco dance floor boasts the contemporary tunes of DJ Folami, spinning nightly. Inquire about the bar menu if you are after a more casual dining experience. Their food is so good that they expanded to run a catering company, as well as Cakes by Caribou for delicious pastries.

Casa Tua

Cuisine: Classic French/Italian
Open: D: Daily, L: Daily: Summers

447 E. Cooper Ave   970.920.7727
Aspen, 81611

Price: $$$$ **Patio:** No
Reservations: Yes   **Brunch:** No

This restaurant focuses on fine Italian fare with French and Swiss influences. In the summer, sit on the scenic, bustling walking mall and enjoy lunch delights like the pinzimonio salad – a medley of crudite and diced chicken or the unique Casa Tua Club Sandwich with the inclusion of scrambled eggs, for a twist. Casa Tua aims to make diners feel like they are in the home of a friend -- a friend with impeccable cooking skills and amazingly attentive service! The menu is robust and flavorful-from seared foie-gras with ginger and tomato marmalade to tagliolini with stone crab and zucchini. Perfect for a date-night or to catch up with friends over a long, fabulous meal -- treat yourself at this Aspen hot spot and you won't be disappointed. The members-only club upstairs boasts a mountain chic vibe and is a great location to throw an event.

CHEFS CLUB by Food & Wine

Cuisine: Regional American

Open: D: Daily, Friday - Saturday: 5:30 P.M. - 11:00 P.M.

chefsclub.com

315 East Dean Street   970.429.9581
Aspen, 81611

Price: $$$$ **Patio:** Yes
Reservations: Yes   **Brunch:** No

CHEFS CLUB by Food & Wine magazine at The St. Regis Aspen Resort brings the Food & Wine brand to life. Each year CHEFS CLUB features several Food & Wine Best New Chefs to consult on a new menu. The rotating menu is decorated with famous dishes from restaurants across the country. Look out for the traveling chef series with Michelin star chefs creating special dinners at this unique restaurant concept. The open kitchen and bright, airy atmosphere of the restaurant welcomes all guests for a night of fun and adventure in dining.

Cloud Nine Alpine Bistro

Cuisine: European

Open: Winter only; L: Daily, D: Thursday nights

Aspen Highlands   970.923.8715
81612
Mid-mountain Aspen highlands

Price: $$$$ **Patio:** Yes
Reservations: Yes   **Brunch:** No

New for the 2015-2016 season expect to see a remodel of Cloud 9. You are invited to a cozy European-style cabin in the Rocky Mountains for fondue! Cloud Nine Alpine Bistro is a legendary Aspen Highlands restaurant that channels authentic European Alpine culture in a warm, welcoming environment. With views of the iconic Maroon Bells - perhaps North America's most recognizable, postcard perfect mountains - dining here is a gastronomic experience. Ski or snowboard to the unique and intimate bistro, located on Aspen Highlands beneath the high-speed quad aptly named 'Cloud Nine.' An alpine ski hut with casual table settings and an outdoor deck, this full-service restaurant with majestic views of the Maroon Bells is open for lunch with a European-style Bistro menu that changes daily. Snow cat dinners are open to the public on Thursday nights, complete with gourmet meals that suit the European flair of the atmosphere and vibe. Choose an entrée and your choice of soup or assorted greens salad. The menu choices include: steak tartar, raclette, fresh game and vegetarian dishes, accented by international wine and fine champagne. Daily, rotating specials are worthy of your consideration - like the coq au vin or schnitzel. Quite often, the mood turns exciting and a ski boot-clad dance party breaks out before everyone suits back up in their winter gear to ski down!

CP Burger

Cuisine: Gourmet Retro-Burger Joint
Open: Daily: 11:00 AM - 8:00 PM
433 E. Durant Ave   970.925.3056
Aspen, 81611

Price: $$ **Patio:** Yes
Reservations: No   **Late Night:** No
*Kid friendly

Food-loving power couple, Craig and Samantha Cordts-Pearce, have brought retro into the modern light. Situated next to the Silver Circle Ice Rink in the heart of downtown Aspen, this walk-up eatery called 'CP Burger' is more than just a burger joint -- it is a gourmet twist to fast food and memorable experiences. If you ever dreamed of ordering a kale salad at a burger joint – this is the place! The notable 'Lulu's kale salad' with currants, pine nuts and parmesan makes for a fiber filler alongside your tasty fries and shakes. From falafel to tuna to veggie to the Chicano fire beef burger combinations, CP Burger's menu boasts variety, including healthier options too. But there's something more to this new eatery than their famed boozy, alcohol infused milkshakes - the experience! Take a lap around the ice rink beneath the twinkling lights and a satisfying family meal; those simple things become life-long memories. In the winter – work off your calories outside on the ice skating rink, in the summer putt them away at the mini golf course.

Creperie Du Village

Cuisine: European
Open: Daily: L - D
400 E. Hopkins Avenue   970.925.1566
Aspen, 81611

Price: $$$ **Patio:** Yes
Reservations: Yes   **Brunch:** Yes

Find yourself at the best seat in town - the corner of Mill and Hopkins, sipping on rose at the sunny patio facing Aspen Mountain. The Creperie is an authentic French café in the heart of Aspen, open daily 11 AM, from lunch through après-ski and dinner. With a full bar, cozy furnishings, rafters stacked with wine bottles and other bric-a-brac lining the walls, a taste of the Alps appears in the ambience and on the menu. Featuring sweet and savory crepes, raclette, fondue, salads, charcuterie and cheese boards, favorites include: the Mountain Club savory crepe with delicious gruyere, turkey and tomatoes. Don't spend long contemplating your dessert crepe – Nutella, lemon and sugar or the ménage a trois, any way you go, you'll end up smiling. This restaurant is for celebrating special occasions or for holing up on a cold winter's day. Be prepared to settle in to this cozy, quaint atmosphere, as the service is designed to have you linger.

El Rincon

Cuisine: Mexican
Open: L - D: Daily

411 East Main Street   970.925.3663
Aspen, CO 81611

Price: $$ **Patio:** Yes
Reservations: Yes   **Brunch:** No
*Kid friendly

Spanish for "the corner," El Rincon is an adaptation from the long run Cantina restaurant - conveniently poised on the corner of Mill and Main Street - Aspen's busiest corner. Such a great tequila selection, so little time! Always a festive and fun atmosphere for casual Mexican dining and drinks, El Rincon is a mainstay as Aspen's favorite lunch, happy hour or dining establishment. Enjoy hot chips and tangy salsa as you mull over their menu and sip on one of the famous margaritas. El Rincon is a great place to swing in anytime - enjoy sporting events on their big screen TVs, a big family get together or happy hour with friends.

element 47 The Little Nell

Cuisine: Contemporary
Open: B-L-D: Daily, Brunch: Sun
thelittlenell.com/dining/element-47

675 E. Durant Ave.   970.920.6313
Aspen, 81611
The Little Nell Hotel

Price: $$$$ **Patio:** Yes
Reservations: Yes   **Brunch:** Yes

The Little Nell hotel is a slice of heaven with incredible rooms and friendly, caring people that know service inside and out. There is a reason why this hotel has a 70% customer return rate and earns the prestigious Forbes Five Star Award every year, as well as the AAA Five Diamond Award. The Nell's fine dining restaurant was remodeled in 2012 and reinvented as element 47 – the periodic number for silver, to play off the town's booming silver mining era. Restaurant architects Bentel & Bentel were behind the renovation with elements that include: fine natural wood booths and tables and a general glow to the restaurant that beckons diners in for a casual meal or a special occasion feast. A collection of commissioned, large-scale, contemporary artwork creates a unique space for dining, socializing and taking in the scene. (A coffee table book about the collection curated by Little Nell owner and artist Paula Crown was published in late 2013, offering a look into each piece and the talent behind them.) Chef de Cuisine Matt Padilla's undeniably fantastic food complements this exciting space with thoughtful, seasonally-driven contemporary cuisine, highlighted with global influences. Favorite "e47" dishes include: the lemon soufflé pancakes and fresh fruit parfait for breakfast; for lunch or dinner, the top sellers include Maine lobster pot pie, the pine nut crusted chicken breast and pan seared ruby red trout. On the dinner menu, staples include the harvest vegetable salad, Chef Matt's pastas, which are fantastic, and an array of shared plates from oysters to blue crab. The cocktail and beer program shares the same local focus as the menu, highlighting some of Colorado's great distillers and brewers. Their Tableside Cocktails, prepared on an elegant cart that's wheeled over for each order, include a Margarita 47 made with top shelf tequila, fresh lime juice and nitrogen oxide for effect. For additional sipping, The Nell's wine list is spectacular, housing over 20,000 bottles found in the wine cellar and prominently showcased in a clear glass wine wall in the dining room, each decanted on their new, custom made gueridon. The Little Nell has had more master sommeliers come through its wine program than any other establishment in the country – ten and counting - including current Wine Director, Carlton McCoy, the second youngest Master Sommelier ever, as well as the second ever Master Sommelier of African American descent. You'll see why element 47 repeatedly receives awards from Wine Spectator and Wine Enthusiast magazines.

Ellina

Cuisine: Italian
Open: D: Daily, L: Summer
ellinarestaurant.com/

430 E. Hyman Ave.   970.925.2976
Aspen, CO 81611

Price: $$$ **Patio:** Yes
Reservations: Yes   **Brunch:** No

Ellina embraces American cuisine with an Italian influence. The warm, elegant decor and strands of Italian wedding lights hung at the entrance invite you in for a cozy experience. The exterior of this space has an intimate veranda and on-the-mall outdoor cafe-style seating, while the interior highlights the original brick and stone work dating back to 1880s. Try the braised artichoke bruschetta with truffles and an egg or the calamari fritti to get things started; next up savor the seared Mediterranean octopus or the famed oven-roasted rabbit. The service is extremely professional, leaving you feeling very pampered. The festive, front bar and bartenders bring the fun! The signature lemon-basil martini is a must to kick off your evening, then dive into Ellina's greatest hits on their masterful, worldly-inspired wine list. Ellina is short for Valtellina, a valley in the Lombardy region of northern Italy, bordering Switzerland. Much like Aspen's Ellina, Italy's Valtellina is known for skiing, food and wine - a combination of three delightful items that work well in both remote areas.

520 Grill

Cuisine: Gourmet Fast Food
Open: L-D: Daily, Seasonal
520grill.com   **facebook.com/520grillaspen**

520 E. Cooper Avenue   970.925.9788
Fat City Plaza

Price: $ **Patio:** Yes
Reservations: No   **Brunch:** No

Aspen's favorite quick-serve joint, 520 Grill is where locals flock for healthy, high-quality eats. Located just a block from the gondola with ample seating and plenty of natural light, 520 Grill boasts the casual family atmosphere of a roadside diner—but one that cooks up homemade fare using premium regional ingredients. Every dish is made to order and you'll find founding owner Troy Selby behind the counter daily. Renowned for half-pound, hand-crafted burgers (no fast food, pre-pressed meats), 520 uses a variety of meats and options including: buffalo, beef or turkey -- and an all- beef kosher franks and turkey hot dogs. A genius idea inspired for meat lovers -- the bacon burger has bacon actually ground into the burger for an explosion of flavor. This hip, hot spot also offers fish tacos, daily specials and an amazing selection of fresh salads, like the Chipotle Caesar and Kale Quinoa, which has received rave reviews from day one. For the more selective palates, enjoy a build-your-own-salad and gluten free menu items as well. 520's fresh-cut fries and their specialty sweet potato fries are something to write home about. Selby's dedication to quality and devotion to friendly service are why 520 Grill has earned top acknowledgements from National Geographic Explorer, Ski magazine, Yelp, Trip Advisor, Lonely Planet and more. Serving fast, affordable fare to eat-in, take-out, or for downtown delivery, 520 Grill will undoubtedly become your go-to spot, too.

Fuel

Cuisine: American, Breakfast
Open: B-L: Daily
Snowmass Village Mall   970.923.0091
Snowmass, 80615

Price: $ **Patio:** Yes
Reservations: No   **Brunch:** No

A favorite quick stop, this little gem of a coffee shop is conveniently located right at the bus stop and entrance to the Snowmass Village mall. Sometimes a good cup of Joe is hard to find, but not at this quaint, coffee shop. Besides good coffee, you will also find unbelievable breakfast burritos and bagel sandwiches, a great selection of teas, a smoothie bar and classic panini pressed specialties for lunch. If you need to fuel up, follow the locals inside from the line outside and you will quickly find out that this is the place to be. This is a perfect way to start your morning on the way up the mountain in Snowmass.

Grey Lady

Cuisine: American/Nantucket cuisine
Open: : D: Daily, L: Summers
greyladyaspen.com/menu/
305 S. Mill Street   Phone: 970.925.1797
Aspen, 81611

Price: $$$ **Patio:** Yes
Reservations: Yes   **Brunch:** No

'Grey Lady' is a nickname for the fog on Nantucket. Over three years ago, the original Grey Lady restaurant opened in the

Lower East Side of Manhattan, serving up Nantucket inspired fare with a nautical ambience. More recently, the Grey Lady opened in Aspen for an outpost in the West. Aspen Chef Kathleen Crook runs the kitchen with seafaring specialties like: lobster rolls, Thai shrimp corncakes, cornmeal fried oysters and surf and turf. In addition to great savory fare, Grey Lady serves up fancy cocktails like the Escobar Mule or the Master Cleanses. Come dine, drink and stay for fun at the Grey Lady - for the nightlife heats up after dark.

Hickory House

Cuisine: American
Open: B-L-D Daily
hickoryhouseribs.com

730 W. Main Street   970.925.2313
Aspen, 81611

Price: $ **Patio:** Yes
Reservations: No   **Brunch:** No
*****Kid friendly**

The big bear on the roof of the Hickory House is a landmark as one drives into Aspen on the S curve. A casual, no frills dining scene makes this rib shack a favorite for local ski bums and tourists. Go in hungry -- and come out fuller than you've ever been. As well as BBQ, the 'Hick House' serves up an unbeatable, hearty "greasy spoon" breakfast, and can be considered the best hangover breakfast in town. The baby back ribs put this local barbeque joint on Oprah's list of her "favorite things." Locals dominate this festive, fun joint -- and Monday night football is an institution. Consider the Hick House for delivery, take out or for catering a party.

Hops Culture

Cuisine: Comfort
Open: L - D: Daily
hopsculture.com/

414 E Hyman Ave, Aspen   Phone #: 970.925.HOPS
Aspen, 81611   (4677)

Price: $$ **Patio:** Yes
Reservations: No   **Brunch:** No

Set in the style of a German Beer garden with long wooden tables on the Hyman Street mall, HOPS brings the feeling of Oktoberfest to the cobble stone streets of Aspen. The long wooden tables fill quickly with tourists ad locals alike on a nice, sunny day. With inviting indoor/outdoor seating at the entrance

– the inside of the restaurant is spacious with a welcoming bar. There are tons of beers on their menu as well as tasty varieties of Moscow Mule drinks with crushed iced, served as they should be in copper mugs. They serve casual salads, sandwiches and pretzel fondue for savory snacks and meals.

Il Poggio Italian Restaurant

Cuisine: Italian
Open: D: Daily
ilpoggio.webs.com/

57 Elbert Lane   970.923.4292
Aspen, 81615
Snowmass Village

Price: $$ **Patio:** No
Reservations: Yes   **Brunch:** No

A favorite amongst the Snowmass crowd, Il Poggio offers authentic Italian cuisine, a lively atmosphere, brick oven fired pizzas, homemade pastas, elegant dining and an extensive wine list. Favorites include sweet potato & goat cheese ravioli, steak topped with gorgonzola, and gnocchi with veal tenderloin, asparagus, roasted tomato and truffle butter. Il Poggio also serves a variety of pasta dishes and entrees such as seared duck breast and pancetta-wrapped chicken breast. Don't forget dessert – Il Poggio is known for the tiramisu and selection of Italian desserts. A real special treat in the heart of the Snowmass mall – this place is a winner.

J Bar

Cuisine: American
Open: L-D: Daily, D: 11:30am - 12am, BR: Sun
hoteljerome.aubergeresorts.com

330 East Main Street   970.920.1000
Aspen, 81611

Price: $$ **Patio:** No
Reservations: No   **Brunch:** Yes

The Hotel Jerome, including the J Bar, have recently undergone a multimillion dollar renovation making it best it has ever been in the last 100 years. Serving a contemporary American take of your favorite ski town food, drawing on regional and modern influences, the Executive Chef, Rob Zack whips up some amazing eats right in tune with the location - the heart and soul of Aspen. From your standard bar food specialties like buffalo wings and shoestring fries, to more off the beaten path specialties like artisanal charcuterie, kogi tacos and a top notch fish and chips. The J Bar is a sports bar, an après ski bar and a place for locals to belly up to the bar, as well as for newcomers to see what the old days were all about. The historic 'Aspen Crud' signature drink from the Prohibition days is a must - a delicious vanilla milkshake laced with bourbon! There is a devoted following for the burgers and little gem salad. New to the J Bar this year is brunch -- with unique offerings like breakfast pho.

Jimmy's

Cuisine: Steakhouse, Seafood
Open: D: Daily 5:00 PM – 11:30 PM for food
jimmysaspen.com   facebook.com/jimmysaspen

205 S. Mill   970.925.6020
Aspen, 81611
Mill & Hopkins

Price: $$$ **Patio:** Yes
Reservations: Yes   **Brunch:** No

Proprietors Jimmy Yeager and Grayson Stover are what makes this place tick. Walk up the outside stairway and enter an exciting and bustling bar area that keeps the crowd returning to the 15 year local tradition that is Jimmy's. Welcoming energy fills the bar area and leads to the outside patio area, and further back to the dining room. Enjoy classic cocktails and "locally-priced" dinners in the bar – including the best tequila and mezcal selections you have ever seen. Or move into the more formal, inviting dining room where you can enjoy top notch service in a comfortable, relaxed setting. Start your meal with the inspired ahi tuna tartar or unique artichoke dip. For dinner, enjoy the signature steak - an 18 ounce big rib-eye on the bone or the organic salmon or Rocky Mountain Trout are lighter, healthy options. There are more than just steakhouse standards - the versatile menu includes items like roasted corn and jalapeno soup (made with local Olathe sweet corn), local farm vegetable nightly gazpacho, and quinoa stuffed zucchini cannelloni. Make sure to share the famed "Jimmy Mac," Jimmy's twist on the cheesy American classic with jalapenos and bacon. For after-hours sizzle, check out Jimmy's steamy salsa night every Saturday at 10:30PM. Hang around Jimmy's bar long enough and you may just run into to everyone you know in the world.

Jimmy's Bodega

Cuisine: Seafood
Open: D: Daily 2:30 PM - 10 PM L: summers, Closed

307 S Mill Street   970.710.2182
Aspen, 81611

Price: $$$ **Patio:** Yes
Reservations: Yes   **Brunch:** No

Step into the fun, friendly atmosphere of Jimmy's Bodega located on the heart of the Mill Street mall by the fountain in Aspen. For sipping, enjoy specialty bottled cocktails and a wine list focused on value and interesting finds. The Bodega features tequila and mezcal hand-selected by Jimmy as his personal favorites. Enjoy lunch, happy hour, and dinner on the best patio in town, and, of course, Jimmy's signature hospitality. Whether you are relaxing on the patio as the kids take on the jungle gym next door - or having a grown up meal inside, the Bodega is all about fun. Seafood, raw bar, tacos, salads, soups, and nightly specials make up the simple and upscale menu.

Justice Snow's

Cuisine: Contemporary
Open: L - D: Daily
justicesnows.com

221 S. Mill Street   970.429.8192
Aspen, 81611

Price: $$ **Patio:** Yes
Reservations: Yes   **Brunch:** No

Justice Snow is named for the Justice of the Peace that was in office when the Wheeler Opera House was built in the 1880s. Owners Marco Cingolani and Michele Kiley teamed up with the best architects and designers in town to preserve and enliven the historic space with mining-camp details like an antique copper-top bar and machine-age light fixtures made from repurposed bicycle parts. Colorado and Western-influenced cuisine are the name of the game at this unique dining and watering hole. The tangy and tart fried pickles help you work up a thirst as your creation is carefully created. Libation Liaison, as he is dubbed, Joshua Peter Smith has crafted an innovative cocktail list unlike anything Aspen has ever seen. This place has an aggressive cocktail program focusing on barman ship - down to the correct type of vessel from which to drink absinthe. Justice Snow's features both small and large plates with moderate prices amidst a lively bar scene. Stick your head in and you won't want to leave this fun, entertaining speak easy.

Kenichi

Cuisine: Japanese, Sushi, Contemporary Asian

Open: D: Daily

533 E. Hopkins Ave.
Aspen, 81611
Hopkins & Hunter

970.920.2212

Price: $$$$
Reservations: Yes

Patio: Yes
Brunch: No

With outposts in Hawaii and Texas and the original location in Aspen, Kenichi embraces innovative twists on sushi and guarantees a raring good time! World-class, upscale fresh Japanese cuisine and smiling, happy wait staff will greet you at this long-standing favorite sushi spot. Locals dine alongside the rich and famous at the crowded sushi bar, in the cozy dining room, or seek solitude in your very own private room. The fun kicks off with your first sip of the sake mojito signature drink. Snag a seat at the sushi bar and friendly sushi chefs will entertain you and create masterpieces of Asian delight especially for you. Start with dynamite shrimp, try the X Games Blake Roll, the nightly dim-sum special, or crab cakes wrapped in a wonton shell. Non-sushi entrées include miso-marinated sea bass, salmon with blue cheese, macadamia-crusted lamb and Oriental roast duck. For dessert, tempt your taste buds with tempura ice cream. If you are looking for an all night dining party – this is the place to be!

Krabloonik

Cuisine: Colorado/Wild Game

Open: L - D: Daily

krabloonik.com

4250 Divide Rd.
Snowmass, 81615

970.923.3953

Price: $$$ (Summer) $$$$ (Ski Season)
Patio: No
Brunch: No

Reservations: Yes

Step into this unique place and you feel like you have stepped back in time. The cozy, cool bar gets you in the mood as you have a glass of something before you sit down to an elegant and fun eating experience. Located on the slopes of Snowmass, with views of Mount Daly and Capitol Peak, just getting here is an adventure in itself. Reservations are required for the ride and recommended for the meal. Start with the famed wild mushroom soup, baked Brie with lingon berries or a wild-boar chop. For your main course, continue to savor the tastes of the wilderness with roasted elk loin, bison or Rocky Mountain trout. Combination plates offer a chance to experience several different meats. The excellent wine list perfectly matches the top rated food. When summertime rolls around, prix fixe menus and "all you can eat ribs and BBQ" nights, accompanied by live music change the dining scene all together. What a crazy combination: dog sledding and fine food. Somehow, the concept works; given the snowy mountains and the crisp mountain air – the fresh fish and the wild game. No matter when you make the trek, dining at Krabloonik is an experience you will never forget.

L'Hostaria

Cuisine: Italian
Open: D: Daily
hostaria.com

620 E. Hyman Ave.   970.925.9022
Aspen, 81611
Spring & Hunter

Price: $$$ **Patio:** Yes
Reservations: Yes   **Brunch:** No

When choosing where to dine in Aspen, one is faced with endless options of exquisite culinary wonders. Tucked away in the east end of town is L'Hostaria, a locals' favorite for authentic Italian cuisine. With 17 years of business, it seems that L'Hostaria, like its wine selections, gets better with age. From the tradition al antipasto selections paired with velvety burrata cheese to the fresh homemade pasta dishes and desserts, you will experience a meal that will leave you wanting to return night after night. Owner, Tiziano Gortan has created a successful restaurant by using his know-how of Italian cooking, pairing simple yet elegant ingredients to create flavorful meals. With Tiziano or Fabrizio, there is always the authentic Italian double kiss when you are arrive and leave - always happier than when you walked in the door. The affordably priced menu at the vibrant bar is one of the best in town, and the tenured, loyal staff keep your wine glasses full well into the night. Watch out for: Mim's Pinot bombs, homemade lemoncello nightcaps and Scotty's espresso martinis! If you are looking for good food, a good time and friendly people, visit L'hostaria and you will see why this place has such a devoted following of locals and tourists alike.

Limelight Lounge

Cuisine: Light Italian

Open: D: Daily 3-11 PM (Après; Dinner)

355 S. Monarch St.   970.925.3025
Aspen, 81611

Price: $$ **Patio:** Yes
Reservations: No (Except for special dinners)
Brunch: No

Head on into your home away from home - the Limelight - to grab a hand-thrown pizza, ever-changing seasonal entrees, fresh salads, drinks or dessert in the living room ambience. The scene is complete with a cozy fireplace and an outside patio with fire pits for roasting s'mores. Whether you're looking to maintain an epic powder day nirvana after the lifts close or seeking to decompress from a challenging road ride up to Independence Pass, the Lounge offers a relaxed atmosphere that's ideal for clicking off a helmet and letting your hair down. Chef Jeff Gundy dishes up delicious, light Italian fare featuring the finest local and organic ingredients. Try the top fave Diavolo or Proscuitto Crudo pizzas --they are a great sharable meal. The Limelight Lounge is home to Aspen's Longest Happy Hour, from 3 - 7 PM. daily. Five nights per week in winter and summer, Aspen's favorite local bands play from 6-9 PM Thursday through Monday. Twice a month, the Lounge hosts popular three-course Beer Dinners sponsored by select breweries, largely from Colorado. Each course is designed to complement a unique, seasonal brew. Come try this unique hotel eatery and you will be hooked.

Lynn Britt Cabin

Cuisine: Eclectic

Open: L - D: Winter, special events

45 Village Square   970.923.0479
Snowmass Village, 81615
Mid-mountain at Snowmass.

Price: $$$ **Patio:** Yes
Reservations: Yes   **Brunch:** No

Hold on to your hat, because you are in for the meal of your life: start with a chair lift or cat ride as your chariot up the mountain for lunch or dinner during the winter at this elegant spot. If romance is your thing, go for the cat ride at night and enjoy live music when you arrive. This quaint cabin, built in the early 1900s is spectacular; the interior is rustic and comfortable and the surrounding scenery is beyond description. The food is upscale gourmet and completely divine, serving Colorado cuisine at its finest featuring elk, lamb and bison. Take in the surroundings and relax in the moment with a glass of wine. Then start the adventure that is dining - enjoy elk chili, bison meatloaf, poached lobster with shallot mignonette, crisp stripe bass with gnocchi, or Asiago stuffed chicken breast on a bed of baby spinach. The menu changes frequently based upon availability of seasonal ingredients. Every dish is magnificent to the eye and even better to taste. Leave room for dessert! The portions are very generous and the service exemplary. This dining experience is a must when you visit Snowmass. Stay tuned for some après ski specials and new seating for winter of 2015-2016.

Matsuhisa Aspen

Cuisine: Japanese, Sushi

Open: D: Daily (Seasonal)

matsuhisaaspen.com

303 East Main Street 970.544.6628
Aspen, Colorado 81611
Corner of Main St. & Monarch St.

Price: $$$$	**Patio:** Yes - Summer
Reservations: Yes	**Brunch:** No

Matsuhisa is Aspen's one and only Nobu-famed gourmet Japanese Seafood & Sushi Restaurant. Set in a historic Victorian house on the Main Street of Aspen, this hip restaurant is the most exciting dining scene in Aspen. Delights range from sushi and sashimi to yellowtail sashimi spiked with jalapenos and cilantro, tuna on a miso chip, the Peruvian influenced new style salmon or the famed blackened cod cooked on a limestone rock. Desserts include a Bento Box filled with molten chocolate cake or the sensational Japanese mochi ice cream flavors that change daily. The world class wine, sake and shochu list will have you coming back for more delightful drinks you can only find in this locale. Matsuhisa offers a downstairs restaurant with a huge sushi bar while upstairs you will find a more relaxed, bar atmosphere and the same impeccable service. At the chic downstairs restaurant bar, the udon noodle bowl warms the soul after a great powder day. The cuisine is worth every bit of the hype Matsuhisa receives. Without a doubt, this is Aspen's best seafood and a worthy visit for both locals and travelers, time and again.

Meat & Cheese

Cuisine: Charcuterie with an Asian twist

Open: L - D

319 E. Hopkins   970.710.7120
Aspen, 81611

Price: $$$ **Patio:** Yes
Reservations: No   **Brunch:** No

Meat & Cheese, the new 'go to' spot is a butcher, frommagerie and specialty food shop pantry all in one with a restaurant attached. It's the best new addition to 'Restaurant Row' in Aspen! Cured meats, local Avalanche Farm cheeses and a bit of Asian flair with spicy Korean flavors, coconut red curry chicken soup and kimchi sandwiches make up the menu. Meat & Cheese has a casual menu and vibe with walk-in seating. You can do your grocery or present shopping on the one side of the market storefront, and enjoy a sit down meal and drinks on the other side. People go crazy over the cauliflower side dish, shared dishes and desserts.

Meatball Shack

Cuisine: Italian

Open: D: Daily, N: Nightly
themeatballshack.com

312 S. Mill Street   970.925.1349
Aspen, 81611

Price: $$ **Patio:** Yes
Reservations: No   **Brunch:** No

The Meatball Shack is a fun and friendly restaurant, hailing from the trendy NYC meatball mania concept. The Buffalo chicken meatballs, or spicy pork balls are delicious, served with the appropriate accompaniments and a healthy salad. Have you ever indulged in macaroni and cheese with tator tots, bacon and jalapenos in a homemade cheese sauce? If not, here's the place to get it! A warm and woodsy interior with a 'U' shaped bar makes this eatery a comfortable and casual place you could stop by any old time and saddle up for a drink, snack or get full on meatballs! Smack dab in the middle of the Mill Street Mall across from the playground and the fountain, this is great place for parents to let the kids run around while they enjoy a civilized drink and hearty snack or meal.

Mezzaluna

Cuisine: Italian
Open: L-D: Daily
mezzalunaaspen.com

624 E. Cooper Ave.
Aspen, 81611
Cooper & Hunter

970.925.5882

Price: $$-$$$
Reservations: Yes
*Kid friendly

Patio: Yes
Brunch: No

Soak up the scene outside on the sunny patio, inside at the U shaped bar or the bustling, open air dining room at Mezzaluna. This is an easy place to make friends and blend in with the Aspen scene. Dine on casual California and modern Italian influenced cuisine that ranges from fresh fish to tasty salads to Italian classics. Appetizers include a classic creamy tomato soup, unique, super-sized calamari flash fried with a spicy chili sauce and ahi tuna carpaccio with pickled seaweed and wasabi caviar. Try Grandma's stuffed shells with Italian sausage or the herb marinated veal chop with wild mushroom demi-glace and creamy corn polenta. The Chinese chicken salad and traditional chicken parmesan are top sellers in the poultry section. There is even a 'steak and fries' plate to please every palate. A cheerful crowd is almost always saddled up to the bar with the fiery pizza oven as the backdrop. Happy hour and après ski deals are found in the form of personal wood-fired pizzas and bottled beer to keep the locals happy. This bustling energetic mainstay keeps the crowds coming back season after season, year after year.

New York Pizza

Cuisine: Pizza/Italian
Open: L - D: Daily

409 E. Hyman Street
Aspen, 81611

970.920.3088

Price: $
Reservations: No
*Kid friendly

Patio: No
Brunch: No

The finest cuisine in Aspen past midnight! New York Pizza is a reliable place to grab a slice and enjoy a beer. Big thin-crust slices start at $3, so this Big Apple-style pizzeria is hard to beat for the budget-conscious. Open until the wee hours and after the bars close, this joint is about as good as late-night eating gets in this one horse town! The line out the door for late night service can be daunting – but if you know the right people, it goes quickly.

Phat Thai

Cuisine: Thai

Open: D: Mon-Sat

343 Main Street
Carbondale, 81623

970.963.7001

Price: $$
Reservations: Yes

Patio: No
Brunch: No

Think Thai inspired street food in a hip, small town atmosphere and you've got Carbondale's Phat Thai restaurant. Set in a "turn-of-the-century" row building complete with exposed brick and hardwood floors, the scene is updated with modern touches like a long, steel bar that welcomes friendly chatter. Just across the road from his fantastic new restaurant Town, Phat Thai takes on an Asian dimension for Chef-Owner Mark Fischer. With authentic recipes full of flavor, taste and unique ingredients, there is reason why the bar is always hopping and the dining room is always packed. Satisfy your Asian craving with traditional favorites like the five-spice BBQ sticky pork ribs, garlic and cilantro steamed crab with celery, green onion, chilies, fish sauce as well as a selection of spicy curry dishes, stir fries, noodles and rice. Try something new and different with Spicy Mama ramen, BBQ pork and a soft poached egg served with shiitake mushrooms and bok choy. The Thai specialties are reasonably priced, a nice wine list, fun cocktail menu and friendly, knowledgeable service to make the experience even more fun. On Friday nights enjoy live entertainment and a totally hip scene that takes over the streets of Carbondale.

Pine Creek Cookhouse

Cuisine: Coloradan

Open: L - D: Daily (Seasonal)

pinecreekcookhouse.com

11399 Castle Creek Road
Aspen, 81611

970.925.1044

Price: $$$
Reservations: Yes

Patio: Yes
Brunch: No

Located 12 miles outside Aspen, past the ghost town of Ashcroft, at the base of the Elk Mountain Range, the Pinecreek Cookhouse is a dining experience to say the least! Gourmet cuisine meets authentic mountain atmosphere, as the restaurant is housed in a log cabin with breathtaking wilderness surroundings. Best known for creatively prepared, naturally raised, local meats and game specialties, this is the place to experience Colorado at its best. In the winter you arrive to the restaurant by horse drawn sleigh or cross country skis, snowshoes or hiking boots from the ghost town. When summertime rolls around, you can drive right up to the door or work up your appetite with a road bike ride in from town. The Pinecreek Cookhouse is a must eat experience if you are in Aspen/Snowmass!

Piñons

Cuisine: Contemporary Colorado Cuisine

Open: D: Daily (seasonal)

105 S. Mill St.   970.920.2021
Aspen, 81611
Mill & Main

Price: $$$$ **Patio:** Yes - full deck
Reservations: Yes (Not in bar)   **Brunch:** No

Piñons is one for the dining history books! Classic, savored eateries like Pinons lay the ground work for establishing Aspen as a food lover's haven. It's no wonder that this Aspen restaurant continues to rate high with locals and travelers. The welcoming distinguished interior, impeccable tenured staff and delicious food remain consistent and irresistible. Enjoy the taste of crème frâiche and caviar on oysters or a salad made with asparagus and burrata, baked brie and pine nuts. Fans return for the specially cooked steaks, buffalo, ruby red trout and even the tofu enchilada has a following at this upscale American steakhouse. A simple filet of beef turns knock out with Hudson Valley foie gras and black truffle sauce. Desserts like the chocolate Nutella banana tart keep the clientele returning often. Piñons makes for a memorable meal. The cozy bar presents a special bar menu that is quite reasonable and walk-ins are encouraged – or the back patio in the summertime cannot be beat for the views.

Plato's

Cuisine: Contemporary, Sustainable, Infusion
Open: D: Nightly 5:30 – 10:00 pm
platosaspen.com/

845 Meadows Road   970.925.4240
Aspen, CO 81611
At the Aspen Meadows Resort

Price: $$$	**Patio:** Yes
Reservations: Yes	**Brunch:** No

Overlooking the Roaring Fork River, the Elk Mountain range and gorgeous groves of Aspen trees, this truly unique dining locale boasts an intimate atmosphere with simple yet elegant Bauhaus-inspired design and décor. Sustainable in practice, products and ingredients are sourced from local and regional farmers and even Plato's very own backyard garden. A noteworthy wine list compliments Plato's award-winning cuisine to reflect the flavors of the season in such dishes as Local Goat Cheese Agnolotti, Crystal River Lamb Tartar and Troyer Farms Brick Roasted Chicken. For more casual fare, try the amazing falafel burger or Chicken club by the pool. Breakfast at Plato's is also a treat with a long list of favorites made to your specifications. Plato's is located at the magnificent Aspen Meadows Resort, home of the venerable Aspen Institute. Sustainable in practice, products and ingredients are sourced from local and regional farmers, and even from Plato's very own backyard garden- because in the end, real, fresh and simple ingredients come together to create unforgettable dishes.

Prospect Hotel Jerome

Cuisine: American
Open: B-L-D: Daily
hoteljerome.aubergeresorts.com

330 East Main Street   970.920.1000
Aspen, 81611

Price: $$$	**Patio:** Yes
Reservations: Yes	**Brunch:** Yes-Sundays

Aspen's newest introduction on the culinary scene is Prospect, an upscale American bistro at the Hotel Jerome. The hotel's restaurant is the centerpiece of the property's top-to-bottom renovation, which debuted in December 2012. For over 120 years, Hotel Jerome has defined the true character of Aspen, drawing visitors from around the world with exquisite accommodations, acclaimed dining and true hospitality. The lobby Living Room is the place to be - designed for après ski, drinks anytime of the day or night, American tapas and small dessert plates. Executive Chef Rob Zack brings classically inspired yet contemporary dishes to the new menus at both Prospect and the new lobby Living Room. Having begun his career at Hotel Jerome nearly 20 years earlier, Zack repeats history and brings his own experience and point of view to the table. The Living Room is designed to feel exactly as it sounds - an open, expansive space for guests to relax and settle in over small plates and drinks from a new lobby bar. The menu consists of light, shareable snacks. The fun and sociable jar selection of snacks and appetizers is top notch. A nod to the town's rich mining history, Prospect offers hearty and diverse American dishes that are meant to be shared. Chef Zack studied the Jerome's old menus from the 1950s and reinterpreted a few of the dishes using contemporary techniques. Family recipes also have place on the menu, such as his Italian grandfather's meatballs. Zack's approach to cooking is simple: fresh, quality ingredients. Much of the menu is locally sourced from Avalanche Cheese Company in Basalt to Aspen's Emma Farms Cattle Company, as well as the local farmers' markets. Complementing the cuisine is a rich and varied wine program. The Hotel Jerome is a step back in time with a contemporary, decorative flair, thoughtful food and drinks -- it is a mandatory stop in Aspen.

The Pullman

Cuisine: American
Open: L - D: Daily
thepullmangws.com/

330 7th Street   970.230.9234
Glenwood Springs 81601

Price: $$ **Patio:** Yes
Reservations: Yes   **Brunch:** No

The hippest thing to hit Glenwood Springs since the Springs themselves! If Glenwood had hipsters, they would hang out here. Amazing, soulful Colorado-based cooking, the Pullman brings great dining and a well-balanced menu to this interesting town. Marc Fisher of Colorado's restaurant empire fame adds this address to his fantastic restaurant resume of: the newest Town in Carbondale, Phat Thai in Carbondale and the new Harman's in Denver. Fischer shows his terrific style as he offers an American menu to entice locals and tourists at The Pullman. The trains rattle by; the setting is high-tech, featuring high ceilings with exposed pipes, brick, big windows, and shades of green and gold on the walls. Totally casual, affordable, fun-- and great food, this place is the spot to be in Glenwood. Small plates include oysters, truffled pork rinds, chevre fritters, grilled calamari, and rellenos stuffed with oxtail and dates. Salads shine with many choices and pasta pleases with mac and cheese, lamb meatballs and feta gnudi, and perogiis. Large plates go from a burger, mussels, and chicken, to hanger steak, Berkshire porchetta, lamb and fish. Sandwiches at lunch are tasty: chicken with gruyere and ham, fried egg on English muffin with bacon and cheese, pulled pork on a bacon biscuit, and a Reuben. Decadent desserts end the meal. The wine list is great, service is excellent. On this Pullman, the dining car is the place to be.

Pyramid Bistro

Cuisine: Health-conscious World Cuisine

Open: L - D: Daily

221 E Main St   970.925.5338
Aspen, 81611

Price: $$ **Patio:** Yes
Reservations: No   **Brunch:** No

In a turn-of-the-century Victorian house, upstairs from the quaint bookseller on Main Street, Pyramid's dining room feels like a romantic, intimate tree house hideaway. A menu that emphasizes a touch of Thai influence, greens, whole grains, berries and beans, Pyramid Bistro is a toast to your health. Dubbed the "first nutritarian restaurant" by Dr. Fuhrman, who calculates the most nutrients per calorie, this healthy hotspot offers organic and conscious cuisine as well as embracing initiatives like 'meatless Mondays.' The menu caters fabulously to the vegan, vegetarian and gluten-free diner, but former chef of the renowned Syzygy restaurant, Martin Oswald, doesn't discriminate. Dishes spotlighting natural chicken, meat and fresh fish, any and everyone is sure to be delighted by the selection of choices, but more importantly, by the incredible savors and flavors. Oswald dishes up some of the most savory dishes around from sweet potato lasagna with roasted peppers and cremini mushrooms to decadent vegan chocolate cake; meals are meant to nourish and that's exactly what Pyramid Bistro strives to do. Pyramid Bistro leads Aspen's "nutritarian" movement with its nutrient-rich menu, presenting dishes to fit vegetarian, vegan, macrobiotic, raw-food and gluten-free diets – even the wines are bio-dynamic, organic and sustainably produced. Start with the kale crunchies, cashew crust and apple butter, then order the stir frys with forbidden rice or one of the fish and chicken specials. Owner Martin Oswald led Aspen's adoption of Meatless Mondays, making it the first city to join the national campaign.

Riverside Grill

Cuisine: American

Open: L: Daily 11:30 am to 2:30 pm. Happy Hour 4-6, D: at 5

181 Basalt Center Circle   970.927.9301
Basalt, CO 81621

Price: $ - $$ **Patio:** Yes
Reservation: No   **Brunch:** Yes
*Kid friendly

Serenely set by a rushing river in the cute town of Basalt, the Riverside Grill is the only place in the valley with outdoor deck seating overlooking the Frying Pan River. Tucked away between Clark's Market and Taylor Creek Fly Shop, "the riv" is open for lunch, happy hour and dinner daily. With its casual atmosphere and one-of-a-kind location, this is a great place to take the family or enjoy the afternoon sun on the patio with co-workers and friends. From juicy angus burgers and grilled rainbow trout, to crispy calamari with sweet chili sauce and a healthy quinoa salad, Riverside's menu is sure to please all. Riverside Grill is a local favorite hotspot, for private parties and events with the "open" design and 360 degree bar. Be sure to stop by for the live music on Friday nights or check out their 'Meatless Mondays' vegetarian offerings, and 'Fat Tuesday' specials. Visit Riverside Grill today, because, without a doubt – you will have fun!

Rustique Bistro

Cuisine: County French

Open: D: Daily

rustiquebistro.com

216 S. Monarch St.   970.920.2555
Aspen, 81611
Monarch & Hopkins

Price: $$$ **Patio:** Yes
Reservations: Yes (not required)   **Brunch:** No

Aspen delights in a little slice of the French Provencal country with the cuisine and charm of Rustique Bistro. The cozy, romantic ambience with soft lighting and a feel for France will have you 'parlez-vous-ing francais' in no time! Start with crispy frog legs with tomato vinaigrette, a divine pâté plate or the best salmon tartar. Don't forget to nibble on an order of pommes frites in a cone or the acclaimed cheese tray. The salad course reaches a new height when herb-marinated goat cheese arrives mounded on arugula salad with summer tomatoes. Endive with arugula, Roquefort and poached pears would please royalty, as would the bowl of onion-soup gratinée. Those who know stop by or call in to inquire of the 'Weird Dish of the Night,' or other specials like the 'Risotto of the Moment', Fish Special or Nightly Plat du Jour. The rest of the menu offers an enormous selection of possibilities to please any normal or weird diner's palate. "Weird" dishes include specials like the sautéed sweetbreads, crispy and delicious with haricots verts and wild mushrooms. The roasted half-chicken and mashed potatoes taste like mother wished she could make, and pot-au-feu of short ribs with roasted carrots, potatoes and horseradish crème falls off the bone. The duck cassoulet and the calf's liver with bacon and onions, potato purée and sauce Dijon, fruítes de mer – say "oui, oui!" The mussels are terrific as each sauce is perfectly blended not to overpower the main part of the dish. Finish with a classic French favorite like the chocolate pot au crème, the apple tarte tatin or almond pear financier...Bon Appetit!

Sam's Smokehouse

Cuisine: Western American

Open: L: Winter only

aspensnowmass.com/events-and-activities/on-mountain-dining/sams-smokehousedining/

130 Kearns Road Mid-Mountain 970.923.8686
Snowmass, Sam's Knob

Price: $ **Patio:** Yes
Reservations: No/Yes during high ski season   **Brunch:** No
*Kid friendly

Deemed as the "best BBQ on a mountain" by local foodies, Sam's Smokehouse is located at the top of the Village Express chairlift on Snowmass at Sam's Knob. Sam's Smokehouse features a wall of windows on the west side with spectacular views of Garret's Peak, Mount Daly, and the surrounding backcountry. Take a break from the slopes and indulge at the quick stop café and dedicated espresso bar; this kind of break will have you geared up and back on the slopes in no time with a jolt of delicious java and a delectable baked good. Or take a load off and sit-down in the lovely dining room with friendly, sit-down service. Here you will dive into barbecue-style smokehouse meats paying homage to Texas, Carolina and St. Louis style BBQs, as well as a variety of other Southern-style delights like fried green tomatoes, hearty salads and interesting soups. Now, it becomes clear why people bother to ski at all!

Steakhouse 316

Cuisine: Steak, American

Open: B-L-D

steakhouse316.com

316 E. Hopkins Avenue
Aspen, 81611

970.920.1893

Price: $$$$ **Patio:** Yes

Reservations: Yes   **Brunch:** No

Steakhouse 316 brings a New-York-vibe to the Aspen dining scene with a boutique steakhouse styled to feel like a 1920s Moulin Rouge style boudoir with velvet banquettes, warm black paneled walls and bordello-style lighting fixtures. The steak-focused menu is overseen by Chef Kathleen Crook. In addition to steaks, custom sauces, decadent side dishes and other steakhouse staples, the restaurant features the famous Lulu kale salad and several seafood dishes. If you are in the mood for a rich evening of steak and fun - this is the place to stop. Tuck into a booth and enjoy some oysters and a steak. Lovely outside seating draws a great crowd in the summertime.

Sundeck

Cuisine: Cafeteria featuring American and International Fare

Open: L: Daily

675 E. Durant Ave.
Aspen, 81611
Top of Aspen Mountain

970.920.4600

Price: $$$ **Patio:** Yes

Reservations: No   **Brunch:** No

Ride the Silver Queen Gondola from downtown to the crest of Aspen Mountain to find this jewel of a restaurant overlooking spectacular peaks in the Rockies. You'll feel like you are on top of the world! Relax under the open sky on the patio, sit inside where you can eat in a dining room rich with copper accents and natural wood or just socialize, drink and grab a meal at the elegant bar. Locavore-centered cuisine is served cafeteria-style and prepared while you watch. The menu ranges from Asian stir fries and salads to freshly fired, hand-tossed pizzas. A variety of baked goods and pastries satisfy all of your sweet cravings. Dining this high never tasted so good. Skiers will love taking a break in this idyllic spot, and in the summer, guests are met with an array of activity from hiking, yoga, Euro bungy and Frisbee golf to classical and bluegrass music, just outside the Sundeck's doorstep. The Sundeck is often used for large events, hosting parties from 30 to 450 with exquisitely themed buffets. Parties or wedding receptions in this location can't be beat.

Town

Cuisine: Contemporary American
Open: L - D: Daily
towncarbondale.com/index.php/restaurant

348 Main St.   970.963.6328
Carbondale 81623

Price: $$$ **Patio:** Yes
Reservations: Yes   **Brunch:** Yes

Happen upon the little town of Carbondale and you'll be surprised to find a foodie mecca, with Chef-Owner Mark Fischer's latest addition, Town, sitting right in the middle. By day, Town is a 'grab and go' bakery, a coffee shop, a lunch room and a gathering spot. By night, Town is something a little more ambitious, yet still accessible - a restaurant and bar that connects a community through eating. Pick a table by the window and pay for the basket of breads and house churned butter when you first sit down - it is worth it! Fiona's baked goods are made in-house at the adjoining bakery that greets you as you walk in the door of Town. Starters like the chile scented hamachi crudo with guacamole or the rabbit tacos with pickled onions, tomatillo and queso fresco are special treats you probably won't find anywhere else in the world. The entree halibut with cauliflower, carrots, oranges and a yellow curry is spectacular. Don't miss the side dish of the artichokes with sage butter and potatoes - it is the best thing on the menu. To wet your whistle, enjoy local beer and a fab selection of wine glasses from $7 to $12. The creative and delectable sticky bun toffee pudding was the icing on top for dessert. What a sweet beginning to end at a fresh new place called Town.

Trecento Quindici Decano

Cuisine: Italian
Open: B-L: Daily, D- Sun-Thurs
stregisaspen.com/trecentoquindici

315 East Dean Street   970.920.3300
Aspen 81611

Price: $$$ **Patio:** Yes (summer months)
Reservations: Recommended, not required   **Brunch:** No

Trecento Quindici Decano is the newest addition to the fabulous St. Regis Aspen Resort. With incredible views overlooking the St. Regis Aspen courtyard, as well as Aspen Mountain, Trecento satisfies in every way. Trecento offers extraordinary contemporary Italian cuisines guaranteed to please food-lovers of all ages. Executive Chef David Viviano mixes bold flavors with traditional cuisine using handmade pastas and pizzas to create an epicurean experience beyond expectation. With a welcoming atmosphere, Trecento brings a homey, yet upscale dining experience with exemplary service to any affair.

Venga Venga Cantina & Tequila Bar

Cuisine: Modern-Mexican
Open: Daily: 10:30 AM – late; Happy hour 3-6; Brunch Sat and Sun; open 10AM-9
richardsandoval.com/vengavenga/

105 Daly Lane   970.923.7777
Snowmass Village, 81615

Price: $$	**Patio:** Yes
Reservations: No	**Brunch:** No
***Kid friendly**	

Panoramic views, a vibrant atmosphere, authentic cuisine and with over 75 different tequilas to choose from, there's no wonder why Venga Venga Cantina and Tequila Bar has received so much press. Famed, globetrotting chef-owner Richard Sandoval was instilled with a passion for the cuisine of his heritage. His approach to cooking is simple and embedded in his mantra, "Old ways, new hands". With interpretations on traditional dishes and adding an innovative twist, this modern Mexican-style cuisine is a popular destination. Enjoy bottomless Bloody Marys, mimosas or house margaritas for $15.99 for two hours! Located at the end of the Snowmass Village Mall, there is no better place to bask in the afternoon sun with afresh margarita in hand and dine on authentic Mexican fare. This is the best Tex Mex food you will find in the Valley.

Viceroy Snowmass: Eight K, NEST

Cuisine: American; Asian; Contemporary Global
Open: B-L-D: Daily
viceroysnowmass.com

130 Wood Road   970.923.8008
Snowmass Village, CO 81615

Price: $$$	**Patio:** Yes
Reservations: Yes	**Brunch:** Yes

Viceroy Snowmass, the uber-hip, luxury ski resort located in the new Base Village development in Snowmass, features two favorite restaurants: Eight K and Nest, along with poolside dining. Eight K – arguably the sexiest room in Snowmass has an ambience that is warm, friendly and cutting-edge with a contemporary feel. The menu features options utilizing local farms' products like the flatbread sandwiches with selections like heirloom tomato, wild mushroom with balsamic onion, fontina, pea shoots, truffle oil and duck confit with caramelized shallots, roasted red grapes, wild arugula and saba. Unique and interesting local greens will tempt your healthy side with wild arugula and endive, red plum, orange, Marcona almonds and plum wine vinaigrette, or the Tatsoy with Fuji apple, goat's milk cheddar, cashews and kimchee dressing. A main entrée favorite is the thyme basted Colorado striped bass with artichoke hearts, sunchoke puree and sizzling balsamic butter. Anything on the menu with a Louisiana twist created by Cajun Chef Will Dolan is sure to be a winning choice.

NEST, decorated by celebrated designer Kelly Wearstler, is located near the pool area in Viceroy Snowmass. Their menu highlights include signature 'Nest rolls', sushi, sashimi and Asian inspired soups and salads. New this year is a 'mix and match, 'create your own' salad and/or burger with a list of tantalizing ingredients. For couples, families and friends, Viceroy Snowmass luxury ski resort offers ski-in/ski-out luxury resort lodging, complimented by imaginative dining and lounging, a Ute-inspired wellness spa, and a year-round pool terrace and café—an ideal setting for a Snowmass mountain vacation during any season.

Village Smithy

Cuisine: Casual American
Open: B, L: Daily D: Wed-Sun
villagesmithyrestaurant.com/

26 South Third Street   970.963.9990
Carbondale, CO 81623

Price: $ **Patio:** Yes
Reservations: No   **Brunch:** Yes
*Kid friendly

Back in the seventies this mom and pop team turned a charming 'black smith' building into a community restaurant. In 2009 their son and a partner took over and continued the tradition that is now Carbondale's gathering place and a true icon with an eclectic and enthusiastic environment. The Smithy's exceptionally friendly wait staff is documented by an old sign in the restaurant say is all: "We reserve the right to serve everyone." The popular breakfast eatery runs the gamut familiar favorite breakfast dishes, like the blueberry cornmeal pancakes to the delightfully unexpected such as our Fresh Spinach and Wild Mushroom omelette. Village Smithy is everyone's choice for the best breakfasts available in the region. Their popular breakfast dishes run the gamut from familiar favorites to the delightfully unexpected such as Santiago skillet, a bed of hash browns with grilled chicken, mild green chilies, black beans, corn, jack cheese and two eggs and cheese blintzes filled with cottage cheese, cream cheese and sour cream topped with fresh fruit. Around lunchtime, there is a fine selection of entree salads, sandwiches, burgers, and Mexican dishes. The Asian Chicken Salad with its homemade Tamari dressing has been a local's favorite for years. The large open air deck, surrounded by gardens, will make it hard for you to leave. Feel free to let your kids run wild on the lawn while you sit back, relax and enjoy an authentic, small town dining treat. The food is delicious and the wait-staff is exceptionally friendly. An old sign in the restaurant says it all: "We reserve the right to serve everyone."

Whitehouse Tavern

Cuisine: American
Open: D: Daily

hillstone.com/whitehousetavern/

302 East Hopkins Avenue   970.925.1007
Aspen, Colorado 81611

Price: $$ **Patio:** Yes
Reservations: No   **Brunch:** No

The White House Tavern resides in the historic A.G. Sheppard House on Restaurant Row in Aspen. The house was built in 1883 on a lot purchased from Isaac Cooper for $300. It served as a miner's cottage at the turn of the century and it remains one of the oldest structures in Aspen. Though it is run by the Hillstone and Houston's' chain of restaurants, the White House Tavern does not feel like a chain at all. Whitehouse offers a tasty selection of appetizers, salads and sandwiches along with distinctive wines, beers, and cocktails with great service - which is hard to find in this town with high turnover. Favorites include the crispy chicken and the fish sandwiches. Their kale salad with crushed peanuts is a big hit as well. Go for the lively and convivial atmosphere with an exposed kitchen and interesting artworks set in a cozy, wood paneled interior. Due to the intimate size and casual nature - they do not accept reservations. Bar seating is always available on a first-come first-served basis. this is a fun place to hang out in Aspen!

Wild Fig

Cuisine: Italian, Mediterranean
Open: D: Daily
thewildfig.com/

315 E. Hyman   970.925.5160
Aspen, 81611
3rd & Hyman

Price: $$$ **Patio:** Yes
Reservations: No   **Brunch:** No

The first restaurant of the Cordts-Pearce Aspen restaurateur empire is the lovely, Mediterranean influenes, Wild Fig. A quaint, well lit spot right in the heart of town, this gem is very small, with a few seats inside and a few seats outside. The atmosphere is casual, with lots of glass, an engaging bar for gathering or dining, and a charm that makes everyone feel at home instantly. The white French subway tiled walls and warm burgundy red banquets add to the Mediterranean, brasserie-type feel. The patio adds additional seating (weather permitting, though there are heaters.) The delicious bread is served in napkins, and the wine list is fantastic with many offerings by the glass or bottle at reasonable prices. The cuisine is Mediterranean, covering Greece, Morocco, Italy, France—or whatever suits the chef's whim of the day. Start with French onion or mushroom soup, baba ghanoush or falafel, or a spinach and feta pie with tzatziki sauce. Terrific flavors leave your taste buds begging for more. Try the daily "fish in a bag" for a seafood dining adventure! Life gets even better if you order the chocolate soufflé or beignets for dessert. The coffee arrives in a French press, which makes the experience so European and special. By Aspen standards, Wild Fig is very affordable; by any standard, this is a restaurant where you want to be. The Mediterranean platter and a bottle of wine and one would be content any night of the week.

Woody Creek Tavern

Cuisine: American

Open: L-D: Daily

#2 Woody Creek Plaza   970.923.4585
Woody Creek, 81656
7 miles west of Aspen

Price: $$ **Patio:** Yes
Reservations: No   **Brunch:** No
*Kid friendly

This laid-back hangout with colorful scenery is the perfect spot to enjoy a fresh lime margarita, kick up your heels and have a good time. Located on the outskirts of Aspen, locals and part-time Aspenites swear by the Mexican specials, like the chicken Estofado served twice a week, the enchiladas, the fish tacos and the guacamole and homemade tortilla chips. The BLT aims to please and does not skimp on the bacon. The locally raised Limousin burgers are tops in town, and more than one has connived, unsuccessfully, to get the recipe for the WCT signature salad dressing. There can be a wait to dine at this distinguished dive, which boasts a menu of sandwiches, Mexican food, soups, salads and appetizers. Bike here in the summer and hang for hours on the sunny patio! Belly up at the bar and you are sure to hear a good yarn or two from the staff or local dwellers, also called "Woody Creatures." Take in the atmosphere by checking out the zillions of photos, mementos and unique artwork that plaster the walls and ceilings. It is no wonder that ranchers, city folk and Hunter S. Thompson pick this spot to refuel and whet their whistle– it has zest, color and delightfully good food.

Zocalito

Cuisine: Latin America, Spain
Open: D: Daily
zocalito.com/

420 E. Hyman Ave.   970.920.1991
Aspen, CO 81611

Price: $$ **Patio:** Yes
Reservations: Yes   **Brunch:** No

This unique, colorful, friendly restaurant is the closest thing you'll get to authentic, traditional Mexican cuisine in Colorado. Start off at the bar and enjoy some amazing queso with chorizo and homemade tortilla chips to go along with a refreshing and tasty mojito, which is made right in front of you with locally grown mint and mashed with fresh lime juice, cane sugar, Appleton's rum and soda. The margaritas are made fresh with lime juice for that sweet taste of Mexico you can only find south of the border. Owner-Chef Michael Beary makes incredibly tasty carnitas, chili rellenos, grilled vegetable chayote and black bean sopes which are thick tortillas topped with black beans, cheese and pork loin that hit the spot for flavors and fun. Several times a year, Beary flies down to Mexico to dig up exotic ingredients like dried chilies from Oaxaca and other specialties like Chapulines (grasshoppers) for us to enjoy locally. Zocalito is the only importer in the U.S. of seven different rare chiles from Oaxaca that are essential to making moles the right way! You will find a variety of different moles, some that you have never even heard of or tasted before. All of the wines in the restaurant are either from Spain or Central

Bob and Lisa Rennick and friends

• • • • • • • • • • • • • • • • • • • •

Two South Food and Wine Bar

Cuisine: Contemporary
Open: D: Mon-Sat, L: Fri-Sun
2southwinebar.com

2 South 25th Street   719.351.2806
Colorado Springs, CO 80904
Corner of Pikes Peak Street & 25th Street

Price: $$ **Patio:** Yes
Reservations: Yes   **Brunch:** Yes
Location: Old Colorado City

What if the TV show "This Old House" was about taking a slightly run down Victorian two-story in a historic part of town, and turning it into a wonderful casual neighborhood restaurant and wine bar, with extremely well selected wines and creative, expertly prepared and gorgeous contemporary food. Bingo! Consider it done. Co-owner Rod Quass is the wine maven, and with Chef James Davis, acclaimed for his former work at The Blue Star, and Sous-and-Pastry Chef Supansa Banker, a rising local star, this is one of the places giving Old Colorado City a reputation as the fun culinary part of town. Their passionate vision of "A place to come often and stay late" seems to be working. Tables under the large oaks in the front yard are popular for relaxing with a drink and tapas on a sunny afternoon. Your best bet is to go with a few friends and do lots of mixing and matching. Charcuterie and Fromage plates are perfect for sharing – you construct them from a list. The big pizza oven out back (don't ask) produces some very tasty items, such as the shrimp, basil, tomato,chevre ricotta, and fontal 'flatbread'. Tapas are delightful, and fish, beef and chicken larger plates are all special taste creations. Save room, because the sweets are outstanding, especially pastry chef Supansa's Lime Pavlova. Be sure to ask about the Sunday Supper Club. Other than the front yard, handicapped access might be a problem, so call ahead.

Adam's Mountain Café

Cuisine: Contemporary
Open: B-L: Daily, D: Tues-Sat
adamsmountain.com

26 Manitou Ave   719.685.1430
Manitou Springs, 80829
East end of Manitou Springs

Price: $-$$ **Patio:** Yes
Reservations: Yes   **Brunch:** No
Location: Manitou Springs

For three decades, three owners, and now in its fourth location following the flood aftermath of the Waldo Canyon Fire, this local treasure has creatively and consistently grown from its roots (sprouts?) in the California natural and green tradition. This has been the go-to spot for vegetarian (70% of the menu) and vegan (20% of the menu) dishes. Adam's is focused on seasonal, local, organic ingredients. Add carefully sourced seafood and fowl (but no beef) and a small but well-chosen and well-paired wine list, and you have the current winner. The cheerful, funky, kid friendly atmosphere and attentive service (please, please ask questions and explore the menu with your server) is further enhanced by a Community Table – sit there if you want to avoid a wait or make new friends. Adam's is well known for a creative breakfast menu as well as delicious lunch and dinner options - all cooked to order, which takes a little while, so relax. Popular breakfast items include Huevos Rancheros, Orange Almond French Toast , omelets, quiches, whole grain pancakes, shrimp and grits, and eggs-to-order (with elegantly presented fruit and Great Harvest toast). Slide right into lunch with fresh soups, salads, sandwiches, noodle dishes, and the baked catch of the day. After a break, dinner adds appetizers, such as lettuce wraps, fig and pear crostini, and crab cakes, as well as three soups, including the ever-popular Cuban black bean and the New England clam chowder. Entrée favorites span the globe - Senegalese Vegetables on rice or udon, Rural Italian Lasagna (a favorite for 30 years) and Smoked Salmon Enchiladas. Newer entrees (only a few years on the menu) include Brazilian style Barramundi, Moroccan fish tacos, East Indian curry, and pozole verde – you get the idea. Check the schedule for live acoustic music on Tuesday, Thursday and Friday. Reservations are recommended on holidays and during the Summer.

Ai Sushi & Grill at Powers

Cuisine: Japanese
Open: L-D: Daily
aisushipowers.com

3215 Cinema Point   719-622-8866
Colorado Springs, 80922
First & Main Town Center – Carefree Circle

Price: $-$$ **Patio:** No
Reservations: Yes   **Brunch:** No
Location: Colorado Springs - Eastside

"AI" is the Japanese word for "love" and this is a sushi experience you can love. The chefs do a great job connecting with guests. AI offers teppan grills, regular tables, booths and a sushi bar where you can be up close and personal. There's a large and varied dinner menu, with some good seafood options, and family-pleasing sushi rolls. One cringe-worthy roll is the "Monkey Brain", a full avocado split into halves, filled with spicy tuna and crab , put back together, dipped in tempura batter, fried ,cut into quarters and drizzled with creamy spicy sauce and teriyaki sauce – a spicy and slightly sweet explosion of flavor. The full line of hot and cold sake wines complements the menu. Just to confuse you, there is another good formerly related "Ai Sushi & Grill" on the west side of town, on Centennial Blvd near Garden of the Gods Rd, very similar to the Powers restaurant.

Amanda's Fonda

Cuisine: Mexican
Open: L-D: Daily
amandasfonda.com/

3625 West Colorado Ave   719.227.1975
Colorado Springs, 80904
Colorado Springs Westside

8050 N. Academy Blvd   719.266.6680
Colorado Springs, 80920
North Academy Blvd near the South entrance of the Air Force Academy

Price: $-$$ **Patio:** Yes
Reservations: No   **Brunch:** No
Location: Colorado Springs-Westside & North Academy Blvd, near the AFA

The rustic original Old Colorado City Amanda's, with the log cabin look, many small rooms, and a dirt parking lot, sits by a babbling (sometimes overflowing) creek, with many large trees.

The newer north Academy Blvd location is more modern and open, with a paved parking lot and babbling traffic. Both are festive places for families to enjoy a lively Mexican meal. The Academy location is convenient to nearby businesses and the Chapel Hills Shopping Mall. The service is quick yet personal. The American-Mexican menu has all the familiar items. Try the mole, enchiladas, chile rellenos, and burritos. The homemade salsa is fresh, zesty, filled with chunks of tomatoes, roasted green chilies, and generous amounts of cilantro leaves. If you like your hot sauce hot, then request the Habenero Hot Sauce! The margarita menu features a variety of top shelf tequilas and options for small, medium, or large glasses or a pitcher for the table. The burritos are delicious with combinations of beef, chicken, pork and vegetables, topped with black olives and automatically served with guacamole and sour cream. The traditional cabbage salad served with all entrees is a crisp rendition of American coleslaw. There is rarely room for dessert, but many options are available to satisfy that sweet tooth. This is perfect for families, couples or friends. Amanda's has received many local awards over the years.

Bhan Thai

Cuisine: Thai
Open: L-D: Mon-Sat
Bhanthai.net

4431 Centennial Blvd.   719.266.1309
Colorado Springs 80907
Garden of the Gods Road & Centennial Blvd.

Price: $	**Patio:** No
Reservations: No	**Brunch:** No
Location: Colorado Springs	

There are at least a dozen reasonably good Thai restaurants in Colorado Springs. All have pretty similar menus and most are inexpensive and plain. There are three just in the area around I-25 and North Academy Blvd - Thai Basil (related to the same names in Denver), Thai Mint (our favorite - 1725 Briargate Blvd, Colorado Springs, CO 80920 , 719.598.7843), and Chaang Thai. The somewhat fancier NaRai Thai, with table cloths, has Rockrimmon area and Broadmoor area locations. Wild Ginger, a Westside winner for decades, has recently moved to a small storefront in Old Colorado City. This Bhan Thai, (there is another Bhan Thai, formerly related – don't ask), is a storefront next to a super market, and in addition to tasty Thai food, has a Glacier ice cream stand – guess who the kids vote for. Diners do not go here for the ambience, fancy wares or service. They flock here for inexpensive traditional Thai food and beverages. Counter service and self-serve fountain drinks keep it quick and simple - please bus your table.. The Pad Thai is classic, simple and delicious with peanuts, sprouts, fried egg, vermicelli, red peppers and as spicy as you want it. The more savory Drunken Noodles is flat, rectangular noodles, cabbage, broccoli, carrots and choice of meat, with a garlic brown sauce and a slight kick at the end. The expected curries, Green, Penang, and Red, with choice of meat, are authentic. The Massamon curry is a favorite, with yellow curry paste, coconut milk, potatoes, bell peppers, onions and peanuts. The soups are very popular. Thai Iced Tea is the perfect way to begin or end a meal—a sweet treat with brewed fresh Thai Tea (a black tea that is orange in color) and sweetened condensed milk floating on top. Did we mention the Glacier homemade ice cream?

BJ's Restaurant and Brewhouse

Cuisine: American
Open: L-D: Daily

bjsrestaurants.com/locations/co/colorado-springs

5150 North Nevada Avenue   719.268.0505
Colorado Springs, CO 80918
University Village Shopping Center

Price: $-$$ **Patio:** Yes
Reservations: No   **Brunch:** No
Location: Colorado Springs – University Village Shopping Center

Yes, with over a hundred locations, it is a chain. However, the something-for-everyone very large menu of well-prepared food and beverages, and the exceptionally good consistency, makes it worth recommending. The service is good, the loyalty program works, the silent TVs with sports events can be seen (or ignored) from everywhere, and the décor is fun art deco 1930's murals. You can choose seating at the bar, the patio, high tables close to the bar, or two other sections of regular tables and booths. Whether you're looking for burgers, pizza, chicken, steaks, ribs, fish, soups, salads, or those deadly "Pizookie" desserts, you'll find a favorite. There is a short but well-selected wine list, a very long list of draft and bottled beer, and an impressive number of tasty lower calorie items. At the regular meal times, the joint is jumping, so speak up, or come at in-between-meals times for quiet conversation.

The Blue Star

Cuisine: Contemporary
Open: L-D: Mon-Fri, D: Sat-Sun
thebluestar.net

1645 S. Tejon St.   719.632.1086
Colorado Springs, 80905
South Tejon and Cheyenne Mountain Blvd.

Price: $$-$$$ **Patio:** No
Reservations: Yes   **Brunch:** No
Location: Colorado Springs – South of Downtown, Just
north of the Broadmoor area

"Contemporary fusion", "fresh, locally grown", "global flavors, harmoniously blended", "casual elegance" .... sound familiar? Like maybe on every upscale restaurant web site these days? Well, good news – The Blue Star really does it. Ignore the uninteresting industrial exterior, walk into The Blue Star and you are struck by the Santa Fe modern decor, the bold paintings and clever sculptures on the brightly colored walls, and the pleasant jazz instrumentals. Good food, quality and attentiveness is the goal at the diverse food enterprises of owner Joseph Campbell –The Blue Star (south of downtown), Nosh (downtown), La'au's Taco Shop (near Colorado College), and 3 in the old Ivywild school building (three blocks from The Blue Star) - The Old School Bakery, The Meat Locker, and The Principal's Office. There are three dining areas - the lounge, the fine dining room and the private wine room. The frequently changing menus are just as interesting and engaging as the art. Layered nuances of taste, complementing and contrasting in Executive Chef Will's well thought dishes, will reward your choices. Appetizers ("Tapas" on the lounge menu) might feature oysters, PEI mussels, ahi tartare, calamari, Shishito peppers, and carrots. (Seriously, a carrot tapa? Think 'seasonal'.) The soup of the day could be called "corn chowder", but consist of a blended cream of roasted tomatoes, peppers and corn, topped with bacon and blue cheese. Entrees have included lamb sumac, lamb burger with sumac fries, lamb loin chops (OK, that month they liked lamb and sumac), duck, Alamosa bass, scallops, halibut and pork chops. Sunday evenings are busy with wine lovers because all bottles are half-price! The staff knows their stuff, so ask for help in pairing from the excellent wine and cocktail list. For vegetarians, there are very nice soups, salads and a quinoa burger (and don't forget the carrot). All the house-made desserts are terrific, but you can't refuse The Corleone. Just go try it – you'll thank us! Perfect for drinks and tapas in the lounge after work or for fine dining, the Blue Star has a loyal following. Just don't get too fond of a menu item - it 'Will' (get it?) be replaced the next time.

Bonefish Grill

Cuisine: Seafood
Open: L-D: Daily
bonefishgrill.com/Locator/details/colorado-springs

5102 North Nevada Avenue   719.598.0826
Colorado Springs, 80918
University Village Shopping Center

Price: $$-$$$ **Patio:** Yes
Reservations: Yes   **Brunch:** Yes
Location: Location: Colorado Springs - north Nevada Ave
near I-25

Bonefish is not the only place in The Springs for reliably good seafood, but it's a good option. They have quality fresh fish, properly prepared and nicely served. There are some really nice appetizers and salads and soups to get you going, then choose your favorite preparation of a fish from the list, or a fancy special, or some lighter dishes. We love the mussels and the Bang-Bang shrimp for starters, and then whatever is in season and approved by the Monterey Aquarium people. 'It ain't cheap, McGee', but it's good. Good wine, beer & martini list, too, and a sports bar area for noisy happiness.

Briarhurst Manor Estate

Cuisine: American
Open: D Tues-Sun
briarhurstdining.com

404 Manitou Ave.   719.685.1864 or
 Manitou Springs, 80829   1-877-685-1448

Price: $$$-$$$$ **Patio:** No
Reservations: Yes   **Brunch:** No
Location: Manitou Springs – just East of downtown Manitou
Springs

This Victorian Tudor manor, built in 1876 by the English founder of Manitou Springs, sits well off the street amid tree-shaded grounds; the setting is ideal for gracious dining, weddings and other special events. Your special occasion dinner, in one of nine plush and cozy dining rooms, will truly be special. Traditional favorites, such as Beef Wellington, Trout Almandine and Steak Diane grace the menu, along with contemporary touches such as Wild Boar "Green Chili" and the Peppermint Patty and Orange "Creamsicle" desserts. In addition to the a la carte choices, several five-course dinners make for easy ordering and are a little easier on the pocketbook. The comprehensive wine list is reasonably priced. The upscale "Youth Menu" makes kids feel more special and grown up, which gets extra points for a birthday celebration. Come enjoy the elegant atmosphere at Briarhurst Manor which has been luring tourists and locals alike since 1975. Use the valet parking – the dirt lot can be muddy in wet weather.

The Broadmoor

Cuisine: Traditional, Contemporary, Italian, Pub
Open: B-L-D: Daily
Broadmoor.com

The Broadmoor,
1 Lake Avenue
South of Downtown

Colorado Springs, CO 80906
844.513.9981

Price: $$$-$$$$$ **Patio:** Yes
Reservations: Yes   **Brunch:** Yes
Location: Colorado Springs

From the moment the valet whisks your car away, you will step into a world class ocean of elegance. The Broadmoor and it's cadre of dining venues are, as a whole, quite special. (Check ahead for dress code for each venue and do not even think of wearing sneakers or a baseball cap, let alone backwards.) The Broadmoor has held a 5 star rating longer than any other resort in America. Pick up a cocktail at the Lobby Bar and stroll around the lake, admiring the magnificent hotel and the view, while building an appetite. This is a major dining operation, with a squadron of executive chefs and an army of supporting cast, drawn from the best hotels and restaurants around the world. The dining rooms vary in style and price. The Penrose Room ($$$$$) captures the essence of formal dining and is complete in every regard. The Summit introduces lighter, innovative cuisine in a modern setting. Ristorante del Lago, on the west side of the lake, strives for the best of many regions of Italy, with a glamorous villa ambience. The Entre Deux section of La Taverne, in the main building, features more of a chophouse menu as well as live dance music at certain times, while the faux al fresco atrium Le Jardin is perfect for ladies who lunch. Natural Epicurean is a casual spot serving organic, healthy food locally grown, partly by The Broadmoor itself. The renovated Golden Bee provides all the spirit of a 19th century British pub should you crave some chips, a scotch egg, a yard of ale, and a jolly sing-along. The Golf Club is for hotel guests and members, overlooking PGA championship golf courses. "PLAY", a retro sports bar, rec room and lounge with an eclectic menu is the newest hangout. The Lake Terrace dining room is where breakfast is served during the week, and a fancy brunch buffets on Sundays. Taken altogether, it's incomparable - it's the Broadmoor!

Brother Luck's Street Eats

Cuisine: Contemporary
Open: L-D: Tue-Sat, B: Sun
chefbrotherluck.com

1005 W. Colorado Avenue   719.434.2741
Colorado Springs, CO 80904
Ten blocks West of Downtown Colorado Springs

Price: $-$$ **Patio:** Yes
Reservations: Yes   **Brunch:** Yes
Location: Old Colorado City

Highly perceptive foodie that you are, you already noticed that the email address names the chef, not the restaurant. Yes, that's his name, and his fans follow him for fresh, imaginative, delicious food wherever he is cooking, be it his former stints at upscale places like the Cheyenne Mtn. Resort and Craftwood Inn, or a kitchen behind a bar, or now this funky little old house in Old Colorado City. Ambience? Don't ask. Well, since you asked, the best part of the otherwise drab interior is the colorful mural of a butcher's diagram of a pig named Fred ... oh, and Brother's Executive Master Chef certificate from the American Culinary Federation. The bowl of bacon flavored popcorn on the table on the table is your second clue about Brother's favorite protein. The menu changes seasonally, but small bites have included Red Snapper Crudo, Tempura Jalapeno Poppers, and Tomatillo Pork Tacos. The Westside Greens can become the whole meal with added protein such as pork belly or chicken. Artfully plated Large Plates and 'Handhelds' have at various times been Pig Ear Ramen, Bacon Jam Burger, Paella, Lamb Merguez Sausage, strip steak, each with accompanying ingredients, spices and sauces that create layers of complementary and contrasting tastes that enhance the basic flavor of the dish. Brunch has included Coffee Croughnuts, Duck Spam Benedict, and Bananas Foster French Toast among many other items, some less unusual. The list of cocktails, wine and beer is short but very well selected.

Carlos' Bistro

Cuisine: Contemporary
Open: D: Winter Wed-Sat, Summer Daily, closed March

carlosbistrocos.com/

1025 S. 21st St.   719.471.2905
Colorado Springs, 80904
21st Street just south of Hwy 24/Cimarron St/Midland Expy

Price: $$$-$$$$ **Patio:** No
Reservations: Yes   **Brunch:** No
Location: Colorado Springs - southwest of downtown

What's in a restaurant name? In this case, it's everything. Carlos is the owner, the executive chef, the pastry chef, the maitre'd, the sommelier, the bartender, and the constant tie-over-the-shoulder presence, warmly greeting you at the door (opening the door most of the time), seating you, explaining everything, and following up to make sure you are having an excellent experience. His accent, the Peruvian (not Chilean) Pisco Sour, the ceviche, and the ribeye lomo saltado, give away his origins. The prices tend toward high and are worth it, without resorting to pretentious ambience and overly fussy food, because of thoughtful recipes prepared with high quality ingredients, properly and consistently. The simple tasteful bistro décor and music are conducive to conversation. The flavor profiles are expertly balanced, and the seasonal items are creatively prepared. A long list of appetizers includes various shellfish preparations, five kinds of nachos, avocado eggrolls and expense account treats such as caviar, abalone steak, Foie Gras, and legs - king crab and frog. Entrees include USDA Prime steaks, from filet to ribeye to hangar, several veal preparations, Colorado lamb chops, calves liver and such treats as filet mignon stroganoff, lobster Fra Diavolo, calamari Genovese, paella and cioppino. Save room for the bread pudding and the Key Lime desserts – they are different and very good. Even before opening his own place, Carlos was well known for his wine expertise, so don't hesitate to ask for help in pairing from the excellent wine list. The Early Bird special menu has many items, in smaller portions, at roughly half price, and half price bottles of wine are offered Wednesdays in the Winter, and Sunday and Monday in the Summer

Caspian Café

Cuisine: Mediterranean
Open: L-D: Mon-Sat, D: Daily
caspiancafe.com

4375 Sinton Road   719.528.1155
Colorado Springs, 80907
Just southeast of the I-25 & Garden of the Gods Road
interchange

Price: $$ **Patio:** No
Reservations: Yes   **Brunch:** No
Location: Colorado Springs

With the inside feel of a secluded villa but just off Interstate
25, Caspian Café was opened in 2004 by Mo Sharifi, a warm
presence in the dining room, who emigrated from Iran in 1977.
Well-known local chef Daniel White skillfully prepares fish,
lamb, beef and vegetarian dishes, using both familiar French
and Greek preparations and more exotic spices and treatments
from North Africa and the Middle East. Whether you prefer
rosemary lamb or lamb tagine, chicken Moroccan style or
Persian style, baba ghanouj, dolmades or Spanish tapas, you
will be happy. The expansive menu's wide range of flavors and
cultures means you could visit the Caspian Café each week for
months and be in a different country each time. The effusive
greeting and attention you will receive from Sharifi and his
staff will keep you coming back.

The Cliff House at Pikes Peak

Cuisine: Colorado Contemporary
Open: B-L-D: Daily
thecliffhouse.com

306 Canon Ave.   719.785.2415
Manitou Springs, 80829
Next street over from the Historic Manitou Spa

Price: $$-$$$ **Patio:** Yes (Veranda)
Reservations: Yes   **Brunch:** Yes
Location: Manitou Springs

This restored historic hotel dates to when upper class
gentlemen from England and 'Back East' enjoyed Western
elegance in Manitou Springs, the jumping off place for their
Rocky Mountain outdoor experience. This is the place to treat
that special someone (or yourself) to a memorable meal in the
Victorian dining room, a leisurely Summer breakfast on the
Veranda, or a gourmet burger and Colorado craft beer in the
Red Mountain Bar and Grill. The dining room features china,
linens and crystal, beautiful artwork, and impeccable service.

Chefs blend classic French cooking styles with modern ideas and fresh Colorado ingredients (including herbs from their own garden). Certified sommeliers guide you through the award-winning wine list. It's the place for elk and Colorado lamb, as well as Fruits de Mer—Black Tiger Shrimp, Maine Lobster, Sea Scallops, and creamy risotto. Take a tip from the regulars, and plan dessert when you place your dinner order – the Cliff House soufflé is mandatory, but the Cake Pops and Crème Brulee Trio are among other winners.

Coquette's Bistro and Bakery

Cuisine: Contemporary Gluten Free
Open: L-D: Mon-Fri, B-L-D: Sat-Sun
Coquettesbistroandbakery.com

321 North Tejon St.   719.685.2420
Colorado Springs, CO
Between Boulder and Platte

Price: $-$$ **Patio:** Yes
Reservations: Yes   **Brunch:** Yes
Location: Colorado Springs - Downtown

The graphic logo promises "Boldly Luscious Gluten Free, Made in Colorado", referring to the food, not the cute coquette winking at you. It's not an empty promise. This family is passionate about gluten and allergen free, hormone free, antibiotic free, locally sourced food. They supply the gluten free cooking flour, baking flour and baked goods to many other restaurants and markets. However, even if you have no special need for GF, go anyhow, because you won't be able to tell the difference from just good food. Many familiar items end up better than the similar ones at non-GF places, just because Coquette's has to make in-house many of the ingredients that others buy in bulk from restaurant supply companies. The current broad contemporary menu includes both savory and dessert crepes, along with many other dishes. Mediterranean and Southwestern flavors work well in the Caprese bites, Mezze plate and Vegan lettuce wrap apps. There is a nice choice of salads, burgers and sandwiches, as well as chicken potpie, fried chicken and exceptionally good fish and chips. There's lavender in a salad dressings and one of the desserts, and truffle flavor in the fries, showing good attention to complementary tastes. The bakery sells fresh breads, rolls, pizza crust, muffins and yummy desserts. There's a full bar, and the non-alcoholic drink menu offers some delicious options including, you guessed it, lavender tea. The restaurant interior is pleasant and very roomy, although a little hollow, waiting for a kitchen expansion that will support more seating and some new furniture. Expect the bakery counters at the front of the restaurant to migrate to a separate new shop next door. Servers are knowledgeable. The nice background music choices reflect the professional music background of the family.

Edelweiss German Restaurant

Cuisine: German
Open: L-D: Daily
edelweissrest.com

34 East Ramona Avenue   719.633.2220
Colorado Springs, CO 80906
Between S. Nevada (Hwy 87) and S. Tejon St.

Price: $$ **Patio:** Yes
Reservations: Yes   **Brunch:** Yes
Location: Colorado Springs – Ivywild area

For many decades, this large, picturesque, German restaurant has been serving tasty traditional favorites such as gulasch, schnitzels, bratwurst, sauerbraten, and roulade (we call them "roly-polies" at home), smothered in traditional sauces, with gemischte salad, and spaetzle or potatoes. The German beer list is extensive and served in the correct glasses. The menu has expanded over several years to include regional specialties such as flammkuchen (tarte flambé), schweinshaxe (roasted pork shank), and maultaschen (filled dumplings, though this version is more like a little lasagna than the pockets in broth you might have had in Germany). Lunch offers many of the same items, as well as traditional and German-style salads and sandwiches. Save room for the house made desserts from Konditor Meister Horst – including strudels, Black Forest Cherry Cake, and even Bienenstich. Multiple dining rooms have fireplaces, and the basement lounge has the shared table where the locals hoist a few and argue politics and sports. Some evenings there's a strolling musician in lederhosen – sing along if you know the words. The partially covered Biergarten is the perfect place for a cool drink and a meal or snack on a sunny day. This is the place where local Germans bring visitors and hold parties, and where you can relive your time in Germany.

The Famous Steak House

Cuisine: American
Open: L: Mon-Fri, D: Daily
thefamoussteakhouse.net/

31 N. Tejon St.   719.227.7333
Colorado Springs, CO 80903
Downtown Colorado Springs – Kiowa & Tejon

Price: $$$-$$$$	**Patio:** No
Reservations: Yes	**Brunch:** No
Location: Colorado Springs	

The piano player knows all the lounge standards, the red-leather booths are comfy, the large, polished-wood and brass bar is busy, and the prime steaks are incredibly tender at this downtown favorite with a late-night Midwestern-urban feel. Your Daddy's favorite martinis and highballs are supplemented by modern updates, and the wine list is impressive. Shrimp cocktail and raw oysters are what you remembered and the Wisconsin Pork Belly app makes a new memory. The filet mignon will melt in your mouth, and the "Maytag bleu cheese" New York strip is huge and flavorful. Perfectly prepared lamb, chicken and seafood dishes round out an evening of quality food in a historic setting. If you can handle dessert, go all the way with the suggested wine pairings. The service is prompt and the atmosphere takes you right back to a 1920's speakeasy. It's an experience not to be missed.

Front Range BBQ

Cuisine: Barbecue
Open: L-D: Daily (Seasonal)
frontrangebbq.com

2330 West Colorado Ave   719.632.2596
Colorado Springs, 80904
Colorado Ave at 24th Street, next to Bancroft Park

Price: $-$$	**Patio:** Yes
Reservations: No	**Brunch:** No
Location: Colorado Springs - Old Colorado City	

What more could we ask for than good Southern BBQ, North Carolina slow-smoked BBQ (dry rub, then add the sauce of your choice), and Cajun staples, plus bluegrass, blues, folk & jazz in an old house in Old Colorado City? Not only does this BBQ joint serve delicious food, but they also boast a heated and covered patio with frequent live and lively music!. The intimate dining room and bar area show the character of the old home that was converted into this restaurant. It's easy to understand why this place is a perennial "Best Of" BBQ winner when you dig into the scrumptious ribs, pulled pork, and beef brisket. Starters include Cracklins', fried Okra, and Old Brunswick Southern Stew. Beyond BBQ, there's catfish, salads, vegetarian burgers and several 'regular' burgers. Sandwiches on "Sweet Po-Tater Buns" are topped with onion straws which add the perfect salty, savory crunch to the sweet and smoky BBQ sauce. In addition to the usual sides, try Louisiana Red Beans and Rice or Mom's Corn 'n Pea Salad, which perfectly complement the unsophisticated but well executed food. Save room for the pecan pie with vanilla sauce, and don't forget the local craft beers on tap!

Garden of the Gods Gourmet, Market & Cafe

Cuisine: Contemporary
Open: B-L: Mon-Fri, D: Tues-Sat, Brunch: Sat-Sun

godsgourmet.com

410 South 26th Street   719.471.2799
Colorado Springs, CO 80904
Southwest Corner of Hwy24 & 26th Street

Price: $$-$$$ **Patio:** No
Reservations: Yes   **Brunch:** Yes
Location: Colorado Springs - Hwy 24 next to Old Colorado City

Beautiful and tasty food and attentive service is exactly what you'd expect from one of the most popular long-time catering operations in town. Being right on Hwy24/Cimarron St./Midland Expressway, if you are on your way to or from Ute Pass, this is a convenient travel stop for a good sit-down meal, ready to eat takeout, and/or supplies for your mountain destination. Enter through the market and gift shop. On the other side of the fieldstone double fireplace is the open, bright, modern casual dining room. The food theme is natural, fresh, local, minimally manipulated ingredients, cooked from scratch. Vegetarian, Vegan and Gluten-Free options are clearly identified. This is not fast food, so relax. Breakfast and Brunch has all the basic eggs and pancakes, as well as some creative Benedicts, hashes, and frittatas. Lunch features many delicious salads, soups, tacos, burgers and panini. The wine and beer list is small but well selected. For dinner, there are pub and bistro-style appetizers such as Mac-and-Cheese, Picnic Board, Crab cakes and smoked pork belly. Soup of the day can be outstanding, especially if it's the Squash and Chorizo, served with "Great Bread" (it is). Fresh salads range from familiar to trendy, such as the Kale-Me-Crazy organic medley and the Beet Love. The short entrée menu does cover all the categories – fish, shellfish, beef, lamb and vegetarian, with appropriate preparations, starches and vegetables. The Cauliflower Steak was a nice surprise, and the Kobe Beef Burger is right up there. There are a half dozen desserts suitable for sharing, all creatively complex except for the pie of the day and the ice cream, and all prettily plated.

Jack Quinn Irish Alehouse and Pub

Cuisine: Irish Pub
Open: L-D: Daily
jackquinnspub.com

21 S. Tejon St.   719.385.0766
Colorado Springs, 80903
Colorado Ave & Tejon St

Price: $-$$	**Patio:** Yes
Reservations: Yes	**Brunch:** Yes

Location: Colorado Springs-Downtown

The Quinn-tessential Irish pub has everything you'd expect—corned beef and cabbage, Irish stew, shepherd's pie, boxtys, bangers, champ potatoes and a wide selection of Irish, Colorado and British brews on tap. For some different pub grub, try "Reuben Fritters" and "Irish nachos." (If they don't survive the next menu cycle, something equivalently weird will.) Live music is available upstairs on most nights, and an Irish jam session is held every Sunday afternoon. It's a true public place with tons of social life and an Irish feeling enhanced by furniture and décor imported from Ireland. Don't miss the Irish ballads and pub songs every Thursday night. Don't be surprised if you get run over on Tuesday evenings as this pub hosts a running club that attracts hundreds of local runners in all weather conditions.

Jake & Telly's Greek Taverna

Cuisine: Greek
Open: L-D: Daily
jakeandtellys.com/

2616 West Colorado Ave   719.633.0406
Colorado Springs, CO 80904
Between 26th and 27th Streets on W. Colorado Ave.

Price: $$-$$$	**Patio:** Yes
Reservations: Yes	**Brunch:** No

Location: Colorado Springs-Westside – Old Colorado City

The talented Topakas brothers, Iakovos and Eleftherios (Jake and Telly), provide Colorado Springs' only full service upscale Greek restaurant. If you can't find the Greek dish or drink you're looking for on their menu, it probably doesn't exist. The dining room, on the second floor of an historic building in Old Colorado City, is colorful and happy, conveying Greek-ness from murals to columns to statuary. There are even Greek newspapers and maps in the restroom. The umbrella-topped tables outside, on the large balcony/patio, look over the street and up at the mountains, as they would on a Greek isle. Telly has sommelier cred, which shows in the wine list and the wait-staff 's ability to explain it. Start off with spanakopita, dolmades, marinated octopus, or kalamari, a cup of egg lemon or lentil soup, and a traditional Greek salad. For lunch, continue with a gyro or souvlaki sandwich, or a lamb entree. For dinner, you can have souvlaki, lamb ribs or shanks or kebobs, casseroles such as moussaka and pastitsio, pasta with seafood or chicken, and many other choices, all in large shareable portions. Save some room for baklava, stuffed figs or cheesecake for dessert. Finish off with a little glass of ouzo – say "Mas, Opa!", down the liquid in one gulp, and slam down the glass! Or something like that – they'll tell you what to do. One special note - there is no elevator, and the stairs from the parking lot are narrow, steep, and possibly slippery in wet weather. Note that their sister restaurant in Denver - Axios Estiatorio –has also won several 'Best Greek' awards.

Joseph's Restaurant

Cuisine: Traditional
Open: L: Mon-Fri, D: Mon-Sat
gazettesites.com/josephsrestaurant/

1603 S. 8th St.   719.630.3631
Colorado Springs, 80905
Near South 8th St. and W. Brookside St.

Price: $$$-$$$$	**Patio–yes**
Reserve–yes	**Brunch:** No

Location: Colorado Springs-South of Motor City

Joseph Freyre, a many decades front-of-the-house veteran of the Colorado Springs high end dining scene, including The Garden of the Gods Club and The Broadmoor, has a new building across the street from the old location where many good Springs restaurants such as Marigold and Walter's built reputations before moving to their own facilities. The lunch menu, still very suitable for both ladies-who-lunch and business people, is expanded, and the TV dominated bar lounge has its own menu. The dinner menu is still pretty much the same – just about the last place in town that does traditional special occasion table-side flambé preparation. If you want to impress with spinach Pernod and flaming pepper steak , this is your place. Some diners have been ordering their favorite, the calf's liver ,veal scallopine, steak Diane, or trout meuniere, once a month for decades. As you might expect, many of the supper clientele tend to be 'mature'. Some of the elegance of the former location seems not to have survived the move across the street – Viennese-plush morphed into Taos-simple; however, the nostalgic sensation of special-dinner-out-with-the-folks endures. The jazz vocals background music is quite pleasant and conducive to table conversation. The wine list is good, the classic menu is competently prepared with standard recipes, the sauces are mostly traditional, a little on the sweet side, and the presentations are very nice. The service is serious and at a thoughtful, special occasion pace. Dessert is fun if you go for the measured excitement of the flaming cherries jubilee or bananas Foster.

Jun Japanese

Cuisine: Japanese
Open: L-D: Daily
jun-japanese.com/

3276 Centennial Boulevard –   719.227.8690
Colorado Springs, CO 80907
West Fillmore St & Centennial Blvd

1760 Dublin Blvd   719.531.9368
Colorado Springs,CO80918
Southwest corner of Dublin Blvd and North Academy Blvd

Price: $$-$$$	**Patio:** No
Reservations: Yes	**Brunch:** No
Location: Colorado Springs - Northwest	

Jun Japanese has won 'Best Sushi' awards for more than a decade, and deservedly so. There's a myth that good sushi is only available in coastal cities - flash bulletin, the good stuff has to be flown into everywhere, even our coastal cities, and Colorado has great air service. The original Jun at Dublin & Academy is diner-compact and plain, with sushi bar, a few American tables and a few Japanese tables with embedded electric burners for Shabu-Shabu – no Teppan grills. The newer and roomier Centennial Blvd. location, with bamboo paneled contemporary ambience, has both American and Japanese seating and several Teppan grills, but no Shabu-Shabu. At both locations, the sashimi and sushi is first class – as good as we've experienced at many top West Coast places. The sushi rolls are excellent and imaginative. Beverages include sakes, beers, specialty drinks and, of course, tea. In addition to the separate sushi and specialty roll menus - with 'real deal' prices during happy hours - there are many appetizer and entrée choices from chicken to steak to seafood, and several combinations. If you like really good cooked fish, give your most winning smile and ask for the off-menu Hamachi Kama (yellowtail collar) – you might get lucky. The Dublin location also offers several Ramen choices, sukiyaki, and Shabu-Shabu with several grades of beef, up to Kobe (get that wallet open). The theatrical Teppan grill chefs at the Centennial location are very entertaining for special occasions (what kids, including those with AARP cards, don't like fire and knives?). We've always been very pleased by the attentive, helpful and well-paced service.

Juniper Valley Ranch

Cuisine: American

Open: D: Fri-Sun (Closed December thru March)

junipervalleyranch.com/

16350 Hwy 115   719.576.0741
Colorado Springs,CO80926
19 miles south of downtown Colorado Springs

Price: $ **Patio:** No
Reservations: Yes (strongly recommended)
Brunch: No
Location: Colorado Springs – way south of downtown

Chances are, if you've never been to Juniper Valley Ranch, you're not a long time Coloradoan. And, if you are about to go, it will be because it's your annual family ritual, or you just finished binge-watching "Little House on the Prairie" or reading a Zane Grey or Karl May western novel. Since 1951, five generations of the same family have been serving the same simple family style dinners, three days a week (except in the Winter) in this very plain adobe ranch house. No alcohol, no credit cards, no asphalt parking, not even a good sign to find it. Always the same just-under-$20 meal - skillet fried chicken, ham and, on Fridays, chicken fried steak, with juice, biscuits, potatoes and gravy, vegetables, and simple desserts. You could get the same at a Denny's for less money, less driving time and less gas, but you wouldn't have a story to tell about how it was just like when you went to Grandma's house on the ranch when you were a child. Make a reservation. Get a map. See you there. Bring cash.

La Baguette Café & Bakery

Cuisine: French
Open: B-L-D: Daily
labaguette-co.com

2417 W. Colorado Ave.   719.577.4818
Colorado Springs, 80904
Old Colorado City between 24th and 25th Streets

Price: $ **Patio:** No
Reservations: No   **Brunch:** Yes
Location: Colorado Springs- In the heart of Old Colorado City

This is the 30-something French bakery cafe in the historic Old Colorado City district, whose three branch locations became independent spin-offs, each with its own personality. (Kids do that, don't they?) This original location has the big steam-injected ovens, supplying them (and many area markets and restaurants) with breads and pastries, all authentic and terrific. Close your eyes and you're in Paris. Think long and crusty baguette loaves, and plate-filling croissants stuffed with fruit, cheese, almonds or chocolate. No trouble finding it in the morning – just follow the aroma of the French bread and coffee. La Baguette is an excellent place for breakfast, lunch, or a full dinner with wine. Order at the counter, take the number and find a table. This Old Colorado City location has also created 'Upstairs at La Baguette', a cozy evening and late night wine bar above the bakery, with a very small menu, open Thurs-Sat.

La Baguette French Bistro

Cuisine: French
Open: B-L: Mon-Sat, D: Wed-Sat
LaBaguetteFrenchBistro.com

4440 N. Chestnut Street,   719.599.0686
Colorado Springs, 80907
Colorado Springs – just west of the I-25 & Garden of the Gods interchange

Price: $-$$ **Patio:** Yes
Reservations: Yes   **Brunch:** No
Location: Colorado Springs

French chef Patrick Garnier, he of the infectious smile and enthusiasm, and his wife Krystyna have transformed this former branch of La Baguette Bakery Café. They added a full bar, an expanded and very reasonable wine list, table service for lunch and dinner, a full décor and lighting makeover, and "voilà!" - a French bistro that would be your regular hangout in Paris if you were lucky enough to have it in your

arrondissement. Added to the original La Baguette breakfast and lunch menu (the authentic French baked goods still come out of the Old Colorado City La Baguette Bakery), there are now many more omelets and casseroles and salads and hot entrees. For dinner, Chef Patrick whips up the full range of French classics - Canard à L'orange, L'Escalope de Veau, Boeuf Bourguignon, Moules à La Maroccain, superb French onion soup, and much more. There are also Pierogies (it's a mixed marriage - Krystyna is Polish). Service is friendly and efficient, and no request is too much for them. It has become one of the most popular places in town, winning 'Best French' every year, so dinner reservations are recommended. Try it, your bouche will be very amused.

The Margarita at Pine Creek

Cuisine: Contemporary
Open: L: Tues-Fri, D: Tues-Sat, BR: Sun
margaritaatpinecreek.com

7350 Pine Creek Rd.   719.598.8667
Colorado Springs, 80919
West frontage road off of Woodmen and I-25

Price: $$-$$$ **Patio:** Yes
Reservations: Yes   **Brunch:** Yes
Location: Colorado Springs

Tucked among the pines, with views of Pikes Peak and the Rampart Range from the patios, and a collection of eclectic original art, this 40-year old white adobe oasis transports you to another time and place. Opened in 1974 serving old Spanish entrées to fit the southwestern architecture, the Margarita has more recently evolved under award winning Chef Eric Viedt into a continental contemporary adventure. Three or five course prix fixe dinners, with or without wine pairings, change nightly built around your preference of vegetarian, meat and fish entrées. The kitchen takes pride in from-scratch preparations, from locally sourced ingredients. They bake bread twice daily and make all of their own desserts. Weekends feature live music on the patio or in the downstairs lounge, and Saturday evenings feature baroque accompaniment on the Margarita's antique harpsichord in the dining room. Summer Fridays offer a dinner and movie on the patio (weather permitting) with the menu inspired by the movie shown. Sunday brunches feature a full menu of egg dishes, and some favorites from the lunch and bar menus, prepared to order. Since founding the restaurant, Pati Davidson Burleson has made The Margarita a hub of community activity, sponsoring public events throughout the year, including farmers markets, wine tastings, art shows and guest chefs.

Marigold Cafe and Bakery

Cuisine: Contemporary
Open: L-D: Mon-Sat
Bakery: 8am-9pm Mon-Sat

marigoldcoloradosprings.com Colorado Springs, 80919
4605 Centennial Blvd.   719.599.4776
Centennial Blvd and Garden of the Gods Road

Price: $$-$$$	**Patio:** No
Reservations: Yes	**Brunch:** No
Location: Colorado Springs	

Chef Dominique, trained in Lyon, France, by legendary chefs, with wife Elaine, a pastry chef graduate and instructor at the Culinary Institute of America, have set the standard for delicious, affordable, and beautiful bistro food and pastries in Colorado Springs for decades. They always have a full house, so make that reservation now, and expect to join the corps of 'regulars'. The lunch menu offers soups, salads, sandwiches, pasta, pizza, and the ever popular fish and chips. Starters include fresh oysters, escargots, crab cakes, classic French onion soup, and excellent seasonal salads. The regular and long specials menus feature steaks, fresh fish, lamb chops, French standards, pastas, and rotisserie chicken. There are many exceptional dishes, including the Spring Salad, a little tower based on roasted beets with goat cheese, and the boeuf bourguignon. Although the to-die-for rack of lamb for two is no longer on the regular menu, in-the-know customers call a couple of days ahead to order it. As befits the protégé of world-class chefs, even Dominique's vegetable and starch sides are memorable. The wine list is excellent and the highly professional wait staff can advise. Do not miss the in-house bakery desserts, and plan on taking some home. From the award winning double and triple chocolate mousse cake to the fruit and citrus tarts, the éclair, and the Napoleon, everything is marvelous. So here's the parlor game – name the one restaurant you would have to have if stranded on a desert island; Marigold is ours.

Momma Pearl's Cajun Kitchen

Cuisine: Cajun/Creole
Open: L-D: Daily
Mommapearls.com

6620 Delmonico Drive   719.471.9222
Colorado Springs, 80919
Corner of N. Rockrimmon and Delmonico streets

Price: $-$$ **Patio:** Yes
Reservations: Yes   **Brunch:** No
Location: Colorado Springs

If you've ever wandered through the steamy backwaters of southern Louisiana and stumbled into a rustic small town family Cajun eatery, this is the very definition of Momma Pearl's Kitchen. The place is tiny, simple, hard to find, delicious, and absolutely authentic. Altogether now, say "Atchafalaya". The full spectrum of Creole/Cajun delights including gator, frog legs, gulf oysters, bugs (crawfish), and etouffee are consistently excellent. Moreover, you can feel the passion of the owner/ chef in every bite of the heaping portions. Make sure to visit the Saturday bug boil, just like a family afternoon barbecue in old Louisiana. So, what wind blew them here? The answer is – Hurricane Katrina. No liquor license as of this report, but an indication that for a small corkage fee they will open your own sealed bottle and provide a glass.

Nosh

Cuisine: Contemporary
Open: L: Mon-Fri, D: Mon-Sat
nosh121.com

121 South Tejon Street   719.634.6674
Colorado Springs, 80903
Tejon St. & Colorado Ave.

Price: $-$$ **Patio:** Yes
Reservations: Yes   **Brunch:** No
Location: Colorado Springs

Located downtown in the Plaza of the Rockies, Nosh has set a name for itself in the inventive creations coming from the kitchen and the bar. Walls at Nosh are covered with art, tables are simply set and there is an overall modern/urban feel. Billing itself as a "Social dining experience", NOSH encourages you to share, and many menu items are suitable for sharing. The focus has shifted somewhat toward Asian items such as noodle bowls Asian spices, and edamame, and away from 'comfort' items like fried chicken and waffles, aiming for flavorful and healthy and fresh. Not to panic – the sweet potato fries are still there for lunch and dinner. Lunch leans toward creative sandwiches, burgers (which are excellent), soups and salads. Dinner leans toward bowls, some of which are spicy, and seafood. The small patio is a beautiful summertime option and it is also dog-friendly. If you can't figure out what drink to enjoy, you can't go wrong with the house made white sangria as it packs a lot of punch for a small price. If you love Sangria and want something different to try, check out the Elderflower, Grapefruit, Melon or Blueberry choices! Nosh is the perfect place to visit on your way to an evening out downtown or for a lazy summer afternoon with your pup. Regardless, you will enjoy the creative selection of small bites and big flavor. Be sure to park underground and tell the attendant you are there to enjoy Nosh and parking will be free.

Odyssey Gastropub

Cuisine: Pub
Open: L-D: Daily
odysseygastropub.com

311 N Tejon St   719.999.5127
Colorado Springs 80903
Between Platte & Boulder streets

Price: $-$$	**Patio:** Yes
Reservations: Yes	**Brunch:** Yes
Location: Downtown Colorado Springs	

Are cute menu item names a draw or a bit much for an upscale pub? How about drinks like The Good Juan, Wake Up With Mary, and Sweet Talker, or food items like Wave-O-Stada (cross between Huevos Ranchero and Tostada) and Cheeky Shepherd (beef cheeks and cheddar mashed potatoes, carrots & rosemary)? Should we get even by misnaming them the Odessa Gastropod (Black Sea snails, maybe?), which is what our auto-spell-check called it. It's all in fun, and this pub (in the former Tony's Bar which is now across the street and still serving Wisconsin Walleye fish-n-chips with cheese curds) gets away with the cuteness because the drinks and food are very satisfying. There are lots of tasty appetizers, salads, sandwiches and entrees to go with the big drink selection and the very long bar. Bold voyages deserve bold flavors, so use the optional condiments. Exposed brick walls, laminated map tabletops, and helpful friendly service complete the pleasant experience. We like the vibe and the motto: "May your journeys be epic and each destination a homecoming."

The Pantry in Green Mountain Falls

Cuisine: American
Open: B-L: Daily Year Round, D-Thu-Sun, Summer
thepantryingreenmtnfallsco.com

6980 Lake Street   719-684-9018
Green Mountain Falls, 80819
Off Hwy 24, center of town by the lake (pond to Easterners)

Price: $ **Patio:** Yes
Reservations: No   **Brunch:** Yes (Summer)
Location: Green Mountain Falls-West of Colorado Springs on Hwy 24

Next to Hwy 24, 15 miles and 1800' added elevation west of Colorado Springs, above the red rock formations and into the pine forest, on the flanks of Pikes Peak, lies the mountain hamlet of Green Mountain Falls. Get ready for some small town hospitality and 'down home' country style food. Colorado Springs folks bring their out-of-town visitors here. Park next to the picturesque pond with the gazebo (popular for weddings), open the Pantry's squeaky screen door, and you are warmly welcomed by several people, usually including 'Nan', the owner. There is nothing fancy about The Pantry, but the basic food is familiar, well prepared, and tasty. Whether you bring the whole family or not, you will feel like family – in fact, you might have been brought here as a child. Sit at the counter or an inside table or the patio. The décor is old fashioned and nostalgic. Coffee mugs are lovingly mismatched and the coffee flows like water – but there is also a full bar. Service is attentive and informal. The homemade cinnamon raisin bread and bread pudding are very popular! The pantry omelet is a great choice, stuffed with ham, onions, mushrooms, cheese, peppers, and diced mild green chili. For potatoes, definitely choose the yummy home fried potato slices, crisp golden brown but soft inside. For pancake fans, try the Mother Lode - it's so big it falls off the plate! For lunch, loosen your belt a notch and go for the "Colossal Burger". Summer weekends, put on your boots, bring your Wranglers and Buckaroos, and join in the "Creekside Cowboy Breakfast Buffet" and/or the evening 'Cowboy BBQ', both with live music.

Paravicini's Italian Bistro

Cuisine: Italian
Open: L-D: Daily
paravicinis.com

2802 W. Colorado Ave.   719.471.8200
Colorado Springs, 80904
Colorado Ave. at 28th Street

Price: $$ **Patio:** Yes
Reservations: Yes   **Brunch:** No
Location: Colorado Springs – Westside - Old Colorado City

Literally a restaurant "for the neighborhood", Paravicini's brings together typical Italian cuisine in a casual and lively atmosphere. Just like a large, loud Italian family, Paravicini's has a lot of love to share with its customers. The food from the open kitchen is both classic and creative with representations from both Northern and Southern Italy. Whether you start with the bruschetta, calamari, fried artichokes, pasta fagioli or Italian wedding soup, there isn't a bad choice. Classic entrees include Veal Tuscano (sic) and Chicken Marsala. For a sometime special, ask for the Basil cream sauce with the lasagna and be pleasantly surprised. The wine list is heavily dotted with Italian favorites spanning 'the Boot' and a sprinkling of new world goodies. Table seating is close but comfortable and the bar overlooks the semi-open kitchen so there is plenty of action to be seen. The Italian posters are fascinating pop art.

Pizzeria Rustica

Cuisine: Italian
Open: L-D: Tues-Sun
pizzeriarustica.com

2527 West Colorado Ave   719.632.8121
Colorado Springs, CO 80904
Old Colorado City between 25th and 26th streets

Price: $-$$ **Patio:** Yes
Reservations: Yes   **Brunch:** No
Location: Colorado Springs - Westside - Old Colorado City

Many claim that the Neapolitan-style pizza served at this rustic yet refined trattoria is the best they have eaten outside of Italy. Authentic, quality ingredients are the only ones used here. The thin dough is made fresh daily and then hand stretched to order and cooked in a pecan wood-fired oven. The pizza flour, San Marzano tomatoes and selected toppings are imported from Italy. Other ingredients are locally sourced from organic and sustainable Colorado growers. The mozzarella cheese is made daily by hand. The chef embraces the slow food movement by

featuring daily pizza and antipasto items that are in peak season. The menu is small, presenting fewer items but deep flavors. Award winning chef Jay Gust is the top toque for both Pizzeria Rustica and sister restaurant Tapateria on the next block. The antipasti di giorno is always a wonderful surprise. A medley made for sharing, it will include marinated vegetables, cheeses, and cured meats. The signature Rustica Pizza features arugula, prosciutto ham, Gran Padano parmesan, house-made mozzarella and a ricotta stuffed crust. Be sure to dip your crust in the truffle infused extra virgin olive oil. Simple but pure flavors are what you can expect in each bite, a true Italian experience. For dessert, try the Limoncello combo - Limoncello sorbetto with balsamic fig glaze, a shot of Amalfi limoncello and biscottini. Be sure to enjoy the lovely al fresco patio dining in the summer and the numerous wine events that occur year round. The atmosphere inside is warm and cozy so, with a limited amount of tables, be sure to call ahead for a reservation during the colder months. It's hard to convey how thoughtful and serious these folks are in their approach to what they do. Pizzeria Rustica was named the 11th 4-Star Certified Green Restaurant ® in the world, and was named to both Top-20 and Top-5 lists of America's most sustainable restaurants in 2014. Bravo!

The Rabbit Hole

Cuisine: Contemporary
Open: D: Daily
Rabbitholedinner.com

101 North Tejon Street   719.203.5072
Colorado Springs, CO 80903
Entrance on Kiowa St. just east of Tejon

Price: $$	**Patio:** No
Reservations: Yes	**Brunch:** No
Location: Colorado Springs - downtown	

You descend into the dimly lit world of Alice's White Rabbit via the steep stairs under the covered Paris subway kiosk on the sidewalk. (There are stairs and an elevator inside the building for a more secure descent.) The underground restaurant layout has several sections and chambers, adding to the hideaway vibe. The décor is all dark tones and fantasy. The "eat me" and "drink me" menus continue the theme, both in the graphic design and the names of drinks and food items. The White Rabbit martini, the Mad Hatter Manhattan, the Fried Bunny Bites, the Rabbit Food salad menu, and the Rabbit Meatloaf don't let you forget where you are. This is one of the few late night spots in town, where other restaurant people can come after work so, as you would expect, there is a creative drink menu and an extensive menu of small to large trendy dishes. 'Nibbles' include onion & gruyere raviolis, glazed duck wings, couscous balls, pork belly tacos and much more. Entrees cover beef, lamb, shellfish, fish and vegetarian items, most with interesting non-standard flavors and sauces, some of which fulfill their expectations – and all are food for conversation. Most evenings it's not the ideal place for a tête–à–tête , but is great for a fun-loving group.

Roman Villa

Cuisine: Italian
Open: D: Tues-Sat

3005 N. Nevada Ave.   719.635.1806
Colorado Springs, 80907
Fillmore St. & North Nevada Ave.

Price: $-$$	**Patio:** No
Reservations: No	**Brunch:** No
Location: Colorado Springs-Northside	

This hole-in-the-wall converted house is one of the best kept secrets of Colorado Springs. Roman Villa is small and crowded inside with bench seating and low lighting. Open since 1959, this family owned and operated restaurant is now run by the third generation. The staff is very friendly, making you feel like family, too. Don't be surprised if they call you by name the next time you come back. Serving up large portions of hearty homemade Italian-American food, you will be glad to take home leftovers. The lasagna is cooked to order (takes 20 minutes) and is served bubbling over in an individual crock. All pasta sauces and raviolis are made from scratch daily. The Roman Villa Chicken will keep you coming back over and over again and the pizza is amazing! Using only fresh ingredients and made to order in a semi-open kitchen at the front of the restaurant, every bite is like a flavor explosion in your mouth. If nothing else, the loyal local following and line that stretches out the door on most nights should tell you that this a neighborhood hot spot for a reason!

Saigon Café

Cuisine: Vietnamese
Open: L-D: Mon-Sat
coloradosaigoncafe.com/

20 E. Colorado Ave.   719.633.2888
Colorado Springs, 80903
Between Tejon & Cascade

Price: $-$$ **Patio:** No
Reservations: Yes   **Brunch:** No
Location: Colorado Springs-Downtown

A longtime downtown lunch favorite, Saigon Café is a fine
choice for dinner after work or before an event at the nearby
Pikes Peak Center. The upscale dining area is bright and
roomy, with simple art adorning the walls and light maple
tables spanning the room. Fresh flavors, crisp and contrasting
textures and healthy options abound on this Vietnamese and
Chinese-based menu. A short but well selected wine list is a
plus. Team service is seamless and attentive, from first greeting
to farewell. The house specialty here is the "bun" noodle bowl,
a huge bowl of fresh vegetables, bean sprouts, rice noodles,
fresh herbs and your choice of meats and topped with crushed
peanuts and a tangy house sauce. Rice bowls are another
choice. Chef's favorites include marinated and grilled shrimp
and pork, hot and spicy squid in lemon grass, and seafood
combinations cooked in a butter-coconut sauce. A variety of
meats are served sate', and vegetarians can delight in various
dishes made to order. Want a quick between-meals snack or a
tasty appetizer? Grab a summer roll; the shrimp, lettuce, rice
noodles and mint densely packed in rice paper and served
with peanut sauce can cure a case of the munchies in a healthy
way. Traditional pho (soup) is also a wonderful representation
of the classic dish with sliced beef or well done brisket and
placed over the steaming broth packed full of noodles, herbs,
jalapeños, and bean sprouts. You will leave with your taste buds
satisfied and your stomach feeling full.

Salsa Brava Fresh Mexican Grill

Cuisine: Mexican/Southwestern
Open: L-D: Mon-Sat
salsabravacolorado.com/

802 Village Center Drive   719.266.9244
Colorado Springs, 80903
Rockrimmon & Vindicator

Price: $$ **Patio:** Yes
Reserve-Call-ahead   **Brunch:** no
Location: Colorado Springs-Northwest of downtown

This was the first of Randy Price's Colorado restaurants, which now include three Salsa Bravas, two Over Easy's, one Urban Egg, and one Sonterra Grill, plus a sizable catering operation. All of them have scored 'Best Of' awards. The food is memorable for its freshness, clarity, consistency and value. Made-from-scratch Mexican fare starts with rolled-to-order Baja rolls stuffed with fish (featuring sea bass), guacamole, cabbage and green chilies. Take your time choosing from the large variety of fajitas, fish dishes, enchiladas, and other entrees – or, like us, just work your way through the menu on multiple visits. Many of the standard entrées come with an unexpected twist. Muy bueno! For the athletic Mexican food fan, they have a 5k Neighborhood run that starts at 6pm on Tuesday nights at the Briargate location and a Cycling Club that starts at 10am on Saturday mornings from this Rockrimmon location. Not so athletic? Don't miss the fresh tortilla chips with two or three different salsas that hit the table right after you sit down, the great Margaritas, and the perfectly prepared early bird tapas.

Shangri-La

Cuisine: Chinese – Mandarin & Szechuan
Open: L-D: Daily

8850 N. Union Blvd   719.495.1738
Colorado Springs, CO 80920
Union Town Center at Union Blvd and Research Parkway

Price: $$ **Patio:** No
Reservations: Yes   **Brunch:** No
Location: Colorado Springs – Briargate area

If you prefer more downscale, run-of-the-mill Chinese food, hurriedly prepared with lots of salt/MSG, in a crowded and noisy place with children running around, this is probably not your place. This is also not the place for self-conscious, elaborately plated, exotic ingredient, gourmet Chinese food. The menu is familiar, with most of the same appetizer, soup, entree, house special and combo dinner names you are used to

seeing, but be prepared to pay an additional 30% or more for food that is fresher, less salty and more flavorful, served in a more elegant, quiet and pleasant atmosphere. One or both of the owners, Ilene and Doug (not married, just friends, really), is there all the time, making sure that the food and service is consistently excellent. Their motto is "Enjoyment Without Regret". Relax, enjoy your meal, and Gong Xi Fa Cai!

Springs Orleans

Cuisine: Cajun/Creole
Open: B-L-D: Daily
SpringsOrleans.com

123 E. Pikes Peak Avenue   719.520.0123
Colorado Springs, 80903
Next to the Wyndham Grand Mining Exchange Hotel

Price: $$-$$$ **Patio:** Yes
Reservations: Yes   **Brunch:** Yes
Location: Colorado Springs-Downtown

This is the downtown (upscale) Cajun/Creole. The uptown (downscale) source is Momma Pearl's Cajun Kitchen (see the review). Confused? The French Quarter décor and classic libations at Springs Orleans – Sazerac, Hurricane, fine wines - will make you not care. At Springs Orleans, for appetizers you'll definitely want to try the excellent crab cakes and oysters (mix and match raw, charbroiled and fried), as well as the creative and tasty "Tower" and "Matchstick" salads, and the delightful seafood and corn chowder. For lunches and dinner entrees, all the expected étouffées, gumbos, po'boys and more oysters are offered – a little mild, so ask for the hot sauce tray. Do not overlook the pastas, which are not expected but are very good - the lobster trotolle is a winner. You won't be allowed back on Bourbon Street if you skip dessert, but you won't be able to choose between the Banana Pudding, Flourless Chocolate Torte, Bread Pudding, and Beignets, so just order the dessert sampler, which has some of each – and add a Bourbon Pecan Tartlet for good measure. As you know, most French coffee is atrocious, which is the reason for Café au Lait, so order some of that. The vibe is lively, so laissez les bon temps rouler!

Tapateria

Cuisine: Tapas
Open: L-D: Tues-Sun
Tapateria.com

2607 W Colorado Ave   719.471.8272
Colorado Springs, 80904
Colorado Ave and 26th

Price: $-$$ **Patio:** Yes
Reservations: Yes   **Brunch:** No
Location: Colorado Springs-Old Colorado City

Tapateria, the next block sister restaurant to Pizzeria Rustica, with the same award winning executive chef, is a cozy, tasty tapas restaurant with a rustic Old Colorado City neighborhood feel. The overall vibe is casual and inclusive, like a scene out of a Hemingway story - the young couple at the bar is in their own little world, the bachelorette group at the corner table is giggly, and friends at the high and low tables are just relaxed and happy, catching up while sipping wine and discussing the subtleties of the menu choices with the knowledgeable wait-staff. The wine list is well-chosen and value priced – don't overlook the sangria. You will think you are back on vacation in Barcelona. The regular menu of 36 tapas in four categories —Bocados/snacks, Verduras/vegetarian, Mariscos/seafood, and Carne/meat—includes garlic mushrooms, goat cheese salad, grilled shrimp, lamb sausage, chorizo & figs and carne Adobada. With optional add-ons like Serrano ham, Manchego cheese, wonderful white anchovies, and daily specials from the chalkboard, everyone will find what they like. Desserts are not emphasized. The menu is 100% gluten free, 50% vegetarian, 25% vegan. Summertime is special with 'grilling on the patio' and once a month patio paella. A small deli case offers special charcuterie and cheeses by the pound to take home.

Uchenna

Cuisine: Ethiopian and Mediterranean
Open: L-D: Tues-Sun
uchennaalive.com

2501 W Colorado Ave, Ste 105   719.634.5070
Colorado Springs, CO 80904
In the little shop cluster at the corner of 25th Street and
Colorado Ave.

Price: $-$$	**Patio:** No
Reservations: Yes	**Brunch:** No
Location: Colorado Springs – Westside – Old Colorado City	

If Linus and Charlie Brown ate at Uchenna, Linus wouldn't
need his blanket and Charlie wouldn't have any hang-ups. The
motto of Maya, the owner/chef, is "Live, Love, Eat Well". All
you really need to know is that there are 'regulars' who drive
down to The Springs from Boulder, Lakewood and Denver to
eat Maya's food and be enveloped in her serenity and love. If
you're not familiar with Ethiopian food, don't worry - all will
be patiently explained when you get there. The web site also has
explanations and photos. The food is made from scratch, and
is almost all Gluten-free. Chef Maya was raised in Ethiopia, and
worked many years in France, so there is a Mediterranean menu
in addition to the Ethiopian one. Typically, one eats Ethiopian
food without utensils, by scooping or pinching bites of the
food using thin, slightly spongy, slightly sour/tangy bread
called "Injera", made from a native Ethiopian grain called
"Teff". Baskets of Injera are provided for the Ethiopian food
and forks for the Mediterranean food. The Ethiopian food is
customarily eaten family style from a large dish or pan in the
middle of the table, in which the food items are laid out side-
by-side on a layer of Injera. As the meal proceeds, that sauce-
soaked Injera becomes very delicious. The best approach is to
order several items to be shared from the common dish. Dishes
can be ordered mild or spicy, and the two standard sauces can
be on the side. Try chicken, lamb, beef and seafood items, along
with lentils and collard greens. Available Mediterranean dishes,
on separate plates, include salads and sandwiches as well as
very flavorful lamb, shrimp and chicken entrees on basmati
rice. Save room for excellent baklava and other delicious
desserts made by Maya's daughter. This is 'slow food', so relax,
ask questions, be patient, and be prepared for hugs. As of this
report, there is no liquor license. Beverages are refreshing teas
and Harar coffee (which is surprisingly tasty), or just water.
This is an oasis of warm food and warm culture. Come join the
circle of friends.

Uwe's

K: Okay. Good, not great food. Didn't like the atmosphere.

Cuisine: German
Open: L-D: Tue-Sun

31 N. Iowa Ave.   719-475-1611
Colorado Springs, 80909
Northeast of Pikes Peak Ave. and Union Blvd.

J: Very nice traditional food w/German speaking staff

3½

Price: $-$$	**Patio:** No
Reservations: Yes	**Brunch:** No

Location: Colorado Springs – Near Memorial Park, the Olympic Training Center, and Memorial Hospital

This is where those-in-the-know go for a good, home-like German meal. After Chef Uwe himself retired, it's been run for a decade by a Swiss chef and his Bavarian wife. This small restaurant, on a side street with other little neighborhood businesses, is plain and casual, relaxed and friendly, with enough German and Swiss decorations that you can't mistake where you are. Sometimes there's even live German folk music. The drink list is short, but covers the bases with German beers and wines and specialty drinks. The menu is also short and authentic – bratwurst, smoked pork chops, goulash, roulade, sauerbraten and Jaeger schnitzel, each with the appropriate spaetzle, potatoes, vegetables and good German bread from Wimberger's Old World Bakery. Most entrees are offered in regular and 'half' portions, with choice of soup or German-style mixed salad. Do your best to save room for desserts such as apple strudel a la mode, rice pudding, and cheesecake, with Schlagsahne (fresh whipped cream) of course. Guten Appetit!

Walter's Bistro

Cuisine: Classical American & European
Open: L: Mon-Fri, D: Mon-Sat
waltersbistro.com

146 E. Cheyenne Mountain Blvd.   719.630.0201
Colorado Springs, 80906
South of downtown, near The Cheyenne Mtn. Resort

3½

Price: $$-$$$	**Patio:** No
Reservations: Yes	**Brunch:** No

Location: Colorado Springs- Country Club Corners, Hwy 115 & Cheyenne Mtn Blvd

Mature fine dining might be defined as familiar cuisine, well prepared, with a good wine list and a warm upscale setting with excellent service, where the owner, the guests, and the salads are all well-dressed. That's Walter's Bistro! Walter Iser himself, trained for fine dining in Austria and Switzerland and having managed at some of the top hotels in the world, has been graciously attentive for decades. You sense that he really wants you to be happy. Start your meal with the signature lobster bisque or a traditional Caesar salad, then choose from steak, fresh fish, chicken, a savory fish stew or lighter fare – everything familiar, and everything reliably good. Save room for crème brûlée.

INDEX BY RATING

. . . .

384

4.0 PIGS

3.5 PIGS

3.0 PIGS

INDEX BY CUISINE

· · · · · · · · · · · · · · · · · · · ·

ASIAN/ASIAN FUSION

405

JAPANESE

411

INDEX BY PRICE

• •

INDEX BY LOCATION

· · · · · · · · · · · · · · · · · · · ·

431

LOHI (LOWER HIGHLANDS) NEIGHBORHOOD -DENVER

LONE TREE

LONGMONT

LOUISVILLE